HISTORICAL DICTIONARIES
OF U.S. POLITICS AND POLITICAL ERAS
Jon Woronoff, Series Editor

1. *From the Great War to the Great Depression*, by Neil A. Wynn, 2003.
2. *Civil War and Reconstruction*, by William L. Richter, 2004.
3. *Revolutionary America*, by Terry M. Mays, 2005.
4. *Old South*, by William L. Richter, 2006.
5. *Early American Republic*, by Richard Buel Jr., 2006.
6. *Jacksonian Era and Manifest Destiny*, by Terry Corps, 2006.
7. *Reagan–Bush Era*, by Richard S. Conley, 2007.
8. *Kennedy–Johnson Era*, by Richard Dean Burns and Joseph M. Siracusa, 2008.
9. *Nixon–Ford Era*, by Mitchell K. Hall, 2008.
10. *Roosevelt–Truman Era*, by Neil A. Wynn, 2008.
11. *Eisenhower Era*, by Burton I. Kaufman and Diane Kaufman, 2009.
12. *Progressive Era*, by Catherine Cocks, Peter C. Holloran, and Alan Lessoff, 2009.
13. *Gilded Age*, by T. Adams Upchurch, 2009.
14. *Political Parties*, by Harold F. Bass Jr., 2010.
15. *George W. Bush Era*, by Richard S. Conley, 2010.

Historical Dictionary of the George W. Bush Era

Richard S. Conley

Historical Dictionaries of U.S.
Politics and Political Eras, No. 15

The Scarecrow Press, Inc.
Lanham • Toronto • Plymouth, UK
2010

Published by Scarecrow Press, Inc.
A wholly owned subsidiary of The Rowman & Littlefield Publishing Group, Inc.
4501 Forbes Boulevard, Suite 200, Lanham, Maryland 20706
http://www.scarecrowpress.com

Estover Road, Plymouth PL6 7PY, United Kingdom

British Library Cataloguing in Publication Information Available

Library of Congress Cataloging-in-Publication Data
Library of Congress Cataloging-in-Publication Data

Conley, Richard Steven.
  Historical dictionary of the George W. Bush era / Richard S. Conley.
    p. cm. -- (Historical dictionaries of U.S. politics and political eras ; 15)
  Includes bibliographical references.
  ISBN 978-0-8108-6063-6 (cloth : alk. paper) -- ISBN 978-0-8108-7077-2
(ebook)
  1. United States--Politics and government--2001-2009--Dictionaries. 2. United
States--History--21st century--Dictionaries. I. Title.
  E902.C6585 2010
  973.931--dc22

                                                                    2009027133

Printed in the United States of America

∞ ™ The paper used in this publication meets the minimum requirements of
American National Standard for Information Sciences—Permanence of Paper for
Printed Library Materials, ANSI/NISO Z39.48-1992.

Printed in the United States of America.

Contents

Editor's Foreword

As the author of this volume explains, we are too close to events to determine how the tenure of George W. Bush as president of the United States will ultimately be judged. But there is no question that, from where we stood at the end of his second term in January 2009, the overall evaluation was rather negative: a conclusion most clearly and graphically illustrated from the chart that shows his public approval rating, which ended in the low 30s after declining gradually and steadily from a high of 90 just after the attacks on the World Trade Center and Pentagon on 11 September 2001. This was not surprising, with the United States engaged in not one but two wars—only one of which was universally regarded as inevitable—and in both of which the body count continued mounting with no end in sight. On top of that, the economy had fallen into its worst recession since the Great Depression, and America was increasingly unpopular in many parts of the world. Meanwhile, in the eyes of some, only limited progress was made on educational, social, and cultural issues, while others complained of backsliding. Some things may turn out better than they seem at present, but the years of the George W. Bush administration are unlikely to go down in history as a particularly happy time.

While we can follow the approval rating, and consider the problems along the way, we certainly are too close to explain just why things turned out this way. But at least we can start looking for explanations. And this *Historical Dictionary of the George W. Bush Era* is an excellent place to start. With commendable clarity and objectivity, it surveys the broad field of activity in which the 43rd president left his mark and shows how America fared in a whole range of fields, including those mentioned above and many others. It also describes his team, those who surrounded him and were entrusted with advising him and carrying out his decisions. Thus, the dictionary is full of useful entries on major persons, places, events, institutions, and policies. The overall situation is summed up in the introduction, and the path from there to here is traced twice, once as regards policy in general and again as concerns the situation in Iraq. The appendixes, one of which was cited above, are particularly revealing in some ways. And the bibliography, even this close to the presidency, is filling up quickly.

The author of this volume, Richard S. Conley, is specialized in American politics more broadly but especially presidential politics, and he has studied both domestic and foreign affairs. Along with this, he has taught comparative politics of other Western countries, giving him a broader view, as well. He is presently associate professor in political science at the University of Florida and has led many study-abroad programs. He has written numerous scholarly articles in leading journals, as well as a number of books, including one on *The Presidency, Congress, and Divided Government* and another dealing with George W. Bush and the War on Terrorism. Most helpful as regards this title is that he also authored the *Historical Dictionary of the Reagan–Bush Era*. Thus, although we and he—as he wisely concedes—are too close to recent history to draw serious conclusions, Dr. Conley does have an excellent vantage point from which to help us all mull over the past decade and decide for ourselves how we feel about it.

Jon Woronoff
Series Editor

Acronyms and Abbreviations

ABC	American Broadcasting Corporation
ABM TREATY	Anti-Ballistic Missile Treaty
ACLU	American Civil Liberties Union
AIDS	Acquired immune deficiency syndrome
AIG	American International Group
ARM	Adjustable rate mortgage
AU	African Union
AUMF	Authorization for the use of military force
BART	Bay Area Rapid Transit
BCRA	Bipartisan Campaign Reform Act (2002)
BNP-Paribas	Banque Nationale de Paris-Paribas (French bank)
CAFTA	Central American Free Trade Agreement
CDU	Christian Democratic Party (Germany)
CENTCOM	U.S. Central Command
CEO	Chief Executive Officer
CIA	Central Intelligence Agency
CNN	Cable News Network
CPA	Coalition Provisional Authority
CTBT	Comprehensive Test Ban Treaty
DHS	Department of Homeland Security
DJIA	Dow Jones Industrial Average
DNC	Democratic National Committee
DNI	Director of National Intelligence
ECU	European Currency Unit
EEC	European Economic Community
EOP	Executive Office of the President
EPA	Environmental Protection Agency
EU	European Union
FANNIE MAE	Federal National Mortgage Association

FBI	Federal Bureau of Investigation
FDA	Food and Drug Administration
FDIC	Federal Deposit Insurance Corporation
FED	Federal Reserve
FEMA	Federal Emergency Management Agency
FHFA	Federal Housing Financing Agency
FISA	Foreign Intelligence Surveillance Act
FREDDIE MAC	Federal Home Loan Mortgage Corporation
GATT	General Agreement on Tariffs and Trade
GDP	Gross domestic product
GOP	Grand Old Party (Republican Party)
HIV	Human immunodeficiency virus
HSPD	Homeland Security Presidential Directive
HUD	Housing and Urban Development, Department of
I-35	Interstate 35
IAEA	International Atomic Energy Agency
ICC	International Criminal Court
IED	Improvised explosive device
IGC	Iraq Governing Council
IMF	International Monetary Fund
INS	Immigration and Naturalization Service
IRA	Irish Republican Army
ISAF	International Security Assistance Force
KGB	*Komitet Gosudarstvennoy Bezopasnosti* (Committee for State Security, former Soviet Union)
MI5	Security Service of Great Britain
MLB	Major League Baseball
NAFTA	North American Free Trade Agreement
NATO	North Atlantic Treaty Organization
NBC	National Broadcasting Corporation
NCTC	National Counterterrorism Center
NFL	National Football League
NSA	National Security Agency
NSC	National Security Council
NSPD	National Security Policy Directive
OAS	Organization of American States
OAU	Organization of African Unity
OHS	Office of Homeland Security

OMB	Office of Management and Budget
ONDCP	Office National Drug Control Policy
PAC	Political Action Committee
PKK	*Partiya Karkerên Kurdistan* (Kurdish Workers Party, Turkey)
PLO	Palestine Liberation Organization
PNAC	Project for the New American Century
POW	Prisoner of war
ROTC	Reserve Officer Training Corps
RPR	*Rassemblement pour la République* (Rally for the Republic, French political party)
SALT	Strategic Arms Limitation Treaty
SDI	Strategic Defense Initiative
SDP	*Soziale Demokratische Partei* (Social Democratic Party, Germany)
SEC	Security and Exchange Commission
TARP	Troubled Assets Relief Program
TIPS	Terrorism Information and Prevention System
UMP	*Union pour la majorité presidentielle* (French political party)
UN	United Nations
UNICEF	United Nations Children's Fund
USA PATRIOT ACT	Uniting and Strengthening America by Providing Appropriate Tools Required to Intercept and Obstruct Terrorism Act of 2001
USTR	United States Trade Representative

Chronology

1999 2 February: Hugo Chávez becomes president of Venezuela. **12 February:** US Senate acquits incumbent President William Clinton of impeachment charges. **18 February:** Republican Senator Bob Smith of New Hampshire announces he is running for the presidency. **2 March:** Republican Pat Buchanan announces his candidacy for the presidency. **9 March:** Republican Governor of Tennessee Lamar Alexander makes official his bid for the White House. **12 March:** Poland, Hungary, and the Czech Republic join the North Atlantic Treaty Organization (NATO). **16 March:** Millionaire publisher Republican Steve Forbes announces his candidacy for the presidency on his website. **14 April:** Former Vice President Dan Quayle announces his candidacy for the presidency. **20 April:** Columbine High School shooting in Littleton, Colorado, leaves 15 dead, including teenage gunmen Eric Harris and Dylan Klebold. **21 April:** Conservative activist Gary Bauer announces his candidacy in Newport, Kentucky. **3 May:** Dow Jones Industrial Average (DJIA) closes over 11,000 for the first time. **9 June:** Kosovo War ends in former Yugoslavia. **12 June:** Republican Texas Governor George W. Bush announces he will run for the White House. **16 June:** Vice President Al Gore announces candidacy for the presidency. **1 July:** Utah Republican Senator Orrin Hatch announces his candidacy for the presidency. **13 July:** New Hampshire Senator Bob Smith leaves the Republican Party, saying it has abandoned core principles. **14 July:** Republican John Kasich leaves the presidential race and throws support to George W. Bush. **14 August:** George W. Bush wins Iowa straw poll. **16 August:** Lamar Alexander withdraws presidential bid after losing Iowa straw poll. **8 September:** Democrat Bill Bradley announces his candidacy for the presidency. **27 September:** Dan Quayle drops out of Republican primaries; Arizona Republican Senator John McCain announces his candidacy for the presidency. **12 October:** General Pervez

Musharraf leads a coup d'état in Pakistan. **13 October:** US Senate rejects Comprehensive Test Ban Treaty. **20 October:** Republican candidate Elizabeth Dole drops presidential bid. **25 October:** Pat Buchanan leaves the Republican Party and joins the Reform Party. **27 October:** First Democratic presidential debate between Al Gore and Bill Bradley in New Hampshire. **28 October:** Senator Bob Smith ends presidential bid and rejoins Republican Party. **3 December:** Republican presidential hopefuls hold first debate in New Hampshire. **15 December:** Presidential candidate George W. Bush affirms at a Republican debate in Des Moines, Iowa, that Jesus Christ has had the most influence in his life, winning praise from Evangelical Christians. **31 December:** United States turns over control of the Panama Canal to Panama.

2000 24 January: Al Gore wins Iowa Democratic Caucuses; George W. Bush wins Iowa Republican Caucuses. **1 February:** John McCain beats George W. Bush in the New Hampshire primary. **19 February:** George W. Bush defeats John McCain in the South Carolina primary. **9 March:** Republican John McCain and Democrat Bill Bradley suspend their presidential campaigns after poor showings in the Super Tuesday primaries. **25 March:** Acting Russian President Vladimir Putin formally chosen for the presidency. **15 June:** Historic agreement to end hostilities signed by North and South Korea. **26 June:** Human genome deciphered. **2 July:** Vicente Fox elected president of Mexico. **25 July:** George W. Bush selects Richard (Dick) Cheney as his vice presidential running mate. **3 August:** George W. Bush accepts the Republican nomination for the presidency in Philadelphia. **8 August:** Al Gore chooses Connecticut Senator Joseph Lieberman as his vice presidential running mate. **17 August:** Al Gore accepts the Democratic nomination for the presidency in Los Angeles. **15 September:** Olympic Games open in Australia. **12 October:** USS *Cole* attacked in Yemen; 17 Navy sailors killed. **7 November:** Election Day yields no victor for the presidency; Florida holds the balance in the Electoral College between Al Gore and George W. Bush, amid allegations of voting irregularities in Palm Beach County; automatic voting recount begins in Florida; Hillary Rodham Clinton wins Senate seat in New York. **11 November:** Republicans file federal lawsuit to halt ballot recounts in Florida. **21 November:** Florida State Supreme Court orders that ballot recounts continue. **26 November:** Florida Secretary of State Katherine Harris certifies George W. Bush as the winner of Florida's Electoral College votes by 537 ballots. **12 December:** By a 5–4 decision in *Bush v. Gore*, the US Supreme Court halts voting recounts in Florida; certification of results from Florida gives Bush the Electoral College victory despite having lost the popular vote nationally. **13 December:** George W. Bush formally accepts the presidency.

2001 16 January: Laurent Kabila, president of Congo, is assassinated. **20 January:** The day he leaves office, President William Clinton issues controversial pardons, including one to fugitive financier Marc Rich; George W. Bush is sworn in as 43rd president of the United States. **9 February:** The submarine USS *Greenville* sinks a Japanese fishing vessel, killing nine. **30 March:** President Bush rejects the Kyoto Protocol, a treaty aimed at fighting global warming. **2 April:** A Chinese commercial jet and a US spy plan collide off the waters of China, after which the American crew is detained for 11 days. **7 April:** Race riots wreak havoc for several days in Cincinnati, Ohio, after white police officers shoot and kill a black suspect. **5 June:** Vermont Republic Senator James Jeffords leaves the Republican Party and throws support to the Democrats, enabling the Democrats to control the majority. **7 June:** President Bush signs into law sweeping tax cuts; Prime Minister Tony Blair is re-elected with a large but slightly diminished Labour Party majority in Great Britain. **11 June:** Oklahoma City bomber Timothy McVeigh is executed. **29 June:** Syrian forces withdraw from Lebanon following major demonstrations. **9 August:** President Bush approves federal funding for stem-cell research but only for the use of existing cells, not from fetal tissue. **11 September:** Terrorists associated with al-Qaeda hijack four commercial aircraft; two of the aircraft are flown into the World Trade Center in New York City, where the towers collapse; a third aircraft is flown into the Pentagon in Washington, D.C.; a fourth aircraft, allegedly bound for the White House, crashes in a Pennsylvania field when passengers learn of the plot. More than 3,000 are killed. **5 October:** Letters containing the deadly agent anthrax are sent to media and government offices in Washington, D.C., and Florida. **7 October:** US and British forces bomb the Taliban government and suspected al-Qaeda terrorist training camps in Afghanistan. **12 November:** Plane crash in Queens, New York, kills 260 passengers and crew. **2 December:** Enron Corporation, an energy company, files for bankruptcy. **9 December:** Taliban government in Afghanistan falls. **22 December:** US-backed interim leader Hamid Karzai heads new Afghan government.

2002 2 January: Twelve nations of the European Union begin use of a single currency, the Euro. **10 January:** United States begins transporting Taliban and al-Qaeda prisoners and "enemy combatants" to Guantanamo Bay, Cuba, for indefinite detention. **18 January:** Defrocked Catholic Priest John Geoghan is convicted of child molestation, sparking nationwide outrage at the Catholic Church's handling of pedophilia among priests. **23 January:** American reporter Daniel Pearl is kidnapped in Pakistan. **24 January:** President Bush gives his first State of the Union address and calls Iran, Iraq, and North Korea an "axis of evil." **12 February:** International war crimes tribunal in The Hague, Netherlands, begins trial of Serbian leader Slobodan Milošević. **13 February:** John Walker Lindh, an American captured with Taliban combatants in Afghanistan, is charged with supporting terrorism. **21 February:** American reporter Daniel Pearl is found dead in Pakistan. **22 February:** Rebel Angolan leader Jonas Savimbi killed. **2 March:** "Operation Anaconda," a joint US–Afghan military effort to root out remaining Taliban in Afghanistan, begins. **4 April:** Angolan civil war ends after 30 years. **11 April:** United Nations ratifies International Criminal Court; the United States rejects it. **5 May:** Jacques Chirac wins the second round of the French presidential election over extreme right-wing candidate Jean-Marie Le Pen; he begins second term with a new five-year mandate. **24 May:** President Bush and Russian President Vladimir Putin sign the Strategic Offensive Reduction Treaty (Treaty of Moscow), reducing US and Russian nuclear arsenals by two-thirds over 10 years. **31 May:** Democratic Governor of Vermont Howard Dean announces formation of an exploratory committee to run for president in 2004. **10 June:** Suspected al-Qaeda convert José Padilla arrested for terrorist plot in Chicago. **13 June:** President Bush signals the United States will no longer adhere to the Anti-Ballistic Missile (ABM) Treaty. **15 June:** Major accounting firm Arthur Andersen is convicted of destroying documents related to the Enron Corporation's bankruptcy. **21 July:** WorldCom, a telecommunications corporation, files largest bankruptcy claim in US history after misstating profits. **28 July:** Workers trapped in a Pennsylvania mine are rescued after more than three days. **30 July:** President Bush signs major legislation dealing with corporate scandals. **12 September:** In an address to the United Nations in New York, President Bush calls for regime change in Iraq; Tyco Corporation's L. Dennis Kozlowski and Mark Swartz are indicted on federal charges for stock fraud. **12 October:** Terrorist bombing in Bali kills 202. **15 October:** ImClone executive Sam Waksal pleads guilty to fraud and perjury in corporate scandal. **16 October:** North Korea announces pursuit of nuclear arms program in defiance of a 1994 agreement. **23 October:** A three-day standoff between Chechen rebels and the Russian military ensues in a Moscow theater; 116 hostages are killed when Russian authorities use gas to oust the rebels. **24 October:** Suspected Washington, D.C.-area snipers John Allen Muhammad and John Lee Malvo are arrested. **5 November:** Mid-term congressional elections yield a majority for the Republicans in the Senate and a solidification of the Republican majority in the House of Representatives. **8 November:** United Nations unanimously passes Resolution 1441 calling for Iraq to disclose weapons of mass destruction (WMDs) to arms inspectors or face "serious consequences." **18 November:** United Nations arms inspectors return to Iraq. **25 November:** Bush signs congressional legislation creating the Department of Homeland Security, the 15th cabinet-level department of the federal government. **1 December:** Democratic Senator John Kerry of Massachusetts announces formation of an exploratory committee to run for the presidency in 2004. **13 December:** Catholic Archbishop Bernard Law resigns over church pedophilia scandals. **16 December:** Al Gore, the Democratic presidential nominee in 2000, announces that he will not seek the presidency in 2004. **20 December:** Republican Senate majority leader Trent Lott of Mississippi resigns his position in the wake of allegedly racist comments in praise of fellow Senator Strom Thurmond; Lott is replaced by Senator Bill Frist.

2003 2 January: Senator John Edwards of North Carolina announces his candidacy for the Democratic presidential nomination in 2004. **4 January:** Richard (Dick) Gephardt of Missouri announces he will run for the Democratic presidential nomination in 2004. **10 January:** North Korea formally withdraws from the Nuclear Non-Proliferation Treaty. **11 January:** Illinois Governor Jim Ryan commutes 167 convictions for death row inmates, citing problems with evidence in capital cases. **13 January:** Senator Joseph Lieberman of Connecticut announces his candidacy for the Democratic presidential nomination in 2004. **28 January:** President Bush gives second State of the Union address and signals the United States is ready to attack Iraq without United Nations support. **29 January:** Ariel Sharon elected as prime minister of Israel. **1 February:** Seven astronauts perish when the Space Shuttle *Columbia* explodes upon re-entry into the Earth's atmosphere, scattering debris over Texas. **18 February:** Former Senator Carole Moseley-Braun announces her run for the Democratic presidential nomination in 2004. **19 February:** Representative Dennis Kucinich of Ohio announces the formation of an exploratory committee to run for the Democratic nomination in 2004. **26 February:** Conflict in the Darfur region of Sudan begins, pitting Arabs against non-Arabs. **27 February:** Senator Bob Graham of Florida announces he is a candidate for the Democratic presidential nomination in 2004. **12 March:** Prime Minister Zoran Djindjic of Serbia is assassinated. **15 March:** Hu Jintao succeeds Jiang Zemin as president of China. **19 March:** United States and Britain begin Iraq War. **9 April:** Allied troops, led by the United States and Britain, capture Baghdad, Iraq. **16 April:** European Union expands membership by 10 countries. **29 April:** Mahmoud Abbas is sworn in as first Palestinian prime minister. **30 April:** President Bush announces a "road map" for comprehensive peace in the Middle East. **1 May:** United States declares an end to military combat operations in Iraq. **7 May:** Vice President Richard (Dick) Cheney announces he will run with George W. Bush on the Republican ticket in 2004. **12 May:** Paul Bremer is appointed civil administrator in Iraq. **28 May:** President Bush signs a $350 billion tax package, the third largest tax cut in US history. **30 May:** Burmese opposition leader Aung San Suu Kyi is placed under house arrest. **23 June:** In two decisions concerning college admissions in Michigan, *Gratz v. Bollinger* and *Grutter v. Bollinger*, US Supreme Court upholds the limited use of affirmative action in higher education. **13 July:** Interim government is inaugurated in Iraq. **22 July:** Iraqi dictator Saddam Hussein's sons Uday and Qusay are killed in a fight with US troops. **27 July:** Three hundred twenty-one troops mutiny in Philippines and take over an apartment complex in Makati City in an unsuccessful coup attempt against President Gloria Macapagal-Arroyo. **6 August:** Terrorist bombing of a hotel in Indonesia kills 10. **11 August:** Liberian President Charles Taylor is forced to flee civil war-torn country. **15 August:** Libya accepts responsibility for the bombing of Pan Am Flight 103 over Lockerbie, Scotland, in 1988 and pays $2.7 billion to victims' families. **19 August:** Brazilian diplomat Sérgio Vieira de Mello is killed in a suicide bombing in Baghdad, Iraq, that destroys the United Nations headquarters in that country. **6 September:** Palestinian Prime Minister Mahmoud Abbas resigns. **17 September:** Former General Wesley Clark announces his candidacy for the Democratic presidential nomination in 2004. **6 October:** Bob Graham ends his bid for the 2004 Democratic presidential nomination. **7 October:** California Governor Gray Davis is "recalled" by voters and replaced by actor Arnold Schwarzenegger. **24 October:** United Nations condemns Israel for building a barrier around the Palestinian territories, but the resolution fails to halt work on the fence. **5 November:** President Bush signs legislation banning "partial-birth" abortions. **12 November:** Ahmed Qurei becomes new Palestinian prime minister. **13 November:** Chief Justice Roy Moore of the Alabama Supreme Court resigns after refusing to remove the Ten Commandments from his office. **18 November:** Massachusetts Supreme Court rules that gay marriage does not contravene state constitution. **23 November:** Eduard Shevardnadze, president of Georgia, resigns after weeks of massive protest. **24 November:** Washington, D.C., "sniper" John Muhammad is found guilty by a Virginia jury, which recommends a death sentence. **12 December:** Paul Martin replaces Jean Chrétien as prime minister of Canada. **13 December:** Iraqi dictator Saddam Hussein is captured by US troops. **19 December:** Libyan leader Mu'ammar Gadhafi scraps nuclear weapons program.

2004 13 January: Andrew Fastow, former chief financial officer for Enron Corporation, pleads guilty to fraud. **15 January:** Carole Moseley-Braun terminates her run for the Democratic presidential nomination. **19 January:** John Kerry wins the Iowa Caucuses with 38 percent of the vote; rival John Edwards culls 32 percent. **20 January:** Dick Gephardt ends bid for the Democratic presidential nomination after receiving only 11 percent of the votes in the Iowa Caucuses. **23 January:** UN weapons inspector David Kay resigns, citing lack of any evidence of WMDs in Iraq. **27 January:** John Kerry wins the New Hampshire Democratic Primary with 38 percent of the vote. **3 February:** After a disappointing showing in the Democratic "Super Tuesday" Primary states, Joe Lieberman ends his bid for the presidency. **4 February:** A. Q. Khan, founder of Pakistan's nuclear weapons program, admits selling plans and information to other countries, including North Korea and Iran. **10 February:** Wesley Clark drops out of the Democratic presidential race. **18 February:** Howard Dean terminates presidential campaign. **2 March:** Democratic Senator John Kerry of Massachusetts effectively wins the nomination for president after primary victories in nine states. **3 March:** John Edwards ends his presidential bid and throws support to John Kerry. **11 March:** Al-Qaeda terrorists bomb a Madrid, Spain, train station, killing 191. **29 March:** The North Atlantic Treaty Organization (NATO) expands by seven countries, including Bulgaria, Estonia, Latvia, Lithuania, Romania, Slovakia, and Slovenia. **12 April:** Israeli Prime Minister Ariel Sharon announces that Israel will withdraw from the Gaza Strip. **30 April:** Film footage of US Army soldiers abusing Iraqi prisoners at Abu Ghraib Prison is broadcast worldwide. **17 May:** Massachusetts becomes the first state to legalize gay marriage. **26 May:** Sudanese rebels and the government end a 21-year-long civil war, even as fighting continues in the Darfur region of Sudan. **28 June:** Iyad Allawi becomes prime minister of Iraq; Supreme Court rules in *Rasul v. Bush* that "enemy combatants" held at the US Marine facility in Guantanamo Bay, Cuba are eligible for habeas corpus; Supreme Court rules in *Hamdi v. Rumsfeld* that holding a US citizen as an enemy combatant is unconstitutional. **29 July:** John Kerry is nominated for president at the Democratic National Convention in Boston. **16 August:** Venezuelan President Hugo Chávez retains power as a recall referendum fails. **2 September:** George W. Bush is nominated for a second term as president at the Republican National Convention in New York City. **3 September:** Chechen terrorists hold more than 1,000 schoolchildren hostage in Beslan, Russia; 340 die when terrorists set off bombs. **2 November:** George W. Bush is re-elected to the presidency with 53 percent of the popular vote. **11 November:** PLO leader Yasser Arafat dies in Paris, France. **7 December:** Hamid Karzai becomes Afghanistan's first elected president. **26 December:** Following massive protests in Ukraine, Viktor Yushchenko is declared the winner and becomes prime minister; tsunami (tidal wave) kills more than 200,000 across Asia.

2005 9 January: Mahmoud Abbas is elected president of the Palestinian Authority; Sudanese rebels sign a peace accord that ends a

20-year-long civil war. **20 January:** George W. Bush officially begins his second term as president. **31 January:** United Nations releases an assessment of the conflict in Darfur but refuses to classify it as genocide. **14 February:** Former Lebanese Prime Minister Rafik Hariri is assassinated. **31 March:** Terry Schiavo, a comatose woman on life support who was at the center of national controversy, dies after her feeding tube is removed. **2 April:** Pope John Paul II dies. **4 April:** Kyrgyzstan plunges into violence following elections considered flawed by international monitoring agencies. **24 April:** Benedict XVI is elected as pope of the Catholic Church and is the first pontiff born in Germany. **26 April:** Syria withdraws from Lebanon after nearly three decades of occupation. **5 May:** Tony Blair and the Labour Party are elected to a third mandate in Great Britain, but with the thinnest majority since taking office in 1997. **16 June:** European Union scraps plans for a constitution after France and the Netherlands reject the treaty in referenda; the defeat is a stinging blow for former French President Valéry Giscard d'Estaing, who championed the document. **24 June:** Mahmoud Ahmadinejad, a hard-line conservative leader with plans to develop a nuclear program, wins the presidential election in Iran. **1 July:** Justice Sandra Day O'Connor announces her retirement from the Supreme Court. **7 July:** Terror attacks rock the London, England, transportation system, killing 52 and wounding 700. **8 July:** US Supreme Court strikes down the "partial-birth abortion" bill supported by President Bush, citing the failure of the bill to allow the procedure when the life of the mother is in danger. **27 July:** The Irish Republican Army (IRA) officially abandons armed struggle for a united Ireland. **2 August:** President Bush signs the Central American Free Trade Agreement (CAFTA), which eliminates trade barriers with six countries. **15 August:** Israel moves more than 8,000 settlers from the Gaza Strip; the Free Aceh Movement signs a treaty with the Indonesian government, ending three decades of civil strife. **25 August:** Hurricane Katrina, a mammoth Category 3 storm on the Saffir-Simpson scale, slams into New Orleans and the Gulf Coast, claiming more than a thousand lives and wreaking unprecedented destruction; federal, state, and local governments' emergency response appalls American and foreign observers. **3 September:** Chief Justice of the Supreme Court William H. Rehnquist dies. **22 September:** John Roberts, Jr., becomes the 17th chief justice of the Supreme Court after Senate confirmation. **23 September:** Hurricane Rita hits the

Gulf Coast, with the Texas and Louisiana coasts bearing the brunt of destruction. **28 September:** Republican House Majority Leader Tom DeLay resigns his position after accusations of election law violations in Texas. **2 October:** A magnitude 7.6 earthquake in Pakistan claims more than 80,000 lives. **3 October:** President Bush selects White House counsel Harriet Miers to replace Sandra Day O'Connor on the Supreme Court, but charges of nepotism and Miers' putative lack of judicial experience later force her withdrawal from Senate consideration. **10 October:** Angela Merkl, leader of the center-right Christian Democratic Union, becomes Germany's first female chancellor after defeating Gerhard Schröder's Social Democratic Party. **27 October:** Paris, France, is plunged into weeks of riots and chaos in northern suburbs after the deaths of two youths pursued by the police. **28 October:** I. Lewis (Scooter) Libby, chief of staff to Vice President Richard (Dick) Cheney, is indicted by a federal grand jury for obstruction of justice. **28 November:** California Republican Congressman Randy (Duke) Cunningham resigns his seat after pleading guilty to taking bribes in excess of $2 million. **15 December:** Iraq holds first parliamentary elections since Saddam Hussein was removed from power in 2003.

2006 5 January: Ehud Olmert is named acting prime minister of Israel after Ariel Sharon is incapacitated by a stroke. **10 January:** Iran resumes work on nuclear program, contending it is for peaceful means. **19 January:** Al-Qaeda leader Osama bin Laden releases a video threatening the United States with terror attacks. **25 January:** Hamas wins Palestinian legislative elections, forcing Prime Minister Ahmed Qurei of Fatah to resign. **31 January:** The US Senate confirms Samuel Alito to the Supreme Court and Ben Bernanke to head the Federal Reserve. **4 February:** Mass protests and riots consume the Muslim world after a Danish newspaper releases negative cartoon caricatures of the prophet Muhammed. **6 February:** Conservative Stephen Harper becomes prime minister of Canada. **9 March:** President Bush signs the renewal of the PATRIOT Act into law. **11 March:** Former Yugoslavian President Slobodan Milošević dies in The Hague, Netherlands, while on trial for war crimes. **29 March:** Lobbyist Jack Abramoff is convicted on fraud charges and sentenced to six years in prison. **4 April:** Iraqi dictator Saddam Hussein is charged by an Iraqi court with genocide over treatment of Kurds. **3 May:** Zacarias Moussaoui is sentenced to life in prison without parole for his role in the 11 September 2001 terror attacks on New York and Washington, D.C. **15 May:** President Bush announces intentions to normalize relations with Libya. **21 May:** Montenegro votes in favor of independence from Serbia. **7 June:** US Senate rejects a constitutional amendment barring same-sex marriage, which was supported by President Bush. **18 June:** Episcopal Church chooses Katharine Jefferts Schori as first woman bishop. **24 June:** Millionaire Warren Buffett announces donation of more than 80 percent of his fortune, worth $44 million, to charities. **29 June:** In a 5–3 decision in *Hamdan v. Rumsfeld*, the US Supreme Court limits President Bush's ability to conduct military tribunals of "enemy combatants" held at Guantanamo Bay, Cuba. **11 July:** Terrorist bombs explode on commuter trains in Mumbai, India, killing 200. **19 July:** President Bush issues the first veto of his administration on a bill that would have expanded federal funding for embryonic stem-cell research. **4 August:** Victor Yanukovich is named prime minister of Ukraine. **29 September:** Florida Republican Congressman Mark Foley vacates his seat after sexually explicit messages from him to congressional pages emerge. **9 October:** North Korea tests a nuclear missile underground. **5 November:** Iraqi dictator Saddam Hussein is sentenced to hang to death for war crimes against the Kurds. **21 November:** Lebanese minister and critic of Syria, Pierre Gemayel, is assassinated. **4 December:** John Bolton, a recess appointment by President Bush as ambassador to the United Nations, resigns when Senate confirmation appears unlikely. **14 December:** Ban Ki-moon replaces Kofi Annan as secretary general of the United Nations. **26 December:** Former President Gerald Ford dies at age 93. **31 December:** US casualties in the war in Iraq reach 3,000.

2007 1 January: Bulgaria and Rumania are admitted into the European Union. **2 January:** Funeral for former President Gerald Ford held in Washington, D.C. **4 January:** California Democrat Nancy Pelosi is sworn in as the first woman speaker of the House of Representatives. **28 January:** Sinn Féin endorses a plan for policing in Northern Ireland. **6 February:** US Senate confirms Mike McConnell as Director of National Intelligence. **8 February:** Palestinian leaders from rival Fatah and Hamas parties reach an accord to end violence. **13 February:** North Korea agrees to suspend its nuclear weapons program in exchange for foreign aid. **1 March:** Furor over patient care at Walter Reed Army

Medical Center forces ouster of General George Weightman as head of the facility. **6 March:** I. Lewis (Scooter) Libby, former chief of staff to Vice President Dick Cheney, is found guilty of lying to a grand jury for his role in exposing undercover CIA agent Valerie Plame Wilson. **26 March:** Gerry Adams and Rev. Ian Paisley agree to a power-sharing government between nationalists and loyalists in Northern Ireland; Iran detains 15 British sailors for putative violation of their waters; Great Britain claims they were in international waters. **4 April:** British sailors held by Iran are released. **16 April:** Mass shooting by student Seung-Hui Cho at Virginia Tech University in Blacksburg, Virginia, claims 32 lives, after which the gunman commits suicide. **18 April:** In *Gonzales v. Carhart*, the US Supreme Court upholds a ban on partial-birth abortions, contending the law does not violate a woman's right to an abortion. **1 May:** President Bush vetoes legislation authorizing spending for wars in Iraq and Afghanistan after Democrats insist on a timetable for the withdrawal of troops from Iraq. **6 May:** Nicolas Sarkozy wins the second round of the French presidential election. **8 May:** Rev. Ian Paisley of the Democratic Unionist Party and Martin McGuinness of Sinn Féin are sworn in as first and deputy-first minister, respectively, in Northern Ireland. **10 May:** British Prime Minister Tony Blair announces plans to resign. **17 May:** Paul Wolfowitz resigns as president of the World Bank due to conflict of interest after overseeing a pay raise for his girlfriend. **4 June:** Democratic Congressman William Jefferson of Louisiana is indicted by a grand jury on corruption charges. **7 June:** In a stinging blow to President Bush, legislation he supported to overhaul immigration fails in the Senate. **11 June:** In *Parhat v. Gates*, a federal appeals court rules that the Bush administration cannot order the military to hold civilian enemy combatants indefinitely. **12 June:** Fighting between rival Palestinian groups leaves Hamas in charge of the Gaza Strip and Fatah in charge of the West Bank. **20 June:** President Bush vetoes a bill that would have eased restriction on federal funding of embryonic stem-cell research. **25 June:** Robert Zoellick succeeds Paul Wolfowitz as head of the World Bank. **27 June:** Gordon Brown becomes British prime minister. **28 June:** In decisions on *Parents v. Seattle* and *Meredith v. Jefferson*, the US Supreme Court rules that Seattle, Washington, and Louisville, Kentucky, school districts' consideration of the race of children when assigning them to schools is unconstitutional; critics charge the ruling is a major setback for affirmative action. **1 August:** Bridge over the Mississippi River on Interstate 35 in Minneapolis, Minnesota, collapses, claiming 13 lives. **5 August:** President Bush signs a bill authorizing eavesdropping on American citizens in the United States and abroad. **13 August:** Karl Rove, confidant and advisor to President Bush, announces plans to leave the White House. **27 August:** Attorney General Alberto Gonzales tenders his resignation. **28 August:** Turkey elects Adullah Gul as its first Islamist president. **24 September:** US Court of Military Commission Review contends that foreign-born unlawful "enemy combatants" should be tried in military courts. **October:** Pakistani leader Pervez Musharraf is elected to a third term amid questions over the constitutionality of his election, which the opposition boycotts. **12 October:** Former Vice President Al Gore receives Nobel Prize for his work on climate change. **18 October:** Exiled leader Benazir Bhutto arrives in Pakistan and narrowly survives a bombing that kills 135. **8 November:** US Senate confirms Michael Mukasey as attorney general. **24 November:** Australian Prime Minister John Howard, an ally in the Bush administration's War on Terror, loses his majority to the Labor Party's Kevin Rudd. **13 December:** Former Senator George Mitchell's panel on steroid use in Major League Baseball accuses dozens of players of violating rules. **27 December:** Pakistani leader Benazir Bhutto is killed in a terrorist attack in the city of Rawalpindi.

2008 2 January: Oil prices reach record $100 per barrel. **8 January:** US forces in Iraq commence large-scale effort, including massive bombing, of Diyala Province to halt insurgency. **21 January:** World markets sink as fear of sub-prime mortgage crisis in the United States escalates. **4 February:** Iran launches a rocket into space, raising worries about its program to develop WMDs. **5–6 February:** Tornados claim 58 lives in US southern states. **17 February:** Taliban insurgents kill 80 in a suicide bombing in Kandahar; Kosovo declares independence from Serbia. **22 February:** Turkey launches major offensive against PKK (Kurdish rebels) in northern Iraq. **24 February:** Fidel Castro resigns as president of Cuba; his brother Raul takes the reins of power. **1 March:** Israel launches air strikes on the Gaza Strip. **25 March:** Iraqi Army launches assault on Mahdi militia rebels in Basra, Iraq. **27 April:** Afghan President Hamid Karzai survives assassination attempt by Taliban insurgents. **12 May:** 69,000 die in devastating earthquake in southwest

China. **12 June:** Voters in Ireland reject the European Union's Lisbon Treaty. **13 June:** Prominent NBC journalist Tim Russert dies of heart attack. **27 June:** Robert Mugabe is re-elected president of Zimbabwe amid allegations of elections fraud. **12 July:** Former press secretary to George W. Bush, Tony Snow, dies of cancer. **21 July:** Radovan Karadžić is arrested for war crimes in Serbia. **28 July:** Insurgent bombs kill 48 and injure nearly 300 in Iraq. **3 August:** Soviet dissident and Nobel prize winner Aleksandr Solzhenitsyn dies. **7 August:** Russia begins offensive against Georgia and the breakaway republics of Abkhazia and South Ossetia. **8 August:** Summer Olympics commence in Beijing, China; President George W. Bush attends opening ceremonies. **18 August:** Pervez Musharraf resigns as president of Pakistan under threat of impeachment. **6 September:** Asif Ali Zardari becomes president of Pakistan. **13 September:** Hurricane Ike makes landfall over Galveston, Texas, causing $20 billion in damage to Texas and Louisiana. **25 September:** China launches third manned space flight, following which it conducts its first spacewalk. **1 October:** President George W. Bush signs legislation for a $700 bailout of troubled banks due to the subprime mortgage crisis. **4 November:** Democrat Barack Obama defeats Republican John McCain in the US presidential election, becoming the 44th president and first African-American elected to the Oval Office. **26–29 November:** Terrorist attacks in Mumbai, India, kill 195 and injure more than 200 more.

2009 3 January: Israel commences ground invasion of Gaza Strip after Hamas militants launch rockets into Israel. **15 January:** US Airways flight loses both engines after taking off from LaGuardia Airport in New York; pilot lands the plane in the Hudson River and all 155 aboard survive. **20 January:** President George W. Bush leaves office; Barack Obama is sworn in as 44th president of the United States amid record crowds.

Time Line of the Iraq War and Occupation

2003 19 March: US and coalition forces launch attack on Iraq to oust President Saddam Hussein. **25 March:** Land battle east of Najaf is one of the most intense of the war, with coalition forces killing 150–200 Iraqis; coalition deaths reach 43. **1 April:** US forces begin major battle for Baghdad; 19-year-old Army Private Jessica Lynch is rescued after being taken hostage following an ambush eight days earlier. **5–6 April:** US forces capture and secure Baghdad airport and begin encircling the city. **9 April:** Citizens of Baghdad loot government buildings and topple a statue of Saddam Hussein; the cities of Kirkuk and Mosul fall to coalition forces. **13 April:** US forces face intense fighting in Tikrit, the last major Iraqi city not under coalition control. **21 April:** Coalition Provisional Authority with executive, legislative, and judicial powers is set up in Iraq. **1 May:** Aboard the aircraft carrier USS *Abraham Lincoln* and standing under a banner reading "Mission Accomplished," President Bush announces the end to major combat operations in Iraq; Paul Bremer takes over as civil administrator of Iraq, replacing Jay Garner. **22 May:** UN Security Council lifts sanctions on Iraq, acknowledging the US-led administration of the country. **30 May:** Secretary of State Colin Powell and British Prime Minister Tony Blair each deny distorting intelligence information on Iraq's potential for WMDs. **7 July:** Bush administration admits that intelligence that Iraq was seeking to buy nuclear material from Niger was unsubstantiated. **13 July:** Interim Governing Council of Iraqis is inaugurated. **17 July:** US casualties in Iraq reach 147, the same number as for the first Persian Gulf War in 1991. **22 July:** Saddam Hussein's sons, Uday and Qusay, are killed in a gun battle with US forces. **9 August:** After 100 days in Iraq, US casualties reach 255. **19 August:** A truck bomb explodes at the UN building in Baghdad and kills 20, including Sérgio Vieira de Mello, UN High Commissioner for Human Rights. **2 October:** Weapons inspector David Kay issues an interim report citing the failure to uncover any WMDs. **16 October:** UN Security Council unanimously backs United States/Great Britain resolution on Iraq reconstruction. **23–24 October:** A conference in Madrid, Spain, to raise funds for Iraq's reconstruction nets $13 billion from donors. **27 October:** Suicide attacks on police stations and the Red Crescent kill 43, injure over 200 in Baghdad. **2 November:** Iraqi guerrillas shoot down a US helicopter, killing 16 and injuring 21; it is the worst attack on US forces since the outset of the war. **14 November:** Bush administration agrees to transfer power to the Iraq Governing Council by 2004. **9 December:** Deputy Secretary of Defense Paul Wolfowitz issues a directive that bars France, Germany, Canada, Mexico, China, and Russia from bidding on Iraq reconstruction contracts. **14 December:** After going into hiding for nine months, Saddam Hussein is captured in a foxhole by US troops.

2004 1 February: Two suicide bombings in Arbil kill 109 and wound more than 200. **18 February:** Suicide bombing kills eight Iraqis on a Coalition base in Baghdad. **21 February:** Red Cross is permitted to visit Saddam Hussein for the first time since his capture in December 2003. **2 March:** Bombs kill nearly 200 Iraqis in Baghdad and Karbala. **8 March:** New Iraqi Constitution is signed. **1 April:** Four US contractors are shot and their car burned in Fallujah. **4 April:** Forces of Shi'ite cleric Muqtada al-Sadr begin four months of extended clashes with Coalition forces. **18 April:** Spanish Prime Minister José Luis Rodríguez Zapatero withdraws his country's participation in military operations in Iraq; reports and images of prisoner abuse by US forces at Abu Ghraib Prison stir international outrage. **1 June:** Prime Minister Iyad Allawi assumes functions in Iraq. **8 June:** UN Resolution 1546 is adopted, which transfers power from the Coalition Provisional Authority to the new Iraqi government. **28 June:** Coalition Provisional Authority officially transfers power to the new Iraqi government, and Paul Bremer leaves Iraq. **16 July:** Philippines government formally withdraws from Coalition forces in Iraq. **20 July:** President of the Philippines Gloria Arroyo confirms that a Filipino hostage's release was conditioned on her country's withdrawal from military operations in Iraq. **1 October:** Intense fighting between Coalition and Iraqi forces against insurgents in Najaf. **7 November:** Iraqi government decrees a countrywide state of emergency.

2005 4 January: The governor of Baghdad Province, Ali al-Haidri, is assassinated. **21 January:** Car bomb in Baghdad Shi'ite mosque kills 14. **26 January:** Helicopter crash near the border of Jordan kills 31 US Marines. **29 January:** Car bombs claim 17 lives in Baghdad; US Embassy is struck by a rocket, killing two Americans and wounding four others. **30 January:** Parliamentary elections in Iraq yield a majority for Shia parties; 30 British soldiers are killed in the crash of transport plane. **7 February:** Bombings at Mosul and Baquba police recruiting stations claim 27 lives. **28 February:** More than 100 Iraqis are killed in a car bombing south of Baghdad. **4 March:** Italian undercover agent Nicola Calipari is killed by fire from US forces as Italian journalist Giuliana Sgrena is freed; four US troops are killed; Italian Prime Minister Silvio Berlusconi announces cutback in his country's troops in Iraq. **10 March:** Suicide bomber at a funeral in Mosul kills 47. **16 March:** New Iraqi National Assembly (legislature) meets for the first time. **20 March:** Intense gun battle between US forces and insurgents leaves 24 dead. **6 April:** Jalal Talabani, a Kurd, is elected to the presidency of Iraq. **9 April:** Fifteen Iraqi troops are killed by insurgents south of Baghdad. **16 April:** Three US troops are killed in attack on their base near Ramadi. **20 April:** Sixty dead bodies are recovered from the Euphrates River in Baghdad, while insurgents execute nearly two dozen Iraqi soldiers at a football stadium in Haditha; Prime Minister Iyad Allawi narrowly escapes an assassination attempt. **21 April:** Insurgents shoot down a commercial jet near Baghdad; the crash claims 11 lives, while one survivor is shot and killed by insurgents. **4 May:** Suicide bombings in Irbil claim 60 lives. **6 May:** Suicide bombing in Suwayra kills 58. **17 May:** Suicide bomber kills 98 in an attack on a mosque in Moussayib. **13 July:** Thirty-four Iraqi boys are killed by a suicide bomber as they scramble for candy thrown on the ground to them from US troops. **31 August:** Nearly a thousand Iraqis are killed during a bridge stampede in Baghdad after pilgrims to a mosque heard rumors of an imminent suicide bombing. **7 September:** US hostage Roy Hallums released. **12 September:** A dozen suicide bombings claim 150 lives in Baghdad; Islamist militant Abu Musab al-Zarqawi declares all-out war against Shia in Iraq. **25 September:** Antiwar rally in Washington, D.C., draws 100,000. **26 September:** Army Private Lynndie England is found guilty of charges relating to the Abu Ghraib prisoner abuse scandal. **29 September:** Suicide bombers claim more than 100 lives in Balad, north of Baghdad. **7 October:** Intense fighting in Western Iraq kills six US Marines and 19 Iraqi troops. **11–12 October:** Insurgent bombs kill 60 in Talafar in two days of violence. **13 October:** Voting in a referendum to ratify the Iraqi Constitution begins. **19 October:** Saddam Hussein's trial by an Iraqi court begins. **25 October:** Iraq's Election Commission certifies passage of the Constitution by referendum. **18 November:** Suicide bombings claim 74 lives at Shi'ite mosques in Kanaqin and Diyala; US House of Representatives rejects a bill to immediately terminate the war in Iraq. **2 December:** Ten US Marines are killed in a roadside bombing in Falluja. **4 December:** Iraqi Prime Minister Iyad Allawi escapes assassination attempt in Najaf. **14 December:** President Bush states that his decision to invade Iraq was the result of faulty intelligence, but stands by the decision nonetheless. **15 December:** Legislative elections are held in Iraq.

2006 4–6 January: Violence in Baghdad claims 200 lives. **4 January:** Suicide bomber in Karbala kills 32. **5 January:** One hundred Iraqis are killed in separate bombings in Karbala and Ramadi. **7 January:** Two Iraqis die after violent demonstrations in Nasiriyah. **22 February:** Mosque in al-Askari is bombed, allegedly by al-Qaeda, severely damaging one of the holiest sites in Iraq. **28 February:** Suicide bomber kills 35 in Baghdad. **24 March:** US Department of Defense alleges, based on intelligence reports seized in Iraq, that Russia aided Saddam Hussein's regime before the 2003 invasion. **25 March:** Violent gun battle in Mahmoudiya kills or injures 40. **26 March:** More than two dozen decapitated bodies are found in Baghdad. **27 March:** Bombing at police recruiting center in Baghdad kills 40. **26 April:** Marines in al-Hamdania shoot an Iraqi man and plant evidence, leading to charges of murder and conspiracy. **20 May:** New Iraqi government fully assumes its functions for provisional government. **5 June:** Two US SEABEEs are killed by an improvised explosive device (IED) near al Asad. **7 June:** Islamist militant Abu Musab al-Zarqawi is killed in Baquba. **1 July:** Sixty-six Iraqis are killed in violence in Sadr City, a slum of Baghdad. **9 July:** Insurgent Shi'ites gun down 40 Sunnis in Baghdad. **18 July:** Car bomb in Kufa kills 53 Iraqis. **20 August:** Sunni gunmen kill nearly two dozen Shi'ites during a pilgrimage in Baghdad. **7 November:** In mid-term congressional elections, the Republican Party loses majorities in the House and Senate; widespread opposition to the Iraq war is cited in exit polls. **8 November:** President Bush announces resignation of Donald Rumsfeld as secretary of defense. **23 November:** Sunni car bombs kill 200 and injure more than 250 in Sadr City. **28 November:** Marine Corps report cites failure to quell insurgency in al-Anbar province. **30 December:** Saddam Hussein is executed by hanging; although the execution was to be private, video recordings of the event are disseminated on the Internet.

2007 6–9 January: US and Iraqi forces kill 120 insurgents in Baghdad in the "Battle of Haifa Street." **10 January:** President Bush announces his plan for a "surge" of 20,000 troops in Iraq to battle insurgency. **16 January:** Car bomb kills 65 Iraqis outside Baghdad's al-Mustansiriya University. **20 January:** Twelve US troops are killed when a helicopter is shot down outside Baghdad; bombings and military engagements claim another 13 troops around the country. **22 January:** Car bombs in Baghdad kill 88. **23 January:** Five employees of military contractor Blackwater are killed when the helicopter in which they were traveling is shot down. **25 January:** Two attacks in the Green Zone in Baghdad claim 26 lives and injure twice as many. **28 January:** Iraqi and Coalition forces engage insurgents near Najaf, killing nearly 300. **3 February:** Truck bomb kills 135 in Baghdad. **6 February:** US Army helicopter crashes and kills seven troops. **12 February:** A series of car bombs are set off in Baghdad, killing 76. **14 February:** Suicide bombers kill more than 60 civilians in Baghdad. **1 March:** Iraqi forces kill 80 insurgents in Anbar province. **6 March:** Two suicide bombers kill 120 pilgrims outside Karbala. **22 March:** UN Secretary General Ban Ki-moon escapes assassination attempt while visiting Baghdad's Green Zone. **27 March:** Truck bombs in Talafar kill 85, injure nearly three times as many. **29 March:** Series of bombings kill more than a hundred in Baghdad. **11 April:** Defense Secretary Robert Gates announces continued deployment of troops past their 12-month tour of duty in Iraq. **18 April:** Series of bombings kills 198 in Baghdad. **6 May:** Eight US troops are killed in roadside bombings around Iraq; bombings also claim 95 Iraqis. **9 May:** Vice President Dick Cheney makes a surprise visit to Baghdad. **3 September:** British forces leave Basra and hand the city over to Iraqi forces. **19 September:** US military contractor Blackwater is involved in a shooting that kills 11 Iraqi civilians. **18 October:** Turkey's Parliament authorizes combat against Kurdish troops in Iraqi territory. **30 November:** New Australian Prime Minister Kevin Rudd

announces the withdrawal of his country's troops by summer of 2008.
16 December: British troops hand over control of Basra Province to
Iraqi forces. **18 December:** Turkish forces launch incursions into northern Iraq to battle Kurdish separatists.

2008 8 January: US forces launch "Operation Phantom Phoenix"
against al-Qaeda in Iraq. **13 January:** Iraqi government announces
former members of the Ba'ath Party are eligible for civilian and military service. **22 January:** Iraqi Parliament adopts a new national flag,
which is minus the three stars of Saddam Hussein's Ba'ath Party.
24–25 January: Bombings in Mosul claim 74 lives. **1 February:**
Several remote-controlled bombs explode in Baghdad markets, killing
nearly a hundred. **13 February:** Iraqi Parliament passes law outlining
federal and provincial powers. **22 February:** 10,000 Turkish forces
incur into northern Iraq to battle PKK separatists. **6 March:** Bombs
kill 53 in Baghdad. **8 March:** Mass grave discovered containing 100
bodies north of Baquba. **17 March:** International Red Cross issues
a report stating Iraq is nearing a full-scale humanitarian crisis. **20
March:** Al-Qaeda leader Osama bin Laden issues a videotape that
airs on Arabic language television station al-Jazeera; bin Laden calls
for a "jihad" in Iraq to liberate the Middle East, including Palestine.
25–30 March: Iraqi forces engage Mahdi Army insurgents in Basra;
the fighting leaves 400 dead. **2 April:** Shi'ite Cleric Muqtada al-Sadr
calls on Iraqis to protest massively against the United States. **8 April:**
General David Petraeus and Ambassador to Iraq Ryan Crocker testify
before Congress on status of US forces in Iraq and planned withdrawal
of "surge" forces in July. **31 May:** US forces suffer 19 deaths in Iraq—
the lowest monthly number since the conflict began in March 2003. **29
July:** US and Iraqi forces mount a significant offensive against insurgents in Diyala Province. **21 August:** United States and Iraq negotiate
agreement for all US forces to leave Iraq by 2011. **29 October:** Polish
troops end mission in Iraq. **4–9 December:** Czech, South Korean, and
Ukranian forces leave Iraq. **14 December:** An Iraqi journalist throws
his shoes at President George W. Bush during a press conference while
the president is in Iraq.

2009 1 January: Iraqi forces take responsibility for the Green Zone
in Baghdad; United States officially opens embassy in Baghdad.

Introduction

A Harris Poll conducted in mid-February 2009 found that 34 percent of Americans thought George W. Bush was the worst president since World War II. Yet any broad assessment of Bush's legacy just a few months after he left the Oval Office is intuitively both premature and precarious. The long-term impact of the 43rd American president's record on domestic and foreign affairs clearly awaits the sobering objectivity that comes with the passage of time, the dispassionate retrospection that will undoubtedly inform future scholarly analyses of the Bush administration's policies and processes, and the ultimate success or failure of the wars in Afghanistan and Iraq and against global terrorism more generally. The proverbial "jury" on Bush's place in history will continue to deliberate for many years to come.

Nonetheless, as George W. Bush left the White House for the last time on that frigid day on 20 January 2009 and ceded the reins of the bully pulpit to a new administration that bitterly opposed so many of his policies, few observers remained neutral about Bush's prospective heritage after eight years in the White House. Bush indubitably failed to accomplish one of the central pledges of his 2000 campaign: To be a "uniter, not a divider."

Political scientist Michael Nelson's tripartite typology of the presidency as "Satan," "Savior," or "Sampson" is quite apropos in placing into sharp relief competing perspectives on Bush's two terms in office.[1]

The Satan model posits a self-aggrandizing, "imperial" presidency run amok. The concept evokes unsettling memories of the most disconcerting abuses of power by the Nixon White House, or the leadership deficits of Lyndon Johnson during the war in Vietnam. The litany of complaints leveled against Bush by his harshest detractors include a wholly unnecessary war in Iraq based on poor or purposefully misinterpreted intelligence; a messianic zeal to "democratize" the Middle

East; a wholesale disregard for civil liberties and contempt for the Constitution and Congress; a suspicion of and disdain for international institutions and conventions; a unilateral foreign policy that placed the United States at odds with long-standing allies; and an irresponsible fiscal policy and a failure to regulate financial markets to the point that the national economy was plunged into the worse and most sudden recession in decades, alongside a burgeoning federal deficit.

The "Savior" model of the presidency, by contrast, envisages a much more benign exercise of presidential power, which is not to be feared but championed. Not only is "energy in the executive a leading character in the definition of good government," as Alexander Hamilton wrote in Federalist 70, but presidential power is inherently benevolent—and necessary to the well-being and security of the Republic. Some scholars go even further to argue that to strengthen the presidency is to buttress democracy itself.[2] The president is the "chief guardian of the national interest not only in foreign policy (because no one else can speak and act for the nation) but also in domestic affairs because of the pluralistic structure of government and society."[3] Instead of conjuring up images of Richard Nixon, Lyndon Johnson, and abuses of power, subscribers to the Savior model look optimistically to the *potential* for presidents to use their powers toward positive ends. The active leadership of Franklin Roosevelt domestically during the New Deal and in foreign affairs during World War II is a case in point.

Bush's staunchest supporters are apt to view his presidency through the lens of the Savior model. Protecting the homeland in the wake of the 11 September 2001 terrorist attacks obliged swift, decisive action both domestically and internationally. Further, the watershed event placed into sharp relief the evil and disregard for human life that radical, Islamist fundamentalism embodies. The response to global terrorism could not wait for congressional dithering. Some civil liberties had to be sacrificed to achieve a greater good—either temporarily or permanently. Moreover the human and financial costs or collateral damage to multilateralism in conjunction with the War on Terror paled in comparison to a failure to act resolutely. From this perspective, Bush did not so much arrogate power but rightly sought to exercise his constitutional authority as commander in chief to its full potential to protect the nation from future terrorist attacks and loss of life. Further, his leadership style combined symbolism and substance as a representation of national unity. His stances on partial-birth abortion and stem-cell research, in conjunction with his view of America's obligation to secure the homeland, stamp out terrorism, and spread global democracy, are part and parcel of a philosophy of "moral clarity" that derives from the nation's unique political culture and historical exceptionalism: Abraham Lincoln's "last, best hope on Earth" and John Winthrop's "shining city on the hill."

While there may be little consensus whether to classify the Bush presidency in "Satan" or "Savior" terms, there is no dispute that Bush and his closest advisors—Vice President Richard B. (Dick) Cheney and Karl Rove, aided by the president's legal counsel staff—subscribed to the "Sampson" model of the presidency. The Sampson model envisions a hobbled presidency with declining substantive authority and power. In 1970, George Reedy wrote of the "twilight of the presidency," an argument that seemed at least partially vindicated by the resurgence of Congress following Watergate and the presidency of Jimmy Carter: A waning of presidential power, influence, and potential for action.[4] Hamstrung by congressional oversight, legal and constitutional barriers to the exercise of authority, and vanishing public confidence in the White House, the presidency appeared emasculated to the point of inefficacy. The presidency of Ronald Reagan may well have reinvigorated the office and invalidated, at least partially, such an overly pessimistic outlook.

But the Bush administration—rightly or wrongly—perceived an increasingly enfeebled chief executive during the presidency of William Clinton. Bush, Cheney, Rove, and other administration officials undeniably set out expressly to reverse constraints on the exercise of executive power via "unitary executive" theory. The reassertion of presidential power took many forms: executive orders, "signing statements" that challenged provisions of congressional legislation, claims to executive privilege, and a host of bold, if controversial, actions taken under the rubric of the president's commander in chief role, including the designation of US citizens and foreign nationals as "enemy combatants" in the waging of war against global terror.

AN ERA OF TRANSFORMATIONS

With Nelson's typology in mind, one useful approach in analyzing the Bush presidency is to consider the multiple transformations that occurred over his eight years in office. Such transformations were in part a product of intent and in part a product of circumstance. Some were successful, others unsuccessful, and many contradictory. Let us consider the transformational nature of Bush's two terms in greater depth, beginning with his election in 2000, as a means of grasping the divergent views of Bush's potential legacy.

The 2000 Election and Bush's Early Agenda

When they cast their ballots on 7 November 2000, few voters could have predicted that the victor would not be known until some 36 days later, after a series of protracted court battles. When the polls closed, Democratic nominee Al Gore culled a half million more votes nationwide than did the Bush–Cheney ticket, thanks largely to a strong showing in California. But popular votes do not determine American presidential elections. The victor must secure a majority of the Electoral College. In the early morning hours of 8 November, it became clear that the race in Florida was too close to call. The Sunshine State's 25 electoral votes held the balance over the election, and voters around the nation held their collective breath.

The closeness of the Florida vote triggered an automatic recount of ballots under state law. Yet, even before this process had commenced, voting irregularities made national and international headlines, adding a critical layer of complexity in determining the next president. In Palm Beach County, the use of a so-called "butterfly ballot" seemingly confused many voters—particularly the elderly—who claimed that while they had meant to vote for Al Gore, they had mistakenly cast their vote for Reform Party candidate Patrick Buchanan. African-American voters around the state complained they had been turned away from polling places because their names were not on the registration lists. Amazingly, some convicted felons ineligible to vote *were* on the lists.

Against this confused backdrop, the state recount got under way. The Gore–Lieberman ticket challenged the results in four counties, including Palm Beach, where voting irregularities appeared most flagrant. Local canvassing boards around the state began the arduous task of examining ballots, some of which were "punch cards" that had not been completely perforated. It fell to local elections workers to analyze "hanging," "pregnant," and other types of "chads" in an effort, surreal at times, to determine the "intention of voters." These ballots became increasingly disputed by Republican and Democratic observers during the recount process.

The Bush–Cheney team never wavered from the contention that it had prevailed in Florida and won the White House. In an initial round of legal wrangling, the state supreme court ordered that the recount continue, notwithstanding Bush's objections. By December, however, the matter had reached the US Supreme Court. The Bush team posited that the lack of uniform standards for the recount process across Florida counties violated the equal protection of the laws. In a 5–4 decision in *Bush v. Gore*, the High Court put an end to the recount. Florida Secretary of State Katherine Harris, an appointee of George W. Bush's brother and governor of Florida, Jeb Bush, had already certified the election for Bush by 537 votes. With 271 electoral votes to Gore's 266, Bush became the nation's 43rd president—and the fourth to win the Electoral College after losing the popular vote.

A clear majority of Americans supported the Supreme Court's pronouncement and accepted Bush as the "legitimate" president. Nonetheless, for a candidate who pledged to unite the country, the narrowness of the Court's decision, recriminations by some Democrats that Bush had "stolen" the election, and Gore's popular vote victory robbed Bush of a significant reservoir of goodwill that usually accompanies a new president into the Oval Office. Bush began his first term with early job approval ratings in the mid-50s, and his first eight months in office were scarcely electrifying.

Bush's early policy victories, significant in their own right, were frequently offset by the controversy that enveloped them. The 2000 campaign had centered primarily on domestic issues, and most notably, what to do with a federal budget surplus. Gore suggested sequestering the funds in a "lockbox" to be used to shore up Social Security. Once in office, Bush remained true to his promise to return the funds as a rebate to taxpayers. He pursued and achieved significant tax cuts, including the removal of the "marriage tax penalty." Fiscal conservatives and some Democrats, however, lamented the possibility of returning to an era of federal budget deficits.

Bush faced his first foreign policy challenge when a US military aircraft collided with a Chinese plane over Hainan Island on 1 April. The crew destroyed sensitive material before being taken by Chinese authorities for interrogation. The crew was held for ten days until the State Department issued letters of apology to the Chinese government. While the exact causes of the collision remain unclear, the Chinese contended that the United States had violated their airspace. Although the incident did not harm bilateral relations in the long term, it nevertheless proved a source of embarrassment for the young administration and did little to bolster Bush's foreign policy credentials.

Bush extended an olive branch to Democrats, working with Senator Ted Kennedy to secure education reform with the passage, in mid-2001, of the No Child Left Behind bill that provided for federal funds to state education programs, contingent on standards and testing. The legislation caused a firestorm of controversy as some states, such as Virginia, challenged the law and contended that their own state standards were higher than the federal mandates.

In August 2001, Bush articulated a federal policy on stem-cell research that restricted the use of human embryos. He won kudos from social conservatives concerned about the production of fetuses for medical research and cemented his commitment to uphold a "culture of life." Yet many in the medical community considered the restrictions an impediment to major advances to solving a host of diseases potentially treatable by stem cells.

As summer 2001 faded into the early days of fall, the Bush administration seemed to drift. Dissatisfied with Bush's economic policy, Republican Senator James Jeffords had abruptly left the Grand Old Party (GOP) in May 2001 and effectively gave Democrats organizational control of the upper chamber, thereby complicating Bush's legislative prospects. The mid-term elections of 2002 loomed just over a year in the offing. Storm clouds appeared on the horizon as signs of an imminent recession mounted. Bush's agenda seemed highly unclear, and observers began to muse whether his fate would parallel his father's—a one-term president with a mixed, lackluster record of achievement on the domestic or international front. The events of 11 September 2001 halted such speculation in its tracks.

9/11 and the Advent of the Wartime Presidency

The tranquil, clear blue skies in New York City and along the eastern seaboard of the United States on the morning of Tuesday, 11 September

2001, betrayed the horror that awaited a nation that had awoken to carry out a typical work- and school day routine. Armed with box cutters, 19 hijackers killed pilots, crew, and passengers to commandeer four commercial aircraft en route to the West Coast from Boston, Newark, and Washington, D.C. In a deadly, coordinated attack, at 8:46 A.M. the hijackers first used American Airlines Flight 11, a Boeing 767, as a flying missile and crashed the fuel-laden aircraft into the North Tower of the World Trade Center in New York City. Seventeen minutes later another aircraft, United Airlines Flight 175, crashed into the South Tower of the World Trade Center. All aboard the aircraft died instantly. Fireballs erupted from the buildings, and the heat from the conflagrations was so intense that the structures began to melt, and collapse became imminent. Hundreds of New Yorkers on the streets who witnessed the horrific sights went scurrying for cover, and many in the towers jumped to their deaths rather than succumb to the flames and smoke. At 9:37 A.M. American Airlines Flight 77, a Boeing 757, crashed into the Pentagon in northern Virginia, killing all on board and 125 at the nation's military headquarters. Passengers aboard hijacked United Airlines Flight 93, when they learned of the attacks, managed to take back the aircraft from the terrorists. The hijackers allegedly planned to crash the jet into the White House. Control of the aircraft was lost, however, and Flight 93 crashed in a farm field near Shanksville, Pennsylvania, at 10:03, killing all on board. By 10:30 A.M. both towers of the World Trade Center had collapsed. The death toll in the worst terror attacks on American soil ultimately reached 2,974.

9/11 was unquestionably *the* defining moment of Bush's presidency. His office was immediately transformed into a wartime presidency—and in times of war, the American constitutional order pivots on the president's commander-in-chief role. In the early days following the terror attacks, the nation rallied around Bush. The president appeared steady, reassuring, and determined to pursue the perpetrators of the attacks.

The terrorist organization al-Qaeda and its ringleader, Osama bin Laden, claimed responsibility—and gleefully noted that the destruction and loss of life from the attacks had exceeded expectations. Within weeks, US intelligence confirmed that the Taliban regime in Afghanistan had provided—and continued to provide—safe haven for al-Qaeda operatives and supported terror training camps. Bush quickly seized goodwill from around the world to assemble a US-led international coalition that attacked the Taliban regime, drove it from power, and began the arduous task of securing peace and establishing some semblance of democracy in Afghanistan. Peace and regime change were not, however, easily achieved. Ultimately faced with a growing insurgency of the variety that had, using guerrilla tactics, successfully chased the Soviets from Afghanistan in the 1980s, US and international forces struggled to complete the task, which remained unfinished seven years later when Bush left office.

The war in Afghanistan cemented elements of the so-called Bush Doctrine that would guide strategy for the War on Terror. The first prong of the doctrine was that the United States would not only target and seek to eradicate non-state terrorist actors such as al-Qaeda, but also take action through military and/or diplomatic means against regimes such as the Taliban that gave terrorist groups succor. The War on Terror was broadened significantly in early 2002, when, in his State of the Union address Bush called Iran, Iraq, and North Korea an "axis of evil" because of these regimes' pursuit of weapons of mass destruction (WMDs)—nuclear, biological, and chemical—and putative state sponsorship of terrorism. Diplomatic efforts were stepped up against Iran and North Korea, while Iraqi dictator Saddam Hussein's failure to comply with United Nations (UN) weapons inspectors as part of the 1991 post-Persian Gulf War agreement loomed large on the administration's agenda for potential military action.

Saddam Hussein's bellicosity and refusal to comply with the UN's terms imposed on his regime became a rallying point for the Bush administration's contemplation of a military invasion of Iraq. In October 2002, Congress passed the Iraq War Resolution, an authorization for the use of military force should Bush decide on military action. By early 2003, controversy in the UN Security Council centered on UN Resolution 1441 and the "serious consequences" for Iraq if Hussein continued a "material breach" of the Resolution. France and Russia contended that "serious consequences" did not mean automatic military action and preferred an extension of harsh sanctions on Hussein's government. The United States and Great Britain favored military action, persuaded as they were by intelligence suggesting that Hussein had stockpiled WMDs. Unconvinced by the intelligence and unwilling to cede to pressure by the United States, French President Jacques Chirac elucidated in March 2003 that France would veto any UN resolution authorizing military action against Iraq. Transatlantic relations became palpably strained as anti-French sentiment grew in the United States. North Atlantic Treaty Organization (NATO) members, including Germany, severely criticized Bush's call to arms. The outpouring of European sympathy for the United States that followed 9/11 had regrettably vanished in the hallways and conference rooms of the UN building in New York, not far from where tragedy had struck just 18 months earlier. Absent a UN mandate for military action, Bush assembled a "Coalition of the Willing" countries—including Great Britain, Poland, Australia, and Denmark—which contributed troops to the US-led invasion of Iraq that commenced on 20 March 2003.

Bush's willingness to take military action despite a lack of international consensus formed the second and third prongs to the Bush doctrine: The United States would act alone, or in concert with other willing nations, if international institutions failed to do so. Moreover, the United States would act *preemptively* in the security interest of the nation if danger of an attack were imminent. Preemptive warfare stands in stark contrast to the doctrine of *containment* that guided US foreign policy during the Cold War with the Soviet Union, and which was the de facto policy in Iraq following the Persian Gulf War. Saddam Hussein's ability to threaten his neighbors had been thwarted by "no-fly" zones in the north and south of the country, patrolled as they were by the United States and Great Britain. Regardless, the second and third prongs of the Bush Doctrine relied on a sense of "moral clarity" in foreign affairs, which essentially couples national security interests with the notion that the United States is a force of righteousness in the world against the evils of despots and terrorism; hence, the United States has not only a right but a responsibility to act if others do not.

The ability of the US military and multinational force to crush Hussein's regime was never in doubt. On 1 May 2003, just six weeks after the invasion, Bush appeared on the USS *Abraham Lincoln* to declare that major military operations had ended in Iraq. Overhead hung a sign: "Mission Accomplished." But critics wondered what, exactly, had been accomplished? Hussein had not yet been captured, but most critically, no WMDs had been discovered. UN chief weapons inspector David Kay and Mohammed ElBaradei of the International Atomic Energy Agency would, of course, later confirm the absence of WMDs in a major embarrassment to the Bush administration that raised the specter of the possibility the president had misled the country about the need for military intervention against Hussein.

In the meantime, the structure of a new Iraqi government had not been well conceived, and worries emerged about how to balance the Sunni, Shi'ite, and Kurdish factions in whatever state institutions replaced Hussein's dictatorship. It seemed to many observers that the administration had not given adequate weight to the hurdles to be overcome following a successful military campaign. Iraq was moving potentially toward civil war. By 2007, Iraq had, in fact, made halting progress toward an institutional framework of power sharing among the major societal groups, but a large scale insurgency against US forces and widespread civilian casualties from random attacks necessitated a troop "surge" to secure Baghdad and other parts of the country. Tellingly, more than 90 percent of the casualties in the War in Iraq—civilian and military—occurred *after* Bush declared an end to major military operations.

The justification for the War in Iraq war will likely remain the most significant point of contention in analyses of Bush's legacy. Critics charge that the "rush" to war was based on faulty interpretations of intelligence at best, and purposeful deceit at worst. The effect, they argue, was to destabilize the Middle East, undermine the UN as a forum for the mediation of international conflict, and divide long-standing NATO and European allies. Critics further point to the 2002 Downing Street Memo penned by the British intelligence organization MI5, leaked publicly in 2005, which posited that Bush "wanted to remove Saddam, through military action, justified by the conjunction of terrorism and WMD. But the intelligence and facts were being fixed around the policy." Whether the buildup to the War in Iraq was a product of "groupthink" or a conspiracy by key White House advisors is a central, unanswered question. Many neoconservatives in the Bush administration—including Vice President Cheney, his chief of staff I. Lewis (Scooter) Libby, Secretary of Defense Donald Rumsfeld, Deputy Secretary of Defense Paul Wolfowitz, Deputy Secretary of State Richard Armitage, Undersecretary of State and later UN Ambassador John Bolton, Chairman of the Defense Advisory Board Richard Perle, and presidential special assistant Elliott Abrams—were members of the Project for the New American Century (PNAC). Members of the PNAC think tank wrote a forceful letter to President William Clinton in 1998 urging military action to remove Saddam Hussein from power. On the basis of the influence of neoconservative voices on the Bush foreign policy team, critics view the unproven linkage of Hussein with al-Qaeda and the question of WMDs as a facile pretext for George W. Bush to complete the mission for which his father, George H.W. Bush, did not have a UN mandate in 1991—forcing regime change in Iraq. Another charge is that the war was not about democracy, but about securing long-term American access to Iraqi fossil-fuel deposits.

As of early 2009, Iraq remains very much a work in progress and faces an uncertain future. US troop casualties declined substantially in the closing months of Bush's second term, and recent Iraqi elections were, on the whole, positive. US forces are scheduled to depart Iraq in 2011 per a bilateral agreement. Whether the regime change precipitated in Iraq amounts to a template for democracy and stability in the Middle East remains very much an open question. The answer to that paramount question may determine whether Bush's legacy in Iraq was his greatest triumph or greatest failure.

CONSTRUCTING HOMELAND SECURITY AND RECONSTRUCTING THE INTELLIGENCE COMMUNITY

The War on Terror fundamentally transformed the federal bureaucracy. Within a month of the 9/11 attacks, Bush used his executive prerogative and discretionary funds to found an Office of Homeland Security (OHS) within the Executive Office of the President (EOP). His appointment of former Pennsylvania Governor Tom Ridge won early acclaim. The affable and competent Ridge was tasked with acting as an "honest broker" to coordinate the work of intelligence agencies, and was assured the full support of and unfettered access to the president. The creation of the OHS was a swift response to criticisms that the Central Intelligence Agency (CIA) and Federal Bureau of Investigation (FBI) had not prevented the 9/11 attacks due to a failure to "connect the dots" in the sharing of intelligence analysis. The fact that these and other agencies had not taken adequate note of the al-Qaeda operatives' flight instruction in Florida, and of Phoenix and Minneapolis FBI agents' concern about potential terrorist activities in the United States, was a case in point.

Ridge's position quickly proved untenable, however. Critics argued that he lacked adequate financial and human resources to carry out sufficiently the enormity of the task that lay before him. Further, he became embroiled in controversy over executive privilege when Congress called upon him to testify about intelligence failures concerning 9/11 and he demurred. His directorship of the OHS did not require Senate confirmation, and he and the Bush administration invoked privilege concerning his advisory role to the president. While a compromise was eventually reached, the controversy only intensified the congressional drumbeat for a full-scale reorganization of governmental intelligence and security functions. Bush initially rebuffed such calls, but in a stunning *volte-face* in early 2002, preempted Congress with his own proposal for the largest reorganization of the federal bureaucracy since the creation of the Department of Defense in the 1940s.

The creation of the Department of Homeland Security (DHS) entailed the reorganization of 22 federal agencies with more than 200,000 employees. The Republican-controlled House quickly passed the reorganization plan on Bush's terms, but the bill languished in the Democratic-controlled Senate. Democrats refused to acquiesce to Bush's call for broad executive latitude on hiring and firing of employees in the new department, and sparred with the White House over labor protections. The bottleneck ultimately worked to Bush's advantage in the mid-term elections of 2002, as Republicans recaptured the Senate by running on the issue of domestic security. The lame-duck 107th Senate relented, as the bill's passage in the new Congress was assured. Nonetheless, the costs of the failure of the Bush White House and Senate Democrats to come to an earlier compromise may well be measured by what was lost during the eight-month-long delay: precious time to meld the agencies together and unify their mission. The reorganization folded the Customs Service, Coast Guard, Immigration and Naturalization Service (renamed the Border Control Service), the Federal Emergency Management Agency (FEMA), and Transportation Security Administration, among others, into a single, streamlined department. But the new, mammoth organization would have to surmount significant turf wars and a historical lack of interagency cooperation in the bid to thwart would-be terrorists on the home front.

The reform of the federal intelligence apparatus did not stop with the creation of the DHS. In 2004, Congress passed the Intelligence

Reform and Terrorism Prevention Act that created a new Director of National Intelligence (DNI). The president's anti-terrorism advisor par excellence on the National Security Council, the DNI oversees the CIA and bridges intelligence gathering across federal agencies, including the DHS. One of the most colossal tasks that fell to the first DNI, John Negroponte, was to reverse the CIA's demoralization in the wake of the 9/11 attacks and professionalize the ailing organization. A flurry of new hiring was undertaken at the CIA, while the FBI shifted thousands of employees from traditional law enforcement activities to counterterrorism programs.

The relative success of the massive reorganization of the federal bureaucracy is difficult to assess. When Bush left office in 2009, the administration could boast that there had *not* been another terrorist attack on US soil since 9/11. But the question remains whether the record was because of or in spite of these changes. The conundrum stems in part from the fact that the greatest successes of DHS and other agencies may never be reported publicly for national security reasons.

Perhaps the greatest verifiable success came in July 2006. DHS Secretary Michael Chertoff, in concert with British authorities, halted a plot by terrorists to use American transatlantic flights originating in London to style another coordinated attack on the United States using civil aviation. On a different front, perhaps the limitations to reorganization, per se, were evident in FEMA's inadequate and unacceptable response to the devastation that Hurricane Katrina wreaked in New Orleans in August 2005. FEMA had been reorganized into DHS, and its mission altered to include preparation for disasters—both natural and man-made—and post-disaster response. The agency's failure to prepare for Katrina was cause for alarm. The mammoth storm remained in the Gulf of Mexico for several days, poised to make landfall somewhere in the southern United States. Terrorists surely would not give authorities such advanced warning.

THE DECONSTRUCTION OF CIVIL LIBERTIES?

The Bush administration's prosecution of the War on Terror raised serious questions about the balance between civil liberties and the goal of securing the nation from terrorist threats. The mobilization of institutional resources to thwart future terrorist attacks had both domestic and international implications, and troubled civil libertarians and human rights activists alike. Bush's broad application of new legislation and executive prerogative to the open-ended War on Terror represented, in the view of critics, the most significant set of challenges to constitutional protections since the dawning of the Cold War, if not since the founding of the republic. Bush and his supporters contended that the application of these and other tools was critically essential to halting another major terror attack—the single, overriding objective of the administration in a new age of global terrorism. Terrorists, Bush argued, only had to "get it right" once to wreak murder and chaos; the government had to get it right 100 percent of the time.

For civil libertarians, the first alarm bells sounded with congressional passage of the PATRIOT Act in the immediate aftermath of the 9/11 attacks. The bill gave enhanced authority to law enforcement to search electronic, financial, medical, and other records, and to gather foreign intelligence domestically. The sweeping bill applied to both foreign and domestic terrorism. Many of the provisions were due to sunset at the end of 2005. Critics of the bill in the Senate pushed for substantive changes when the legislation came up for renewal. To the chagrin of civil libertarians, most of the changes were excluded as the House and Senate reconciled the bill in 2006 and extended many of the objectionable provisions related to privacy.

Bush's announcement, in July 2002, of his plans for the "TIPS" Operation, or Terrorist Information and Prevention System, further disconcerted civil libertarians. The program was to rely on government employees, such as postal workers, and ordinary citizens to report suspicious activities to authorities. For critics, the program was tantamount to domestic spying of the variety that was rampant under the Soviet or East German systems during the Cold War. The program was ultimately excluded from, and prohibited in, congressional legislation—but suggested the lengths to which the administration seemed willing to go in the War on Terror, whatever the implications for social capital or constitutional freedoms.

Confirmation that the Bush administration had engaged in warrantless wiretaps of US citizens and had circumvented the Foreign Intelligence Surveillance Act (FISA) Court, buttressed concerns that the White House and the national security bureaucracy had overstepped its constitutional authority. Before Congress approved the Protect America Act in 2007 (which authorized limited warrantless surveillance), Bush argued that warrantless wiretaps were implicitly authorized in the Authorization of the Use of Military Force (AUMF) legislation to battle terrorism, which was passed after 9/11. Following a *New York Times* investigation published in 2005, one FISA Court judge resigned in protest, and critics posited that the administration continued to violate essential liberties guaranteed under the Fourth Amendment.

The Bush administration's detention of suspected terrorists brought domestic as well as international criticism. The issue of habeas corpus was front and center in the debate, both for US citizens accused of plotting terror attacks, as well as for foreign "enemy combatants" captured in Afghanistan and held at Guantanamo Bay, Cuba.

The quintessential case involving a US citizen was that of José Padilla. An al-Qaeda sympathizer, Padilla was accused of planning a "dirty bomb" attack, and was arrested in Chicago after traveling to the Middle East in 2002. He was held as a "material witness" by federal authorities. As a material witness, he was not privy to legal counsel since he was not yet charged with anything. And since he was not immediately charged with anything, habeas corpus—the right to appear before a judge and have criminal charges heard—did not apply. The logic was tantamount to indefinite detention and troubled many in the legal community. Amid the furor, Bush designated Padilla an "enemy combatant," and he was transferred to a military facility where he was held. A federal court ruled against Padilla's petition for habeas corpus on technical legal grounds. An appeal overturned the initial ruling, and a federal court found not only that Padilla must be granted habeas corpus but also that as president, Bush did not have the constitutional authority as commander in chief to detain US citizens on US soil outside a zone of combat. An appellate court then overturned that decision, ruling in favor of Bush. The matter was not put to rest until Padilla was ultimately indicted on criminal counts including conspiracy to commit murder, and was convicted and sentenced to federal prison.

Padilla's detention raised the larger question of the administration's detention and prosecution of foreign, illegal enemy combatants. Bush contended that noncitizen detainees held at Guantanamo Bay who were not part of a state-sponsored military were not subject to the Geneva Conventions or constitutional protections, including habeas corpus.

He subsequently authorized military tribunals to conduct trials of the detainees, who would have no recourse to civilian courts for appeal. Bush's unilateral actions were challenged in the Supreme Court. In *Hamdan v. Rumsfeld* (2006), the justices ruled that the president did not have the authority to set up the tribunals, which further violated the Geneva Conventions. As a result, Congress passed the Military Commissions Act (2006), legislating such military tribunals. The law was subsequently challenged in *Boumediene v. Bush* and *Al Odah v. U.S.*, which were consolidated into one case. The Supreme Court struck down the military commissions as unconstitutional and held that detainees did have the right to habeas corpus and recourse to civilian courts.

Whatever the Supreme Court's actions, human rights organizations, such as Amnesty International, deplored the detention facility; so too did European allies—including German Chancellor Angela Merkel—who otherwise supported Bush and the War on Terror. Detainees claimed they had been tortured and subjected to "enhanced interrogation techniques" including "waterboarding," or simulated drowning. Such procedures were, in fact, confirmed by the administration. Allegations of torture prompted congressional action, including the Detainee Treatment Act of 2005, sponsored by Senator John McCain of Arizona, to preclude inhumane treatment of prisoners.

Boumediene clearly did not settle the question of what to do with other suspected terrorists held at Guantanamo. Nor did the Detainee Treatment Act reconcile the need for balance between intelligence that might stop a future terrorist attack and enemy combatants' recourse to rights provided for under the Geneva Conventions or the US Constitution. That task fell to Barack Obama, who pledged to close the facility within a year of taking office and prohibited torture as one of his first symbolic actions as president in 2009.

Surely some of the detainees are innocent. Others *are* terrorists, as evidenced by the fact that estimates suggested one of ten detainees released returned to the battlefield to aid insurgencies against US forces in Afghanistan or Iraq. Other detainees, if released, face persecution or death if returned to their home countries. Still others are prohibited from returning to their home countries and cannot find asylum elsewhere. There is little support for any of the detainees to take up residence in the United States. In short, while in the long term legal debates will take place surrounding Bush's designation of "enemy combatants," their constitutional rights, the line between "enhanced interrogation techniques" and torture, and the appropriateness of the detention facility, the shorter-term conundrum of what to do with detainees at Guantanamo is likely to be one of the major tests and an ongoing *casse-tête* for President Obama.

RESURRECTING EXECUTIVE POWER

More than any other administration in the last quarter century—including Reagan's—the Bush White House expressly set out to enhance the powers of the president. Bush's Office of Legal Counsel articulated a theory of the "unitary executive." The theory goes much further than Theodore Roosevelt's belief that the president could take any action unless not explicitly prohibited by the Constitution. Rather, the unitary executive theory holds that the president's "executive power" outlined in Article I of the Constitution gives him complete control of the executive branch of government and limits congressional interference, within statutory boundaries. Moreover, the theory posits that the president enjoys inherent powers as commander in chief that give him sweeping authority beyond the reach of other branches of government. Critics charge that the theory conflicts with basic tenets of constitutional law and dangerously hampers executive accountability.

The application of unitary executive theory translated into a host of controversies. The administration was scarcely hesitant to invoke executive privilege, resurrecting memories of the Nixon years. Early in Bush's presidency, Vice President Dick Cheney headed an energy task force—and refused to disclose publicly not only the members of the group but also its proceedings. Bush also attempted to overturn unilaterally the Presidential Records Act by signing an executive order authorizing him to claim privilege over presidential papers and prevent public disclosure. As noted earlier, Office of Homeland Security Director Tom Ridge refused to "testify" before Congress because his position did not require Senate approval. And when Bush's Attorney General Alberto Gonzales fired a host of federal attorneys, the administration invoked privilege and refused to cooperate with congressional inquiries.

Bush also argued that his commander in chief role superseded the reach of Congress. In carrying out the War on Terror, the White House contended that it did not have to comply with the FISA Court, and authorized warrantless wiretaps. The president also posited that he had the authority to designate enemy combatants, independently set up military tribunals, and carry out enhanced interrogation techniques that critics charged were tantamount to torture.

Consistent with a practice begun during the Reagan presidency, Bush employed a host of "signing statements" to lodge his disagreement publicly with select provisions of congressional laws and challenge them even as he gave them his signature. The Congressional Research Service analyzed Bush's signing statements in 2007 and determined that he had leveled objections to 118 bills up to that point. In many cases, Bush took the opportunity to give his interpretation of the bills and suggest that he would not enforce some provisions. Although the Supreme Court has not accepted the validity of such signing statements, critics—including the American Bar Association—contend that Bush essentially arrogated a de facto line-item veto that contravenes the sole constitutional power of Congress to make laws, placing the president in conflict with his duty to carry out such laws.

THE VICE PRESIDENCY: CHENEY AS VEEP OR VICEROY?

The office of vice president arguably reached the apex of influence under Dick Cheney. A strong case can be made that Cheney built upon the foundation his predecessors had laid, at least back to the Ford presidency when Nelson Rockefeller headed the Domestic Council. Each subsequent vice president played a significant, if variable, role in domestic and/or foreign affairs. George H.W. Bush, for example, was a critical advisor to Ronald Reagan on foreign affairs. Al Gore engaged in substantial policy entrepreneurship ranging from "Reinventing Government" to technology issues involving the Internet.

Yet Cheney's extensive roots in the Republican establishment, his prior experience in Congress—as Gerald Ford's chief of staff, and as secretary of defense under George H.W. Bush—provided the footing for the vice president to become an indispensable and key advisor to the younger Bush in ways even his predecessors could not necessarily envision. Cheney headed Bush's presidential transition, vetting appointments, and even convincing Donald Rumsfeld to take the position of secretary of defense. Given his health conditions (a poor heart), Cheney made it clear he had no interest in pursuing the presidency, further shoring up Bush's confidence in his counsel.

The immediate aftermath of the terror attacks on 9/11 confirmed Cheney's pivotal role in the Bush White House. The president was in Florida at the time of attacks, and it was Cheney who told him to remain there. He ordered the evacuation of Capitol Hill and then moved to a "secure location" outside public view where he made key national security decisions.

Cheney was both a mouthpiece and an intellectual anchor for Bush's neoconservative foreign policy stances and decisions. Many observers contend he used his influence to manipulate policy debates in the White House and silence dissent. Like Bush, he shunned public criticism, disregarded public opinion polls, and focused on resolute action based on notions of moral clarity, including the War in Iraq, for which he was the major administration proponent.

Critics view Cheney as a Machiavellian figure who would go to great lengths to "punish" detractors of the White House. The role of his chief of staff, I. Lewis (Scooter) Libby, in the "outing" of covert CIA agent Valerie Plame (the spouse of Ambassador Joseph Wilson, an outspoken critic of the War in Iraq) and Libby's conviction on obstruction of justice charges seemingly confirmed the suspicions of Cheney's critics. Yet to his supporters, and perhaps most importantly to Bush himself, the vice president was a savvy, indispensable advisor who brought a policy acumen that buttressed the successful prosecution of the War on Terror.

Whether the vice presidency-centric advisory system in the White House survives the Bush presidency is an open question. Joe Biden's role under Barack Obama, and the policy and advisory role of Biden's successors, will determine whether Cheney's profound influence was a singular, fleeting transformation or a longer-term trend.

BUSH'S RHETORICAL PRESIDENCY

The Bush presidency marked a curious, if ephemeral, transformation of the rhetorical presidency. For his supporters, Bush's unsophisticated, plain-spoken verbal style lent an authenticity to his personage that enabled him to connect to the average American. Even his sometimes bizarre locutions, better known as "Bushisms," endeared him to many who viewed his folksy and frequently halting manner of communication as a positive attribute. His penchant for malapropisms and creating new words, such as "misunderestimate" and "strategery," or his contention that the French did not have a word for *entrepreneur*, added a certain amount of levity to his two terms in office—and certainly fodder for late-night comedians.

To his detractors, however, Bush's semantics represent something far more nefarious. It is not just a matter of those occasions in which the president used incorrect syntax or made verbal gaffes. Rather, those incidents were symbolic of a larger, more disturbing anti-intellectualism that permeated his administration. Fiscal conservatives found cause for alarm when, on the campaign trail in May 2000, Bush commented on his economic policy by stating that "It's clearly a budget. It's got lots of numbers in it." For critics, Bush's alleged oversimplification of issues and use of phrases such as the "axis of evil" and "evildoers" reflects a Manichean approach to politics and international relations that reduces complexities to a question of "good versus evil." Many were stunned when the White House first suggested that constitutional protections did not apply to enemy combatants held at the detention facility in Guantanamo Bay, Cuba, because the military base is not located in the United States proper.

Nevertheless, Bush's strategic use of oratory, with much emphasis on faith and values and replete with dramatic language emphasizing the wickedness of terrorism and the virtue of the American democracy, comprises the key narrative for his two terms in office. From the War on Terror and the buildup to the War in Iraq to Bush's concept of the role of government in society, his rhetorical presidency demands greater scholarly attention in the years to come.

THE PARADOXES OF POPULARITY

Since job approval ratings were first regularly mapped in the 1950s, George W. Bush was at once the most popular and the most disliked president in the post–World War II era. Like his father before him, "rally events" caused his popularity to soar in the wake of external crisis. For the elder Bush, Gallup placed his approval at 89 percent following the invasion of Iraq in early 1991, up some 30 points from just three months earlier. For George W. Bush, the rise was far more swift and dramatic. In summer 2001, his public approval languished in the low 50s. A week after the 9/11 attacks, his approval reached 90 percent—an all-time record.

George W. Bush's approval ratings are axiomatic. When the president takes military action, or a national security crisis grips the nation, the country tends to rally around the president as a symbol of national unity. At the same time, protracted wars tend to drive public approval lower. And presidents cannot escape blame for poor economic conditions.

Bush's two terms ran the gamut of factors that pushed his approval rating to the upper limits and back down to a nadir. His job approval never dipped below 50 percent during his first term. But as casualties mounted in the War in Iraq, the loss of support was palpable. Shortly after his second inauguration, the slow, steady decline in public confidence lowered his job approval to the 40s and into the 30s. The economic chaos that accompanied the sub-prime mortgage crisis beginning in September 2008 sealed Bush's fate as one of the most unpopular presidents as he left office. These two factors—an open-ended war and economic decline—largely parallel the experience of Lyndon Johnson from 1965 to 1968 and underscore the fleeting and mutable nature of public support for American chief executives.

COMPASSIONATE CONSERVATISM, BUDGET DEFICITS, AND ECONOMIC CRISIS

On the campaign trail in 2000 Bush called his political philosophy "compassionate conservatism." The term implies a reliance on compromise and private charity, rather than government, to achieve balance and compromise. One application of Bush's compassionate conservatism involved the establishment of the White House Office of Faith-Based and Community Initiatives. The goal was to extricate the federal government from the provision of some social welfare programs by allowing religious organizations to carry them out. Yet the operationalization of the faith-based program proved difficult, was the subject of a fair amount of attrition in staff, and raised constitutional issues concerning the separation of church and state.

Another implication of Bush's compassionate conservatism was that government *did* have a positive and substantial role to play in certain policy areas. Bush made education reform a top priority early in his administration, and was not averse to increased federal spending on that front. Further, Bush alienated many traditional fiscal conservatives by advocating and ultimately achieving Medicare reform, including a prescription drug plan for senior citizens. Bush and supporters of the admirable program did not clarify how the federal government would pay for it. The administration initially estimated a cost of $500 billion, which soon doubled to a trillion dollars.

Education and Medicare reform were at least partially responsible for the dramatic growth of budget deficits over the course of Bush's two terms. So too was the burgeoning cost of the War in Iraq. Much of the rest of the responsibility rests with corporate and individual tax cuts Bush advocated, and ultimately, a significant slowdown in the US economy. The pace of federal spending only increased under unified Republican control of the White House and Congress from 2001 to 2004. The federal budget was transformed from a surplus of 2.4 percent of gross domestic product (GDP) in 2000 to a deficit of 3.6 percent of GDP—the high-water mark—in 2004. Figure 1 traces the transformation in dollar terms across Bush's two terms. The deficit started to come under somewhat greater control beginning in 2005, but by 2008 the economy and financial markets faced unprecedented tumult, sending the balance of outlays to receipts back to 2004 levels.

The national economy is *the* central criterion by which voters judge presidential performance, even if chief executives have precious few resources to manipulate economic trends. Fiscal policy and deficits aside, Bush's legacy is marred by the crisis in the housing market that ultimately translated into a global economic meltdown beginning in September 2008. Critics posit that poor oversight of the financial services industry led to catastrophe as banks offered consumers "subprime" mortgages (loans below the prime rate) that entailed adjustable rates and balloon payments they were unable to afford later. Others hold congressional legislation to account for encouraging lending institutions to make risky loans to low-income individuals for the purchase of homes. Whatever the case, the cataclysm of the sub-prime mortgage crisis spread throughout the national and global economy with alarming speed. At the end of his second term, Bush prompted Congress to pass

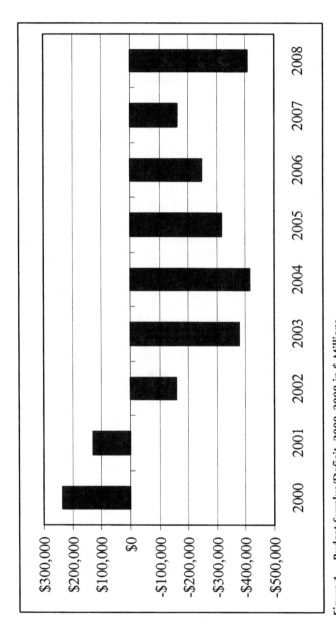

Figure 1. Budget Surplus/Deficit, 2000–2008 in $ Millions

Source: Historical Tables, Budget of the United States Government, Fiscal Year 2009. http://www.gpoaccess.gov/usbudget/fy09/pdf/hist.pdf

an emergency bailout for banks to the tune of $700 billion, which only added to deficit spending. Whether budget deficits incurred during the Bush presidency mark a return to the seemingly structural deficits of the 1970s and 1980s will determine a significant component of his legacy.

THE GRAND OLD PARTY: FROM MAJORITY TO PERMANENT MINORITY?

The fortunes of the Republican Party closely tracked those of President Bush over the course of his two terms. The transformation of the GOP from a majority to a minority party in Congress and nationally marks an astounding development of potentially historic proportions. Remarkably, at the turn of the millennium some in the party spoke of its electoral invincibility and the creation of a permanent majority. Such overconfidence, however, contravened the relative parity in support for the two parties that was evident in the 2000 election and the declining fortunes of the Republican Party nationally.

Bush's narrow election victory in 2000 was paralleled in the Senate, where Republicans held a bare majority with the aid of Vice President Dick Cheney's tie-breaking vote—until Vermont Republican James Jeffords threw his support to Democrats and gave them majority control in May 2001. Bush used the issue of national security, the War on Terror, and most importantly, the delay in the passage of the bill creating the Department of Homeland Security to aid Senate Republicans in recapturing the upper chamber in the mid-term elections of 2002. In 2004, House and Senate Republicans maintained their control of both chambers in a national election that again centered on national security and the War in Iraq.

By 2006, the congressional GOP's fortunes had waned as Bush's approval tumbled in light of heavy casualties of US forces in Iraq and a slowing economy. The backlash against Bush and congressional Republicans was dramatic. Nancy Pelosi led Democrats to a majority in the House, and Harry Reid rallied Democrats to a majority in the Senate in the mid-term elections that heralded a significant decline of support for the GOP nationwide.

In 2008, Republicans not only lost the White House, but watched in shock as the once mighty party of the 1990s, which had gained majority status in the House after 40 years of uninterrupted Democratic control, saw its numbers dwindle to just 178 after a staggering loss of 21 members. In the Senate, Democrats almost reached a filibuster-proof majority with 59 seats after the GOP lost a total of eight members. With the aid of a handful of moderate Republicans in the upper chamber, President Barack Obama and his congressional colleagues stood poised to govern within an institutional context not seen since Lyndon Johnson's and the Democrats' sweeping victory in 1964.

As Bush left office, the GOP was clearly in disarray. Reconstructing the party's message and image fell to the ever soft-spoken yet firm Senate parliamentarian, Mitch McConnell, and a new set of younger Republican leaders in the House of Representatives and governors such as Louisiana's Bobby Jindal. How they set about this task will speak volumes about Bush's legacy. Will the GOP remain a largely southern, Evangelical party, or broaden its base by tempering anti-immigrant sentiment and appealing to Hispanics, the fastest growing segment of new voters? Will the party repudiate the deficits and "big government," including the national security state, built under Bush's watch and return to the themes of sound fiscal management and civil liberties? Will Republicans embrace Bush's neoconservative foreign policy, or hark back to the internationalism of Dwight D. Eisenhower, and his warnings of a "military–industrial complex" as they contemplate strategy in the open-ended War on Terror? The message a new generation of Republican leaders articulates, and how those leaders respond to the policies of the Obama administration, are likely to secure Bush's ultimate place in history. They will also determine whether a diminished and demoralized GOP will rise from the ashes of the 2008 elections or find itself relegated to quasi-permanent minority status, as it was for much of the post-World War II era.

REFERENCES

1. Nelson, Michael. 2006. "Evaluating the Presidency." In Michael Nelson (ed.), *The Presidency and the Political System*, 8th ed. Washington, D.C.: CQ Press, pp. 3–27.

2. Burns, James MacGregor. 1965. *Presidential Government: The Crucible of Leadership*. Boston: Houghton Mifflin.

3. Nelson, p. 3.

4. Reedy, George E. 1970. *The Twilight of the Presidency*. New York: World Publishing.

The Dictionary

– A –

ABBAS, MAHMOUD (1935–). Also known as Abu Mazen, Abbas was born in Safad, Palestine (British Protectorate of). At the age of 13, his family moved to **Syria**, where he later gained employment as a school teacher. He earned a bachelor's degree in law from Damascus University and a doctoral degree in history from the Oriental College in Moscow, **Russia**.

Along with **Yasser Arafat**, Abbas was a founding member of the Palestinian political movement **Fatah**. After serving in several positions for the **Palestine Liberation Organization** (PLO), including chairman of the Occupied Territories, Abbas became prime minister of the **Palestine National Authority** in March 2003. He resigned as prime minister six months later, in October 2003, citing lack of support from **Israel** and the United States toward a peaceful settlement to the Israeli–Palestinian conflict.

On 9 January 2005, Abbas was elected to the presidency of the Palestinian National Authority. In January 2006, Fatah lost the parliamentary elections in the Palestinian Territories. Abbas called upon the Hamas leader, **Ismail Haniya**, to form a national unity government conditioned upon Hamas's acceptance of the state of **Israel** and renunciation of violence. Abbas eventually declared a state of emergency, dismissed Haniya, and replaced him with **Salam Fayyad** in June 2007. His dismissal of Haniya, however, was of dubious constitutionality. Haniya was deemed by many to be the rightful prime minister, and after seizing control of various governmental positions and militias, Haniya remained in control of the **Gaza Strip** in the aftermath of fighting known as the "Battle of Gaza." Fatah remained in charge of the **West Bank**. The de facto division of the Palestinian

1

Territories complicated US and international efforts to find a settlement to the Israeli–Palestinian dispute.

The administration of **George W. Bush** supported Abbas for his moderate policies and opposition to both Hamas and **Islamic Jihad**'s call for **terrorism** against Israel, considering him a vital element in the **Road Map for Peace** elaborated by the White House, **European Union**, and Russia in 2002. Abbas eschewed armed conflict with the Israelis and advocated negotiation with Israel in the 1970s. However, Israel remains suspicious over allegations of Abbas's involvement in the 1972 Munich kidnappings of the Israeli Olympic team. Abbas threatened to resign his position as president if a peace deal were not reached with Israel by the end of 2008. In January 2009, however, he extended his term for another full year under the Palestinian Basic Law, ahead of scheduled legislative and presidential elections.

ABIZAID, JOHN (1951–). Born in Coleville, California, Abizaid graduated from West Point in 1973 and later earned a master's degree from Harvard in Middle Eastern Studies. He trained in the special forces in Jordan, is fluent in Arabic, and is the highest ranking military officer of Arab ancestry to date.

Abizaid started his career with the 504th Parachute Infantry Regiment at Fort Bragg, North Carolina, where he served as a rifle and scout platoon leader. He commanded companies in the 2nd and 1st Ranger Battalions, leading a Ranger Rifle Company during the invasion of Grenada. He commanded the 3rd Battalion, 325th Airborne Battalion combat Team in Vicenza, Italy, during the **Persian Gulf War** (1991), and deployed with the battalion to protect the **Kurds** in northern Iraq. His brigade command was the 504th Parachute Infantry Regiment of the 82nd Airborne Division. He served as the assistant division commander, 1st Armored Division, in Bosnia–Herzegovina. Following that tour, he served as the 66th commandant at West Point. He also commanded the 1st Infantry Division, the Big Red One, in Würzburg, **Germany**. That division formed the core of Task Force Falcon in Kosovo during the civil war in the former **Yugoslavia** in the 1990s.

Abizaid served as deputy commander of **CENTCOM** (US Central Command) in the invasion of **Iraq** in March 2003. Following the ouster of Iraqi dictator **Saddam Hussein**, he took control of CENTCOM from retiring General **Tommy Franks**. Abizaid retired from his position four years later in March 2007 and was replaced by Admiral **William J. Fallon**.

Abizaid's decorations include the Distinguished Service Medal, the Defense Superior Service Medal, the Legion of Merit with five Oak Leaf Clusters and the Bronze Star. He earned the Combat Infantryman's Badge, Master Parachutist Badge with Gold Star, Ranger Tab, and the Expert Infantryman's Badge. *See also* ARMED FORCES.

ABKHAZIA. *See* GEORGIA.

ABORTION. Defined as the medically induced termination of a pregnancy, abortion was legalized by the US **Supreme Court** in the landmark *Roe v. Wade* decision of 1973. The justices who wrote the majority opinion contended that a **woman's** right to choose whether to terminate a pregnancy was protected by an inherent "right to privacy" in the Constitution. Prior to *Roe,* states had legislated varying degrees of access to abortion services, and some banned abortion procedures altogether.

Like his Republican predecessor **Ronald Reagan**, and his father **George H.W. Bush**, President **George W. Bush** steadfastly opposed abortion throughout his presidency. In the 2000 election debates, he emphasized the need to build a "culture of life" and respect for the rights of the unborn. In 2004, he criticized his Democratic opponent, **John Kerry**, for opposing a ban on the procedure known as partial-birth abortion, whereby a fetus is aborted in the third trimester.

Early in his presidency Bush reversed the policy of his immediate predecessor, **William Clinton**, and blocked federal funding of international family planning organizations that advocated abortion. Bush also opposed federal funding of embryonic **stem-cell research** derived from fetuses, and vetoed two bills on the matter, one in July 2006 (HR 810) and another in June 2007 (S. 5). Bush supported the **Partial-Birth Abortion Ban Act** adopted by the Republican Congress in 2003. In a major victory for the Bush administration in April 2007, the Supreme Court ruled by a 5–4 margin in *Gonzales v. Carhart* that the legislation did not violate the Constitution, despite failing to provide an exception to allow the procedure when the life of the mother is in danger. Significantly, the two justices Bush appointed during his term, **Samuel Alito** and Chief Justice **John Roberts**, voted to uphold the ban.

ABRAHAM, SPENCER (1952–). A native of Lansing, Michigan, Abraham earned a BA from Michigan State University in 1974 and graduated with a law degree from Harvard University in 1978. He was a founding member of the legal *Federalist Society*, a conservative organization that favors judicial restraint and constitutional interpretations based on the founders' original intentions. He served as the chair of the Michigan Republican Party from 1983 to 1990, deputy chief of staff to Vice President Dan Quayle from 1990 to 1991, and was elected to a single term in the US Senate from 1995 to 2001. He lost his re-election campaign for the US Senate in 2000 to Debbie Stabenow. Abraham, who is of Lebanese ancestry, was the only Arab-American to serve in the upper chamber of Congress.

Abraham was appointed as secretary of energy during **George W. Bush**'s first term. During his tenure, he was a member of the president's controversial **Energy Task Force**, worked to open the Yucca Mountain, Nevada, site as a repository for nuclear waste, and was particularly active in efforts to prevent the international proliferation of nuclear weapons. He was succeeded by **Samuel Bodman** in February 2005. Abraham is a fellow at Stanford University's Hoover Institution and serves on the board of Areva, Inc., a subsidiary of a French nuclear power corporation.

ABRAMOFF, JACK (1959–). A native of Atlantic City, New Jersey, Abramoff received a BA degree from Brandeis University in 1981 and graduated with a law degree from Georgetown University in 1986. He was chair of the College Republican National Committee in the early 1980s, a supporter of **Ronald Reagan**'s presidential campaign in 1980, and an outspoken proponent of Reagan's **foreign policy** aimed at stopping the spread of communism in Nicaragua, **Afghanistan**, and **Angola**. Reagan appointed Abramoff a member of the US Holocaust Memorial Council in 1986.

Following the mid-term elections of 1994, which gave Republicans their first majority in the US House of Representatives since

1954 and their first majority in the US Senate since 1986, Abramoff was hired by the Seattle, Washington-based lobbying firm of Preston, Gates, Ellis & Rouvelas, Meeds. He lobbied on behalf of American Indian tribes, gaining significant influence over Indian affairs with top Republican leaders in Congress, including Speaker Newt Gingrich, House majority leader Dick Armey, and majority whip **Tom DeLay**. He was also actively engaged in lobbying for the Commonwealth of the Mariana Islands and a Russian pharmaceutical company.

In 2001, Abramoff was hired by the law firm of Greenberg, Traurig in governmental relations. Abramoff focused his lobbying efforts on behalf of Indian tribes as well as foreign governments. He reportedly gained unprecedented access to Bush administration officials, including presidential advisor **Karl Rove**. In 2004, Abramoff's activities came under scrutiny by the US Senate Indian Affairs Committee, later chaired by Senator **John McCain** from 2005–2007. Abramoff was investigated by federal and state authorities, and was indicted on fraud and conspiracy charges for the purchase of SunCruz Casinos in Florida, the seller of which, Konstantinos "Gus" Boulis, had been murdered.

The Senate investigation and federal and state charges stemmed from accusations that Abramoff and his colleagues, including conservative activist **Ralph Reed** and an associate of congressman Tom DeLay, Michael Scanlon, had bribed members of Congress and paid for trips that violated ethics rules, defrauded Indian tribes of an estimated $85 million, and illegally funneled money into bogus corporations for their own profit. Among the most egregious allegations were that Abramoff surreptitiously used Indian tribal moneys to fund antigambling campaigns and then collected more funds from the tribes to lobby lawmakers to reverse restrictions on casino gambling.

In November 2005, Michael Scanlon pleaded guilty to conspiracy to bribe public officials and agreed to reimburse Indian tribe clients more than $19 million. A month later, another Abramoff associate, Adam Kidan, pleaded guilty to conspiracy charges.

In January 2006, Abramoff himself pleaded guilty to fraud, tax evasion, and conspiracy to bribe public officials in a Florida federal court. He was sentenced to six years in prison, and as part of the plea agreement, agreed to cooperate with further bribery investigations of public officials. As of 2008, Abramoff has not been sentenced on other charges, including mail fraud.

The Abramoff scandal had far-reaching consequences for public officials. **J. Steven Griles**, the deputy secretary of the Department of the Interior in the Bush administration, pleaded guilty to obstruction of justice in the Senate investigation into Abramoff's activities and received a 10-month prison sentence. David Safavian, head of the Office of Federal Procurement Policy and the White House **Office of Management and Budget** (OMB), was convicted of lying to federal investigators and received a prison sentence of 18 months, which was later overturned by an appeals court. The scandal also precipitated the resignations of two Republican members of Congress, Tom DeLay of Texas and **Robert Ney** of Ohio, in 2006 and 2007, respectively. Ney was convicted in 2007 of conspiracy charges and making false statements, and was sentenced to 30 months in prison. The scandal is believed to be one of the factors for Republicans' loss of a majority in the House of Representatives in the **mid-term elections** of 2006.

ABU GHRAIB PRISON. This prison, built in 1960, is located approximately 20 miles west of **Baghdad, Iraq**, and was renowned under Iraqi dictator **Saddam Hussein** for the **torture** and death of political dissenters. Under Hussein, the prison was frequently referred to as "Torture Central."

With the March 2003 invasion of Iraq and ouster of Hussein by American and coalition forces, the US Army used Abu Ghraib as a detention center for captured Iraqi soldiers and insurgents. The US Army had launched a criminal investigation of prisoner abuse at Abu Ghraib by American personnel as early as 2003 and issued findings in the Taguba Report of 2004. The Taguba Report detailed physical and mental torture, forced sodomy, and even murder of prisoners. The CBS television news program *60 Minutes* aired graphic pictures of prisoner abuse in late April 2004, followed by *New Yorker* magazine author **Seymour M. Hersh**'s detailed account of prisoner abuse. Two perpetrators depicted in the reports, Private First Class Lynndie England and Private Charles Graner, Jr., were at the heart of the scandal, which also implicated another 15 service personnel. International and domestic outrage swiftly ensued.

As a result of the Army investigation and scandal, England and Graner were court-martialed, dishonorably discharged, and each received a 10-year prison sentence. Five other Army personnel were also dishonorably discharged and convicted. The commander in charge of Abu Ghraib, Brigadier General **Janis Karpinski**, denied any knowledge of prisoner abuse and alleged that the interrogation techniques used at the prison were sanctioned by Secretary of Defense **Donald Rumsfeld**. Karpinski was nevertheless demoted to the rank of colonel. The **American Civil Liberties Union** later obtained documents that showed that the top military officer in Iraq, Lieutenant General **Ricardo Sanchez**, had approved a number of interrogation techniques such as sleep and sensory deprivation, as well as subjecting prisoners to extreme temperatures. Sanchez was not prosecuted, but retired in 2006, a casualty of the scandal.

President **George W. Bush** and Vice President **Richard (Dick) B. Cheney** were quick to repudiate the prisoner abuse at Abu Ghraib. Regardless, critics of the Bush White House, and particularly detractors of Vice President Cheney and Secretary of Defense Donald Rumsfeld, contended that the scandal was in part a product of the administration's blurring of the lines between acceptable interrogation techniques and torture more generally. Critics charged that the administration had facilitated prisoner abuse by failing to adhere to the rules of the **Geneva Convention** concerning the treatment of detainees held at **Guantanamo Bay, Cuba**, practicing **"rendition"** of suspected **terrorist**s and **insurgent**s to countries without civil liberties protections where they could be interrogated by methods illegal under US law, and arguing that the technique of **"waterboarding,"** or simulated drowning, was not tantamount to **torture**. The US Army announced plans to close Abu Ghraib in Spring 2006. *See also* DETAINEE TREATMENT ACT (2005); MCCAIN, JOHN.

ACQUIRED IMMUNE DEFICIENCY SYNDROME (AIDS). The Federal Centers for Disease Control published a report on 5 June 1981 that identified AIDS as a disease that destroys the human immune system. The term *AIDS* was adopted by the scientific and medical communities in 1983. AIDS is the result of infection from the human immunodeficiency virus (HIV). The infection devastates the immune system's T cells, preventing the body from warding off infection. The disease is believed to have originated in Africa and jumped species from nonhuman primates to humans. In the 1980s, AIDS infections in the United States became widespread among gay men and intravenous drug users, who are at high risk for transmission of the disease. The disease has since spread to heterosexual populations, and had reached staggering proportions in Africa by the turn of the millennium.

The administration of **George W. Bush** aggressively pursued an Emergency Plan for AIDS relief in Africa. The program, begun in 2003, pledged foreign aid in the amount of $15 billion over five years to stem the tide of the pandemic largely through new antiretroviral treatments now available. The number of Africans receiving treatment rose from 50,000 in 2003 to 1.3 million by 2007. The program was widely hailed as saving thousands of lives. Detractors, however, noted that the program did not include **abortion** or contraception as a means of AIDS prevention.

ADAMS, GERRY. *See* NORTHERN IRELAND.

ADDINGTON, DAVID S. (1957–). A graduate of Georgetown University's School of Foreign Service and Duke University Law School, Addington worked for the **Central Intelligence Agency (CIA)** as assistant counsel, for several House of Representatives committees, and for **Ronald Reagan** as deputy assistant during the 1980s. In the administration of **George H.W. Bush**, he served as assistant counsel to then Secretary of Defense **Richard B. (Dick) Cheney** and then as general counsel for the Department of Defense. In the 1990s, he worked in private law practice.

In the administration of **George W. Bush** Addington served as a legal advisor to Vice President Cheney. He articulated the administration's theory of the "unitary executive," which contends that during wartime the president, as commander in chief, has unfettered authority and that the president controls the entire executive branch of government within statutory guidelines set by Congress. He played a significant role in analyzing congressional bills and advising Bush on "**signing statements**," during which the president challenged legislative provisions and went so far as to suggest he would either not enforce them or interpret them consistent with his commander in chief role. Addington also drafted legal opinions concerning the use of "enhanced interrogation techniques" and suggested **torture** was not necessarily out of the question in gathering intelligence from **enemy combatants** detained at **Guantanamo Bay, Cuba**. Finally, Addington is thought to have been averse to the **Foreign Intelligence Surveillance Act** (FISA) Court and a proponent of warrantless **wiretapping** by the **National Security Agency**, in addition to support for broad-ranging **executive privilege**.

Addington became Vice President Cheney's chief of staff in 2005 following **I. Lewis (Scooter) Libby**'s resignation. Addington was named in the investigation of the "outing" of **Valerie Plame** as a covert CIA agent.

AFFIRMATIVE ACTION. Affirmative action falls under the rubric of constitutional civil rights, and may be defined as programs at the federal, state, and local levels designed to remedy past injustices, discrimination, or otherwise aid disadvantaged minority groups in employment and education. Much of the contemporary debate over affirmative action centers on whether such programs should be temporary or institutionalized, whether "quotas" in education and employment are constitutional, and whether race- or ethnicity-based criteria for such programs should be replaced by economic means testing.

President **George W. Bush** supported "diversity" in education and employment but opposed affirmative action programs. The Bush administration took positions on three key affirmative action cases on which the **Supreme Court** ruled over the course of his two terms. Bush's stance prevailed in two of three cases.

The issue in *Gratz v. Bollinger* involved admissions rules at the University of Michigan. The university used a system in which applicants were "scored" on numerous criteria, including race. Historically underrepresented groups at the institution, including Hispanics, African-Americans, and Native Americans were given a "bonus score" in the final calculation. Two white students who were denied admission challenged the system, contending that the University of Michigan had violated the "equal protection of the laws" clause in the Fourteenth Amendment of the US Constitution. George W. Bush publicly argued in a speech on 15 January 2003 that the Michigan admission policy was "fundamentally flawed". The administration subsequently filed an amicus curiae brief with the Supreme Court outlining its stance. In a 6–3 decision, Chief Justice **William Rehnquist**, writing on behalf of the majority, contended that Michigan's admissions policy was not narrowly tailored enough to achieve diversity, and that the policy contravened the Fourteenth Amendment.

The case of *Grutter v. Bollinger* involved the University of Michigan Law School's admission policies. In similar fashion to *Gratz*, a white student, Barbara Grutter, who had been denied admission to the university, posited that the admission policy that took race into account had violated her Fourteenth Amendment rights and further violated the 1964 Civil Rights Act. The Bush administration filed a brief with the Supreme Court in support of Ms. Grutter. However, in a 5–4 decision, Justice **Sandra Day O'Connor** wrote for the majority that "The Law School's narrowly tailored use of race in admissions decisions to further a compelling interest in obtaining the educational benefits that flow from a diverse student body is not prohibited by the Equal Protection Clause." Whereas the Supreme Court had found in *Gratz* that the admission policy based on race was too broad and mechanistic, the Law School's admission policy was consistent with the precedent in *Regents v. Bakke* (1978), whereby race could be *one* consideration in deciding admissions because educational institutions have a compelling interest in attaining diversity. Race-based quotas, however, are deemed unconstitutional.

In *Parents Involved in Community Schools v. Seattle School District No. 1*, decided by the Supreme Court in conjunction with *Meredith v. Jefferson County Board of Education* in 2007, the issue of affirmative action centered on local school boards in Washington and Kentucky that had reassigned students to different schools in order to achieve racial integration and ethnic diversity. In a 5–4 opinion, the majority on the Supreme Court contended that the use of race-conscious criteria in assigning school locations to students was unconstitutional because there was no evidence of de jure or state-sponsored discrimination in the past. Writing for the majority, Chief Justice **John Roberts** argued that the Washington and Kentucky policies did not pass the "strict scrutiny" test and were too broad to pass constitutional muster. Since neither school district had practiced racial segregation in the past, there was no compelling state interest to assign students to schools solely on the basis of race. In briefs filed with the High Court, the Bush administration had pressed the Supreme Court to strike down voluntary school-integration programs.

AFGHANISTAN. This central Asian country was invaded by the **Soviet Union** in 1979 in an attempt to prevent an Islamist government from displacing the Communist leadership. Soviet troops remained in Afghanistan for a decade, sinking into a quagmire of guerrilla warfare by **mujahideen insurgent**s backed by the United States. Soviet troops began pulling out of Afghanistan in May 1988 and completed their withdrawal in 1989, after which time the country descended into civil war. In 1996, the **Taliban** clerics seized power and imposed Islamic Sharia law.

The United States, along with a coalition that included **Great Britain**, invaded Afghanistan on 7 October 2001 in response to the 11 September 2001 (**9/11**) terrorist attacks on the **World Trade Center** in New York and the **Pentagon** in Washington, D.C. President **George W. Bush** contended that intelligence showed that the Taliban had allowed the **terrorist** organization **al-Qaeda** to train in Afghanistan and otherwise gave material support and succor to supporters of the suspected mastermind of the 9/11 attacks, **Osama bin Laden**. The invasion of Afghanistan marked the effective beginning of Bush's **War on Terror**.

The first leg of the campaign was titled Operation Enduring Freedom. A total of 20,000 troops, comprised of approximately 18,000 US troops, invaded Afghanistan and toppled the Taliban regime. The coalition was aided by the anti-Taliban Afghan **Northern Alliance**. The air campaign, led by the United States and Great Britain, swiftly destroyed al-Qaeda training facilities, and Taliban leaders fled the capital, **Kabul**, on 12 November 2001. Some of the most intense air bombing occurred in the **Tora Bora** region in eastern Afghanistan beginning in early December 2001, as US forces attempted to oust al-Qaeda forces hiding in extensive cave systems in the rugged, mountainous terrain near the Kyber Pass. Upon their capture, many Taliban prisoners were relocated by US forces to **Guantanamo Bay, Cuba**, for indefinite detention or eventual trial by **military tribunals**.

The second leg of the military campaign, Operation Anaconda, was launched in early 2002 and was aimed at strengthening gains made against al-Qaeda and securing the cities of Kabul and Khandahar. In December 2001, **Hamid Karzai** formed an interim government in Kabul as part of the Transitional Administration in Afghanistan until his election as president in 2004.

Despite the early success of US and coalition forces in Afghanistan, the Taliban, under leader **Mullah Omar**, launched a prolonged insurgency, beginning in 2003 with guerrilla tactics that had proved successful under Soviet occupation two decades earlier. A particular frustration of the Bush administration was the pouring in of Taliban sympathizers from **Pakistan**, and Pakistani President **Pervez Musharraf**'s refusal to allow US troops into his country to battle al-Qaeda.

By January 2006, **North Atlantic Treaty Organization** (NATO) troops, as part of the **International Security Assistance Force** (ISAF), began replacing US troops to secure and engage in reconstruction of the country. Progress was slow and suffered major setbacks. Coalition casualties in Afghanistan numbered about 900 by mid-2008. The number of civilians killed in the conflict is estimated between 1,000 and 5,000, and the number of displaced civilians is estimated in the tens of thousands. As of 2008, opium trade from the production of poppies has flourished in post-invasion Afghanistan, and the United States was largely unable to convince tribal leaders to convert to other crops. Taliban insurgents continued to use **improvised explosive devices** (IEDs) against NATO and US troops. The issue was central in the 2008 US presidential election, with Democratic candidate **Barack Obama** suggesting in the summer of 2008 that more troops were needed in Afghanistan. Obama also suggested that Afghanistan, not **Iraq**, was the pivotal battle in the War on Terror due to increased al-Qaeda resistance and insurgency.

President Bush visited Afghanistan several times over the course of his two terms. In March 2006, he made an unannounced visit to bolster support for Hamid Karzai. He also visited Afghanistan in December 2008, met again with Karzai and US troops, and lauded progress in the fight against insurgents. *See also* ARMED FORCES; *BOUMEDIENE v. BUSH*; FOREIGN POLICY; HABEAS CORPUS; *HAMDAN v. RUMSFELD*; *HAMDI v. RUMSFELD*; IRAQ WAR; RENDITION.

AFRICAN-AMERICANS. *See* AFFIRMATIVE ACTION.

AFRICAN UNION (AU). The AU is an organization of 53 African nations that grew out of the Organization of African Unity (OAU). The AU describes its goals as the promotion of socioeconomic integration of the African continent and greater solidarity between African countries and peoples. As an intergovernmental organization, the AU also focuses on the promotion of peace, security, and stability on the continent.

During the presidency of **George W. Bush**, the AU was involved in several peacekeeping operations in Togo, Mauritania, and Somalia. The most significant peacekeeping operation began in 2004, when the AU sent 150 troops to the **Darfur** region of **Sudan**. By 2005, the AU's presence swelled to some 7,000 troops whose charge it was to protect civilians from the *janjaweed* militias, accused of genocide in Sudan's civil war. Human rights organizations contended that the AU's force was poorly trained and ill-equipped to succeed in its mission, despite the US Congress having appropriated $173 million in June 2006 to support the AU. In July 2007, the **United Nations** (UN) passed a resolution to integrate the AU forces into a joint AU–UN peacekeeping mission in Darfur. *See also* FOREIGN POLICY; INTERNATIONAL CRIMINAL COURT; MORENO-OCAMPO, LUIS.

AHMADINEJAD, MAHMOUD (1956–). Born in Garmsar, **Iran**, Ahmadinejad attended the Iran University of Science and Technology and earned a degree in civil engineering. He joined the Revolutionary Guard after the Iranian Revolution of 1979, led by Ayatollah Khomeini. When students occupied and held captive employees of the US Embassy, some of the captives claimed Ahmadinejad was one of the perpetrators—an allegation he denies. He was a provincial governor from 1993 to 1997. He returned to the academy to teach until his election as mayor of Tehran in 2003. In June 2005, he successfully ran for the presidency of Iran on a populist, religiously conservative platform.

Ahmadinejad is a dogged opponent of US **foreign policy**. In October 2005, he stated that **Israel** should be "wiped off the map," and later that year contended that the Jewish Holocaust in World War II was a "myth." He steadfastly pursued Iran's nuclear program, which he claimed was for peaceful, civilian purposes only. In April 2006, Ahmadinejad announced that Iran had successfully refined uranium to a stage suitable for the nuclear fuel cycle. In television interviews with American media he reemphasized the putatively peaceful nature of the nuclear program, but President **George W. Bush**, his advisors, and Congress remained circumspect. In July 2007, concerns that Iran was funding **al-Qaeda** operations in **Iraq** prompted the US Senate to adopt a unanimous resolution warning Ahmadinejad about attacks in Iraq coming from his country. In September 2007—the same month Ahmadinejad attended a controversial leadership forum at Columbia University in New York City—the Senate passed a second resolution calling the Iranian military a **terrorist** organization.

President George W. Bush named Iran, along with **North Korea** and Iraq, as part of an **"axis of evil"** in his State of the Union speech in 2002, a year before the US invasion of Iraq. Bush accused Iran and the other countries of being state sponsors of terrorism and seeking to procure **weapons of mass destruction** (WMDs). In particular, Bush accused Iran of supporting the radical Islamist terrorist organization **Hezbollah**.

The Bush administration pursued domestic and international sanctions against Iran to force Ahmadinejad to halt the pursuit of nuclear technology. The United States had imposed a general embargo on trade with Iran dating to 1995. In September 2006, the US government imposed sanctions of the Iranian Bank Saderat Iran and barred the institution from relations with US banks. Bush steadfastly advocated **United Nations** (UN) sanctions against Iran. The UN Security Council adopted sanctions in 2006, and successively sought to strengthen them to force Ahmadinejad to scrap Iran's nuclear program—to little avail as of late 2008.

AIDS. *See* ACQUIRED IMMUNE DEFICIENCY SYNDROME.

AIG. *See* AMERICAN INTERNATIONAL GROUP.

AL-ANBAR PROVINCE. Bordered by Jordan, Saudi Arabia, and **Syria**, Al-Anbar is the geographically largest province in **Iraq**. The province has a Sunni Muslim majority, which was intensely opposed to the US invasion and occupation of Iraq in March 2003. The province was subject to some of the most intense battles and highest US military casualties, in addition to continuous and considerable violence from 2003 to 2006. The new Iraqi government eventually took control of the province in June 2008. Violence abated significantly after the US negotiated directly with tribal leaders to enlist their support against **al-Qaeda** fighters and other **insurgent** groups. *See also* WAR IN IRAQ.

AL-HAMDANIA. This village west of **Baghdad, Iraq**, was the site of the unlawful shooting death of a suspected **insurgent** Iraqi by US forces on 26 April 2006. Seven Marines and one Navy corpsman faced a variety of charges, including conspiracy and kidnapping. The Naval Criminal Investigation Service alleged that the servicemen kidnapped Hashim Gowad, placed him next to a hole near a road to show that he was about to plant an **improvised explosive device (IED)**, and shot him. While many of the charges against the servicemen were dropped, two of the accused struck plea deals for conspiracy, kidnapping, and aggravated assault. Sergeant Lawrence Hutchins was court-martialed and found guilty of murder and sentenced to 15 years in prison.

AL-JAAFARI, IBRAHIM (1947–). Born Ibrahim al-Eshaiker in Karbala, **Iraq**, al-Jaafari is a Shi'ite Iraqi politician who opposed the regime of **Saddam Hussein** and worked for its overthrow, beginning in 1968 when he joined the **Islamic Dawa Party**. He was later exiled in **Iran** and moved to London, England, in 1989. Al-Jaafari became a member of the **Iraq Governing Council** in summer 2003 and served as a vice president in the interim government following the US invasion of Iraq in March 2003. He became the Iraqi prime minister after the elections of January 2005 and a razor-thin majority vote in the Iraqi legislature. However, the loss of confidence among Sunni and **Kurdish** parties in Iraq, which blamed him for failing to end escalating violence, led to governmental deadlock. President **George W. Bush** also became highly critical of al-Jaafari. Prompted by **Ayatollah Ali al-Sistani**, al-Jaafari ultimately stepped aside and was succeeded by **Nouri al-Maliki** as prime minister.

AL-JAZEERA. Located in Doha, Qatar, this satellite news and information service broadcasts in Arabic and other languages, and was launched in 1996. Al-Jazeera has frequently disseminated video messages by the **terrorist** organization **al-Qaeda**, including those from leader **Osama bin Laden**. Following the terror attacks on Washington, D.C., and New York on 11 September 2001, al-Jazeera broadcast worldwide a message from bin Laden, who praised the attacks. The administration of President **George W. Bush** was sharply critical of al-Jazeera for its negative coverage of the March 2003 invasion of **Iraq** by the United States.

AL-MALIKI, NOURI MOHAMMED HASSAN (1950–). Born in Abu Gharaq, **Iraq**, al-Maliki is a graduate of Baghdad University, with a degree in literature. He joined the **Islamic Dawa Party** in the 1960s. Iraqi dictator **Saddam Hussein** called for al-Maliki's death in the 1980s because of his active role against his regime, at which time al-Maliki fled into exile in **Syria**. He was elected to the position of chairman of the "Joint Action Committee," a grouping of US-backed dissident exiles that would be transformed into the Iraqi National Congress in the 1990s. Following the US invasion of Iraq in March 2003 and Hussein's ouster, al-Maliki returned to Iraq to oversee the purge of **Ba'ath Party** officials from Iraq's government, and he was elected to the Iraqi National Assembly in 2005. He became Iraq's prime minister in April 2006 when **Ibrahim al-Jaafari** stepped down; al-Jaafari's leadership was unacceptable to Sunni and **Kurdish** factions in the legislature.

Al-Maliki's term as prime minister ends in 2010. His premiership has been marked by strong support for eradicating armed resistance groups, or **insurgents**, in Iraq. He has at times, however, criticized the US-led military coalition's occupation with respect to the deaths of civilians. Al-Maliki, who is known also by the name "Jawad," signed the warrant for Saddam Hussein's death in late 2006 and refused clemency for the former dictator.

AL-QAEDA. Derived from the Arabic word for "base," al-Qaeda is a pan-Islamic, fundamentalist Muslim, international **terrorist** organization founded in 1988. Its members cleave to Sunni Muslim doctrines that consider non-Muslims infidels. The organization's presumptive leaders are Saudi-born **Osama bin Laden** and Egyptian-born **Ayman al-Zawahiri**.

Al-Qaeda boasts a nontraditional organizational arrangement, organized as it is into small "cells" around the world that actively recruit Muslims willing to perpetrate acts of violence and **terrorism** against Western and US targets. The organization views American influence in the Arab world, and particularly the stationing of US forces in Saudi Arabia, as unacceptable. The organization also calls for the destruction of **Israel** and all those who support the Jewish state.

What is today known as al-Qaeda began with the Soviet occupation of **Afghanistan** in the 1980s. Bin Laden and other prominent pan-Islamists funded and partook in the **mujahideen jihad** (holy war) against the Soviets to force their ouster, with an eye to establishing an Islamic state under Sharia law. When the Soviets finally withdrew, a civil war in Afghanistan enabled the **Taliban** clerics to assume control of the country. Many of those involved in the armed struggle, including bin Laden, turned their attention to inciting the cause of Islamic fundamentalism in other parts of the Muslim world.

Although the United States supported the mujahideen's resistance to Soviet forces of occupation in Afghanistan, the **Persian Gulf War** in 1991 placed into sharp relief al-Qaeda's growing resentment at US influence and presence in the Middle East. Al-Qaeda objects to foreign (US) troops in Saudi Arabia, which is home to two of the most sacred mosques in the Arab world—Mecca and Medina. President **George H.W. Bush** used US bases in Saudi Arabia, in particular, to force Iraqi dictator **Saddam Hussein** to retreat from Kuwait, the tiny, oil-rich kingdom Hussein had invaded in August 1990.

Al-Qaeda has claimed responsibility for, or is suspected of, hundreds of acts of terrorism across the globe from the early 1990s through to the present day. Attacks on American civilian and military targets, both in the United States and abroad, include the **World Trade Center** bombing in New York City in 1993; bombings of US embassies in Dar es Salaam, Tanzania, and Nairobi, Kenya, in 1998; the attack on the USS *Cole* in Yemen in 1998; and most dramatically, the use of hijacked commercial aircraft on **11 September 2001**, which were flown into the World Trade Center in New York City and the **Pentagon** in Washington, D.C., killing more than 3,000.

President **George W. Bush**'s subsequent **War on Terror** has focused intensely on eradicating al-Qaeda's domestic and international operations. A US-led coalition invaded Afghanistan and toppled the Taliban regime in the autumn of 2001. The Taliban government had given succor to bin Laden, who used Afghanistan as a base to establish terrorist training camps. Bush also tied Saddam Hussein to al-Qaeda—which many critics doubt—to justify the March 2003 invasion of Iraq. Whatever the status of al-Qaeda in Iraq before the US invasion, al-Qaeda fighters were drawn into the **War in Iraq** and joined the **insurgency** with which the United States had to contend. Al-Qaeda tactics ranged from active military engagement to suicide bombing attacks on civilians in Iraq. The United States has been particularly frustrated by al-Qaeda activity and suspected training grounds in **Pakistan**, which under President **Pervez Musharraf** refused to allow the United States access to search for bin Laden or engage openly in military operations in that country. By 2006, al-Qaeda and Taliban insurgents in Afghanistan, many of whom are suspected to have entered the country through Pakistan, began mounting significant offensives against US and coalition forces.

Al-Qaeda has actively targeted US allies in the War on Terror, including Spain and **Great Britain**. The Spanish government attributed the 11 March 2004 bombings of the **Madrid** commuter train system, which killed 191, to al-Qaeda. A suicide bombing of the **London, England**, transportation system on 7 July 2005 killed more than 50.

Al-Qaeda's leaders have, nonetheless, increasingly been forced underground. The organization has turned to the Internet as a tool for disseminating its stances and recruiting operatives. To date, the group's putative ringleader, bin Laden, has not been located and captured. Al-Zawahiri, who is believed to be al-Qaeda's operational leader, is thought to be hiding in Pakistan. *See also* AL-ZARQAWI, ABU MUSAB; ATTA, MOHAMED; GADHAN, ADAM YAHIYE; LINDH, JOHN WALKER; MOHAMMED, KHALID SHEIKH; MOUSSAOUI, ZACARIAS; OMAR, MULLAH MUHAMMED; PADILLA, JOSÉ.

AL-SADR, MUQTADA (1973–). A Muslim religious and militia leader in **Iraq**, al-Sadr headed the **Mahdi Army**, which battled coalition forces in the city of Najaf in August 2004. **Ayatollah Ali**

al-Sistani successfully persuaded the Mahdi Army to turn in its arms. Al-Sadr has been a vocal critic of the **Coalition Provisional Authority** established after the March 2003 invasion of Iraq by the United States. His newspaper, *al-Hawza*, was closed by coalition authorities in Spring 2004 for allegedly inciting violence. US Administrator of Iraq **L. Paul Bremer** described al-Sadr as an outlaw. Al-Sadr had been the subject of an arrest warrant on suspicion of assassinating fellow Shi'ite cleric Abdul Majid al-Khoei, but the warrant was sealed by the Coalition Provisional Authority. Al-Sadr consistently called for Iraqis not to cooperate with US forces. In April 2007, followers loyal to al-Sadr left the government of **Nouri al-Maliki**. In August 2007, he called upon his militia to halt armed confrontation for six months following violence in Karbala, Iraq. In 2008, he urged his followers to engage in civil disobedience to protest the arrest and incarceration of members of the Mahdi Army.

AL-SISTANI, AYATOLLAH ALI (1930–). Born in Mashad, **Iran**, al-Sistani is a Shi'ite Muslim religious scholar who moved to Najaf, **Iraq**, in 1951. He rose to the position of Grand Ayatollah in 1992. He was repressed by the **Ba'ath Party** of **Saddam Hussein**, and his mosque was forcibly closed in 1994. Following the US invasion of Iraq in 2003, al-Sistani became a highly influential political figure. In August 2004, al-Sistani brokered negotiations to end violence in Najaf between US forces and the **Mahdi Army** of cleric **Muqtada al-Sadr**. Al-Sistani consistently urged Shia Muslims in Iraq to spurn violence and retribution against their Sunni countrymen, and has played a constructive role in calling upon Shia to vote in Iraqi elections since the ouster of Saddam Hussein. Al-Sistani opposed an agreement between the US and Iraqi governments for a long-term presence of US forces in Iraq, but did not call for armed resistance.

AL-ZARQAWI, ABU MUSAB (1966–2006). A Jordanian national, al-Zarqawi joined the **terrorist** organization **al-Qaeda** in 2004 and became one of its key operatives in the **insurgency** against US forces that invaded **Iraq** in March 2003. He was believed to have been an associate of **Osama bin Laden**. A Sunni Muslim, al-Zarqawi had a base of operations in the **Kurd**ish area of northern Iraq, and has masterminded bombings of Shi'ite areas of the country that have claimed the lives of at least 700 people. He is believed responsible for the deadly bombing of the **United Nations** (UN) headquarters in **Baghdad** in August 2003 that claimed 22 lives, including the UN envoy to Iraq, **Sérgio Vieira de Mello**. Al-Zarqawi was killed by US forces on 7 June 2006.

AL-ZAWAHIRI, AYMAN (1951–). Born in Egypt, al-Zawahiri was trained as a surgeon. As a teenager, al-Zawahiri formed an underground movement called the "Muslim Brotherhood" to oppose and overthrow the Egyptian government and establish Islamic Sharia law in the country. Egypt had executed al-Zawahiri's uncle, Sayyid Qutb, in 1966. Qutb had been convicted on charges of conspiracy after contending that the regime had become so corrupt that Islamic law allowed for the assassination of government officials for their spurning the ideals of Islam.

Al-Zawahiri's Muslim Brotherhood had connections with (Egyptian) **Islamic Jihad**, of which he became head in 1991. Islamic Jihad's stated goal was not only to overthrow the Egyptian government but also to oppose the United States and **Israel**. In 1981, al-Zawahiri was convicted on weapons charges and imprisoned for three years following the assassination of Egyptian President Anwar Sadat. In the 1990s, he traveled throughout the Middle East, met **al-Qaeda** leader **Osama bin Laden** in **Pakistan**, and fostered relations with radical Islamists in **Iran**. In 1996, he was expelled from **Sudan** and ultimately found his way to **Afghanistan**. In 1998, he joined bin Laden in issuing a *fatwa*, or religious edict, which called for the murder of Americans and Jews around the world. In 2001, it is believed that Islamic Jihad merged with **al-Qaeda**, and al-Zawahiri overtook operational command of the organization.

Al-Zawahiri tops the list of **terrorist**s wanted by the **Federal Bureau of Investigation** (FBI) for his suspected connection to the **11 September 2001** attacks on the **World Trade Center** in New York City and the **Pentagon** in Washington, D.C. With information supplied by the **Central Intelligence Agency** (CIA) in January 2006, US forces in Afghanistan launched an air strike on a nearby Pakistani border town where it was thought that al-Zawahiri had been hiding. He survived the attack, and is believed to be somewhere in Pakistan. Al-Zawahiri continued to release written and audio statements through 2009.

ALEXANDER, LAMAR (1940–). Alexander was born in Maryville, Tennessee, and is a graduate of Vanderbilt University and New York University Law School. Following law school, he served as a clerk for John Minor Wisdom of the US Court of Appeals in New Orleans, as a legislative assistant to US Senator Howard Baker, and he worked for Bryce Harlow, counselor to President Richard Nixon. After an unsuccessful campaign for Tennessee governor in 1974, he rebounded in his second bid for the office in 1978. Walking 1,000 miles across the state in his trademark plaid shirt, Alexander won election in 1979 and re-election four years later. Following his governorship, he held the presidency of the University of Tennessee (1988–1991). President **George H.W. Bush** appointed him as secretary of **education** in 1991, and he served out the president's term. Alexander made two unsuccessful bids for the Republican nomination for president (1996, 2000). He won election to the US Senate from his home state in 2002. He was re-elected in 2008 with nearly two-thirds of the statewide vote.

ALITO, SAMUEL ANTHONY, JR. (1950–). Born in Trenton, New Jersey, Alito earned an undergraduate degree from Princeton University in 1972 and graduated from Yale Law School in 1975, where he was editor of *Yale Law Review*. His legal career began with a clerkship for Leonard I. Garth of the Third Federal Circuit. He was later assistant to the US attorney for New Jersey and an assistant to Solicitor General Rex Lee. He served as a US attorney for New Jersey (1987–1990) and as a judge on the US Court of Appeals for the Third Circuit (1990–2006). He was also adjunct professor of law at Seton Hall University (1999–2004).

President **George W. Bush** nominated Alito to the US **Supreme Court** in October 2005 to fill the seat vacated by justice **Sandra Day O'Connor**. He was confirmed by the Senate by a vote of 52–42. Critics of Alito nicknamed him "Scalito," suggesting his conservative stances on **abortion** and support for the **War on Terror** mirrored the positions of justice Antonin Scalia. To date, Alito has compiled a relatively conservative voting record on the High Court, but he did not vote in lockstep with Scalia or Clarence Thomas, another conservative justice. On issues ranging from abortion to government regulation of campaign finance, Alito's opinions were narrowly tailored and did not reflect ideological extremes on either side of the Court.

ALLAWI, IYAD (1945–). Trained in medicine in **Iraq** and Great Britain, Allawi joined Iraqi dictator **Saddam Hussein**'s **Ba'ath Party** in 1961. He was later exiled in Beirut, Lebanon, and London, England, for his opposition to Hussein's regime, and he organized opposition to Hussein among other exiled Iraqi dissidents. Allawi was appointed as a member of the Iraq Governing Council by the **Coalition Provisional Authority** following the invasion of **Iraq** and the ouster of Hussein by US forces in 2003. He later held the position of president of the governing council. Between May 2004 and April 2005, he was prime minister of Iraq. During his premiership, Allawi lost favor among many Iraqis for his support of US and coalition forces' decision to bomb the cities of Fallujah and Najaf. Allawi was replaced by **Ibrahim al-Jaafari** following the January 2005 election in Iraq.

AMERICAN CIVIL LIBERTIES UNION (ACLU). Founded in 1920, the ACLU's stated mission is to protect First Amendment constitutional rights (freedom of speech, association, assembly, press, and religion), equal protection under the law, the right to due process of law, and the right to privacy. To achieve its goals, the organization files class action lawsuits at state and federal levels of government and frequently files amicus curiae (friend of the court) briefs to convey its position on cases that it is not litigating.

The ACLU was a dogged opponent of the administration of **George W. Bush** with respect to electronic surveillance and **wiretapping** policies implemented by the president in the **War on Terror**. Bush signed an executive order enabling the **National Security Agency** (NSA) to intercept telephone and other electronic communications originating abroad from suspected **terrorists**, even if the recipients were in the United States. The ACLU filed suit against the NSA in January 2006, contending that the program was unconstitutional. The organization won a case in Michigan state court, but the ruling was stayed, allowing the president to continue the program. In 2008, the **Supreme Court** refused to hear an appeal from the ACLU.

Critics, such as the ACLU, contended that wiretapping required authorization from the **Foreign Intelligence Surveillance Act** (FISA) Court, which President Bush disputed. The Bush administration contended that authority for warrantless wiretapping, dubbed the "Terrorist Surveillance Program" by the White House, was superseded by the **Authorization for Use of Military Force Against Terrorists** law passed in September 2001 following the **11 September 2001** attacks on New York City and the **Pentagon** in Washington, D.C. Further, the USA **PATRIOT Act**, which was passed in 2001 and reauthorized in 2006, also expanded the ability of the president and law enforcement agencies to use wiretaps in intelligence gathering from suspected foreign terrorists. The Supreme Court weighed in on the issue to some degree in *Hamdan v. Rumsfeld* in 2006 by suggesting that Bush had overstepped his executive authority under the Constitution when he authorized warrantless wiretaps. In 2007, Attorney General **Alberto Gonzalez** stated that the Bush administration would ensure judicial oversight of the surveillance program.

AMERICAN INTERNATIONAL GROUP (AIG). This major insurance company received a loan of $85 billion from the **Federal Reserve** in September 2008 to save the corporation from failure, which Fed Chairman **Ben Bernanke** argued would have had severe consequences that would affect the entire US economy. The bailout, which represented the largest of its kind for a private corporation in US financial history at the time, came weeks after the government intervened to save the **Federal National Mortgage Association** (Fannie Mae) and the **Federal Home Loan Mortgage Corporation** (Freddie Mac)—both government corporations. AIG suffered a severe liquidity crisis stemming, in part, from an economic downturn and its investment in **sub-prime mortgages**. *See also* BEAR STEARNS; PAULSON, HENRY MERRITT, JR.; TROUBLED ASSETS RELIEF PROGRAM (TARP).

AMNESTY INTERNATIONAL. This international human rights organization was founded in Great Britain in 1961. Amnesty International claims 2.2 million supporters, whose focus is on prisoner rights, human rights abuses, fair trials, and more generally on economic and social rights for the oppressed, including **women** and children. The organization carries out its mission through a combination of public demonstrations, letter-writing campaigns, education, and lobbying of governmental and nongovernmental agencies. Amnesty International also sends activists to countries in which human rights abuses may be occurring to interview and work with local officials.

Amnesty International criticized the administration of **George W. Bush** for the detention facility at the naval base in **Guantanamo Bay, Cuba**, which held suspected **Taliban** and **al-Qaeda** fighters following the US-led invasion of **Afghanistan** in 2001. In 2005, Amnesty International's secretary general, Irene Khan, suggested that the detention facility was tantamount to a Soviet "gulag." The organization argues that the detentions violate the **Geneva Convention** on prisoner treatment, and has also criticized the Bush administration for the practice of **"rendition"**—sending suspected terrorists to countries with fewer guarantees of civil liberties for interrogation using techniques illegal in the United States. *See also BOUMEDIENE V. BUSH* (2008); DETAINEE TREATMENT ACT (2005); ENEMY COMBATANT; *HAMDAN V. RUMSFELD* (2006); *HAMDI V. RUMSFELD* (2004); MCCAIN, JOHN SIDNEY III; TORTURE; WAR ON TERROR; WATERBOARDING.

ANGOLA. A former Portuguese colony, this southwest African country gained independence in 1975. Civil war immediately followed and ravaged the country for nearly a quarter century as Marxist and anti-Communist, nationalist factions battled for power. In March 2002, anti-Communist rebel leader Jonas Savimbi was killed by government forces. A cease-fire between the government and opposition groups was reached later that year, effectively ending a quarter century of civil war.

ANNAN, KOFI ATTA (1938–). Born in Ghana, Annan studied economics in his home country as well as in Switzerland and the United States. He worked for the World Health Organization in the 1960s, and in Ghana as the director of tourism in the 1970s. He returned to the **United Nations** (UN) in the 1980s and ultimately became head of peacekeeping operations in the war-torn African country of Rwanda in 1993–1994. Annan became secretary general of the UN in January 1997 and held the position through December 2006, at which time he retired.

Annan was a strong supporter of human rights, and he sought to address issues of poverty, disease, and the plight of **women** and children in the developing world during his two terms as secretary general. During his tenure, he confronted issues of genocide in the

Darfur region of **Sudan**, sought to reform the UN's budget, and made **acquired immune deficiency syndrome** (AIDS) in Africa a top priority. On these issues cooperation between the administration of **George W. Bush** and Annan was generally positive. One of Annan's major successes was the establishment in 2006 of World Diabetes Day, which, by UN consensus, brought significant attention to the disease.

The Bush administration's growing calls for a **preemptive** invasion of **Iraq** to oust dictator **Saddam Hussein**, beginning in 2002, however, caused a growing rift between the Bush administration and Annan. The secretary general repeatedly cautioned the United States not to invade Iraq unilaterally and was thrown into the spotlight in the debate over **United Nations Resolution 1441**, which called for severe consequences if the Iraqi regime failed to cooperate with UN weapons inspectors in their search for **weapons of mass destruction** (WMDs). Annan pressed for the return to Iraq of UN weapons inspectors, previously expelled by Hussein, and called for diplomatic efforts to resolve the crisis. When the United States invaded Iraq in March 2003 with a **Coalition of the Willing** nations and absent a UN mandate, Annan criticized the **War in Iraq**. Although he expressed grave concern about mounting civilian casualties and significant instability in Iraq following the invasion, he attempted to maintain positive relations with the United States and emphasized cooperation over conflict. Regardless, Bush's interim appointment as ambassador to the UN, **John Bolton**, like many **neoconservatives** in the administration, repeatedly expressed highly negative opinions of Annan and the UN more generally.

Annan's secretariat was marked by several other minor controversies. The first, in 2004, involved the Dutch UN High Commissioner for Refugees, Ruud Lubbers, who was accused of sexual harassment of an American staff member. Annan declared Lubbers innocent of the charges, but the General Assembly later found Lubbers guilty, and he resigned in 2005. The second controversy erupted in late 2004 over the **Oil for Food Scandal**. The Oil for Food program had been initiated in 1995 to allow the government of **Saddam Hussein** of **Iraq**, which was under significant international sanctions and an economic embargo, to buy a limited amount of food and medicine with oil revenues. Media reports surfaced that linked a lucrative UN contract with a Swiss company that employed Annan's son, Kojo. Cotecna Inspection (SA) was charged with overseeing elements of the Oil for Food program. A commission set up to investigate the claims, headed by former **Federal Reserve** chairman **Paul Volcker**, criticized the management of the UN program under Annan but stopped short of levying criminal allegations against him. Finally, in June 2007, Annan supported comments made by his undersecretary, who was sharply critical of the US media and allegedly negative coverage of UN peacekeeping missions. Annan's comments exacerbated tensions between him and US Ambassador to the UN **John Bolton**. Annan's successor to the secretary of the UN was **Ban Ki-moon** of South Korea, who took up the position in January 2007.

ANTHRAX (ATTACKS). Anthrax is a bacterial disease most commonly found among grazing animals, which inhale or ingest the spores. Humans can contract the disease from infected animals. Some forms of the bacterium are treatable in humans if identified early. Pulmonary anthrax infection is most deadly to humans, resulting in respiratory collapse and death in most cases. Anthrax may be cultured in vitro for use as a biological weapon.

Beginning exactly one week after the **11 September 2001 terrorist** attacks on New York City and the **Pentagon** in Washington, D.C., letters laced with anthrax were sent via the US Postal Service to news media offices in New York City and Florida, as well as to the offices of US Senators **Thomas Daschle** (D-South Dakota) and **Patrick Leahy** (D-Vermont) on Capitol Hill. The letters bore a postmark from Trenton, New Jersey, and a return address from an elementary school in Franklin Park, New Jersey. The anthrax-infected letters referenced the 11 September 2001 attacks, called for the death of **Israel** and the United States, and praised Allah. All told, 22 people exposed to the letters developed anthrax infections, and five died.

The **Federal Bureau of Investigation** (FBI) began investigating the mailings in earnest but had few leads. President **George W. Bush** and Vice President **Richard B. (Dick) Cheney** publicly did not rule out a connection between the anthrax attacks and **al-Qaeda terrorists**; Arizona Senator **John McCain** surmised that **Iraq** might have been behind the attacks. The FBI suspected and doggedly pursued **Stephen Hatfill**, a physician and virologist who had worked at the United States Army Medical Research Institute of Infectious Diseases. Hatfill filed suit against Attorney General **John Ashcroft** and settled a lawsuit with the Department of Justice for more than $5 million in June 2008.

In July 2008, the FBI acknowledged a new suspect, Bruce Ivins, whom the Bureau had traced to an anthrax contamination breach at Fort Detrick, Maryland, in 2002. Ivins had previously cooperated in the investigation. Ivins was suffering from depression as the investigation unfolded, and was briefly committed to a psychiatric facility for evaluation. He was found unconscious on 27 July 2008 following a drug overdose and died two days later. FBI investigators were never able to conclusively link Ivins to the attacks, of which Ivins' attorney claims he was innocent. *See also* BIOTERRORISM; WEAPONS OF MASS DESTRUCTION (WMDs).

ANTI-BALLISTIC MISSILE (ABM) TREATY. The ABM Treaty between the United States and the **Soviet Union** was signed by President Richard Nixon and Soviet General Secretary Leonid Brezhnev in May 1972. The purpose of the treaty was to prevent either country from developing or deploying systems capable of destroying incoming nuclear weapons. Both the United States and Soviet Union viewed ABM systems as destabilizing the doctrine of "mutually assured destruction" during the **Cold War**, whereby neither country had an incentive to launch a first strike against the other. Paradoxically, precluding deployment of ABM systems left both countries vulnerable but restored confidence in deterrence; neither had a strategic advantage in starting a nuclear war.

President **Ronald Reagan** proposed the Strategic Defense Initiative (SDI) in the 1980s, dubbed "Star Wars," which would have violated the ABM Treaty by implementing a space-based missile defense system to protect the United States from incoming Soviet missiles. SDI was never fully developed or deployed.

With the collapse of the Soviet Union, the ABM Treaty remained in force between the United States and the Russian Federation until June 2002, when President **George W. Bush** announced that the United States had withdrawn from the treaty. Bush proposed a land-based missile defense system to protect the United States and Europe from potential nuclear threats from **terrorists**. The plan called for a radar system in the **Czech Republic** and missile interceptors to be based in **Poland**, which **Russia** opposed. More generally, Russia opposed the admittance of many former Soviet satellite states, including the Czech Republic and Poland, into the **North Atlantic Treaty Organization** (NATO). Russia traditionally considered these former **Warsaw Pact** nations within its sphere of influence.

In February 2007, a Russian military general suggested that US bases in Poland and the Czech Republic could be targeted by Russian missiles if the United States carried out plans for its missile defense program; in June 2007, Russian President **Vladimir Putin** reiterated the point that Europe could be targeted by nuclear weapons. Presidents Bush and Putin met in April 2008 in Sochi, Russia, to discuss the missile defense program, but the summit did not yield agreement. Bush invited Russia to participate in the program and called it entirely defensive. Prospects for a resolution to the dispute diminished significantly following the Russian invasion of **Georgia** in August 2008, which chilled US–Russian relations. Bush supported Georgia's petition to become a NATO member state.

ARAFAT, YASSER (1929–2004). Born in Cairo, Egypt, Arafat founded the **Fatah** political party in 1959 in the Palestinian Territories, which was dedicated to armed struggle for the establishment of a Palestinian state. Arafat's Fatah party was secular, prompting rival leader Abu Nidal to break away and form an Islamist movement for independence in 1974. Arafat headed the **Palestine Liberation Organization** (PLO) from 1969 until his death in 2004.

Under Arafat the PLO based many of its paramilitary operations in Lebanon and used guerrilla tactics to challenge **Israel**'s dominance in the **West Bank** and **Gaza Strip**. The United States and Israel considered Arafat a **terrorist**. In 1988, in a watershed development, Arafat accepted Israel's right to exist in exchange for Palestinian statehood as part of a set of **United Nations** resolutions aimed at resolving the Israeli–Palestinian conflict. Arafat continued to negotiate with Israel in the 1990s. US President **William Clinton** acted as a mediator in the 1993 Oslo Accords and the 2000 Camp David Summit. For his efforts to secure peace at Oslo, Arafat received the Nobel Peace Prize in 2004. In the Palestinian Territories, however, Arafat was increasingly opposed by radical Islamists who formed **Hamas** in 1987 and called for jihad (holy war) against Israel. Arafat died in Paris, France, in 2004 of complications arising from the flu. *See also* ABBAS, MAHMOUD; FAYYAD, SALAM; HANIYA, ISMAIL; ISLAMIC JIHAD; LEBANON; PALESTINIAN NATIONAL AUTHORITY; ROAD MAP FOR PEACE; SYRIA.

ARMED FORCES. The armed forces of the United States comprise the Air Force, Army (including Army National Guard), Marines, and Navy, and are civilian-controlled. The headquarters for the armed forces is at the **Pentagon** in Arlington, Virginia.

Following the **Persian Gulf War** and the end of the **Cold War** with the dissolution of the **Soviet Union** in 1991, troop levels in the armed forces dropped substantially, as did congressional funding absent a major threat to national security. The point was not lost on **George W. Bush**, who as a presidential candidate in 2000 pledged to revitalize the military if elected. Nonetheless, between 1991 and the **11 September 2001 terrorist** attacks on the **World Trade Center** in New York and the Pentagon, the armed forces invested heavily in sophisticated, "smart technology," including robots and drones in lieu of heavy machinery and nuclear weapons. The conventional wisdom was that in a multipolar world with the United States as the only remaining superpower, probable theaters of military operation would be regional in nature, and would require both rapid deployment and precision targeting of tactical conventional weapons. The United States' bombing of select Serbian targets in the former **Yugoslavia** in the 1990s was a case in point. The **North Atlantic Treaty Organization** (NATO) followed similar protocols in its strategic operational plans.

The US armed forces were unquestionably the most powerful of any nation. Bush was confident in their ability when he elaborated the **neoconservative Bush Doctrine** in **foreign policy** following 9/11: The United States would take action not only against terrorists but the countries that harbored them. Moreover, the United States. would take **preemptive** action if the nation were under imminent threat of attack and would do so unilaterally if necessary. Bush implemented the new doctrine swiftly. In October 2001, Congress passed the **Authorization for the Use of Military Force** (AUMF) that enabled Bush to take military action against the **Taliban** regime in **Afghanistan**, which had provided aid and training camps for **al-Qaeda** terrorists responsible for the 9/11 attacks. In October 2002, Congress passed the **Iraq War Resolution**, which authorized the president to take military action against Iraqi dictator **Saddam Hussein**, who Bush believed was stockpiling **weapons of mass destruction** (WMDs) that could be used against the United States and its allies.

In the initial phases of the invasion of Afghanistan in October 2001, which quickly toppled the Taliban regime, and the US-led campaign of **shock and awe** that swiftly decimated Iraqi dictator Saddam Hussein's army in Spring 2003, there was little doubt of victory. With the Taliban driven underground, the **United Nations** (UN) placed the task of rebuilding Afghanistan under the aegis of the **International Security Assistance Force** (ISAF) only a few months after US and NATO troops ended major military operations. In May 2003, President Bush declared an end to major combat operations in **Iraq**, just six weeks after the US-led invasion by the **Coalition of the Willing** nations.

Despite these stunning—if anticipated—initial victories, the armed forces that occupied Afghanistan and Iraq were increasingly ill-equipped to handle the guerrilla warfare tactics of **insurgents** in the months and years that followed. In Afghanistan remnants of the Taliban, alongside al-Qaeda terrorists, perfected the use of roadside bombs, **improvised explosive devices** (IEDs), and rocket-propelled grenades against US troops. Insurgents also targeted civilians in urban areas by planting bombs in markets, mosques, and other high-density population areas. Many of the Taliban insurgents had learned these tactics as **mujahideen** fighters against the Soviet Union's occupation of Afghanistan in the 1980s—an insurgency that eventually drove Soviet troops out of the country by 1988. One major frustration of the armed forces was increasing attacks launched by insurgents from border areas, including **Waziristan** in **Pakistan**. Pakistani President **Pervez Musharraf** would not allow US troops to hunt for suspected terrorists in Pakistan, and the US military's use of drones to attack terrorist strongholds in Waziristan strained relations with Pakistan.

Afghan insurgents' tactics were replicated in post-invasion Iraq, but with even deadlier consequences as Shi'ites, Sunnis, and **Kurds** battled each other for control over the direction of new governmental institutions. Al-Qaeda fighters poured over the unsecured border with **Iran** and **Syria** following the initial invasion by US and coalition troops. The death toll on US troops was staggering, reaching more than 4,000 by the end of 2008. More than 90 percent of troop deaths occurred after President Bush's 1 May 2003 declaration of the end of major combat operations. The toll on Iraqi civilians reached the proportions of a full-scale humanitarian crisis. In 2006, estimates suggested more than 27,000 Iraqi civilians had been killed that year alone.

Many critics of the Bush administration's handling of postwar Iraq, including Arizona Senator **John McCain**, faulted the assumptions made by Secretary of Defense **Donald Rumsfeld** that the country could be secured with fewer than 200,000 troops. Other critics charged that the Bush administration's eschewing of **multilateralism** and its decision to invade Iraq without the aid of international troops that might have been available had he procured a UN mandate were to blame and underscored why the Bush Doctrine was unsustainable. Some blamed the death toll of US troops on the lack of adequate protection, including insufficient **body armor** available to protect them from surprise guerrilla attacks. Yet others were critical of the Bush administration's extensive use of private contractors, such as **Blackwater**, to provide vital security services.

Regardless, successive chairmen of the **Joint Chiefs of Staff**— **Richard Myers** (2001–2005), **Peter Pace** (2005–2007), and **Michael Mullen**—along with **CENTCOM** Commanders **Tommy Franks** (2000–2003), **John Abizaid** (2003–2007), and **William Fallon** (2007–2008) struggled to find a way to quell the violence and fashion an "exit strategy" in Iraq. The armed services implemented an unpopular policy of **stop loss**, which involuntarily extended the tours of duty of US troops. Army reserve units were called up and sent to Iraq. As the war became increasingly unpopular in the United States, protests grew and were symbolized by those of antiwar activist **Cindy Sheehan**, whose son had been killed in Iraq. One eventual casualty of the insurgency was Secretary of Defense Rumsfeld, who announced his resignation in November 2006.

Rumsfeld's departure, and the Republicans' loss of Congress in the 2006 **mid-term elections**, convinced the president and his new secretary of defense, **Robert Gates**, to fight the insurgency with a "surge" of troops. In 2007, the United States sent an additional 20,000 troops to Iraq to halt the violence in the area of **Al-Anbar**, the **Sunni Triangle**, and most importantly the capital, **Baghdad**, and its **Green Zone**, where most international organizations were located. By 2008, the surge had proven largely successful, particularly in Baghdad, although sporadic violence and instability continued throughout the country.

The armed forces' handling of **enemy combatants** captured in Afghanistan and prisoners of war captured in Iraq came under intense scrutiny. In 2003, allegations of **torture** at the **Abu Ghraib** detention facility outside of Baghdad drew national headlines and international outrage. The commander of the facility, **Janis Karpinski**, was demoted; the commander of coalition troops in Iraq at the time, **Ricardo Sanchez**, resigned under a cloud of suspicion that he had given his accord to "enhanced interrogation techniques" that allegedly violated the **Geneva Conventions**.

Concern over the treatment of enemy combatants held at **Guantanamo Bay, Cuba**, also placed the armed forces in the spotlight of media attention. Some detainees, including **Abu Zubaydah**, claimed to have been subject to **waterboarding** (simulated drowning). Others claimed they had been subject to a policy of **rendition**, whereby they were sent to countries without constitutional protections against torture where they were interrogated by **Central Intelligence Agency** (CIA) operatives, in violation of the Geneva Conventions. In 2005, Congress passed the **Detainee Treatment Act**, which forbade inhumane treatment of prisoners and mandated that interrogations follow the Army Field Manual. The longer-term issue was the indefinite detention of suspected terrorists at Guantanamo Bay. The Bush administration planned to use **military tribunals** to try them and contended that enemy combatants were not subject to **habeas corpus** and had no recourse to federal civil courts. Successive **Supreme Court** decisions in *Rasul v. Bush* (2004), *Hamdi v. Rumsfeld* (2004), and *Boumediene v. Bush* (2008), however, overturned the Bush administration's claims and found the military tribunals, including the **Military Commissions Act** (2006) passed by Congress, unconstitutional. The status of enemy combatants at Guantanamo Bay—many of whom could not return to their home countries because they would surely be executed—remained unresolved at the end of Bush's presidency.

The postwar insurgencies in Afghanistan and Iraq underscored the limitations of the armed services in the larger **War on Terror** waged by Bush. As a result, the president and Congress worked to strengthen intelligence and counterterrorism programs by creating a host of new agencies. Bush began by creating the **Office of Homeland Security**, headed by former Pennsylvania Governor **Tom Ridge**, in the **Executive Office of the President** (EOP) just a month after 9/11. Ridge's mandate was to coordinate counterterrorism programs across the federal government, but scarce resources and his lack of accountability to the legislative branch prompted Congress to create the 15th Cabinet-level agency, the **Department of Homeland Security** (DHS), in 2003. DHS merged 22 different agencies under its roof. Ridge headed the agency until 2005, when he was succeeded by **Michael Chertoff**. Moreover, Congress created a National Counterterrorism Center (NCTC) and a new **Director of National Intelligence** (DNI) position in the **Intelligence Reform and Terrorism Prevention Act** of 2004. The DNI coordinates intelligence-gathering with other federal agencies, including the **Federal Bureau of Investigation** (FBI), and the CIA director reports to him. **John Negroponte** was the first DNI; he was succeeded two years later by **Michael McConnell**. *See also* AXIS OF EVIL; ODIERNO, RAYMOND; PETRAEUS, DAVID; POWELL, COLIN; RICE, CONDOLEEZZA; UNITED NATIONS RESOLUTION 1441.

ARMITAGE, RICHARD LEE (1945–). A native of Boston, Massachusetts, Armitage served in the Vietnam War. He became a defense attaché at the US embassy shortly before the fall of Saigon. He later worked for the Department of Defense as a consultant in **Iran** and Thailand. Armitage served as a foreign policy advisor to both Senator Robert Dole of Kansas and President **Ronald Reagan**. He had a role in the administration of **George H.W. Bush** as well, negotiating the status of military bases in the Philippines and managing aid to the former **Soviet Union**. A signatory of the **Project for the New American Century** (PNAC) letter to President **William Clinton** calling for the ouster of **Saddam Hussein** in **Iraq** in 1998, Armitage was a foreign policy advisor to President **George W. Bush** during the 2000 presidential election. Bush appointed him deputy secretary of state in 2001. He served under Secretary of State **Colin Powell** until February 2005.

Armitage was implicated in the **Valerie Plame** affair. The identity of Plame, a covert **Central Intelligence Agency** agent, had been leaked in late 2005, and the source was believed to be someone in the White House. Plame was the wife of ambassador **Joseph Wilson**, a critic of the **War in Iraq**. Armitage was thought to have been the source of the leak, which was revealed to journalist **Robert Novak** in 2003. Special prosecutor **Patrick Fitzgerald** investigated the claims, and Armitage cooperated. In September 2006, Armitage revealed publicly that he was indeed the source of the leak. He was not charged with any criminal wrongdoing.

ARTHUR ANDERSEN (LLP). One of the Big Five accounting firms in the United States, Arthur Andersen was convicted in federal court for its role in the **Enron** scandal in 2002. The firm had been responsible for an audit of the failed energy corporation, for which accountants were ordered by top managers to destroy documents. Arthur Andersen voluntarily ceded its licenses to practice before the US **Securities and Exchange Commission**, which put the firm out of business.

The United States **Supreme Court** overturned the company's conviction in May 2005 on technicalities relating to the judge's instructions to jurors, which the High Court deemed vague with respect to the threshold to convict on grounds of obstruction of justice. Nevertheless, the firm had already sold much of its business to rival accounting firms and its reputation was thoroughly discredited. Arthur Andersen was also implicated in a substandard audit of **WorldCom**, a company that failed in July 2002, in the largest bankruptcy in US history at the time. The Arthur Andersen, Enron, and WorldCom failures were part of a larger series of corporate scandals that occurred during the presidency of **George W. Bush**. *See also* IMCLONE.

ASHCROFT, JOHN DAVID (1942–). Born in Chicago, Illinois, Ashcroft earned an undergraduate degree from Yale (1964) and a law degree from the University of Chicago (1967).

After an unsuccessful bid for Congress in 1972, Ashcroft worked as an assistant attorney general in Missouri. In 1976, he was elected attorney general in Missouri and re-elected in 1980. He successfully ran for the governorship in Missouri in 1984 and was re-elected in 1988, after which time he chaired the National Governors Association.

Ashcroft won election to the US Senate in 1994. In 2000, he was challenged by incumbent Missouri Governor Mel Carnahan, a Democrat, who perished in a plane crash shortly before election day. Carnahan's name remained on the ballot, and Ashcroft was defeated by a narrow margin of 2 percent. Carnahan's widow, Jean, was appointed to take the seat won by her deceased husband. Ashcroft was subsequently appointed by President **George W. Bush** to serve as attorney general of the United States. Ashcroft's appointment was approved in the Senate by a 58–42 margin. He served as attorney general from 2001 until his resignation in February 2005.

Ashcroft was a controversial figure during Bush's first term. Civil libertarians criticized his support of the USA **PATRIOT Act**, which weakened the standards for warrantless searches and **wiretapping**, as well as his support for Bush's **Terrorism Prevention and Information System** (TIPS) proposal that citizens report suspicious activities of their neighbors and coworkers to government officials as part of the **War on Terror**. Following the **11 September 2001** terrorist attacks on New York City and Washington, D.C., Ashcroft publicly raised the specter of the possibility of new attacks by **al-Qaeda**. A devout Christian, Ashcroft had a nude statue called the "Spirit of Justice," situated in a hallway frequently used for press conferences in the Department of Justice, covered with drapes in 2002.

After leaving his post as attorney general Ashcroft worked in consulting and as a lobbyist for technology and communications firms. His books include *Lessons From a Father to His Son* (1998), *On My Honor: The Beliefs that Shape My Life* (2001), and *Never Again: Securing America and Restoring Justice* (2006). Ashcroft has penned a number of gospel and other types of songs, including "Let the Eagle Soar," which was sung at President Bush's inauguration in 2005 and was the subject of many comedians' jokes.

ASIAN BIRD FLU. This virus, known as H5N1 or avian influenza, is common in many bird species in Asia. The virus has the ability to jump species and affect humans. The first cases of human deaths caused by the virus occurred in 2003, when poultry in Hong Kong, **China**, apparently caused three deaths. The virus spread rapidly throughout southeast Asia and parts of Africa, prompting concerns of a potential pandemic that could spread worldwide. Between 2004 and 2008 the World Health Organization reported 391 cases of Asian bird flu in humans and a mortality rate of 63 percent.

ATTA, MOHAMED (1968–2001). An Egyptian national who studied in Hamburg, **Germany**, from 1992 to 1999, Atta was the leader of the **al-Qaeda terrorist** attacks on the **World Trade Center** in New York City and the **Pentagon** on **11 September 2001**. He and 18 other al-Qaeda operatives hijacked four commercial aircraft, which they used as missiles. Atta flew the first airplane, American Airlines Flight 11, en route from Boston to Los Angeles, into one of the two towers at the World Trade Center in New York. All 92 passengers aboard the aircraft, a Boeing 767 with nearly full fuel tanks, perished.

Atta formed what is called the al-Qaeda "Hamburg Cell" in Germany by recruiting other fundamentalist Islamists to the organization. He is believed to have spent time in **Afghanistan**, where he met **Osama bin Laden**. He came to the United States in 2000 to enroll in aviation courses, and he received his pilot's license in August 2000. The day before the 11 September 2001 attacks, Atta and another hijacker were in Maine; they took a flight from Portland to Boston on a small regional carrier, where they subsequently boarded American Airlines Flight 11. The hijackers overpowered the crew and took control of the aircraft. Atta is thought to have been piloting the jumbo jet when it crashed into the World Trade Center. *See also* MOUSSAOUI, ZACARIAS.

AUSTRALIA. *See* HOWARD, JOHN WINSTON; RUDD, KEVIN.

AUTHORIZATION FOR THE USE OF MILITARY FORCE AGAINST IRAQ RESOLUTION OF 2002. *See* IRAQ WAR RESOLUTION.

AUTHORIZATION FOR THE USE OF MILITARY FORCE AGAINST TERRORISTS (AUMF). This bill was a joint resolution passed by the United States Congress on 18 September 2001 that authorized President **George W. Bush** to use "necessary and appropriate force" as commander in chief against the perpetrators of the **11 September 2001** attacks on the **World Trade Center** in New York City and the **Pentagon** in Washington, D.C. The bill passed in the House of Representatives 420–1 and in the Senate 98–0. Passage of the bill marked the opening chapter in President Bush's **War on Terror**.

The Bush administration cited the AUMF as a basis for the establishment of **military tribunals** and the holding of suspected terrorists at **Guantanamo Bay, Cuba**. The **Supreme Court** rejected this logic in *Hamdan v. Rumsfeld*. The High Court contended that the legislative intent of the authorization did not include such measures.

The Bush administration also used the AUMF as a partial justification for warrantless **wiretapping**, over which the **American Civil Liberties Union** (ACLU) unsuccessfully filed suit. *See also* AFGHANISTAN; AL-QAEDA; FOREIGN INTELLIGENCE SURVEILLANCE ACT (FISA); IRAQ; OMAR, MULLAH MUHAMMED; OSAMA BIN LADEN; TALIBAN; TERRORIST.

AXIS OF EVIL. In his 29 January 2002 State of the Union address, President **George W. Bush** used this phrase to describe **Iran**, **Iraq**, and **North Korea**, and contended that the three regimes were actively seeking **weapons of mass destruction** (WMDs) and were facilitating the activities of **terrorists**. The phrase is attributable to author and former White House speech writer David Frum, who was tasked with constructing a simple locution that would convey Bush's belief that the regime of Iraqi dictator **Saddam Hussein** had to be toppled. Frum drew from President Franklin Roosevelt's speech to the nation on 8 December 1941, the day after the Japanese attack on Pearl Harbor, Hawaii, in which the president described the attack as a "date which will live in infamy." Bush's use of the phrase signaled a critical juncture in the **War on Terror** as the president attempted to link Hussein to the terrorist group **al-Qaeda** and build the case for a **preemptive** attack on Iraq—a fundamental component of the **Bush Doctrine** in foreign policy.

AYERS, WILLIAM CHARLES (BILL) (1944–). A native of Chicago, Illinois, Ayers protested against the Vietnam War in the 1960s and 1970s. He formed an organization called Weather Underground in 1969, which embarked on a series of domestic bombing campaigns that included New York, the Capitol building in Washington, D.C., and the Pentagon. Ayers escaped federal prosecution on procedural technicalities. He became a professor of education at the University of Illinois at Chicago after earning a doctorate in education from Columbia University (1987). He is author of *Fugitive Days: A Memoir* (2001).

Ayers's ties to 2008 Democratic presidential nominee **Barack Obama** came under intense scrutiny during the latter's campaign against Republican Senator **John McCain**. Obama met Ayers in the 1990s, served on several community boards together, and Ayers held a "coffee" in support of Obama's bid for a seat in the Illinois legislature. McCain's vice presidential running mate, Alaska governor **Sarah Palin**, suggested that Obama had consorted with a known **terrorist**. Ayers never expressed regret over his past actions. Obama contended that his relationship with Ayers was not close, and had repudiated the Weather Underground organization's militant bombings decades earlier.

AZNAR LÓPEZ, JOSÉ MARÍA ALFREDO (1953–). Born in Madrid, Spain, Aznar is a right-wing politician who headed Spain's "People's Party." He became prime minister in 1996 and led his party to victories in 1996 and again in 2000. He was a strong supporter of President **George W. Bush** and the **War on Terror**. Aznar committed Spanish troops to the **War in Iraq**. He was prime minister during the bombings of the Madrid rail lines that killed 191 just three days prior to the 2004 elections. Many blamed Spain's support for the US-led invasion of **Iraq** for the attacks, and Aznar's party lost the elections. He was succeeded by **José Luis Rodríguez Zapatero**, who pulled Spain's forces out of Iraq within a month of assuming the prime ministership.

– B –

BA'ATH PARTY. Ba'ath is the Arabic language term for "resurrection." The Ba'ath Party was originally formed in **Syria** in 1941. The party espouses an anti-Western philosophy, pan-Arab unity, secularism, and socialist principles. Ba'ath has been the primary ruling party in Syria since the late 1950s.

The Ba'ath Party achieved political success in **Iraq** in 1963, but linkages with the Syrian party were strained amid tensions between moderate and extreme elements, and the Syrian party's alignment with the former **Soviet Union**. **Saddam Hussein** took over the leadership of the Iraqi Ba'ath Party in 1979, ruling for more than two decades. During his reign, Hussein transformed the Ba'ath Party into a much more militaristic organization.

Following Hussein's ouster in March 2003 with the US-led invasion of Iraq, US Administrator of Iraq **L. Paul Bremer** pursued a policy of "de-Ba'athification," or the purge of former Ba'ath Party members from senior governmental positions and the Iraqi military. While the policy succeeded in ousting former Ba'athists from positions of authority, critics charged that the expulsion of former Ba'ath Party members in the military slowed efforts to recruit and train a new Iraqi army capable of controlling internal security without a significant US military presence.

BAGHDAD, IRAQ. With a population of approximately 7 million, Baghdad is not only the capital of **Iraq** but also the third largest city in the Middle East. The city traces its founding to the eighth century. The majority of Baghdad's residents are Sunni Muslims.

During the **Persian Gulf War** in 1991, led by President **George H.W. Bush** and an international coalition sanctioned by the **United Nations**, Baghdad suffered sustained aerial bombing and significant damage.

When President **George W. Bush** launched a **preemptive** invasion of Iraq in March 2003 to topple the regime of **Saddam Hussein**, Baghdad once again suffered considerable damage, casualties, and civilian loss of life. US troops attempted to secure the city by April 2003 and established the "**Green Zone**," a three-square-mile block from which the **Coalition Provisional Authority** governed Iraq for more than a year. Nonetheless, attacks on US troops and civilians by insurgents around Baghdad, largely through the use of **improvised explosive devices** (IEDs), remained a frequent occurrence even as an Iraqi interim government under **Iyad Allawi** took office in June

2004. The Baghdad Morgue reported that between March 2003 and mid-2006, the death toll in the city reached nearly 50,000, including civilians and insurgents.

BAKER, JAMES ADDISON III (1930–). A native Texan, Baker has been a prominent figure in Republican presidential administrations and elections since the mid-1970s. Baker graduated from Princeton University in 1952, and after two years in the Marine Corps, attended the University of Texas, where he received a law degree in 1957. President Gerald Ford appointed him undersecretary of commerce in 1975, and later chairman of his national election committee in 1976. Baker was chairman of **George H.W. Bush**'s 1980 campaign for the presidency.

When **Ronald Reagan** clinched the Republican nomination and chose Bush as his running mate, Baker subsequently joined Reagan's campaign as senior advisor for the general election. He served as Reagan's White House **chief of staff** from 1981 to 1985, after which he was appointed secretary of the treasury (1985–1989). He was also a member of the **National Security Council** and the Economic Policy Council during Reagan's second term. George H.W. Bush appointed him secretary of state in 1989, and Baker held that position until August 1992, when he became the White House chief of staff. In 1991, he was awarded the Presidential Medal of Freedom for his leadership in the Communist transitions of 1989 following the collapse of the **Soviet Union** and the fall of the Berlin Wall. He was also commended for his service with respect to the reunification of **Germany** and the allied invasion of **Iraq** in the **Persian Gulf War** in 1991.

Baker published *Politics of Diplomacy* in 1995. In 1997, he served as the personal envoy for the **United Nations** secretary general for the Western Sahara. After returning to the private sector as a senior partner in his law practice of Baker Botts and as senior counsel to the Carlyle Group, he was one of President **George W. Bush**'s principal legal advisors during the **Florida recount** controversy following the 2000 election. Bush appointed him as a special envoy in 2003 to work with foreign countries to relieve Iraq's debt after dictator **Saddam Hussein**'s regime was toppled by American and coalition forces earlier that year. In 2006, alongside former Representative Lee Hamilton, Baker cochaired the **Iraq Study Group**, which was commissioned by Congress to study potential alternative governmental arrangements in Iraq. The same year Baker published *"Work Hard, Study. . . And Keep Out of Politics!": Adventures and Lessons from an Unexpected Public Life.*

BALI, INDONESIA. This small Indonesian island has a population in excess of 3 million, most of whom are Hindus. Bali suffered two **terrorist** bombings, one in 2002 and another in 2005, that were directed at the primary tourist district of Kuta. The 12 October 2002 attack killed 202 people and was the deadliest terrorist attack in Indonesian history. The radical Islamist group Jemaiyaa Islamiya claimed responsibility for the attack. The 1 October 2005 attack killed 20, including three suspected bombers, and injured more than 100. Jemaiyaa Islamiya was suspected of having carried out the attacks.

BAN, KI-MOON (1944–). Born in the village of North Chungcheong in what is now South Korea, Ban earned an undergraduate degree from Seoul National University (1970) and a master's degree in public administration from Harvard University (1985). He worked as a career diplomat for the South Korean government beginning in the 1970s. He was deputy ambassador to the United States from 1993 to 1994, and was appointed ambassador to Austria in 1998. From 2004 to 2006, he served as South Korea's foreign minister. In October 2006, he was elected secretary-general of the **United Nations** to succeed **Kofi Annan**. In the closing days of President **George W. Bush**'s second term, Ban's secretariat was dominated by the issue of genocide in the **Darfur** region of **Sudan**, the **War in Iraq**, efforts to find a peaceful settlement to the conflict between **Israel** and **Palestine** including the **Road Map for Peace**, and global warming.

BASRA, IRAQ. An ancient city in the southeastern corner of **Iraq** near the Persian Gulf, Basra was the site of intense battles between US and British troops and insurgent forces in the early stages of the **War in Iraq** led by the US in March 2003. The city was secured by British troops in early April 2003. However, Basra became the focal point for **insurgent** attacks that mounted in 2008, prompting Iraqi Prime Minister **Nouri al-Maliki** to launch a security crackdown in March 2008 that ultimately resulted in more than 200 deaths and hundreds of arrests of suspected insurgents.

BAUER, GARY LEE (1946–). A native of Covington, Kentucky, Bauer is a major figure of the **Evangelical Christian** Right within the Republican Party. He received a bachelor's degree from Georgetown College (1968) and a law degree from Georgetown University (1973). He worked in the administration of **Ronald Reagan** from 1982 to 1987 under Secretary of Education William Bennett and was named chair of the president's Special Working Group on the Family.

Bauer is best known for his leadership of various not-for-profit groups concerned with the interplay of traditional Christian values and issues of **education**, marriage, and family. He served as vice president of Focus on the Family from 1988 to 1992 and founded the Campaign for Working Families in 1996, a political action committee with the goal of electing conservative, pro-life candidates to offices across the country. He served as president of the Family Research Council from 1988 to 1999. He left that position to run unsuccessfully for the Republican presidential nomination in 2000. In 2001, he founded American Values, a nonprofit education organization.

Bauer is also considered a **neoconservative** on **foreign policy**. In 1997, he signed the statement of principles for the **Project for the New American Century** (PNAC), cofounded by many officials who would play pivotal roles in the administration of George W. Bush, including **Richard (Dick) Cheney**, **I. Lewis (Scooter) Libby**, **Richard N. Perle**, **Donald Rumsfeld**, and **Paul Wolfowitz**. PNAC's goal, harkening back to President Reagan's positions, was to promote American global leadership based on military strength and moral clarity. Bauer is also a strong supporter of the state of **Israel** and cofounded the American Alliance of Jews and Christians in 2002.

BEAR STEARNS. Bear Stearns was an investment and stock trading firm that collapsed in 2008 due to problematic **sub-prime mortgage** loans, as well as alleged securities violations by its managers. In 2008, the **Federal Reserve** loaned Bear Stearns $29 million—the largest bailout of a private corporation until the **American International Group** (AIG) in 2008. Bear Stearns was ultimately purchased by JP Morgan Chase. *See also* BERNANKE, BEN SHALOM; PAULSON, HENRY MERRITT, JR.; TROUBLED ASSETS RELIEF PROGRAM (TARP).

BELTWAY SNIPER. Also sometimes referred to in the press as the "Washington Sniper" or the "D.C. Sniper," this term refers to the shootings around the Washington, D.C., metropolitan area in October 2002. Using a modified passenger car, **John Allen Muhammad** and his 17-year-old accomplice, Lee Boyd Malvo, killed 10 individuals and injured three others before both were arrested on 24 October 2002. Many of the shootings took place in the parking lots of shopping malls and gas stations. The random shootings were perpetrated in Montgomery and Prince George's Counties in Maryland, and Spotsylvania, Arlington, and Prince William Counties in Virginia. Muhammad was convicted of murder in a Virginia court and was sentenced to death; Malvo, who was a minor at the time of the murders, was sentenced to multiple life sentences without the possibility of parole.

BENEDICT XVI (1927–). Born Joseph Alois Ratzinger in Bavaria, **Germany**, Benedict XVI succeeded Pope **John Paul II** as the pontiff of the Catholic Church on 19 April 2005. A prolific writer, Benedict XVI is widely regarded as a traditionalist and a conservative in his policy and faith-based positions, including opposition to **abortion**. President **George W. Bush** visited Pope Benedict at the Vatican in June 2007. Pope Benedict visited the United States in April 2008, including the site of the **11 September 2001 terrorist** attacks on the **World Trade Center** in New York City.

BERLUSCONI, SILVIO (1936–). Born in Milan, Italy, Berlusconi is Italy's longest-serving prime minister, having served in 1994–1995, 2001–2006, and 2008– . He heads a coalition of center-right/right parties in Italy. A wealthy businessman who owns a media conglomerate and the soccer team *AC Milan*, Berlusconi was a stanch supporter of President **George W. Bush** and the **War in Iraq**. Under Berlusconi, Italy committed more than 3,000 troops to the war, the third largest contingent after the United States and **Great Britain**.

Berlusconi lost his parliamentary majority in the elections of May 2006 to Romano Prodi, the former president of the **European Union** Commission (1999–2004). Berlusconi had pushed for a time frame during which to withdraw Italy's troops from **Iraq**. Prodi hastened the withdrawal as the war became increasingly unpopular in Italy. In

2005, an Italian military general, **Nicola Calipari**, was accidentally killed by US troops while escorting an Italian journalist, Giulana Sgregna, to the **Baghdad** airport. In Spring 2006, one Italian soldier was killed and four others wounded during an ambush by insurgents while they were escorting a British logistics convoy. All Italian soldiers left Iraq in December 2006. Berlusconi won re-election in 2008 as Prodi's government fell into disarray over economic issues.

BERNANKE, BEN SHALOM (1953–). A Georgia native who grew up in South Carolina, Bernanke graduated from Harvard College (1975) and completed a doctorate in economics at the Massachusetts Institute of Technology (1979). He taught at Stanford, New York University, and Princeton before joining the Board of Commissioners of the **Federal Reserve** in 2002. In 2006, he was appointed by President **George W. Bush** to chair the Federal Reserve and replace **Alan Greenspan**, who held the position for 19 years.

Bernanke's tenure was overshadowed by the crisis of **sub-prime mortgage**s, which caused the failure of many Wall Street firms and sent the federal government scrambling to save them to avoid a collapse of the US financial system. Under Bernanke's watch, the Federal Reserve loaned $29 million to **Bear Stearns**, which was consequently purchased by JP Morgan Chase in 2007. Along with Treasury Secretary **Henry Paulson**, Bernanke supported the bailout of **American International Group** (AIG) for a sum of $85 billion in 2008, as well as congressional efforts to loan more money to troubled financial firms on the brink of failure. *See also* TROUBLED ASSETS RELIEF PROGRAM (TARP).

BESLAN, RUSSIA. A city of 35,000 in the Russian Republic of North Ossetia-Alania, Beslan was the site of a bloody hostage-taking incident by more than 30 Chechen **terrorist**s at a secondary school beginning 1 September 2004. Two days later, 334 civilians—of which 186 were children—were killed when armed Russian security forces confronted the terrorists. President **George W. Bush** did not reproach Russian President **Vladimir Putin** for the ill-fated military intervention, but rather linked the Beslan incident to the global **War on Terror** in his 2006 State of the Union address. *See also* CHECHNYA; GEORGIA.

BHUTTO, BENAZIR (1953–2007). Leader of the Pakistani People's Party, Benazir Bhutto was the first woman to be elected prime minister of **Pakistan**. She was elected twice—once in 1988 and again in 1993. Both times she was removed from office by the incumbent Pakistani president on alleged corruption charges, which she disputed. In 1998, she left Pakistan and relocated to Dubai. Bhutto did not return to Pakistan until 2007, when President **Pervez Musharraf** granted her immunity from prosecution. She quickly organized opposition and was placed under house arrest just a month after her return, following Musharraf's decision to call a state of emergency. She was assassinated by a car bomb in Rawalpindi on 27 December 2007, several weeks before scheduled legislative elections. **Al-Qaeda** in Pakistan claimed responsibility for the bombing.

BIDEN, JOSEPH ROBINETTE, JR. (1942–). A native of Scranton, Pennsylvania, Biden graduated from the University of Delaware (1965) and earned a law degree from Syracuse University (1968). He entered politics by winning a seat on the New Castle County, Delaware, County Council in 1970. Biden ran successfully in Delaware for the US Senate in 1972. He was subsequently elected five times through 2002. He served on the Senate Foreign Relations and Judiciary Committees throughout his legislative career, chairing Foreign Relations twice (2001–2003, 2007–2008) and chairing Judiciary from 1987 to 1994. In **foreign policy**, Biden is widely hailed for his knowledge and experience, particularly during the regional conflicts in the former **Yugoslavia** in the 1990s. Biden initially supported the US-led **War in Iraq** in 2003. He later used his position as Senate Foreign Relations chair to explore alternative governing arrangements for postwar **Iraq** and was critical of President **George W. Bush**'s handling of the war.

Biden made two unsuccessful bids for the presidency. His 1988 campaign ended when it was revealed that he had plagiarized parts of a speech from British Labour Party leader Neil Kinnock. He announced his candidacy for the 2008 election a year earlier in January 2007. Biden was unable to compete successfully against Democratic front runners **Hillary Clinton** and **Barack Obama**. He withdrew from the 2008 race after garnering less than a percent of the vote in the **Iowa Caucuses**.

After clinching the Democratic Party's nomination for the presidency, Barack Obama chose Biden as his vice presidential running mate in August 2008. He did so ostensibly for Biden's experience in foreign policy matters in the Senate, and his potential ability to reach out to blue-collar voters. Obama's choice of Biden angered many supporters of Hillary Clinton, who had won 18 million votes during the 2008 primaries and caucuses. Moreover, Biden had once remarked of Obama during an interview that "I mean, you got the first mainstream African-American who is articulate and bright and clean and a nice-looking guy . . . " Biden immediately apologized, but the gaffe was characteristic of Biden's often troubled, "foot-in-mouth" political style according to his critics. Supporters of Republican nominee **John McCain** set up Biden "gaffe-o-meters" on their Internet Web pages to monitor Biden's peculiar comments during the campaign.

Potentially more problematic was the comment that Biden reiterated about Obama at a Democratic candidates' debate in August 2007. Biden had stated that Obama was not ready to be president, and accentuated his belief that "The presidency is not something that lends itself to on-the-job training." Regardless, Biden was sworn in as vice president on 20 January 2009. President Obama placed him in charge of economic recovery matters.

Biden is author of a memoir entitled *Promises to Keep* (2007).

BIN LADEN, OSAMA (1957–?). Born in Riyadh, Saudi Arabia, bin Laden inherited a fortune from his father's construction business. In the late 1980s, he established Maktab al-Khadamat (Office of Order), which supported and supplied the **mujahideen** fighters with money, arms, and human resources following the **Soviet Union**'s invasion of **Afghanistan**. The extent of US support for or covert involvement of bin Laden's organization and its **jihad** (holy war) against the Soviets in Afghanistan is a matter of speculation. From the extremist elements of Maktab al-Khadamat, bin Laden formed a new group of militant Islamists called **al-Qaeda** in 1988. Following the **Persian Gulf War** in 1991 he called for the ouster of US troops from Saudi Arabia, which contains the Muslim holy cities of Mecca and Medina. The Saudi royal family expelled bin Laden from the country in 1991, and he fled to **Sudan**. Bin Laden's family disowned him in 1994, the same year Saudi Arabia formally revoked his citizenship. After Sudan expelled him under international pressure, bin Laden took up refuge in Afghanistan, where the **Taliban** clerics had come to control the country following the Soviet's withdrawal of troops in 1988 and a subsequent civil war.

Bin Laden is suspected of masterminding widespread **terrorist** activities around the globe, including hotel bombings in Egypt and Yemen; the US embassy bombings in Dar-es-Salaam, Tanzania, and Nairobi, Kenya, in 1998; and most importantly, the hijacking of four commercial aircraft used in the **11 September 2001** terrorist attacks on the **World Trade Center** in New York City and the **Pentagon** in Washington, D.C.

President **George W. Bush** vowed to capture bin Laden and bring him to justice in earnest following the 11 September 2001 attacks as part of the **War on Terror** that began with the US-led invasion of Afghanistan in the autumn of 2001. While the invasion successfully toppled the Taliban regime, bin Laden was never located. US intelligence suggested that bin Laden may have been hiding in the area of **Tora Bora** region of Afghanistan, which was the site of intense fighting between US troops and insurgents loyal to bin Laden and the Taliban in 2001. Bush was criticized for not committing ground troops in the battle, which might have produced bin Laden. Further, the **Central Intelligence Agency** (CIA) closed the subunit dedicated solely to finding bin Laden in 2005. In 2004, Democratic presidential candidate **Bob Graham** suggested that the Bush administration had given up trying to capture bin Laden, to whom he referred as "Osama Been Forgotten."

As of 2008, it was unclear whether bin Laden was alive. International press accounts dating to 2006 speculate that he was killed in either Afghanistan or **Pakistan**. Further, he is suspected of needing long-term dialysis treatments for failing kidneys, and may be deceased from lack of such treatment. The last major video of bin Laden was broadcast on the **al-Jazeera** television network in 2004, in which he claimed to have assigned the hijackers to carry out the 11 September 2001 attacks against the United States. The authenticity of subsequent videos and audiotapes of bin Laden, whether broadcast by al-Jazeera or on the Internet, has been disputed.

BIOTERRORISM. Bioterrorism may be defined as the use of any biological agents by **terrorist**s to harm or kill civilian populations. Examples of deadly pathogens that may be used for such purposes include bubonic plague, **anthrax**, and measles. Preventing terrorists from locating, producing, and delivering such pathogens as a potential **weapon of mass destruction** (WMD) figured significantly into President **George W. Bush**'s **War on Terror** following the **11 September 2001** attacks. The **Department of Homeland Security**, as well as the Food and Drug Administration and the Department of Agriculture, have significant responsibility for guarding against bioterror threats.

BIPARTISAN CAMPAIGN REFORM ACT (BCRA) (2002). This law, sponsored by Senators **John McCain** and Russell Feingold (D-WI), sought to reform campaign finance laws originally passed in the 1970s. The bill abolished so-called "soft money" contributions to national party organizations (Democratic National Committee, Republican National Committee). In the past, the national party organizations used soft money not only to fund campaigns, but for other activities such as advertising and voter registration. BCRA, however, raised the limit of contributions to individual candidates or a political party (i.e., "hard money"). Finally, BCRA banned the use of corporate or union money from being used in non- or for-profit organizations' election advertisements. State political parties, independent groups, and several US senators challenged the law due to its limitations on spending, which the bill's detractors contend is a First Amendment right to free speech. The law was upheld by the **Supreme Court** in 2003 in a 5–4 ruling in *McConnell v. FEC*.

BLACKWATER WORLDWIDE. Blackwater is a North Carolina-based private military security contracting firm founded in 1997. Following the initiation of the **War in Iraq**, the US government hired Blackwater in 2003 to secure the protection of **L. Paul Bremer**, head of the **Coalition Provisional Authority**. The company was also hired to provide protection to other US officials in **Iraq**, and received a contract to guard the US Embassy in **Baghdad, Iraq**.

Blackwater's involvement in Iraq raised significant controversy over the role of private military contractors, which some critics charge are tantamount to mercenary operations. The US Congress investigated Blackwater's conduct in October 2007, a month after the Iraq government rescinded the company's license to work in the country after 17 civilians were killed by Blackwater employees in **Baghdad**. Critics charged that Blackwater personnel, who were involved in nearly 200 shootings in Iraq, had a "shoot-first" policy. Blackwater personnel were also involved in a gunfight involving insurgents in Fallujah, Iraq, in 2004 that resulted in the death of four contractors. The congressional committee investigating Blackwater in 2007 charged the company with delaying the investigation, but the company escaped criminal prosecution.

BLAGOJEVICH, MILORAD (ROD) R. (1956–). Born to Serbian immigrants in Chicago, Blagojevich graduated from Northwestern University (1979) and earned a law degree from Pepperdine University (1983). He entered the legal profession as an assistant state's attorney in Illinois before successfully seeking a seat in the Illinois legislature in 1992. He won election as governor of Illinois in 2002 and was re-elected in 2006.

Blagojevich was at the center of controversy following the election of **Barack Obama** to the presidency in 2008. At issue was the appointment to fill Obama's vacant Senate seat. Federal authorities, led by prosecutor **Patrick Fitzgerald**, charged that Blagojevich had attempted to "sell" the Senate seat. Blagojevich was subsequently impeached by the Illinois legislature in January 2009 not only on this matter, but also for other alleged abuses of power. He was convicted by the Illinois Senate on a unanimous vote and removed from office on 29 January 2009. As of that date, the federal investigation continued.

BLAIR, CHARLES LYNTON (TONY) (1953–). Born in Edinburgh, Scotland, and educated at Oxford University in England, Blair became the British Labour Party leader in 1994. He was first elected to the British House of Commons in 1994 from the constituency of Sedgefield in northeastern England, and subsequently re-elected in 1997, 2001, and 2005. He became prime minister in 1997 and remained in that position until his resignation in June 2007, at which time he was succeeded by **Gordon Brown**. Blair is the only British prime minister to have successfully waged three consecutive elections to the premiership.

Blair was an indefatigable supporter of President **George W. Bush**'s **War on Terror**. Under Blair's premiership, **Great Britain** provided the second-largest contingent of troops for the invasion of **Afghanistan** in 2001 and the **War in Iraq** in 2003. Under Blair, **Great Britain** was also targeted by **al-Qaeda terrorist**s. A suicide bombing of the **London** transportation system on 7 July 2005 killed more than 50. Three days after Blair left office, terrorists with suspected links to al-Qaeda drove a car bomb into the terminal at Glasgow International Airport, killing the driver of the car.

Blair's public esteem and political capital in Britain nevertheless waned as the unpopular War in Iraq continued, and with revelations in 2005 of the so-called **Downing Street Memo**, which was leaked to the press. The memo allegedly reported details of a secret meeting of Labour party officials in July 2002 in which they argued that President Bush had "framed" intelligence in such a way as to link the Iraqi regime of **Saddam Hussein** to **weapons of mass destruction**, and used the data as a justification to remove the dictator militarily. Foreign Secretary **Jack Straw** was reported to have stated that Bush had "made up his mind" on a military invasion of Iraq in spite of questionable evidence. Both Bush and Blair disputed the memo's allegations.

In domestic politics Blair advocated "New Labour," and transformed the image and policy substance of his party. He focused on "centrist" politics and market solutions, all the while pursuing improvements and greater public expenditures for education and health. He also oversaw the devolution of powers to Scotland and Wales, and was a pivotal player in the negotiation of the Good Friday Accord in 1998, along with US President **William Clinton**, in **Northern Ireland**. Upon leaving the prime minister's office in 2007, Blair was appointed as an envoy by the so-called "Quartet" of nations—the United States, Great Britain, **Russia**, and the **European Union**—to find a comprehensive solution for peace in the Middle East. *See also* ISRAEL; PALESTINIAN NATIONAL AUTHORITY; ROAD MAP FOR PEACE.

BLANCO, KATHLEEN BABINEAUX (1942–). Born in New Iberia, Louisiana, and educated at the University of Louisiana at Lafayette (formerly University of Southwestern Louisiana) in business, Blanco got her start in politics in 1984, when she ran successfully for a state representative as a Democrat. She was elected twice as public service commissioner (1988, 1994) and served as lieutenant governor of Louisiana from 1996 to 2004. She was elected to the governorship of Louisiana in 2004—the first woman to be elected to the position in the state's history. Her term ended in January 2008, at which time she exited politics.

Blanco was governor when the costliest natural disaster in US history, **Hurricane Katrina**, struck New Orleans and the Gulf Coast as a Category 3 storm on the Saffir-Simpson scale. Much of the multibillion dollar damage came from the storm surge, which broke levees built to protect New Orleans and adjoining parishes, which are several feet below sea level. Blanco was roundly criticized for her public statement that Louisiana was prepared for the storm when many citizens were later stranded for days or perished in the storm. Some critics posited that she prioritized "law and order" over rescue and aid of victims of the storm when she ordered the state National Guard to secure flooded areas in New Orleans and elsewhere and to halt looters by deadly force if necessary. She is alleged to have placed less emphasis on requisite human and financial resources, such as medical aid, for first-responders. Further, news organizations reported that the American Red Cross had been denied access to the city of New Orleans by the state homeland security agency, under Blanco's control, immediately following the hurricane. Finally, criticism of her handling of federal relief funds in 2006 and 2007 dissuaded Blanco from seeking re-election.

Blanco had a thorny relationship with New Orleans Mayor **Ray Nagin** and President **George W. Bush** before and after Hurricane Katrina. Nagin, a Democrat, had supported her opponent for Governor, Bobby Jindal, in 2004 and was publicly critical of Blanco's leadership after Katrina. Blanco blamed the **Federal Emergency Management Agency** (FEMA) director **Michael D. Brown** for incompetent relief efforts, while Nagin accused Blanco of failing to enable the president to "federalize" the National Guard to hasten military relief efforts. While ultimately accepting responsibility for the lackluster state-level response to Katrina, Blanco remained critical of the Bush administration, contending that neighboring Mississippi had received preferential treatment in the aftermath of the storm because its governor was Republican.

BLIX, HANS MARTIN (1928–). A doctor in law from Stockholm University, Blix was born in Uppsala, Sweden. He served as a career diplomat in the Swedish Ministry of Foreign Affairs (1963–1976), and was minister of foreign affairs from 1978 to 1979. He became the director of the **International Atomic Energy Agency** (IAEA) in 1981 and held the position until 1997. **United Nations** (UN) General Secretary **Kofi Annan** appointed Blix as the head weapons inspector (or formally, head of the United Nations Monitoring, Verification, and Inspection Commission) in **Iraq** from 2000 to 2003. Blix's charge in Iraq was to ensure that the regime of **Saddam Hussein** was complying with the terms of UN Resolution 687 (following the **Persian Gulf War** in 1991), which mandated that Iraq disarm.

Blix began searching for alleged **weapons of mass destruction** (WMDs) in Iraq in 2002. He encountered some resistance from Hussein's regime, of which he was critical. However, he never uncovered any WMDs and was recalled from his mission in early 2003. Following the US-led **War in Iraq** that began in March 2003, Blix turned his criticism to President **George W. Bush** and British Prime Minister **Tony Blair**, whom he accused of an unnecessary rush to armed conflict despite little evidence that Hussein's regime had stockpiled weapons. *See also* AXIS OF EVIL; ELBARADEI, MOHAMMED; DOWNING STREET MEMO; KAY, DAVID A.; NIGER; WILSON, JOSEPH CHARLES.

BODMAN, SAMUEL WRIGHT (1938–). A native of Chicago, Illinois, Bodman graduated with a BS degree in chemical engineering from Cornell University (1961) and a doctor of science from the Massachusetts Institute of Technology (1965). He worked as a professor of chemical engineering before moving to the venture capital firm American Research Development Corporation and Fidelity Investments. In 1987, he moved to Cabot Corporation, an international chemical company, where he held the positions of chair, director, and chief executive officer. His public service record includes service as director of the Massachusetts Institute of Technology (MIT) School of Engineering Practice and the MIT Commission on Education. He is a member of the American Academy of Arts and Sciences and a trustee of the Isabella Stewart Gardner Museum in Boston and the New England Aquarium.

Bodman joined the administration of President **George W. Bush** in 2001, when he became deputy secretary of the Department of Commerce. He moved to the Department of the Treasury in 2004, where he was also deputy secretary. In 2005, he was unanimously confirmed as secretary of energy, succeeding **Spencer Abraham**.

BODY ARMOR. The concept of body armor dates to the Middle Ages and earlier. It is simply a suit or layers of protection made of metal or other types of material that protects a soldier's body during combat. During the **War in Iraq** the **Pentagon** came under intense scrutiny on the issue of body armor. Allegations ranged from the Pentagon's failure to provide soldiers with body armor, forcing them or their families to find non–military-issued body armor, to charges that the military-issued body armor was substandard. During the War in Iraq the Pentagon confirmed that between 40,000 and 130,000 troops had not been issued the Kevlar Interceptor vests or ceramic plates required for full protection against shrapnel from explosive devices and firearms as powerful as AK-47s. In 2004, during a visit to troops awaiting deployment to Iraq in Kuwait, Secretary of Defense **Donald Rumsfeld** was questioned publicly by troops on the issue. Massachusetts Senator **John Kerry**, during the 2004 presidential election, accused **George W. Bush** of going to war in Iraq "on the cheap."

In 2006, one Pentagon study found that 74 of 93 fatal wounds in soldiers serving in Iraq were due to inadequate body armor. Under pressure from soldiers, veterans groups, and soldiers' families, the armed services scrambled to order sufficient body armor. In 2008, the Marine Corps alone reportedly ordered 28,000 vests from a Florida-based company. *See also* IMPROVISED EXPLOSIVE DEVICES (IEDs).

BOLTEN, JOSHUA BREWSTER (1954–). A graduate of Princeton (1976) and Stanford Law School (1980), Bolten worked as general counsel in the Office of the US Trade Representative under President **George H.W. Bush**. From 1994 to 1999, he worked for the investment firm of Goldman Sachs in London, England.

Bolten was policy director for President **George W. Bush**'s campaign for the presidency in 2000. He became the president's deputy chief of staff in 2001. In 2003, he was appointed to serve as the director of the **Office of Management and Budget** (OMB). In 2006, Bolten succeeded **Andrew Card** as Bush's White House **chief of staff**.

BOLTON, JOHN ROBERT (1948–). A Baltimore, Maryland, native educated at Yale University (BA, 1970; law degree, 1974), Bolton held the positions of assistant secretary in the State Department, assistant attorney general in the Justice Department, and assistant program coordinator for the US Agency for International Development under Presidents **Ronald Reagan** and **George H.W. Bush**. President **George W. Bush** appointed him undersecretary of state for arms control and international security in 2001, a position he held until 2005.

In the administration of George W. Bush, Bolton was a highly controversial figure. A supporter of the **neoconservative Project for a New American Century** (PNAC), Bolton was sharply critical of the **United Nations**, as well as **Iraq, Iran**, and Cuba. He was deeply concerned about rogue regimes developing **weapons of mass destruction** (WMDs). Critics of Bolton suggested that he had misinterpreted intelligence to support and encourage President Bush's policies leading up to the invasion of Iraq in 2003, and his criticism of the United Nations was superciliously **isolationist**.

President Bush nominated Bolton as ambassador to the United Nations, to replace John Danforth, in 2005. Senate Democrats filibustered Bolton's nomination and precluded a floor vote. President Bush then made a "recess appointment" of Bolton to fill the post — appointing him to the post when Congress went into its summer recess in August. Bolton held the position in the interim from August 2005 to December 2006. Although some of Bolton's supporters lauded his efforts to reform the United Nations, particularly on human rights issues, his style was abrasive, and he often criticized General Secretary **Kofi Annan**. After Democrats swept the 2006 **mid-term elections** Bush planned to renominate Bolton for confirmation. However, it became clear to Bolton and President Bush that Senate Democrats would continue to oppose his nomination, and Bolton resigned. *See also* INTERNATIONAL CRIMINAL COURT.

BOUMEDIENE V. BUSH (2008). This **Supreme Court** case concerned the rights of suspected **terrorists** to challenge their indefinite detention at **Guantanamo Bay, Cuba**, and their prospective trial by military courts. The plaintiff, Lakhdar Boumediene, a Bosnian national born in Algeria, was arrested by US troops in Bosnia for alleged ties to **al-Qaeda** after the Bosnian courts found no grounds to hold him. He was subsequently transferred to and detained at the military detention facility in Cuba as an **enemy combatant**.

Boumediene's petition to the High Court was a writ of **habeas corpus**, or the right to appear before a judge in a civilian court. By a 5–4 decision, Boumediene's petition was granted. Prior to this case, the Supreme Court held in *Rasul v. Bush* (2004) that US courts did have the authority to determine whether detainees were unlawfully imprisoned and dismissed the argument that the facility in Cuba was beyond the reach of US law. In *Hamdan v. Rumsfeld* (2006), the Court had also decided a habeas corpus petition by a detainee, concluding that the **military tribunals** set up by the Bush administration were unconstitutional and could only be founded by an act of Congress. As a result, Congress passed the **Military Commissions Act**. The ruling in *Boumediene* found that the Military Commissions Act, as well, violated detainees' rights to habeas corpus, and was a major setback to Bush administration policy in the **War on Terror**. *See also HAMDI V. RUMSFELD* (2004).

BRADLEY, WILLIAM (BILL) WARREN (1943–). A native of Crystal City, Missouri, Bradley attended Princeton University, as well as Oxford University in England, and was a Rhodes Scholar. He was a professional basketball player for the New York Knicks in the 1960s and 1970s, leading them to championships in 1970 and 1973. He retired from the National Basketball Association in 1977.

Bradley ran successfully for the US Senate in 1978 as a Democrat in New Jersey, and was re-elected twice. Race relations and poverty informed much of his political agenda. In 1999, he announced his candidacy for the presidency, making environmental issues a cornerstone of his platform. He was defeated by his rival **Al Gore** in the 2000 Democratic primaries. He subsequently left politics and is a corporate consultant. Bradley is author of *The Journey from Here* (2000) and *The New American Story* (2007).

BREMER, LEWIS PAUL III (1941–). Bremer, a career diplomat, was born in Hartford, Connecticut. He earned a BA degree from Yale University (1963) and a master's degree in business administration from

Harvard (1966). He also studied at the prestigious *Institut d'Études Politiques* in Paris, France. He joined the foreign service and was stationed in **Afghanistan** and Malawi until 1971. He served as an assistant to Secretary of State Henry Kissinger from 1972 to 1976, was stationed in Norway from 1976 to 1979, was a deputy executive secretary in the Department of State from 1979 to 1981, and an assistant to Alexander Haig from 1981 to 1983. He retired from the foreign service in 1989 to work in consulting after serving as the ambassador to the Netherlands and ambassador-at-large for counterterrorism in the administration of **Ronald Reagan**.

Following the **11 September 2001 terrorist** attacks on New York and the Pentagon in Washington, D.C., Bremer coauthored a report from the conservative think tank the Heritage Foundation, which would ultimately serve as a design for President **George W. Bush**'s proposal for the creation of a new **Department of Homeland Security** to combat terrorism in 2002. In June 2003, following the US-led invasion of **Iraq** three months earlier, President Bush appointed Bremer US administrator in Iraq until a provisional government could be founded by the Iraqis. As US administrator in Iraq, Bremer purged former **Ba'ath Party** officials of **Saddam Hussein**'s regime from senior government positions and the Iraqi Army ("de-Ba'athification"). Bremer also ordered that the newspaper of insurgent **Muqtada al-Sadr** be shut down. In June 2004, the **Coalition Provisional Authority** formally transferred power in Iraq to an interim government, led by **Iyad Allawi**, and Bremer returned to the United States. Ambassador **John Negroponte** replaced Bremer as the highest ranking governmental official in Iraq.

Bremer was awarded the Presidential Medal of Freedom Award in 2004, and currently serves on several boards. He is author of *My Year in Iraq: The Struggle to Build a Future of Hope* (2006).

BROWN, JAMES GORDON (1951–). Born in Glasgow, Scotland, Brown earned a PhD in history in 1972. He was first elected to the British parliament in 1983 under the Labour Party banner from the constituency of Dunferline East (Scotland). He served as chancellor of the exchequer (finance minister) under Prime Minister **Tony Blair** from 1997 to 2007. When Blair retired in June 2007, Brown took over leadership of the Labour Party and became prime minister.

He currently holds the seat for the constituency of Kirkcaldy and Cowdenbeath in Scotland (elected in 2005), which includes elements of the old constituency of Dunferline.

Brown continued the British policy of support for the **War in Iraq**. However, early in his premiership he appeared cooler to the continued presence of British troops in **Iraq**. He suggested that Great Britain would learn from the mistakes of the Iraq War, but would continue to support the United States and President **George W. Bush**, with whom Brown claimed a cordial, if less openly convivial relationship compared to his predecessor, Blair.

BROWN, MICHAEL DEWAYNE (1954–). Born in Guymon, Oklahoma, Brown earned a BA from Oklahoma State University (1978) and a law degree from Oklahoma City University (1981). After law school he worked for the finance committee of the Oklahoma legislature. He practiced and taught law before unsuccessfully running for Congress in 1988. He was a commissioner for the International Arabian Horse Association from 1989 to 2001. Brown took up a position as general counsel to the **Federal Emergency Management Agency** (FEMA) in 2001. He became FEMA director in April 2003.

Brown was widely criticized for the insufficient federal response in the aftermath of **Hurricane Katrina**, which devastated New Orleans and the Gulf Coast when the mammoth storm made landfall on 29 August 2005. FEMA had been folded into the new **Department of Homeland Security** (DHS) in March 2003, and Secretary of DHS **Michael Chertoff** appointed Brown to oversee federal relief efforts following the storm. President **George W. Bush** stated his confidence in Brown on 2 September 2005, when he said, "Brownie, you're doing a heck of a job."

But as the death toll from the storm mounted, search-and-rescue efforts were painstakingly slow, and New Orleans residents were left stranded on freeways or in the Superdome in unsanitary conditions, Brown's handling of the federal response appeared inefficient and unacceptable. Calls for Brown's resignation multiplied, and on 9 September Chertoff relieved Brown of his responsibilities; Coast Guard Vice Admiral Thad Allen took over responsibility for the relief efforts. Brown resigned on 12 September. He was later replaced by R. David Paulson.

Critics charged that Brown had lied about his experience on his résumé and had no emergency management experience. Brown testified before Congress about the mishandling of the federal response to Hurricane Katrina and held New Orleans Mayor **Ray Nagin** and Louisiana Governor **Kathleen Babineaux Blanco** responsible for failing to coordinate relief efforts at the local and state levels, or to coordinate properly with the federal government. After leaving FEMA, Brown worked for companies in the private sector in security and disaster relief.

BUCHANAN, PATRICK JOSEPH (1938–). A native of Washington, D.C., Buchanan served in the administrations of Richard Nixon, Gerald Ford, and **Ronald Reagan**. He ran unsuccessfully for the presidency three times—twice as a Republican (1992, 1996) and in 2000 under the Reform Party banner after a bitter court battle over that party's internal nomination politics.

A conservative Catholic and graduate of Georgetown University in English and philosophy (1961) and Columbia University in journalism (1962), Buchanan entered politics during Richard Nixon's first presidential campaign. He joined the Nixon administration as a speechwriter in 1969. When Nixon resigned in August 1974, Buchanan stayed on briefly in the same capacity under President Ford before leaving to take up a career in broadcast and print media. He became a regular contributor and host on television programs such as the *McLaughlin Group* (Public Broadcasting Corporation) and the Cable News Network's (CNN) *Crossfire*, where he elaborated his traditionalist conservative views on social and **foreign policy**. Buchanan was also a widely read syndicated columnist before joining the White House during Ronald Reagan's second term (1985–1988). From 1985 to 1987 he served as director of White House communications.

Buchanan was a staunch critic of President **George W. Bush**'s **neoconservative** foreign policy and the **War in Iraq**, which he contended verges on imperialism. He also opposed illegal **immigration** and championed greater border security with **Mexico**.

Buchanan was the **Reform Party** candidate for the presidency in 2000. Nationally, he received less than a half million votes. But he was thrown into the spotlight in **Palm Beach County**, Florida, where he culled 3,407 votes. Many voters allegedly cast their votes mistakenly for Buchanan due to the so-called "**butterfly ballot**" designed by county elections supervisor **Theresa LePore**. Democratic presidential nominee **Al Gore** challenged the Palm Beach County results during the **Florida recount**, which lasted 36 days. Ultimately, the **Supreme Court** halted the recount in its decision of *Bush v. Gore* (2000), and George W. Bush was certified as the victor in Florida by 537 votes.

Buchanan is a prolific writer. His recent books include *Churchill, Hitler, and "The Unnecessary War": How Britain Lost Its Empire and the West Lost the World* (2008); *Day of Reckoning: How Hubris, Ideology, and Greed Are Tearing America Apart* (2007); *State of Emergency: The Third World Invasion and Conquest of America* (2007); and *Where the Right Went Wrong: How Neoconservatives Subverted the Reagan Revolution and Hijacked the Bush Presidency* (2004).

BUCKLEY, WILLIAM FRANK, JR. (1925–2008). A native of New York City, Buckley was a prominent conservative author and commentator. A second lieutenant in the Army during World War II, Buckley later graduated from Yale University (1950). He worked briefly for the **Central Intelligence Agency**. He founded the influential political weekly *National Review* in 1955, and remained its editor until 1990. He also hosted the weekly television show *Firing Line* from 1966 to 1999. He was known for his friendship with and support of presidential candidate and Arizona senator Barry Goldwater. Buckley authored more than 50 books, including the Blackford Oakes novels. In 2008, he published *The Reagan I Knew* and *Flying High: Remembering Barry Goldwater*.

BUFFETT, WARREN EDWARD (1930–). Born in Omaha, Nebraska, Buffett is a philanthropist and billionaire chief executive officer of Berkshire Hathaway, a financial holding company. *Forbes* magazine declared him to be the fourth-richest man in the world, with assets in excess of $60 billion. In 2008, in the midst of the **subprime mortgage** crisis, Buffett purchased $5 billion in shares of the troubled financial firm Goldman Sachs to shore up the firm's viability and avoid a potential government bailout. *See also* AMERICAN INTERNATIONAL GROUP; BEAR STEARNS; BERNANKE, BEN

SHALOM; PAULSON, HENRY MERRITT, JR.; TROUBLED AS-
SETS RELIEF PROGRAM (TARP).

BULGARIA. This former Soviet-bloc country was invited to join the
North Atlantic Treaty Organization (NATO) at the Prague Summit on 21 November 2002. Along with Estonia, Latvia, Lithuania,
Slovakia, Slovenia, and Romania, Bulgaria formally joined NATO
in March 2004. President **George W. Bush** visited Bulgaria in June
2007.

BUSH, BARBARA PIERCE (1925–). First Lady Barbara Bush was
born in Rye, New York. She married her husband, President **George
H.W. Bush**, in early 1945, shortly after he shipped off to the South
Pacific as a navy pilot in World War II. She is mother to six children,
including President **George W. Bush**, former Florida Governor **John
Ellis (Jeb) Bush**, Pauline Robinson (1949–53), Neil, Marvin, and
Dorothy Walker.

As first lady, Barbara Bush's role in the White House was more
understated than her immediate predecessors, but her strong support
of the causes of literacy and homelessness exemplified her husband's
calls for voluntarism. She worked with the Project Literacy US
(PLUS) and became a board member of Reading Is Fundamental.
From the White House in 1989 she established the Barbara Bush
Foundation for Family Literacy. She engaged in fund-raising activities for such organizations as the United Negro College Fund and
Morehouse College School of Medicine. She also actively volun-
teered in various hospitals and clinics. She is author of three books,
namely *C. Fred's Story* (1984), *Millie's Book* (1990), and *Barbara
Bush: A Memoir* (1994). She used the proceeds from her first book,
a story about the Bush family dogs, to support literacy causes. She
resides with her husband in Houston, Texas, and at their family compound in Kennebunkport, Maine.

BUSH, BARBARA PIERCE (1981–). Born in Dallas and raised in
Texas, Barbara is the daughter of President **George W. Bush** and
First Lady **Laura Bush**, and the older fraternal twin sister of **Jenna
Welch Bush**. She graduated from Yale in 2004 with a degree in
humanities. She also actively campaigned for her father's re-election

in 2004. She lives in New York, and has been active in **acquired immune deficiency syndrome** (AIDS) campaigns in Africa.

BUSH DOCTRINE. The so-called Bush Doctrine refers to President **George W. Bush**'s declared position on **terrorists** and the **War on Terror** through a series of speeches and statements that followed the **11 September 2001** terrorist attacks on New York and the **Pentagon**. The "doctrine" entails not only targeting terrorists and the regimes that may give succor to them, but also the right to **preemptive warfare** if an attack is imminent. The doctrine conflicts with the policy of *containment*, which was employed not only against the **Soviet Union** during the **Cold War**, but was also the de facto policy regarding **Iraq** following the **Persian Gulf War**.

Many observers regard Bush's 2002 State of the Union address to the nation as the main articulation of the doctrine. In his speech, Bush stated that with respect to nations that harbor terrorists or seek to develop **weapons of mass destruction** (WMDs) against the United States ". . . the United States will, if necessary, act preemptively in exercising our inherent right of self-defense." This policy was used as a justification for the invasion of **Afghanistan**, which, under the **Taliban**, had given safe haven to **al-Qaeda** terrorists including **Osama bin Laden** prior to 11 September 2001. The principle was also used to justify the beginning, in March 2003, of the **War in Iraq** against the regime of **Saddam Hussein**, as Bush believed that Hussein had stockpiled WMDs.

Critics argue that "preemptive warfare" runs against the principles of the founders of the United States, who viewed the president's commander-in-chief role as defensive—to "repel sudden attacks." Moreover, critics charge that the Bush Doctrine buttresses a unilateralism in **foreign policy** that threatens relations with American allies in the **North Atlantic Treaty Organization** (NATO) and other longstanding allies, such as **France** (whose president **Jacques Chirac** opposed the invasion of **Iraq**) and undermines dialogue and action, as well as American leadership, through international organizations like the **United Nations** (UN).

In September 2008, Republican vice presidential candidate **Sarah Palin**, Senator **John McCain**'s running mate, was criticized following an interview with ABC News in which she seemed unfamiliar with the precepts of the Bush Doctrine. *See also* MULTILATERALISM; NEOCONSERVATISM.

BUSH, GEORGE HERBERT WALKER (1924–). The 41st president of the United States was born on 12 June 1924 in Milton, Massachusetts, to Dorothy Walker and Prescott Bush. His father was a US senator from Connecticut from 1952 to 1963. He attended the prestigious Phillips Academy in Andover, Massachusetts, and joined the US Navy in 1942 on his 18th birthday. As a naval aviator, Bush's plane was shot down by the Japanese during an otherwise successful raid on Chi Chi Jima in the South Pacific. Bush survived a crash landing in the sea and was rescued, but the other three members of his crew perished. He received the Distinguished Flying Cross for his mission. He subsequently flew 58 combat missions in the Philippines and also received medals of valor for his service aboard the USS *San Jacinto*.

After World War II he enrolled in Yale University, where he became president of the Delta Kappa Epsilon fraternity and was inducted into the secret Skull and Bones society. Bush married Barbara Pierce on 6 January 1945. His children include **George Walker Bush** (Texas governor and 43rd president of the United States), Pauline Robinson (died 1953), **John Ellis (Jeb)** (Florida governor), Neil, Marvin, and Dorothy Walker.

Following his degree at Yale, Bush moved to Texas and joined Dresser Industries to pursue oil exploration. He entered Republican politics in Texas in 1964, unsuccessfully challenging incumbent Senator Ralph Yarborough. He turned his attention to the seventh district of Texas in 1966, and won election to the House of Representatives twice. Yet his second run at the Senate ended in defeat against Democrat Lloyd Bentsen in 1970. Bush caught the attention of President Richard Nixon for his support of Nixon's agenda in Congress. Nixon appointed him ambassador to the **United Nations** (1971–1972). Bush returned to the United States to chair the Republican National Committee in 1972. His assignment was a difficult one, as he sought to minimize the damage to Republican electoral politics as the Watergate scandal unfolded. In 1974, President Gerald Ford appointed him to the US liaison office in Beijing, **China**, where he remained until he assumed the directorship of the

Central Intelligence Agency (CIA) in 1976. Bush returned to the private sector in Texas following the 1976 election of President **Jimmy Carter**.

In 1980, Bush entered the Republican presidential primaries, only to lose to **Ronald Reagan**. The primary contests became bitter when the more moderate Bush called Reagan's tax cut program "voodoo economics"—a phrase that would surface time and again following the massive deficits of the 1980s. Nevertheless, Reagan chose Bush as his vice presidential candidate, largely because of his **foreign policy** experience. After eight years as vice president, Bush ran for the Oval Office in 1988, beating back early primary challenges from prominent Republican Senator Robert (Bob) Dole and television evangelist Pat Robertson. The dynamics of the 1988 Republican convention were especially important for Bush. In a surprise move, he chose a relatively unknown conservative—Senator J. Danforth (Dan) Quayle—of Indiana as his running mate. He also made a commanding speech in which he outlined his vision of America as a "thousand points of light" and pledged not to raise taxes in a phrase that would later haunt him: "Read my lips: no new taxes." The general campaign pitted the Bush–Quayle ticket against Democratic presidential nominee Michael Dukakis of Massachusetts and vice presidential candidate Lloyd Bentsen of Texas.

The campaign was notable as one of the most bitter and negative in recent history. The Bush–Quayle team used scathing television ads that lambasted Dukakis's record on crime as Massachusetts governor. Particularly controversial was the Willy Horton ad, which portrayed an African-American man serving a life sentence who was released on a weekend furlough and committed rape. Another ad depicted the furlough program as a "revolving door" of criminals coming and going to and from prison. Despite a slow preconvention start in the polls, Bush ultimately prevailed in the election with 54 percent of the popular vote and 426 Electoral College votes. Yet Democrats retained both chambers of Congress, and Republicans actually lost seats in the House of Representatives in 1988.

Bush did not have a far-reaching domestic agenda. Nevertheless, Congress passed a minimum wage increase, the Americans with Disabilities Act, and a federal bailout of the failed savings and loan industry during his first two years in office. Relations with the

Democratic Congress became more strained as time passed, and Bush turned increasingly to the veto to halt objectionable legislation. In 1990, he became the first president to veto a civil rights bill, which he argued placed quotas for the hiring of minorities. A compromise version of the bill passed a year later. Bush's apparent reneging on his pledge not to raise taxes in the Budget Agreement of 1990 cost him much political capital among conservative Republicans in Congress and in the electorate. Foreign policy drove the more successful side of Bush's term. The president cautiously approached the disintegration of the **Soviet Union**, lending his support to an aid bill for the Commonwealth of Independent States.

When Iraqi dictator **Saddam Hussein** invaded Kuwait, Bush built an impressive international coalition through the United Nations and drove Iraqi forces out of the country. The **Persian Gulf War** of 1991 boosted his public approval to unprecedented heights following successful resolution of the conflict. Some critics suggest that Bush squandered his high approval—over 90 percent—by failing to translate the "rally effect" of the war into tangible domestic programs, although there is little evidence the Democratic Congress would have necessarily followed his lead. As the electorate turned to domestic issues following the Gulf War, Bush came under increased scrutiny for rising unemployment and an economic slowdown.

The entry of **Reform Party** candidate and millionaire H. Ross Perot confounded Bush's re-election bid in 1992, as Perot and Democratic candidate **William J. Clinton** indefatigably criticized him on the economy. Perot also criticized Bush's negotiation of the North American Free Trade Agreement (NAFTA) with **Canada** and **Mexico**, arguing that the trade bill would export American jobs to Mexico where labor is cheaper. Perot's candidacy cost Bush a sizable number of votes among disaffected Republicans. With 19 percent of the popular vote, Perot arguably enabled Clinton to prevail in the election with a plurality—43.3 percent to Bush's 37.7 percent. Upon leaving office, Bush made the controversial decision to pardon six key figures in the Iran–Contra scandal. He granted pardons to Caspar Weinberger, Elliott Abrams, and Robert McFarlane along with three employees of the Central Intelligence Agency. Bush's autobiography, *All The Best, George Bush*, was published in 1994. The George Bush Presidential Library opened in 1997, situated on the campus of Texas A&M University in College Station, Texas. The former president and his wife, Barbara, reside in Houston and at the family compound in Kennebunkport, Maine.

BUSH, GEORGE WALKER (1946–). The 43rd president of the United States, George W. Bush is the oldest son of **George H.W. Bush** and **Barbara Bush**. He was born in New Haven, Connecticut, on 6 July 1946. He attended the Phillips Academy in Andover, Massachusetts, just as his father had. He earned a bachelor's degree in history from Yale University (1968). He served in the Texas Air National Guard during the Vietnam War. He later completed a Master's of Business Administration degree at Harvard (1975).

Bush got his start in politics in 1978 with an unsuccessful bid for a Texas seat in the US House of Representatives. Between oil ventures, he worked on his father's campaigns—including his successful race against **Michael Dukakis** in 1988. The younger Bush bought a large holding in the Texas Rangers baseball club and became general manager in 1989. In 1994, he defeated incumbent Democrat Ann Richards for the Texas governorship. In 1998, Bush improved significantly on his earlier margin, winning re-election handily with nearly two-thirds of the state vote. He forged a working relationship with the Democratic legislature and lieutenant governor, and was a promoter of **education** reform.

Bush announced his plans to run for the presidency in 1999. He faced competition in the primaries from Arizona Senator **John McCain**, and acrimony developed between the two candidates throughout the campaign. McCain accused Bush of lying about his record and suggested that Bush lacked moral character. Bush, a Methodist, appealed to **Evangelical Christians** and arguably won their firm support when, in a primary debate, he contended that Jesus Christ had had the greatest impact on his life.

Bush won the Republican nomination for the presidency in 2000 and chose **Richard B. (Dick) Cheney**, who had served as secretary of defense under his father, for vice president. Bush ran on a platform of tax cuts and the pledge to be a "uniter, not a divider." The Bush–Cheney ticket faced Democratic nominee **Albert Gore** and his vice presidential running mate, **Joseph Lieberman**, in the general election. The outcome ultimately hinged on Florida's 25 Electoral

College votes. Ballot disputes in **Palm Beach County** and elsewhere cast doubt on the winner, and a protracted, 36-day recount ensued. The **Florida recount** culminated in a **Supreme Court** case, *Bush v. Gore*, which effectively ended the controversy. **James Baker** and **Theodore Olson** represented the Bush campaign in the electoral dispute, aided by **Benjamin Ginsburg**, and the Supreme Court found that the lack of standards for the recount across counties violated equal protection of the laws. Florida Secretary of State **Katherine Harris**, an appointee of **John Ellis (Jeb) Bush**, who was governor of Florida, certified that George W. Bush had received 537 more votes than Gore. Despite losing the popular vote by more than 500,000 nationally, Bush won a majority of the Electoral College and thus the presidency. The administration of George W. Bush included many figures from his father's presidency early in his first term, including Elliott Abrams, Howard Baker, **Andrew Card**, and **Colin Powell**.

Bush won re-election in 2004 on the theme of national security. He and Vice President Cheney faced the Democratic ticket of **John Kerry** and **John Edwards**. The election pivoted largely on the **War in Iraq**, begun a year earlier. Kerry, a Vietnam War veteran, was harshly criticized by an independent group, **Swift Boat Veterans for Truth**, which contended that he was unfit to be commander in chief. Bush won the general election with 53 percent of the popular vote — the first president to win a majority of the popular vote since his father in 1988.

Bush ran for office in 2000 as a domestic president. He focused on **education** reform and, with Democratic support, passed the **No Child Left Behind** bill that mandated federal education funds to the states contingent upon testing of students. Bush also passed sweeping **tax cuts** during his first six months in office, and enunciated a policy on federal funding for **stem-cell research**. His first and only real major crisis in foreign affairs during his first eight months in office occurred in April 2001, when a US spy plane collided with a Chinese aircraft over Hainan Island. In an embarrassing turn of events, the US airmen were detained by **China** for 10 days and released only after the State Department issued two letters of apology over the incident.

Bush's presidency was profoundly transformed by the 11 September 2001 **terrorist** attacks on the **World Trade Center** in New

York City and the **Pentagon** in Washington, D.C. Nineteen terrorists belonging to the organization **al-Qaeda** hijacked four commercial aircraft en route to the West Coast from Boston, Newark, and Washington, D.C. They used the fuel-laden aircraft as flying missiles, slamming them into both towers of the World Trade Center and into the Pentagon. A fourth commandeered flight, United Airlines **Flight 93**, was allegedly destined for the White House. When passengers learned of the attacks, they seized the plane from hijackers but ultimately lost control of it and crashed into a field near Shanksville, Pennsylvania. 9/11 was the worst terrorist attack on US soil, claiming more than 2,700 lives and causing structural damage to the Pentagon and the collapse of the Twin Towers in Manhattan. The watershed event marked the beginning of the **War on Terror**.

Bush was in Florida during the attacks, and was told to stay there by Vice President Cheney. Cheney in turn ordered the evacuation of Capitol Hill, and then proceeded to an "undisclosed location" where he made key national security decisions. In the weeks following 9/11, Congress passed the **Authorization for the Use of Military Force** (AUMF) bill to enable the president to track down and take action against the terrorists responsible for the attack. Intelligence showed that the **Taliban** regime in **Afghanistan** had given safe harbor to al-Qaeda terrorists, including **Osama bin Laden**, and had allowed operatives to establish terrorist training camps. Bush assembled an international coalition that invaded Afghanistan in October 2001 and quickly toppled the Taliban. The conflict in Afghanistan marked one central component in the so-called **Bush Doctrine**—that the United States would not only target terrorists wherever they operated, but also the regimes that gave them support.

Afghanistan began a halting trajectory toward peace and democracy under **Hamid Karzai**, a key ally of the United States in the War on Terror. A significant **insurgency**, however, by al-Qaeda operatives and remnants of the Taliban, placed US and **International Security Assistance Force** (ISAF) troops in continuing peril following the successful invasion. As Bush left office in January 2009, peace and stability in Afghanistan had not been fully achieved.

Nor had debate ended about what to do with suspected terrorists captured in Afghanistan and detained at **Guantanamo Bay, Cuba**, as Bush's second term came to a close. Bush contended that the detainees were foreign illegal **enemy combatants** who were not protected by the **Geneva Conventions** for prisoners of war because they did not belong to a national army, or by the US Constitution. Some detainees claimed they had been subjected to **torture**, including the practice of **waterboarding** or simulated drowning. Others had been subjected to **rendition**—having been sent to so-called "black ops" sites abroad where they had been interrogated by the **Central Intelligence Agency** (CIA). Congress ultimately became concerned and passed the **Detainee Treatment Act** (2005), which prohibited inhumane treatment of prisoners and mandated that interrogations conform to the US Army Field Manual.

Bush planned on trying the detainees at Guantanamo Bay by **military tribunals**. A series of Supreme Court cases ultimately determined the question of whether detainees had recourse to civilian courts and the right to **habeas corpus**. In *Rasul v. Bush* (2004), the Supreme Court ruled that detainees did have recourse to US civilian courts to challenge their detention. In *Hamdi v. Rumsfeld* (2004), the High Court confirmed that enemy combatants could be detained, but US citizens who were detained at Guantanamo had the right to habeas corpus. In *Hamdan v. Rumsfeld* (2006), the Supreme Court struck down the military tribunals set up by the president, asserting that they violated the Uniform Code of Military Justice as well as the Geneva Conventions. Congress subsequently passed the Military Commissions Act authorizing tribunals. In *Boumediene v. Bush* (2008), the Supreme Court struck down the Act, contending that the law violated rights to habeas corpus and reconfirming that detainees were subject to constitutional protections.

The War on Terror also had significant domestic ramifications. Civil libertarians became highly concerned about new governmental policies, including the **PATRIOT Act** that gave law enforcement new tools to gather intelligence on suspected domestic terrorism. Bush had even suggested a program of domestic spying by citizens. But the holding of **José Padilla**, a US citizen suspected of plotting a "dirty-bomb" attack, as a "material witness" indefinitely without charge raised considerable concerns about the abrogation of essential constitutional freedoms. Finally, revelations in 2005 that the National Security Agency (NSA) had engaged in warrantless **wiretapping** in defiance of the **Foreign Intelligence Surveillance Act** (FISA) Court prompted one court member to resign in protest and congressional legislation that clarified the parameters of compliance with warrantless wiretapping.

The War on Terror was expanded considerably with Bush's State of the Union address in January 2002. He called **Iran, Iraq,** and **North Korea** an "**axis of evil**" because of these regimes' pursuit of **weapons of mass destruction** (WMDs). Diplomatic pressure to impose sanctions on these countries was stepped up by the administration. However, the Iraqi regime of **Saddam Hussein** appeared the most likely potential target for further military action. The bellicose leader had expelled **United Nations** (UN) weapons inspectors, who were to ensure that he was complying with the terms of the **Persian Gulf War** agreement. The Bush administration suspected that Hussein was stockpiling WMDs and attempted to link him to al-Qaeda terrorism. The intelligence, as the **Downing Street Memo** suggested, was thin at best on both counts. Bush, his national security advisor, **Condoleezza Rice**, and secretary of state, **Colin Powell**, began making a public case for military action. Their case was somewhat bolstered by the chief UN weapons inspector, **Hans Blix**, who noted that some chemicals and toxins that could be used for WMDs were unaccounted for. But just prior to the US-led invasion in March 2003, Blix contended that some progress had been made in moving forward with inspections.

There was no consensus in the UN Security Council on military action against Iraq. The United States and **Great Britain** were in favor of an invasion, while **Russia** and **France** were particularly opposed. The US Congress passed a joint resolution (the **Iraq War Resolution**) in October 2002 authorizing the use of force against Iraq. But by early March 2003, French President **Jacques Chirac** promised to veto any Security Council resolution authorizing UN-sanctioned military action. At issue was interpretation of the "serious consequences" contemplated by **UN Resolution 1441** if Hussein remained in material breach of his obligations to comply with UN weapons inspectors. The French, like many European and **North Atlantic Treaty Organization** (NATO) members including **Germany**'s **Gerhard Schröder**, interpreted "serious consequences" to be an extension and solidification of harsh economic sanctions. Absent a UN mandate for military action, Bush assembled a **Coalition of the Willing** nations alongside US forces to invade Iraq on 20 March 2003.

The US invasion of Iraq solidified two additional elements of the Bush Doctrine as part of a **neoconservative foreign policy**. First, the United States could act unilaterally if other nations or international institutions failed to act. Second, the United States would act *pre-emptively* in the wake of an imminent threat to national security. The latter notion conflicted with the policy of *containment* that was followed against the **Soviet Union** during the **Cold War** and also was the de facto policy against Iraq following the Persian Gulf War. The United States and Great Britain imposed "no-fly" zones on Hussein's regime to ensure his inability to threaten neighboring countries in the Middle East.

The US and coalition forces quickly overran Hussein's **Ba'ath Party** regime, despite heavy fighting in areas such as **Al-Anbar** Province. More than 16,000 Iraqis are believed to have died in the fighting, including moe than 7,000 civilians. There were 139 US casualties from the beginning of the conflict until Bush declared a halt to major military operations on 1 May 2003. Bush appeared on the USS *Abraham Lincoln* to declare "mission accomplished." Saddam Hussein was captured in a makeshift underground shelter seven months later outside his native city of **Tikrit**, and was ultimately hanged by Iraqi authorities in December 2006 for, among other things, his mass killing of **Kurds** following the Persian Gulf War in 1991.

The US occupation of Iraq proved far more difficult than the initial hostilities that chased Hussein from power. While the United States, the **Coalition Provisional Authority** under **L. Paul Bremer**, the **Iraq Governing Council**, and new leaders, including Prime Ministers **Iyad Allawi**, **Ibrahim al-Jafaari**, **Nouri al-Maliki**, and President **Jalal Talabani**, worked to secure new governmental institutions and reconcile historical divides among the Sunni, Shi'ite, and Kurdish populations in Iraq, a significant insurgency took its toll on US troops. Between May 2003 and December 2003, a total of 344 US troops died in Iraq. 2004 and 2007 would turn out to be the deadliest years of the conflict, with 849 and 870 deaths, respectively. In January 2007, Bush announced a new counterinsurgency strategy with the deployment of 20,000 additional troops in Iraq. The strategy ultimately paid off, particularly in **Baghdad**, but took time to implement. By the time Bush left office in January 2009, 4,139 US troops had died and more than 30,000 had been wounded. Many of the attacks that killed or wounded soldiers were from random and roadside bombings or **improvised explosive devices** (IEDs). More than 90 percent of all civilian and military casualties from the War in Iraq occurred after Bush announced the termination of major military operations.

The protracted war took a heavy toll on Bush's popularity, which had soared to 90 percent following the 9/11 attacks. Following the 2004 election, Bush's public approval dropped into the 40s and 30s. Critics of the war charged that it was waged under false pretenses. Proponents of the war, including Arizona Senator **John McCain**, suggested the war was mismanaged by Secretary of Defense **Donald Rumsfeld**, who did not anticipate the insurgency and did not originally send enough troops for the mission. Protesters of the war, including **Cindy Sheehan**, the mother of a US soldier in Iraq, gained national attention. The clamor for Rumsfeld's resignation grew louder and, following the 2006 **mid-term elections** in which Democrats won a majority in both the House and Senate, Rumsfeld resigned and was succeeded by **Robert Gates**. Nonetheless Bush left office one of the least popular presidents, largely due to the situation in Iraq and a worsening economy. The last Gallup Poll taken in mid-January 2009 showed his approval at 34 percent, up five points from December 2008.

If the War in Iraq was one of the most controversial elements of Bush's foreign policy, his dedication to foreign aid for the **acquired immune deficiency syndrome** (AIDS) epidemic in Africa won worldwide acclaim. The Bush administration promised billions of dollars over five years for AIDS treatment and prevention, and is credited with saving hundreds of thousands of lives.

In domestic policy, Bush described himself as a **compassionate conservative**. The philosophy entailed an emphasis on private charity that was exemplified by the creation of the **Office of Faith-Based and Community Initiatives** to allow religious organizations to engage in the provision of social welfare and services. Bush was also not adverse to governmental spending on education, as noted earlier, in the passage of the No Child Left Behind legislation. Moreover, the passage of **Medicare** reform, including a new prescription drug program for senior citizens, represented the largest new entitlement program in decades. Bush also accentuated a "culture of life," as he sought to find a compromise on stem-cell research and signed the **Partial-Birth Abortion Ban Act** of 2003, which was upheld by the Supreme Court in 2007. He was unable, however, to achieve significant reform of Social Security, including the privatization of part of the program, or comprehensive **immigration** reform in a bid to secure the southern border with **Mexico**.

By 2002, the federal budget was transformed from a surplus to a deficit that reached a high point first in 2004. Deficit spending again accelerated during Bush's second term—a product of individual and corporate tax cuts as well as the War in Iraq. In September 2008, the **sub-prime mortgage** crisis plummeted the economy into a rapid recession and necessitated a $700 billion rescue bailout package for banks. The crisis spread globally, resulting in a significant worldwide economic downturn.

Against this backdrop, Democratic presidential nominee **Barack Obama** and his vice presidential nominee **Joe Biden** campaigned against Republican nominee **John McCain** and his running mate, Alaska Governor **Sarah Palin**. The Obama ticket ran against the Bush economic record and the failures of the War in Iraq, and attempted to tie McCain to that record. Obama ultimately triumphed in the election, winning the popular vote in 2008 by a margin of more than 9 million ballots. Congressional Democrats improved their margins in the House and Senate, and reached a near filibuster-proof majority in the Senate. In light of his lack of popularity, Bush did not actively campaign for McCain.

Bush retired with his wife, **Laura Bush**, to a $2 million home in Dallas, Texas. Groundbreaking for Bush's presidential library on the campus of Southern Methodist University in Dallas is scheduled for 2010, with a target date for completion of 2013.

BUSH, JENNA WELCH (1981 –). The daughter of President **George W. Bush** and First Lady **Laura Bush**, Jenna Bush is the younger fraternal twin sister of **Barbara Pierce Bush**. She is a graduate of the University of Texas at Austin (2004) with a degree in English. In Spring 2001, she fell under intense media scrutiny when she was charged with two separate misdemeanors—underage drinking and attempting to use fake identification—while at college. She pleaded no contest to both charges, and the Bush family attempted to keep the matter private. In August 2007, she married Henry Chase Hager and changed her name to Jenna Welch Hager. She is a teacher, educational advocate, and writer. She published *Ana's Story—A Journey of Hope* (2007) and, with her mother, *Read All About It!* (2008).

BUSH, JOHN ELLIS (JEB) (1953–). Born on 11 February 1953, Jeb is the second son of President **George H.W. Bush** and younger brother to **George W. Bush**. A graduate of the University of Texas at Austin (1973), he married Columbo Garnica Gallo, a Mexican national, in 1974, with whom he has three children.

Bush gained business experience in Texas, south Florida, and Latin America in banking and real estate ventures. Although he aided his father's failed bid for the Republican presidential nomination in 1980, he did not enter politics until a few years later when he became chair of the Dade County, Florida, Republican Party. In 1986, he used his position to help elect Robert (Bob) Martinez to the governorship. In 1988, he again supported his father's electoral bid for the presidency, and a year later worked on south Florida congresswoman Ileana Ros-Lehtinen's successful campaign.

Bush lost the 1994 governor's race in Florida by a narrow margin to popular incumbent Lawton Chiles. He returned to the campaign trail in 1998 to defeat Lieutenant Governor Buddy MacKay handily and was re-elected in 2002. Bush billed himself as an environmentalist, and played an important role in the restoration of the Florida Everglades as governor. Nevertheless, he found himself at the center of controversy in the 2000 presidential election when the secretary of state he appointed, **Katherine Harris**, certified that his brother George W. Bush had defeated Democratic candidate **Al Gore** by just 537 votes. The certification gave all of Florida's Electoral College votes to George W. Bush and enabled him to win the presidency, despite having lost the popular vote. Harris's certification came in the midst of allegations that a flawed "**butterfly ballot**" used in **Palm Beach County** had confused elderly voters, and that black voters around the state had been erroneously placed on a felons list that annulled their right to vote. Critics charged that Jeb Bush had also aided his brother during the **Florida recount** through a lack of cooperation from the state government.

Bush finished his term as governor in Florida in 2006, and was replaced by Republican Charlie Crist. He was rumored to be a potential

Republican candidate for the presidency in 2008 but did not run. In 2007, he joined Tenet Healthcare and also served as an advisor to the investment firm of Lehman Brothers. *See also BUSH V. GORE* (2000).

BUSH, LAURA LANE WELCH (1946–). A native of Midland, Texas, First Lady Laura Bush is the wife of President **George W. Bush**, whom she married in 1977, and mother to **Jenna Welch Bush** and **Barbara Pierce Bush**. She is a graduate of Southern Methodist University (1968) in education. She worked as a schoolteacher in Dallas and Houston before completing a master's degree from the University of Texas at Austin (1973).

Laura Bush has actively taken part in her husband's political campaigns, from his unsuccessful bid for a congressional seat in 1978 to his successful election as governor of Texas in 1994. She gave the keynote address at the Republican National Convention in 2000, when her husband was formally nominated as the presidential candidate.

As first lady, she was deeply involved in **education**, **women**'s, and national and world health issues. She promoted reading among children with the National Book Festival, launched in 2001. She also organized the White House Salute to American Authors Series. Following the US-led invasion of **Afghanistan**, she gave her husband's weekly radio address—the first time a first lady had done so—and she drew public attention to the treatment of women in that country. In 2003, she joined the "Heart for Truth" campaign to raise awareness of heart disease in women. She also traveled throughout Africa during her husband's second term to raise awareness of **acquired immune deficiency syndrome** (AIDS) and support the president's efforts to bring more international funding to combat the disease on the African continent. She also was the honorary ambassador for the **United Nations** Literacy Decade, and directed President Bush's "Helping America's Youth" initiative, which was a nationwide effort to support programs that help children avoid risky behaviors including drugs, alcohol, sex, and violence.

First Lady Laura Bush has received numerous awards and recognition for her work in education and health. She was honored by the Elie Wiesel Foundation (2002), the American Library Association

(2005), the Kuwait-American Foundation (2006), and the Nichols-Chancellor's Medal from Vanderbilt University (2006).

***BUSH V. GORE* (2000).** This **Supreme Court** case effectively halted the **Florida recount** of votes between **George W. Bush** and **Al Gore** in the contested presidential election of 2000. Following the 7 November 2000 election, Florida's 25 **Electoral College** votes, and consequently the presidential election, hung in the balance because of the closeness of the state election and disputed ballots. Early results from Florida's 67 counties on 8 November showed that Bush had defeated Gore by a margin of less than a half percent, which triggered an automatic machine recount of ballots under state law. Using the discretion afforded him under Florida law, Gore petitioned four counties to conduct manual recounts: Broward, Miami-Dade, **Palm Beach**, and Volusia. Florida Secretary of State **Katherine Harris** noted on 14 November that she was in receipt of the results from all 67 counties, but since recounts in Broward, Miami-Dade, and Palm Beach continued, she would not certify the results until 26 November.

On 26 November, Harris certified that Bush had won Florida by 537 votes. She determined that there was no basis to amend the results of the disputed counties. Litigation ensued, and on 8 December the Florida Supreme Court, in a 4–3 decision, ordered a statewide manual recount of all votes. The next day, the US Supreme Court halted the recount on a 5–4 decision and scheduled oral arguments on the case. On 12 December, the Court made an expedited decision, and in a 7–2 vote, contended that the methods used in the recount violated the Equal Protection Clause (Fourteenth Amendment) of the Constitution. The Court's rationale was that the standards used across precincts and counties for the recount varied substantially. Moreover, the Court followed Bush's argument that the state supreme court had erred in its interpretation of Florida election law and essentially pre-empted the intentions of the state legislature. *See also* BUTTERFLY BALLOT.

"BUSHISM." The term "Bushism" has been used to describe the incorrect grammar or syntax, malapropisms, or otherwise strange and sometimes humorous phrases and locutions used by President **George W. Bush**. Examples include: "You're working hard to put food on your family" (Nashua, NH, 27 January 2000); "I know the human being and fish can coexist peacefully" (Saginaw, MI, 29 September 2000); "Families is where our nation finds hope, where wings take dream" (LaCrosse, WI, 18 October 2000); "You teach a child to read, and he or her will be able to pass a literacy test" (Townsend, TN, 21 February 2001); "I'm the master of low expectations" (aboard Air Force One, 4 June 2003); "Our enemies are innovative and resourceful, and so are we. They never stop thinking about new ways to harm our country and our people, and neither do we" (Washington, D.C., 5 August 2004).

BUTTERFLY BALLOT. The so-called "butterfly ballot" was used in **Palm Beach County**, Florida, in the 2000 presidential election. The ballot, which had been approved by Democratic supervisor of elections **Theresa LePore**, was confusing for some elderly and other voters because names of candidates appeared across two pages, with arrows pointing to a middle column for the voter to punch. Some voters suggested they had meant to vote for Democratic presidential candidate **Al Gore** but worried the design of the ballot had led them to punch the wrong hole in the ballot for **Reform Party** candidate **Patrick Buchanan** or, worse yet, double-punch the holes, which invalidated their ballot altogether. The butterfly ballot was just one of the controversies surrounding the **Florida recount** of votes following the November election. Ultimately the **Supreme Court** effectively halted the recount in its decision on *Bush v. Gore*, and **George W. Bush** was certified as the winner of Florida's 25 Electoral College votes. *See also* HARRIS, KATHERINE.

BYRD, ROBERT CARLYLE (1917–). Born Cornelius Calvin Sale, Jr., in North Carolina, Byrd was renamed by his aunt and uncle who raised him after his mother died when he was one year old. He grew up in Raleigh County, West Virginia. He studied at several colleges—Beckley, Concord, Morris Harvey, and Marshall—all in West Virginia—but had to support his family as a young man. He did not actually receive his BA degree from Marshall College until 1994. During World War II, he worked at various jobs and as a shipyard welder. He entered politics in 1946, winning a seat to the West Virginia House of Delegates. In 1950, he won a seat to the West Virginia Senate. His congressional career began in 1952, when he won a seat to the US House of Representatives as a Democrat. He won re-election to the House twice.

Byrd's long career in the US Senate began in 1960, and he was re-elected eight times. In 1963, after attending night classes, he received a law degree from American University. His current seat expires in 2012. Byrd has served in numerous leadership positions in the Senate, including secretary of the Senate Democratic Conference (1967–1971); Democratic whip (1971–1977); majority leader (1977–1980, 1987–1988); minority leader (1981–1986); president pro tempore (1989–1995, 2001–2003, 2007–); and chair, Committee on Appropriations (1989–1994, 2001–2003, 2007–).

Often referred to as the "dean" of the Senate, Byrd's legacy is controversial. He joined the Ku Klux Klan in 1942 and was elected the local chief but claims he quit the racist organization a year after joining. A segregationist, he famously filibustered the Civil Rights Act supported by President Lyndon Johnson in 1964 and was generally committed to "states rights" in civil rights matters. Byrd has since recanted his earlier stances against civil rights for African-Americans and, in 2008, endorsed his party's first black presidential candidate, **Barack Obama**, before the Democratic convention.

Byrd was an ardent opponent of several of President **George W. Bush**'s cornerstone policies regarding the **War on Terror**. First, he opposed Bush's plans for a **Department of Homeland Security** after the **11 September 2001** attacks on New York City and the **Pentagon**. Like many Democrats, Byrd contended that Bush's call for a massive reorganization ceded too much authority to the president. Second, he rejected the "**Bush Doctrine**," understood as the president's case for **preemptive warfare** in **Iraq**. Byrd attempted, without success, to filibuster the vote giving the president authority to intervene militarily in Iraq (**Iraq War Resolution**). Finally, a resolute protector of legislative prerogatives, Byrd wrote a book entitled *Losing America: Confronting a Reckless and Arrogant Presidency* (2004) in which he severely criticized Bush for the **War in Iraq**.

– C –

CALIPARI, NICOLA (1953–2005). A major general in the Italian intelligence service, Calipari was accidentally killed in **Iraq** by US troops while taking a former hostage, journalist Giulana Sgregna, to the **Baghdad** airport. Calipari apparently threw himself over Sgregna to protect her from gunfire. Calipari was hailed as a hero in Italy for his bravery, but his death caused a major diplomatic incident between the United States and Italy. Italian parliamentarians led investigations into the death, and some called for charges of voluntary manslaughter against Mario Lozano, the troop who allegedly shot Calipari.

CANADA. The United States' largest trading partner, a member of the **North Atlantic Treaty Organization** (NATO), and a major contributor to the **International Security Assistance Force** (ISAF) in **Afghanistan**, Canada had three different prime ministers during President **George W. Bush**'s two terms. After leading his party to three electoral mandates, Liberal **Jean Chrétien** stepped down as prime minister in 2003 following a campaign finance scandal. Chrétien was critical of Bush, calling him "naïve" and ignorant of Canada. Traditionally, the first trip US presidents make abroad after winning an election is to Canada. Bush chose instead to go to **Mexico**. He canceled a visit to Canada scheduled in May 2003 due to the **War in Iraq**.

Bush did not make his first official visit to Canada until December 2004. He sought to smooth relations with Chrétien's successor, **Paul Martin**, who took over the Liberal Party's reins in 2003. Chrétien had been a vocal critic of the US military intervention in **Iraq**.

Martin, who led his party into a minority government in 2004, had a closer working relationship with Bush, particularly on trade issues, and met with him and Mexican President **Vicente Fox** in Texas in 2005. Martin also expelled a member of parliament from his party for trampling on a "doll" of the president in protest of the War in Iraq and Bush's **foreign policy**.

Martin's government was defeated in the election of 2006. **Stephen Harper** led his newly established Conservative Party to victory, albeit as a minority government in Ottawa; in October 2008, Harper called a snap election that yielded yet another minority government. In 2003, while in parliamentary opposition, Harper and his party supported the US-led invasion of Iraq. The Conservative Party was the only Canadian political party to do so.

CARD, ANDREW HILL, JR. (1947–). A graduate in engineering from the University of South Carolina, Card's career has spanned the public and private sectors. Card got his start in politics by serving in the Massachusetts statehouse from 1975 to 1983, where he was active in ethics issues. In 1980, he was campaign chair for **George H.W. Bush**'s presidential bid. He served in President **Ronald Reagan**'s White House as special assistant to the president for intergovernmental affairs and later as director of intergovernmental affairs, charged with developing relations with governors and state officials.

Card served President George H.W. Bush as his deputy chief of staff (1988–1992) before he was appointed secretary of transportation (1992–1993). Card won praise for his oversight of federal disaster relief efforts following Hurricane Andrew, which devastated south Florida in 1992. Following Bush's defeat to **William Clinton** in the presidential election of 1992, Card returned to the private sector. He was president and chief executive officer of the American Automobile Manufacturers Association (1993–1998).

President **George W. Bush** appointed Card his **chief of staff** following the 2000 presidential election. Card remained in that post until 2006. He won bipartisan acclaim for his professionalism and generally smooth management of White House operations. It was Card who informed Bush of the **11 September 2001 terrorist** attacks on New York City and the **Pentagon** while the president was on travel to Florida that day. **Office of Management and Budget** (OMB) director **Joshua Bolten** succeeded Card as Bush's chief of staff in 2006.

CASTRO RUZ, FIDEL ALEJANDRO (1926–). An iconic revolutionary and communist, Castro came to power in the island nation of Cuba in 1959 and ruled the country for 47 years. He quickly became an ally of the **Soviet Union**, and relations between the United States and Cuba were subsequently strained. In 1961, President John F. Kennedy agreed to a plan for US forces to back Cuban exiles in a bid to oust Castro from power. The "Bay of Pigs" invasion was a military failure and embarrassment to the Kennedy White House.

Just a year later, in 1962, Castro agreed to allow the Soviet Union to place nuclear missiles in Cuba. President Kennedy demanded that Soviet leader Nikita Khrushchev withdraw the missiles, and imposed a naval blockage of Castro's Cuba. The tense standoff, often referred to as the "missiles of October," brought the United States and Soviet Union to the brink of nuclear war. Khruschev ultimately withdrew the missiles in exchange for US concessions on missiles in Turkey and Italy.

Castro continued his support for the Soviet Union and worldwide communism in the 1970s and 1980s. He sent Cuban troops to **Angola** and Mozambique to aid leftist forces engaged in civil war, and he supported the Marxist rebellion in Nicaragua.

The US Congress adopted an economic embargo against Castro's regime in 1962, which remains in effect in 2008 with the strong support of Cuban-Americans, particularly concentrated in south Florida. With the collapse of the Soviet Union in 1991, Castro lost a major trading partner and significant financial support. He found common cause with some Latin American leaders, including Venezuela's **Hugo Chávez**, who is an ardent critic of the United States.

Rumors of Castro's illness or possible death surfaced in 2006. That year, he underwent surgery for intestinal problems and temporarily transferred power to his brother, Raúl Castro. In February 2008, Fidel Castro formally announced he would not return to lead the country, and the Cuban legislature handed the reins of power to Raúl. *See also* FOREIGN POLICY.

CENTRAL AMERICAN FREE TRADE AGREEMENT (CAFTA). The goal of this agreement between the United States and Costa Rica, the Dominican Republic, El Salvador, Guatemala, Honduras, and Nicaragua is to reduce tariff and nontariff barriers to trade between member countries. President **George W. Bush** strongly supported CAFTA. United States Trade Representative **Robert Zoellick** signed the agreement in May 2004. The agreement was approved by Congress in August 2005. Critics of the agreement contend that it does not include adequate labor and environmental protections and favors large corporations over small enterprises.

CENTRAL INTELLIGENCE AGENCY (CIA). The Central Intelligence Agency was created by the National Security Act of 1947 under President Harry Truman. The director of the CIA heads the agency, coordinates foreign intelligence-gathering activities, and advises the president on intelligence matters. The CIA is precluded from domestic intelligence gathering.

The **11 September 2001 terrorist** attacks on the **World Trade Center** in New York City and the **Pentagon** in Washington, D.C.—and the CIA's putative failure to prevent the attacks—prompted substantive changes to the organization of the national intelligence structure as part of the **War on Terror**. In the **Intelligence Reform and Terrorism Prevention Act** of 2004, Congress created a **Director of National Intelligence** (DNI) to whom the CIA director now reports, and who is charged with liaising with other federal agencies, such as the **Federal Bureau of Investigation** (FBI), to thwart terrorist attacks.

President **George W. Bush** appointed **John Negroponte** as the first DNI; he was succeeded two years later by **Michael McConnell**. Three CIA directors served under Bush across his two terms: **George Tenet** (1997–2004), **Porter Goss** (2004–2006), and General **Michael Hayden** (2006–2008).

Under George Tenet, in particular, the CIA fell under acute scrutiny and criticism. Tenet testified before the **9/11 Commission** to detail the CIA's efforts to track the terror group **al-Qaeda** and its leader, **Osama bin Laden**. The agency was blamed not only for failing to prevent the 9/11 attacks but also for intelligence failures surrounding the US-led invasion of **Iraq** in 2003—namely that no **weapons of mass destruction** (WMDs) were found following the ouster of Iraqi dictator **Saddam Hussein**.

CHALABI, AHMED ABDEL HADI (1944–). Exiled from his native **Iraq** in 1956, Chalabi lived in Great Britain and the United States. He earned a doctoral degree in mathematics from the University of Chicago.

Chalabi was a dogged opponent of the regime of **Saddam Hussein** and was the leader of the Iraqi National Congress, an organization whose goal was to overthrow Hussein. Prior to the US-led invasion Iraq in 2003, Chalabi and his associates had furnished intelligence information on alleged **weapons of mass destruction** (WMDs) in Iraq, as well as possible links between Hussein's regime and the **terrorist** organization **al-Qaeda**. The information later turned out to be false. Once hailed as a pivotal, future leader in a democratic Iraq, Chalabi subsequently fell out of favor with the administration of **George W. Bush**.

Chalabi returned to Iraq and served as oil minister in 2005 and 2006. He served as deputy prime minister for eight months in 2005, but in the December 2005 elections his party, the Iraqi National Congress, failed to win a single seat. In October 2007, Iraqi Prime Minister **Nouri al-Maliki** appointed Chalabi to oversee a committee charged with improving basic municipal and governmental services in **Baghdad**.

CHAO, ELAINE LAN (1953–). Born in Taiwan, Chao emigrated to the United States with her family as a child. She earned a bachelor's degree from Mount Holyoke College (1975) and a master's degree in business administration from Harvard University (1979). Chao's governmental service spans three decades. Under President **Ronald Reagan** she served as deputy administrator and administrator of the Maritime Administration (Department of Transportation, 1986–1988). President **George H.W. Bush** tapped her as his deputy secretary of transportation (1989–1991). In the 1990s, she directed the Peace Corps (1991–1992) and then headed the United Way from 1992 to 1996. She became a distinguished fellow at the conservative Heritage Foundation in 1996. President **George W. Bush** appointed Chao as his secretary of labor in 2001. His first choice for the position, **Linda Chavez**, withdrew her nomination from congressional consideration.

Chao is the first Asian-American woman to be appointed to a president's cabinet. She is also the only secretary of the 15 federal cabinet departments to have served President Bush through the entirety of his two terms.

CHÁVEZ FRÍAS, HUGO RAFAEL (1954–). A 17-year veteran of the Venezuelan Army, Chávez attempted to overthrow the Venezuelan government in 1992. He spent two years in prison before he was pardoned. He subsequently embraced politics, and was elected president of Venezuela in 1998 on a populist platform known as the

"Bolivarian Revolution" (named for Simón Bolívar, the 19th-century Venezuelan leader), which promised to aid the poor by using the country's oil revenues. Chávez was re-elected to the presidency in 2000 and 2006. He survived a coup attempt in 2002, which he alleged involved the United States, and a recall vote in 2004. His call for indefinite re-election of the president was narrowly defeated in a referendum in 2007.

An ardent critic of President **George W. Bush**, Chávez cultivated strong relationships with Cuba's **Fidel Castro** and fellow populist leader Evo Morales in Bolivia as part of his campaign for Latin American solidarity. Chávez frequently accused the Bush administration of "neocolonialism" in **foreign policy**. In 2006, he upset the Bush administration by announcing Venezuela would import arms from **Russia**, and by accusing **Israel** of a holocaust relative to its attacks on **Lebanon**. In September 2006, Chávez made worldwide headlines by referring to Bush as the "devil" in a speech at the **United Nations** in New York. Chávez's insistence on keeping oil prices high placed him at further odds with the Bush administration. In November 2008, the Venezuelan military engaged in joint maneuvers with Russia.

Critics of Chávez accuse him of corruption and attempting to concentrate excessive power in the presidency to the detriment of democracy. In 2005, Chávez's anti-American rhetoric prompted television evangelist **Pat Robertson**'s suggestion that he be assassinated, a comment for which Robertson later apologized.

CHAVEZ, LINDA (1947–). A native of Albuquerque, New Mexico, Chavez is a prominent Hispanic conservative. She worked for President **Ronald Reagan** as White House director of Public Liaison (1985), and as staff director for the US Commission on Civil Rights (1983–1985). She ran unsuccessfully for the US Senate seat from Maryland in 1986. President **George H.W. Bush** appointed her to chair the National Commission on Migrant Education (1989–1992). From 1992 to 1996, she served as an expert to the **United Nations** subcommittee on discrimination and minorities.

In 2000, Chavez chaired President **George W. Bush**'s task force on **immigration** while he was running for the White House. Bush nominated Chavez for secretary of labor in 2001. The nomination made national headlines, as Chavez was the first Hispanic woman to be nominated for a cabinet position. She withdrew her nomination over controversy that she had helped an illegal alien from Guatemala procure work with her neighbor. Bush subsequently nominated **Elaine Chao**, who was confirmed by the US Senate without incident.

CENTCOM. Acronym for central command, or Unified Combatant Command of US armed forces for the Middle East and Central Asia. It was established in 1983 and is headquartered at MacDill Air Force Base in Tampa, Florida. CENTCOM coordinated the US military operations in the **Persian Gulf War**, the war in **Afghanistan**, and the **War in Iraq**. Commanders of CENTCOM under President **George W. Bush** included **Tommy Franks** (2000–2003), **John Abizaid** (2003–2007), **William Fallon** (2007–2008), and **David Petraeus** (2008–).

CHECHNYA. Chechnya is a republic of **Russia** located in the Northern Caucasus Mountains. Following the collapse of the Soviet Union in 1991, Chechnya sought independence. Russia lost control of the territory in armed conflict with Chechen rebels from 1994 to 1996. Russian forces began a military campaign against the breakaway republic in 1999 and established direct rule from Moscow in 2000 under President **Vladimir Putin**. In September 2004, Chechen **terrorist**s took over a secondary school in **Beslan**, Russia. After a two-day siege, Russian forces confronted the terrorists, resulting in the deaths of 334. *See also* FOREIGN POLICY.

CHEMICAL ALI. *See* HASSAN AL-MAJID, ALI.

CHENEY, RICHARD BRUCE (DICK) (1941–). Born in Lincoln, Nebraska, Cheney was raised in Casper, Wyoming. After beginning and halting his studies at Yale, he eventually completed undergraduate and graduate work at the University of Wyoming in political science. His early political experience included service in the Richard Nixon White House on the Cost of Living Council and the Office of Economic Opportunity. Cheney was named President Gerald Ford's **chief of staff** in 1975, and managed Ford's election campaign in

1976. He later won a seat to Congress from Wyoming in 1978, and was re-elected five times, serving as chair of the House Republican Policy Committee (1981–1987), chair of the House Republican Conference (1987), and minority whip (1988). In 1989, President **George H.W. Bush** selected Cheney as secretary of defense. Cheney was instrumental in directing military operations in Panama and in **Iraq** in the **Persian Gulf War** (1991).

Exiting public service in 1993 following the election of **William Clinton** to the presidency, Cheney joined the conservative think tank the American Enterprise Institute. He later became chair and chief executive officer of **Halliburton**, an energy corporation. In 1997, he cofounded the **Project for the New American Century** (PNAC), a **neoconservative foreign policy** think tank. He resigned from Halliburton in 2000, when President **George W. Bush** asked him to run on the Republican ticket as the vice presidential candidate.

Cheney was a highly visible and energetic vice president relative to campaigning and fund-raising during Bush's two terms. He also played a pivotal role in developing Bush's neoconservative foreign and defense policy. Many observers contend that he was the most influential vice president to date.

Cheney led Bush's transition team in 2000. He was instrumental in recruiting cabinet members, including Secretary of Defense **Donald Rumsfeld**, with whom he had served during the administration of Gerald Ford. Early in Bush's first term Cheney led the **Energy Task Force**. Neither the proceedings nor the members of the task force were made public. Despite a **Supreme Court** ruling to the contrary, Cheney and the White House claimed **executive privilege**. Critics suggest that the task force included members of **Enron Corporation**, including **Kenneth Lay**, with whom Cheney is known to have met numerous times. Moreover, critics questioned Cheney's chairing of the committee, given his past connections and deferred compensation from Halliburton Corporation.

Following the **11 September 2001 terrorist** attacks on New York and the **Pentagon**, Cheney played a critical role in decision-making. He told Bush to remain in Florida, where the president had been in a classroom promoting **education**, and ordered the evacuation of Capitol Hill. Cheney subsequently proceeded to an "undisclosed location" where he made key national security decisions.

Perhaps of all of Bush's top advisors, Cheney was the most steadfast in his belief that the powers of the presidency should be expanded. Cheney subscribed to the so-called "unitary executive" theory, which held that the president controlled the entirety of the executive branch and should be beyond the reach of congressional interference. Moreover, Cheney believed that the president's constitutional status as commander in chief enabled him to interpret legislative provisions relative to his role to protect the nation. Cheney's second chief of staff and White House advisor **David Addington** was critical in articulating the administration's views on this account, including the use of "**signing statements**" to challenge congressional laws.

Cheney was a major proponent for the president's **War on Terror** and a vocal supporter of the US-led invasion of **Iraq**. He is believed to have been a lead advocate for the **War in Iraq** in cabinet deliberations, where he allegedly countered Secretary of State **Colin Powell**'s reservations about armed conflict. When the **United Nations** (UN) Security Council failed to sanction military action against Iraqi dictator **Saddam Hussein** following French President **Jacques Chirac**'s pledge to veto any resolution authorizing the use of force, Secretary of Defense Donald Rumsfeld—a close Cheney confidant—suggested that **France** and **Germany** were part of the "old Europe," putatively deepening divisions within the **North Atlantic Treaty Organization** and the **European Union** and threatening transatlantic relations. Cheney was front and center in making claims about alleged links between **al-Qaeda** and Hussein, as well as the Iraqi dictator's alleged stockpiling of **weapons of mass destruction** (WMDs). Critics charge that Halliburton Corporation, a firm Cheney formerly headed, gained substantial advantage from defense contracts associated with the rebuilding of Iraq following the US-led invasion in March 2003.

Cheney was also at the center of controversy concerning **enemy combatants** and detainees captured in **Afghanistan** and held at **Guantanamo Bay, Cuba**. He helped articulate the administration's policy of "enhanced interrogation techniques" used to gain intelligence from detainees as well as those subject to **rendition**, or questioning by the **Central Intelligence Agency** (CIA) at so-called "black ops" sites outside the United States. Cheney did not believe that extraordinary techniques were tantamount to **torture**, and in 2006 made public his view that **waterboarding** or simulated drowning was an acceptable practice. In 2005, Congress passed the **Detainee Treatment Act** that prohibited inhumane treatment of prisoners and clarified that interrogations must be conducted consistent with the US Army Field Manual.

Cheney was implicated in the **Valerie Plame** affair. Plame was the spouse of former ambassador and critic of the War in Iraq **Joseph Wilson**. Her status as a covert agent for the CIA was revealed in an article published by **Robert Novak** in July 2003, allegedly after the White House "outed" her as a means of political retribution against Wilson. Cheney's chief of staff, **I. Lewis (Scooter) Libby** was thought to be the source, until Deputy Defense Secretary **Richard Armitage** later revealed that he had disclosed her name publicly.

In February 2006, Cheney accidentally shot a friend, lawyer Harry Whittington, with birdshot while on a hunting trip in Texas. Whittington survived, and no criminal charges were filed against Cheney, who publicly regretted the incident. In February 2007, Cheney survived an assassination attempt at Bagram Air Force Base in Afghanistan.

Cheney exited public service at the end of Bush's second term. He suffers from heart disease, and made clear in 2000 that he did not plan to seek the White House himself. Observers suggest that this fact only strengthened Bush's trust in his counsel.

CHERTOFF, MICHAEL (1953–). A native of Elizabeth, New Jersey, Chertoff earned an undergraduate degree (1975) as well as a law degree (1978) from Harvard University. He was a law clerk for federal appellate judge Murray Gurfein (1978) and for Chief Justice of the US **Supreme Court** William Brennan (1979–80). He worked in private practice briefly before New York City Mayor **Rudolph Giuliani** hired him as a district attorney; he later became a US attorney for New Jersey and for New York. In the 1990s, Chertoff returned to the private law firm of Latham and Watkins.

As a prosecutor, Chertoff was a dogged opponent of the Mafia. His reputation earned him an appointment by President **George W. Bush** to head the criminal division of the Department of Justice in 2001. Following the **11 September 2001 terrorist** attacks on the **World Trade Center** in New York and the **Pentagon** in Washington, D.C., Chertoff focused on prosecuting suspected terrorists, including **Zacarias Moussaoui**. He was also involved in the investigation of the accounting firm **Arthur Andersen**'s involvement with the collapse of the **Enron Corporation**, and he helped the Bush administration draft the **PATRIOT Act**. Chertoff was the principal architect of the Bush administration's policy of detaining terror suspects as "**material witnesses**"—the controversial policy of binding them over for grand jury testimony without charging them with a crime—in an effort to root out potential coconspirators. Bush subsequently appointed Chertoff to a judgeship on the federal court of appeals in 2003.

Chertoff succeeded former Pennsylvania Governor **Tom Ridge** as secretary of the **Department of Homeland Security** (DHS) in 2005. Just months into his tenure, Chertoff was criticized for the federal government's handling of **Hurricane Katrina**. While many critics blamed **Federal Emergency Management Agency** (FEMA) head **Michael D. Brown** for the inadequate response, FEMA had become part of DHS when the new department was created in 2003, and Chertoff took a very low-key approach to the disaster. Chertoff's greatest public success at DHS was arguably the thwarting of the plot by **al-Qaeda** operatives to blow up airliners en route from Europe to the United States in August 2006. His coordination with British authorities, who foiled the terror operation, received uniform praise.

CHIEF OF STAFF. The White House chief of staff serves at the president's pleasure and does not require confirmation by the Senate. The chief of staff manages personnel in the White House, oversees the president's calendar, and supervises access and paper flow to the president. For this reason, the function of the chief of staff is frequently referred to as "gatekeeper." Chiefs of staff also variably take on other roles, including that of personal and political advisor to the president. During President **George W. Bush**'s two terms, the chiefs of staff were **Joshua Bolten** and **Andrew Card**.

CHINA. With a population of 1.2 billion, China is a major trading partner of the United States, as well as an economic and military rival. President **George W. Bush**'s first **foreign policy** challenge involved China in April 2001, when a US naval aircraft collided with a Chinese jet, killing a Chinese pilot. The US jet made an emergency landing on Hainan Island, and the flight crew was detained for 10 days by the Chinese, who contended that the United States had violated Chinese airspace. The United States issued an apology to the Chinese government, ultimately defusing the tense situation.

Relations with China were solidified following the **11 September 2001 terrorist** attacks on New York and Washington, D.C. The Chinese governments of Jiang Zemin and **Hu Jintao** were generally supportive of Bush's **War on Terror**. Many of the deaths at the **World Trade Center** were Chinese nationals. Jiang visited President Bush at his Crawford, Texas, ranch in 2002. Hu visited the White House in 2006. President Bush visited China in 2002 and 2006, and attended the Summer Olympics held in Beijing, China, in August 2008.

The Bush administration was nevertheless critical of China on its human rights record and concerned over its investments in **Sudan**, which was wracked by ethnic strife in the **Darfur** region. Bush was also concerned with the United States' negative trade deficit with China, or the balance of American exports to Chinese imports, and Chinese monetary policy that devalued the *yuan*. Finally, China increased its military and defense expenditures during Bush's two terms, raising alarm among some administration officials and members of Congress. Bush attempted to balance concerns over greater Chinese military influence in Asia with China's assistance in mediating **North Korea**'s pursuit of nuclear power and **weapons of mass destruction** (WMDs).

CHIRAC, JACQUES RENÉ (1932–). Born in the south central department of Corrèze in **France**, Chirac was nicknamed the "bulldozer" by Prime Minister Georges Pompidou for his candor and penchant for action. Once a proponent of the Left, Chirac quickly became a "Gaullist"—a follower of the uniquely conservative and nationalist philosophy of the first president of the French Fifth Republic, founded by Charles de Gaulle in 1958 and continuing to the present. Chirac served as an advisor to Prime Minister Pompidou in the 1960s, and later ran successfully for the French parliament in 1967. He held several ministries in his early legislative career, and was prime minister under President **Valéry Giscard d'Estaing** (1974–1976) and under President François Mitterrand (1986–1988). He also served concurrently as the popular mayor of Paris (1977–1995). He was elected to a seven-year term as president in 1995, and to a second five-year term in 2002 after France changed the length of the president's term by referendum.

Chirac had a tumultuous relationship with President **George W. Bush**. Following the **11 September 2001 terrorist** attacks on New York and Washington, D.C., Chirac gave an impassioned statement in which he said "today, we are all Americans" to show his solidarity with the United States. However, Chirac rejected Bush's stance on **Iraq** as part of the **War on Terror** several years later. France is a permanent member of the **United Nations** (UN) Security Council, and Chirac rebuffed Bush's push for military intervention in Iraq in 2003, when **Saddam Hussein** expelled UN weapons inspectors from the country. Chirac made it clear that France would veto any Security Council resolution of UN authorization for an invasion of Iraq for its failure to comply with UN Resolution 1441, which mandated that Iraq disarm following the **Persian Gulf War**. Diplomatic relations subsequently became tense between the United States and France. Many Americans displayed outwardly hostile gestures toward France, such as the pouring of French wine into gutters, to protest Chirac's position. French fries were even renamed "Freedom Fries" in the US House of Representatives.

Chirac's position on military intervention in Iraq was ostensibly driven both by principle and pragmatics. France had a long-established economic relationship with Iraq and stood to lose much. But many of Chirac's **European Union** counterparts, including German Chancellor **Gerhard Schröder**, generally rejected the tenets of Bush's **neoconservative foreign policy** and opposed US military action against Iraq. They instead supported economic and other sanctions to force Hussein to comply with arms inspections. Chirac's Security Council position prompted Bush to take action against Iraq without a UN mandate. The countries that took part in the **War in Iraq** beginning in March 2003 became known as the **Coalition of the Willing**.

Chirac left office in 2007 under a cloud of scandal relating to his finances and allegations that his prime minister, **Dominique de Villepin**, had attempted to spy on presidential candidate—and ultimately Chirac's successor to the presidency—**Nicolas Sarkozy**. *See also* ANNAN, KOFI; BLAIR, TONY; GREAT BRITAIN.

CHRÉTIEN, JOSEPH JACQUES JEAN (1934–). Born in Shawinigan, Québec, **Canada**, Chrétien studied law at the Université Laval (Québec City). A member of the Liberal Party, he served as a minister under Canadian Prime Ministers Lester Pearson and Pierre Trudeau in the 1960s, 1970s, and 1980s. He succeeded John Turner as the leader of the Liberal Party in 1990. He led the Liberals to victory in the elections of 1993, 1997, and 2002. He served as prime minister of Canada from 1993 to 2003. He was succeeded by his rival **Paul Martin** in 2003.

Chrétien's relationship with President **George W. Bush** ranged from cordial to cool. Trade relations as part of the North American Free Trade Agreement (NAFTA) marked a more solid working relationship early in Bush's term. Chrétien was highly critical of Bush's **foreign policy** inexperience and lack of knowledge about Canada following a meeting in April 2001. After the **terrorist** attacks on New York and Washington, D.C., on **11 September 2001**, Chrétien urged Canadians to help stranded US passengers when North American airspace was temporarily shut down in the immediate wake of the crisis. Later, however, he stirred international controversy when he stated in an interview that "I believe the West is too rich in relation to the poor world. We are inevitably regarded as arrogant, self-absorbed, greedy, and boundless. For me, September 11 was a chance to realize this more strongly."

Chrétien opposed the **War in Iraq** and refused to send Canadian troops to **Iraq** in the absence of a **United Nations** (UN) mandate. Bush had been unable to obtain such a mandate after French President **Jacques Chirac** threatened to veto any UN resolution authorizing the use of force in Iraq. Canadian public opinion overwhelmingly supported Chrétien's decision. Chrétien did, however, support the US-led, multinational force that invaded **Afghanistan** in the autumn of 2002 in search of **al-Qaeda** terrorists. As of 2008, Canadian troops number more than 2,000 as part of the **International Security Assistance Force** (ISAF) in Afghanistan.

Chrétien retired from politics in 2003 under a cloud relating to a financial and lobbying scandal. He is author of *My Years as Prime Minister* (2007), *Straight from the Heart* (2007), and *Finding Common Ground* (1995).

CINCINNATI (RACE RIOTS). Riots in Cincinnati, Ohio, broke out on 7 April 2001 several days after police officers shot Timothy Thomas, a 19-year-old African-American during a foot pursuit. Thomas was unarmed. Many black residents were angry at the handling of the shooting investigation by city commissioners, which followed more than a dozen deaths of black youths in the preceding six years either while in custody of the Cincinnati Police or during pursuit. Rioters caused more than $3 million in damage to downtown Cincinnati over a three-day period. The riots ended after the third day, by which time the mayor had imposed a citywide curfew.

The officer involved in the Thomas shooting was eventually acquitted in court. However, the US Department of Justice under Attorney General **John Ashcroft** investigated police practices in Cincinnati and aided the city in developing a collaborative agreement with citizens' groups in 2002 to improve policing and community relations.

CINO, MARIA (1957–). A native of Buffalo, New York, Cino was chief of staff for New York Republican Representative Bill Paxon before working as executive director for the National Republican Congressional Committee (1993–1997). She worked as a public policy and government affairs consultant for the law firm of Wiley Rein before she became the national political director for **George W. Bush** in Austin, Texas, during the 2000 presidential election. During Bush's first term, Cino served as assistant secretary and director general of the United States and Foreign Commercial Service at the US Department of Commerce. She served as deputy chairman of the Republican National Committee in the election of 2004. President Bush appointed her deputy secretary of the Department of Transportation in 2005; upon **Norman Mineta**'s resignation as secretary and the Senate's confirmation of **Mary Peters** as secretary, Cino served as acting secretary of the Department of Transportation between July and September 2006.

CLARK, WESLEY KANNE (1944–). Born in Chicago, Illinois, Clark grew up in Little Rock, Arkansas. He graduated from West Point as his class's valedictorian, and later was awarded a Rhodes Scholarship to the University of Oxford (1968). He later earned a master's degree in military science from the Command and General Staff College.

Clark's military career spanned 34 years, and he retired as a four-star general. Clark served in Vietnam and worked for the **Office of Management and Budget** (OMB) in 1975 under President Gerald Ford. While on detail at the White House, he later helped secure a Vietnam Veterans Memorial. He worked for Supreme Allied Commander Alexander Haig (1978–1979) and in the offices of the chief and deputy chiefs of staff of the United States Army (1983–84). His major command included appointment by President **William Clinton** as US commander of the North Atlantic Treaty Organization (NATO) forces in Kosovo that battled the Serbian regime of **Slobodan Milošević** during the war in the former **Yugoslavia**. Controversy surrounded Clark for his handling of an incident at the airport in Pristina, Kosovo, when Russian forces arrived. Further, although Clark denied such rumors, it was alleged in the media that he had been forced into retirement by then Secretary of Defense William Cohen over disagreements with the Clinton administration. He was, nevertheless, awarded the Presidential Medal of Freedom in 2000.

Clark sought the Democratic Party's nomination for president in the 2004 election. He entered the race in September 2003. Although he won the Oklahoma primary, Clark's campaign failed to gain traction in other state primaries, and he withdrew his candidacy in February 2004. He threw his support to the eventual Democratic nominee, **John Kerry**.

Clark played an important role in the 2006 **mid-term elections**, which gave Democrats a majority in the House and Senate for the first time since they had lost control of Congress in 1994. He formed a political action committee titled "WesPAC: Securing America" that he used to support Democrats running for Congress. Clark was rumored to have considered running for president again in 2008, but in Fall 2007 instead endorsed New York Senator **Hillary Clinton**'s campaign.

A vocal critic of President **George W. Bush**'s **foreign policy**, Clark was also critical of 2008 Republican presidential candidate **John McCain**. Clark suggested that McCain's military service, per se, did not qualify him to be commander in chief. Since his retirement from the military, Clark pursued consulting and wrote several books: *Waging Modern War* (2002), *Winning Modern Wars* (2004), and *A Time to Lead* (2007).

CLARKE, RICHARD ALAN (1950–). A native of Dorchester, Massachusetts, and a graduate of the University of Pennsylvania (1972), Clarke has an extensive résumé of governmental service in defense and counterterrorism. He began his career with the Department of Defense in 1973. President **Ronald Reagan** appointed Clarke to the position of deputy secretary of state for intelligence (1985), where he worked on **Libya**. He was a key advisor to President **George H.W. Bush** during the **Persian Gulf War** as assistant secretary of state for political and military affairs. Clarke also served in the administration of **William Clinton** on the **National Security Council** (1992–2000), advising the president and secretary of state on issues ranging from the genocide in Rwanda to Middle East **terrorism**.

Clarke remained on the National Security Council as a special counterterrorism expert under President **George W. Bush**. He reported to Secretary of State **Condoleezza Rice**, and was in charge of key aspects of the governmental response to the **terrorist** attacks of **11 September 2001** on New York and Washington, D.C.

Clarke left governmental service in 2003 to author a book entitled *Against All Enemies: Inside America's War on Terror*, which was published in March 2004. The book made startling allegations that the administration of George W. Bush had ignored warnings about the terror group **al-Qaeda** and its leader, **Osama bin Laden**, that Clarke, as well as former Clinton administration officials, had made in advance of the 9/11 attacks. Instead, Clarke contended, the Bush administration had been more concerned with **Iraq** and its dictator, **Saddam Hussein**. Just weeks after the book's publication, Clarke testified before the **9/11 Commission**; he was the only official in the Bush administration to publicly apologize for the intelligence failures leading to the terrorist attack. Clarke also alleged that he had showed Bush administration officials intelligence, signed by the **Central Intelligence Agency** (CIA) and the **Federal Bureau of Investigation** (FBI), that underscored that no connection existed between Saddam Hussein's regime and the 9/11 attacks perpetrated by al-Qaeda. Vice President **Richard B. (Dick) Cheney** categorically denied Clarke's allegations, as did Republican Senate Majority Leader **Bill Frist**, in various television interviews.

Clarke has since been a contributor to the American Broadcasting Corporation (ABC). He is author of two other books, *Scorpion's Gate* (2005) and *Breakpoint* (2007).

CLINTON, HILLARY DIANE RODHAM (1947–). Born in Chicago, Illinois, Clinton graduated from Wellesley College (1969) and Yale Law School (1973). Clinton stirred controversy at Wellesley when she gave the commencement address and criticized the keynote speaker for not addressing the concerns of young people. She met President **William Clinton** in 1971, moved to Arkansas in 1974, and married him in 1975. She and Bill have one daughter, Chelsea, born in 1980.

Hillary Clinton worked indefatigably to support her husband's political career in the 1970s and 1980s, aiding him in his successful election as governor twice. In 1979, she became a partner in the Little Rock Rose law firm. As the first lady of Arkansas, she was particularly active in children's issues.

Following her husband's election to the presidency in 1992, she headed his failed health care initiative. It was the first time in modern presidential history that a first lady had been named to a paramount policy position in an administration. Later in Bill Clinton's presidency, she became mired in controversy over Whitewater, a failed land development scheme in Arkansas. She was not indicted on any wrongdoing. She remained publicly supportive of her husband during the Monica Lewinsky scandal and his subsequent impeachment, as well as when Paul Jones brought accusations of sexual harassment against him.

As her husband's second term came to a close, she moved hurriedly to New York, established residency, and won an open seat in the US Senate, defeating Republican Ric Lazio. Her election marked the first time a former first lady had successfully been elected to public office. She was re-elected to the Senate in 2006 with 67 percent of the statewide vote. Although she supported President **George W. Bush** and the **War on Terror**, including the authorization for military action in **Iraq** (**Iraq War Resolution**), Clinton became a vocal critic of Bush's administration in **foreign policy**, as well as in domestic and economic matters.

In January 2007, she announced that she would seek the Democratic Party's nomination for the presidency in the election of 2008. She competed with fellow senator **Barack Obama** in a hard-fought primary campaign that was highly competitive. Clinton won 18 million votes nationwide and generally carried larger, heterogeneous states with primaries, while Obama was more successful in states that held caucuses, or meetings of party activists. Controversy erupted during the campaign over the Michigan and Florida delegates to the Democratic Party convention in Denver when Democratic National Committee leaders made it clear that delegates from those two states would not be seated because they had moved their primary election dates up, in violation of party rules. Clinton won both states. However, neither she nor Obama campaigned in Michigan or Florida, and Obama's name was not on the ballot in Michigan. Ultimately, Clinton suspended her campaign in June 2008, rather than risk a convention battle over the nomination, and backed Obama. Her term in the US Senate was set to end in 2012. However, President Obama appointed her secretary of state in early 2009. *See also* BIDEN, JOSEPH ROBINETTE; LIMBAUGH, RUSH HUDSON III; WAR IN IRAQ.

CLINTON, WILLIAM JEFFERSON (1946–). Born William Jefferson Blythe III and adopted by Roger Clinton, his mother's second husband, the 42nd president of the United States graduated from Georgetown University, was a Rhodes Scholar at Oxford University in Great Britain, and later earned a law degree from Yale University. After serving as an assistant to Arkansas Senator J. William Fulbright, Clinton ran unsuccessfully for the House of Representatives in 1974. Two years later, he was elected attorney general of Arkansas, which he used as a springboard to the governor's mansion. Clinton was elected to five terms as governor of the state of Arkansas from 1978 to 1980 and from 1982 to 1992. He headed the National Governors' Association and then the centrist Democratic Leadership Council from 1990 to 1991.

Clinton's presidential aspirations were aided by President **George H.W. Bush**'s extremely high popularity following victory in the **Per-**

sian Gulf War, which convinced many senior Democrats to eschew a run for the White House in the 1992 election. Clinton emerged as a Democratic challenger following Bush's slide in public approval as the electorate and the media focused intensely on domestic politics and a sluggish economy. Clinton lost the Iowa Caucuses to rival and Iowa native Tom Harkin and finished second behind favorite-son Massachusetts Senator Paul Tsongas in New Hampshire. Clinton's early primary campaign was marred by scandals surrounding Vietnam and his draft deferral, as well as allegations of extramarital affairs that he and his wife, **Hillary Clinton**, would address candidly on national television. His strong showing in New Hampshire despite these obstacles gave him a label he would carry through his two terms—the "comeback kid." Clinton swept subsequent primaries and won the Democratic nomination. He chose Tennessee Senator **Albert Gore, Jr.**, as his running mate.

The general campaign pitted Clinton and **Reform Party** candidate **H. Ross Perot** against George H.W. Bush. Like Perot, Clinton's campaign focused on domestic politics. His campaign strategist James Carville hung a sign in the "war room" of the Clinton campaign headquarters that read "It's the economy, stupid—and don't forget health care" to keep the message on track. Clinton focused on the need for change, and promised to address rising health care costs, while Perot criticized Bush for his economic policies and the risks of further job losses through the North American Free Trade Agreement (NAFTA). Bush emphasized his steady leadership in **foreign policy** and his broad experience from World War II to his days in the **United Nations**, calling into question Clinton's fitness to be commander in chief. Clinton ultimately won the 1992 election with 43 percent of the popular vote to Bush's 37 percent. Perot's 19 percent was the best showing for a third-party candidate for president since Teddy Roosevelt's "Bull Moose" Party in 1912 and is believed to have cost Bush more votes than Clinton.

Despite a Democratic majority in both chambers of Congress, Clinton's first two years in the Oval Office were scarred by battles over gays in the military, gun control, the federal budget, and his health care proposal, which gave a far-reaching regulatory role to the national government—but never came to a vote in Congress. By 1994, Clinton's popularity reached a nadir, and in the 1994 **mid-term**

elections Republicans won a stunning victory by gaining control of the House of Representatives for the first time in 40 years and a majority in the Senate, which they had lost in 1986. House Speaker Newt Gingrich supplanted Clinton's legislative agenda with the GOP's conservative program entitled the "Contract with America," much of which Clinton eventually vetoed. Clinton won re-election in 1996 against Republican candidate Robert Dole largely on a defensive campaign that emphasized the need to keep the GOP majority in Congress in check. He achieved victory again with only a plurality of the national vote—49 percent—to Dole's 41 percent and Perot's 8 percent. Clinton faced a Republican majority in Congress for the duration of his second term.

He became only the second president in US history to be impeached. Following his denial of an affair with White House intern Monica Lewinsky, the House of Representatives approved two articles of impeachment against Clinton: perjury and obstruction of justice. He was acquitted by the Senate on both counts in February 1999. Despite the scandal and impeachment, Clinton did negotiate a compromise budget in his second term that reduced the deficit and a bill that fundamentally altered federal welfare programs. He also turned his attention to foreign policy, attempting to broker peace negotiations in Northern Ireland and between **Israel** and the Palestinians. Clinton maintains a high profile in the Democratic Party alongside his wife, Hillary, whom he helped successfully campaign for the junior Senate seat from the state of New York in 2001. He published his memoirs, *My Life*, in 2004.

COALITION OF THE WILLING. This term was coined by President **George W. Bush** in November 2002. Bush suggested that if Iraqi dictator **Saddam Hussein** did not disarm and halt his pursuit of **weapons of mass destruction** (WMDs), the United States would head a coalition of willing nations to force him to do so. When Bush was unable to procure a **United Nations** mandate to invade **Iraq** after French President **Jacques Chirac** threatened to veto any such move, the term was used to denote those nations that supported the US-led invasion in March 2003, namely Australia, Denmark, Netherlands, **Poland**, and **Great Britain**, which contributed troops to the invasion, as well as other countries that supported intelligence and materiel for the invasion and aftermath. *See also* BLAIR, TONY; BROWN, GORDON; DE VILLEPIN, DOMINIQUE; EUROPEAN UNION; SCHRÖDER, GERHARD; WAR IN IRAQ.

COALITION PROVISIONAL AUTHORITY. Following the March 2003 invasion of **Iraq** and ouster of dictator **Saddam Hussein**, the United States established the Coalition Provisional Authority as a transitional government until new Iraqi political institutions could be formulated. It was headquartered in the so-called **Green Zone** of **Baghdad**. The Authority was set up several months before the invasion, and was originally headed by Army Lieutenant General **Jay Garner**. Following the invasion, Garner became administrator for the Authority, but his refusal to purge former **Ba'ath Party** members from the Iraqi military and government led to his dismissal after just one month. Garner was replaced by former ambassador **L. Paul Bremer**. Bremer served as administrator from April 2003 to June 2004, at which time power was transferred to an interim Iraqi government headed by **Iyad Allawi**.

COLD WAR. Coined by Bernard Baruch, an advisor to Presidents Woodrow Wilson, Franklin Roosevelt, Harry Truman, and John Kennedy, the term "Cold War" connotes the ideological, technological, and military rivalry between the United States and the **Soviet Union** following World War II, and by extension, between the countries of the **North Atlantic Treaty Organization** (NATO) and **Warsaw Pact** nations. The Cold War arguably began when President Truman called upon Congress to support efforts to rebuild Europe following the war and preclude Communist victories in Greece and Turkey. The fall of the Berlin Wall in 1989 signaled the closing stages of the Cold War, which ended with the dissolution of the Soviet Union in 1991. President **George H.W. Bush** and Russian President Boris Yeltsin declared the Cold War over in 1992.

COLUMBIA (SPACE SHUTTLE). First launched in April 1981, *Columbia* undertook a total of 28 missions into space. On 1 February 2003, *Columbia* reentered the Earth's atmosphere after a 16-day scientific mission. Upon reentry, the thermal protectors on one of the wings was damaged. The wing overheated, broke apart, and all seven crew members aboard the shuttle were killed. The accident spread significant debris over Texas.

COMPASSIONATE CONSERVATIVE. This term was coined in the 1970s by author Doug Wead, and it occasionally circulated during the administrations of **Ronald Reagan** and **George H.W. Bush**. **George W. Bush** frequently referenced "compassion" on the campaign trail in 1999 and 2000, which won the support of many **Evangelical Christians**. In December 2000, as president-elect, he defined his understanding of the term: "Together, we will address some of society's deepest problems one person at a time, by encouraging and empowering the good hearts and good works of the American people. This is the essence of compassionate conservatism, and it will be a foundation of my administration." Bush's attempt to operationalize "compassionate conservativism" was reflected in the White House **Office of Faith-Based and Community Initiatives**, which was tasked with encouraging welfare and assistance solutions through private donations and religious organizations.

COMPREHENSIVE TEST BAN TREATY. The Comprehensive Test Ban Treaty (CTBT) was signed by 71 countries. Under the terms of the treaty, signatories are prohibited from testing nuclear weapons. President **William Clinton** signed the CTBT in 1996. However, the US Senate, at the time controlled by Republicans, failed to ratify the treaty in a vote in October 1999. President **George W. Bush** opposed ratification of the CTBT on national security grounds, although the United States abided by the moratorium on testing during his presidency.

CONGO, DEMOCRATIC REPUBLIC OF. The Congo (formerly Zaire) was the site of a bloody, five-year-long war that began in 1998 and ended in 2003. The conflict, which pitted several ethnic groups against one another, involved eight African nations, including Namibia, Zimbabwe, **Angola**, Chad, Uganda, Rwanda, and Burundi. With more than 5 million dead, the war was the deadliest conflict since World War II. *See also* FOREIGN POLICY.

CORPORATE SCANDALS. *See* ABRAMOFF, JACK; ARTHUR ANDERSEN; IMCLONE; TYCO CORPORATION; WORLD-COM.

COX, CHARLES CHRISTOPHER (1952–). Born in St. Paul, Minnesota, Cox is a graduate of the University of Southern California (1973). In 1977, he graduated with both a master's in business administration and a law degree from Harvard. He worked in private law practice in Southern California from 1977 to 1986 for the firm of Latham and Watkins. He then joined the administration of President **Ronald Reagan** as senior White House counsel (1986–1988).

Cox began his congressional career in 1988, winning election from a wealthy district in Orange County, California. He was elected to eight more terms. A Republican, Cox was chair of the House majority leadership and the chair of the House Republican policy committee. He specialized in security and international affairs, in addition to economic matters. He served on all major congressional committees regarding finance issues, including the House Energy and Commerce, Financial Services, Government Reform, Joint Economic, and Budget Committees. In 1995, he authored the Private Securities Litigation Reform Act, which sought to protect investors from fraudulent lawsuits. He also served as chair of President **William Clinton**'s Bipartisan Commission on Entitlement and Tax Reform. He chaired the House Committee on Homeland Security following the establishment of the **Department of Homeland Security** in 2003.

Cox left Congress when President **George W. Bush** appointed him to chair the **Securities and Exchange Commission** (SEC) in June 2005. As SEC chair, Cox was responsible for enforcing those laws that govern the securities and stock trade. He quickly earned a reputation for pursuing fraudulent trading practices. Nevertheless, by 2008, calls for Cox's resignation escalated in the wake of the **sub-prime mortgage** crisis that gripped the nation and forced Congress to adopt a $700 billion financial bailout for the banking and investment industry. Republican presidential nominee **John McCain** stated he would have fired Cox had he been president when the crisis erupted. An internal report by the SEC suggested that the agency's oversight of the failed firm **Bear Stearns** had been inadequate. Cox contended that the congressional legislation adopted in 1999 had not given the agency the tools or authority to regulate large investment holding banks like Bear Stearns. *See also* AMERICAN INTERNATIONAL GROUP; LEHMAN BROTHERS.

CRAIG, LARRY EDWIN (1945–). A native of Council, Idaho, Craig is a graduate of the University of Idaho (1969) in political science. He began his career in public service in 1974, when he was elected to the Idaho Senate. He was re-elected twice, in 1976 and 1978. In 1980, he ran for Congress, winning an open seat race as a Republican. He won re-election to the House of Representatives four times. He ran successfully for the US Senate in 1990. He was re-elected twice, in 1996 and 2002. While in the Senate he served as Senate Republican Policy Committee chairman (1997–2003), and on the Veterans' Affairs and Energy Committees.

Craig made national news in August 2007, when a news report surfaced that he had been arrested two months earlier for lewd conduct at the Minneapolis airport. Police officers alleged that Craig had been caught in the men's room attempting to solicit gay sex. Craig pleaded guilty to a lesser charge of disorderly conduct. When the news reports surfaced, he attempted to recant his guilty plea and fight the original charges, but a court denied his petition. He refused to resign his seat from Congress, but later announced he would not run for re-election in 2008. Craig had been the subject of allegations in 1982 that he had engaged in sex and illicit drug use with male pages on Capitol Hill, which he dismissed as gossip. No formal charges were ever filed.

CROCKER, RYAN CLARK (1949–). Born in Spokane, Washington, Crocker grew up in Canada, Morocco, and Turkey. He graduated from Whitman College in Walla Walla, Washington, in 1971. A career foreign service officer, Crocker specialized in the Middle East and served in the US State Department in Qatar, **Baghdad, Iraq**, **Lebanon**, and Egypt. He was appointed by President **George H.W. Bush** as ambassador to Lebanon in 1990; President **George W. Bush** appointed him as ambassador to **Pakistan** in 2006. He received a Presidential Distinguished Service Award in 1994.

Crocker succeeded **Zalmay Khalilzad** as the US ambassador to Iraq in March 2007. Crocker was ambassador when the United States opened its embassy in Baghdad, Iraq, in Spring 2008. As ambassador, Crocker was particularly active in attempting to negotiate with the new Iraqi government about the long-term presence of American troops in Iraq.

CUBA. *See* CASTRO, FIDEL; GUANTANAMO BAY.

**CUNNINGHAM, RANDALL HAROLD (RANDY "DUKE")
(1941–).** A Los Angeles native and graduate of the University of
Missouri, Cunningham joined the Navy in 1967 and served in Vietnam. A skilled pilot, he received the Navy Cross, Silver Star, Air
Medal, and Purple Heart for his military service. After serving at the
naval flight school, Cunningham retired from the military with the
rank of commander in 1987. In 1990, he ran successfully for the US
House of Representatives as a Republican from a district in northern
San Diego County, California. He was re-elected in every election
through 2004. He served on the House Intelligence and Appropriations Committees.

Known for his gruff and sometimes off-putting style in politics,
Cunningham was caught in a political scandal that made national
headlines. He pleaded guilty to accepting more than $2 million in
bribes concerning defense contracts, and further pleaded guilty to
conspiracy to commit bribery, mail fraud, wire fraud, and tax evasion. He resigned his seat in Congress in late November 2005. In
March 2006, he was sentenced by a federal court to eight years and
four months in prison. He was further ordered to pay $1.8 million in
restitution.

CZECH REPUBLIC. A former **Warsaw Pact** nation during the **Cold
War** between the United States and the **Soviet Union**, the Czech
Republic joined the **North Atlantic Treaty Organization** (NATO)
in 1999. After President **George W. Bush** announced that the United
States had withdrawn from **Anti-Ballistic Missile Treaty** in 2002,
he proposed a land-based missile defense system in **Poland** and the
Czech Republic to protect the United States and Europe from potential nuclear threats from terrorists. **Russian** President **Vladimir
Putin** opposed the plan. In February 2007, a Russian military general
suggested that US bases in Poland and the Czech Republic could be
targeted by Russian missiles if the United States carried out plans for
its missile defense program. In June 2007, Putin reiterated the point
that Europe could be targeted by nuclear weapons. President Bush
and Putin met in April 2008 in Sochi, Russia, to discuss the missile
defense program, but the summit did not yield agreement.

– D –

DARFUR. A region in western **Sudan**, Darfur has been the subject of an ethnic conflict since 2003 that pitted the Arab tribes and the *janjaweed* militia, the latter with government backing, against other tribes that oppose the Sudanese government. The janjaweed militias were accused of genocide by Secretary of State **Colin Powell** in 2004, but a **United Nations** report a year later contradicted findings of genocide, and the matter was referred to the **International Criminal Court**, which the Sudanese government does not recognize. Nevertheless, between 2003 and 2008, estimates of civilian deaths ranged from 200,000 to 500,000, with more than 2 million others displaced.

By 2005, combined forces numbering 7,000 from the **African Union** (AU) were sent to Sudan on a peacekeeping mission. Critics argued that the AU's force was inadequately trained for the mission. In 2006, the US Congress appropriated $173 million to support the AU troops, but did not send US troops. In July 2007, the **United Nations** (UN) passed a resolution to integrate the AU forces into a joint AU–UN peacekeeping mission in Darfur.

DASCHLE, THOMAS ANDREW (1947–). Born in Aberdeen, South Dakota, Daschle graduated from South Dakota State University with a degree in political science in 1969. He served for three years in the US Air Force before becoming an aide to Democratic Senator James Abourezk. Daschle was first elected to the US House of Representatives in 1978 as a Democrat. He won re-election three times before successfully running for the US Senate from South Dakota in 1986. While in the Senate he cochaired the Democratic Policy Committee (1989–1999), was minority leader (1995–2001, 2003–2005), and was majority leader (2001–2003). He also served on the Agricultural, Veterans Affairs, Indian Affairs, Finance, and Ethics Committees.

Daschle became majority leader in 2001 due to a strange turn of circumstances. Following the 2000 election, Republicans and Democrats were evenly divided in the US Senate, with 50 seats each. As president of the Senate, Vice President **Richard B. (Dick) Cheney** could cast a tie-breaking vote, which enabled the Republicans to govern as a majority. However, in May 2001, Vermont Republican Senator **James Jeffords** left the Republican Party, became an independent, and threw his support to the Democrats, which allowed them to control the majority in the upper chamber. Republicans regained the majority in the **mid-term elections** of 2002, which **President George W. Bush** fought on the issue of the **War on Terror**.

In October 2001, following the **11 September 2001 terrorist** attacks on New York and Washington, D.C., Daschle's office was one of several on Capitol Hill that received an **anthrax**-laced letter, which authorities believe Bruce Ivins was guilty of sending. Several of Daschle's staff aides were exposed to the potentially deadly anthrax spores.

Daschle lost his re-election bid for the Senate in 2004 in a narrow race against Republican candidate John Thune. Daschle has since taught at Georgetown University, is advisor for the law firm of Alston & Bird, and is a fellow at the Center for American Progress. He also headed DASHPAC, a political action committee formed in 2005, which some speculated he might use for a presidential bid in 2005. Daschle supported **Barack Obama** in the 2008 presidential election. Obama tapped Daschle to head the Department of Health and Human Services in his new administration, but Daschle withdrew his nomination after revelations that he had not paid his taxes.

DAVIS, JOSEPH GRAHAM (GRAY), JR. (1942–). A graduate of Stanford University and Columbia Law School, Davis is a decorated Vietnam Veteran (Bronze Star). A Democrat, he was elected governor of California in 1999. He had previously served as a state assemblyman (1983–1987), state controller (1987–1995), and lieutenant governor (1995–1999).

A popular governor with presidential aspirations, Davis suffered a radical change in fortune when California faced a huge budget shortfall. He was formally recalled as governor in a vote held on 7 October 2003. One month later, Republican **Arnold Schwarzenegger** succeeded Davis in a statewide election. Davis has since taught at the University of California, Los Angeles, and joined the law firm of Loeb and Loeb.,

DE VILLEPIN, DOMINIQUE MARIE FRANÇOIS RENÉ GALOUZEAU (1953–). Born in Rabat, Morocco, de Villepin is a career French diplomat. He specialized in African affairs and served in the French Embassy to the United States in Washington, D.C., from 1984 to 1989. De Villepin served as foreign minister under President **Jacques Chirac** from 2002 to 2004. He articulated French opposition to the US plan to invade **Saddam Hussein**'s **Iraq**. In February 2002, he gave a speech in the **United Nations** (UN) in which he called for weapons inspections to continue. The French threatened to veto any resolution authorizing military action under UN auspices, and won support from **Russia**, **Germany**, and **China**. De Villepin became prime minister of France in May 2005. He was succeeded by François Fillon in May 2007, when Jacques Chirac finished his second term and **Nicolas Sarkozy** acceded to the presidency. *See also* ANNAN, KOFI; BLAIR, TONY; BLIX, HANS; COALITION OF THE WILLING; WAR IN IRAQ; WAR ON TERROR.

DEAN, HOWARD BRUSH, III (1948–). A native of East Hampton, New York, and a graduate of Yale University in political science (1971), Dean earned a medical degree from Yeshiva University (1978) and moved to Vermont for his residency. He entered politics in 1982, winning a seat as a Democrat in the Vermont legislature. He continued to practice medicine early in his political career. He was elected lieutenant governor in 1986. Dean became governor in 1991, when the incumbent, Richard Snelling, died suddenly. Dean won five subsequent elections over 10 years. He gained national attention for implementing a program to provide health insurance for children in Vermont. He was chair of the National Governors Association (1994–1995). In 2000, Dean signed the first state legislation in the nation authorizing civil unions for same-sex couples.

A strong critic of President **George W. Bush** and the **War in Iraq**, Dean launched his bid for the presidency in 2003. He raised significant amounts of money for his campaign through Internet donations. Despite endorsements from many key Democratic leaders, including **Al Gore**, Dean performed poorly in the **Iowa Caucuses** in January 2004, placing third behind rivals **John Kerry** and **John Edwards**. At a rally event held the evening of the caucuses, at which Dean gave a concession speech for his supporters, he uttered a loud, uncharacteristic yell in front of the cameras that became known as the "Dean Scream" and received substantial negative media attention. He contested New Hampshire and Wisconsin and failed to win either state. He suspended his campaign in February 2004 and endorsed John Kerry a month later.

Dean founded the organization "Democracy for America" in 2004, an operation aimed at using his Internet resources to fund other Democratic candidates. He became chair of the Democratic National Committee (DNC) in February 2005.

DELAY, THOMAS DALE (1947–). A native of Laredo, Texas and a graduate of the University of Houston (1970), DeLay entered politics in 1978 by winning a seat in the Texas legislature. He won a congressional seat as a Republican for a district in Houston in 1984, succeeding Ron Paul, who made an unsuccessful bid for the Senate. DeLay won re-election 10 times and rose quickly in the House Republican leadership. He earned the nickname "Hammer" after serving in the Republican whip operation from 1988 to 2002. He became House majority leader in 2003 and served until 2005. DeLay was both a loyal lieutenant to House Speaker Newt Gingrich in the 1990s and a strong supporter of President **George W. Bush** in his first term.

DeLay was indicted by a Texas grand jury in 2005 for allegedly violating campaign finance rules. He resigned as House majority leader and was succeeded by Roy Blunt of Missouri. DeLay's image suffered when his congressional communications director, Michael Scanlon, and another aide, Tony Rudy, pleaded guilty to conspiring to bribe a member of Congress in the scandal involving **Jack Abramoff**. DeLay was also implicated in the Department of Justice investigation surrounding Abramoff's activities. Delay won the Republican primary in his district in 2006 but later announced he would not seek election to Congress. DeLay is author of *No Retreat, No Surrender: One American's Fight* (2007). As of 2008, DeLay awaited trial on the campaign finance indictments in Texas after having one count dismissed by the court.

DEMOCRATIC UNIONIST PARTY. *See* NORTHERN IRELAND.

DEPARTMENT OF HOMELAND SECURITY (DHS). The 15th cabinet department created in the executive branch, the Department of Homeland Security opened its doors on 1 March 2003. DHS is the third largest department, with more than 200,000 employees. The creation of the department was a direct result of the **terrorist** attacks on New York and Washington, D.C., on **11 September 2001**. DHS was established as the institutional cornerstone in President **George W. Bush**'s **War on Terror**. The department's objective is to prevent the United States from terror attacks and to respond to domestic emergencies.

The creation of the DHS represented the largest reorganization of federal responsibilities since the Department of Defense was created in the 1940s. The department absorbed an amalgam of 22 federal agencies, some of which were renamed or broken apart into subagencies, including the Coast Guard, the old Immigration and Naturalization Service (INS), the Customs Service, and the **Federal Emergency Management Agency** (FEMA). DHS shares responsibility for **terrorism** prevention with other federal departments and agencies, including Justice (**Federal Bureau of Investigation**), Energy (e.g., chemical and nuclear plants), Health and Human Services, Agriculture (e.g., food supply), and Defense.

DHS grew out of the **Office of Homeland Security** (OHS), which President Bush created in the **Executive Office of the President** (EOP) in the immediate aftermath of the 9/11 attacks. Bush appointed **Tom Ridge** to direct the OHS, and his charge was to coordinate programs across federal agencies to combat terrorism. However, many in Congress suggested that a massive reorganization of federal agencies was necessary because Ridge did not have the financial or human resources to succeed, and because he was furthermore beyond accountability to Congress. Bush first rejected such calls, then in early 2002 announced his own plan for a reorganization. For much of 2002, Bush and Senate Democrats could not agree on personnel rules that would govern the new DHS, and legislative action was halted. Finally, in November 2002, following the **mid-term elections** that gave control of the Senate back to Republicans, the Democratic majority passed the Homeland Security Act on terms favorable to Bush's stance that DHS employees not be subject to standard civil service protections. The former OHS was melded into the DHS, but left behind a Homeland Security Council in the EOP that is the equivalent of the **National Security Council** to provide advice and coordination in the White House. House and Senate committees were also established to provide legislative oversight of the DHS.

Bush appointed Ridge to head the DHS, and he was unanimously confirmed as secretary in January 2003. He was succeeded by **Michael Chertoff** in February 2005.

DETAINEE TREATMENT ACT (2005). Sponsored by Republican Senator **John McCain** of Arizona, the Detainee Treatment Act was passed as an amendment to a defense appropriations bill. The law took aim at allegations that "enhanced interrogation techniques," including **waterboarding** of suspected **terrorists** held at **Guantanamo Bay, Cuba**, or subjecting suspects to **rendition** to other countries, had been torture. The act specifically prohibited the inhumane treatment of **enemy combatants** and required that all interrogations be undertaken according to the US Army Field Manual. The act also precluded detainees from recourse to US civil courts via **habeas corpus** petitions. The latter part of the act was struck down in *Boumediene v. Bush* (2008), in which the **Supreme Court** ruled that the **Military Commissions Act** (2006) passed by Congress, which set up military tribunals, was unconstitutional. The High Court further reaffirmed the rights of detainees to habeas corpus. When President **George W. Bush** signed the bill into law, he challenged it through a **signing statement**, contending that he would interpret the language of the act vis-à-vis his role as commander in chief to do all that is necessary in the **War on Terror** to prevent another terrorist attack. *See also* AMNESTY INTERNATIONAL; TORTURE.

DIRECTOR OF NATIONAL INTELLIGENCE (DNI). The **terrorist** attacks of **11 September 2001** on New York and Washington prompted calls for the federal government to streamline counterterrorism programs. In the **Intelligence Reform and Terrorism Prevention Act** of 2004, Congress created a Director of National Intelligence (DNI) to whom the director of the **Central Intelligence Agency** (CIA) now reports, and who is charged with liaising with other federal agencies, such as the **Federal Bureau of Investigation** (FBI), to thwart **terrorist** attacks.

President **George W. Bush** appointed **John Negroponte** as the first DNI; he was succeeded two years later by **Michael McConnell**.

DOLE, ELIZABETH HANFORD (1936–). A North Carolina native and wife of former senator and Republican presidential candidate Robert J. (Bob) Dole (1996), Elizabeth Dole earned an undergraduate degree at Duke University (1958) before pursuing a graduate and law degree at Harvard (1965). She worked as a public defender in Washington, D.C., was deputy assistant for consumer affairs for President Richard Nixon (1971–1973), and was a member of the Federal Trade Commission (1973–1979). Before President **Ronald Reagan** appointed her secretary of transportation in 1983 (a post she held until 1987), she was his assistant for public liaison from 1981 to 1983. President **George H.W. Bush** appointed her secretary of labor in 1989, a position from which she resigned in 1991 to become president of the American Red Cross. In 1999, she announced her run for the 2000 Republican presidential nomination, but terminated her campaign before any primaries due to inadequate fund-raising. She won a seat in the US Senate from North Carolina in 2002. In 2004, she was elected as chair of the Republican Senatorial Committee. She served on the Armed Services and Banking Committees. Dole is author of *Unlimited Partners: Our American Story* (1996) and *Hearts Touched by Fire: My 500 Most Inspirational Quotations* (2004). She lost her Senate seat in 2008 by 9 percent to Democrat Kay Hagan in a campaign that turned on Dole's allegations that her opponent was "godless."

DOW JONES INDUSTRIAL AVERAGE (DJIA). The DJIA is a composite index of the stock values of the 30 largest companies in the United States. The DJIA suffered its two largest single-day point losses in the history of the index under President **George W. Bush**. The index lost 684 points (7.1 percent of its value) on 17 September 2001, when markets reopened following the **terrorist** attacks on **11 September 2001**. The index lost 777 points (6.9 percent of its value) on 29 September 2008 as a result of the **sub-prime mortgage** crisis. *See also* AMERICAN INTERNATIONAL GROUP; BEAR STEARNS; BERNANKE, BEN SHALOM; PAULSON, HENRY MERRITT, JR.; TROUBLED ASSETS RELIEF PROGRAM (TARP).

DOWNEY, MORTIMER LEO (1936–). A graduate of Yale (1958), New York University (1966), and Harvard University (1988), Downey was an assistant secretary in the Department of Transportation under President Jimmy Carter (1977–1981) and was secretary of the Department of Transportation for eight years under President **William Clinton** (1993–2001). He is the longest-serving secretary of transportation. He served briefly (four days) as acting secretary of transportation in the transition between the administration of William Clinton and **George W. Bush** in January 2001. He was succeeded by **Norman Mineta**.

DOWNING STREET MEMO. Leaked to the press and published in the **London** *Sunday Times* on 1 May 2005, the so-called Downing Street Memo is a note made by the head of the British Secret Intelligence Service (MI6) describing a meeting of top officials in the Labour Party government of **Tony Blair** in July 2002. The memo reported that President **George W. Bush** had "framed" intelligence in such a way as to link the Iraqi regime of **Saddam Hussein** to the stockpiling of **weapons of mass destruction** (WMDs) and use the data as a justification to remove the dictator militarily, which led to the protracted **War in Iraq**. British Foreign Secretary **Jack Straw** was reported to have stated that Bush had "made up his mind" on a military invasion of Iraq in spite of questionable evidence and intelligence. Both Bush and Blair disputed the memo's allegations. Critics also questioned the timing of the memo's leak, just days before **Great Britain's** election on 5 May 2005.

"DUBYA." President **George W. Bush**'s widely known nickname, which is derived from his middle initial.

– E –

EDUCATION. Education policy became one of the most heated issues during President **George W. Bush**'s two terms. As a presidential candidate in 2000, Bush endorsed increasing federal funds for local schools contingent upon the adoption of testing standards. He also supported the creation of a greater number of charter schools, and proposed school "vouchers" so that parents whose children attended substandard public schools could move them to private schools with the help of governmental funding.

The centerpiece of George W. Bush's education policy was the **No Child Left Behind** legislation, which was passed by the Republican Congress in 2001 and signed into law in early 2002. The legislation, which reauthorized the Elementary and Secondary Education Act, mandated standardized tests at the state level and called for schools to improve test score performance over time. Emphasis was placed on basic skills, including reading and mathematics. One important aspect of the bill was to target failing schools with large minority populations. Although the bill did not go so far as to create a "voucher" system, the legislation did provide that students enrolled in schools that failed to reach testing targets for two consecutive years could change schools and receive other benefits, including tutoring and after-school programs.

Critics of the legislation, including many Democrats and educators, contended that No Child Left Behind focused too much on standardized testing to the detriment of other aspects of general education. Moreover, critics charged that the bill contained incentives for school districts to lower test expectations to show improvement. Schools that did not show improvement were subject to funding cuts and other penalties. Other detractors of the bill argued that the legislation undermined local control of school curricula.

On a more symbolic level, First Lady **Laura Bush** was a steadfast advocate for reading during her husband's two terms. She spent much time visiting local schools and aiding efforts to recruit qualified teachers. Her high-profile projects included a partnership with the Library of Congress to launch a National Book Festival. The **United Nations** (UN) named her as honorary ambassador for the Decade for Literacy, and she used her position to plan an international conference on global literacy in 2006. Her youngest daughter, **Jenna Bush**, was also a visible proponent of education issues and sometimes accompanied the first lady to promote education. Jenna Bush worked for the UN's Children's Fund and later took a position as a teacher in Washington, D.C.

President Bush's two education secretaries were **Rod Paige** (2001–2005) and **Margaret Spellings** (2005–2008). *See also* AFFIRMATIVE ACTION.

EDWARDS, JOHN REID (1953–). Born in Seneca, South Carolina, Edwards graduated with a bachelor's degree from North Carolina State University (1974) and a law degree from the University of North Carolina, Chapel Hill (1977). From 1978 to 1993, Edwards worked as a litigator in private law practice for firms in Nashville, Tennessee, and Raleigh, North Carolina, before establishing his own firm.

Edwards's notoriety in winning a high-profile medical malpractice lawsuit aided his entry into North Carolina and national politics. In 1998, he successfully challenged incumbent Republican North Carolina Senator Lauch Faircloth. He served on the Judiciary Committee in the Senate. He voted in favor of the **War in Iraq**, but later became a proponent of removing US troops. As Edwards's term in the Senate came to a close, he announced he would not seek re-election, to focus his efforts on the 2004 presidential race. His populist platform and emphasis on poverty issues enabled him to maintain significant support in Democratic primaries, but of the early contests he won only South Carolina. He ultimately suspended his campaign in March 2004 and threw support to his rival, **John Kerry**. In July 2004, Kerry chose Edwards as his vice presidential running mate. The Kerry–Edwards ticket lost to President **George W. Bush** and **Richard B. (Dick) Cheney** by nearly 3 million votes nationwide in November 2004.

In December 2006, Edwards announced his candidacy for the presidential election of 2008. His campaign focused again on poverty, and he made health care a central issue. His wife, Elizabeth, was diagnosed with breast cancer in 2004. Edwards failed to win any of the early primary contests in 2008, placing either second or third behind **Barack Obama** or **Hillary Clinton** in Iowa, New Hampshire, and South Carolina. He withdrew from the race in January 2008. He endorsed Obama in May 2008.

Edwards made national headlines in August 2008, when the media reported he had an affair with a campaign worker, Rielle Hunter, and fathered her child. Edwards first denied the allegations, and then admitted the affair in a televised interview. The revelations of the affair damaged Edwards's political ambitions insofar as he had made family values a centerpiece of his prior campaigns. Edwards is author of

Four Trials (2003), *Home: The Blueprints of Our Lives* (2006), and *Ending Poverty in America: How to Restore the American Dream* (2007).

ELBARADEI, MOHAMMED MOSTAFA (1942–). Born in Cairo, Egypt, ElBaradei worked in the Egyptian foreign ministry before joining the **United Nations** (UN) in 1980. He became the director of the UN's **International Atomic Energy Agency** (IAEA) in 1997. Along with chief weapons inspector **Hans Blix**, El Baradei led the effort to uncover **weapons of mass destruction** (WMDs) in **Iraq** in 2002, prior to the US-led invasion of that country in March 2003. Not only were no WMDs uncovered, but ElBaradei also disputed allegations made by the administration of **George W. Bush** that Iraqi dictator **Saddam Hussein** had attempted to procure uranium from Niger for a nuclear weapons program. The Bush administration attempted to have ElBaradei removed from his position but failed. ElBaradei was critical of the **War in Iraq** and the justification for military action. He continued to spar with the Bush administration on other matters, most notably **Iran**'s nuclear program. The United States contended that ElBaradei was focused too much on diplomatic efforts to halt Iran's nuclear program without supporting tougher economic sanctions. *See also* KAY, DAVID A.

ENEMY COMBATANT (UNLAWFUL, ILLEGAL). The administration of President **George W. Bush** used the term "enemy combatant" in conjunction with the **War on Terror**. The term was first employed after the **terrorist** attacks on **11 September 2001**, and referred to **Taliban** and **al-Qaeda** members, operatives, or associates captured in **Afghanistan** following the US-led invasion of that country.

Bush's use of the term must be distinguished from prior definitions and contexts. The term "enemy combatant" may be traced to the 1942 **Supreme Court** case *Ex parte Quirin* during World War II. The Court then wrote that "Citizens who associate themselves with the military arm of the enemy government, and with its aid, guidance, and direction enter this country bent on hostile acts are enemy belligerents within the meaning of the Hague Convention and the law of war." There are two subcategories of enemy combatants: lawful and unlawful. Lawful enemy combatants, such as soldiers serving in a national army, are afforded protections as prisoners of war under the **Geneva Convention**. Unlawful enemy combatants are nonstate actors for whom the Geneva Convention—and prisoner of war status—do not apply.

It is the latter definition of unlawful enemy combatants that President Bush applied to suspected Taliban and al-Qaeda operatives captured in Afghanistan, in **Iraq**, and elsewhere. Under this view, the president can detain unlawful enemy combatant prisoners indefinitely, and they are not protected under the US Constitution by **habeas corpus** (the right to go before a civil judge). Detainees were sent to the US naval base in **Guantanamo Bay, Cuba**. The Bush administration planned on trying the suspects in **military tribunals** of the variety that were used in World War II.

The Supreme Court made three major rulings on the status of enemy combatants in Cuba. The high court held in ***Rasul v. Bush*** (2004) that the Bush administration did not have the authority to deny habeas corpus, and dismissed the argument that the military facility in Cuba was beyond the reach of US law. In ***Hamdan v. Rumsfeld*** (2006), the Court decided a habeas corpus petition by a detainee, concluding that the military commissions set up independently by the Bush administration were unconstitutional and could only be founded by an act of Congress. As a result, Congress passed the **Military Commissions Act**. That act was ruled unconstitutional in ***Boumediene v. Bush*** (2008) when a detainee filed a habeas corpus petition challenging the law.

ENERGY TASK FORCE. Formally known as the National Energy Policy Development Group, President **George W. Bush** appointed Vice President **Richard B. (Dick) Cheney** chair of the Energy Task Force, which was charged with developing a national energy policy. The Energy Task Force was the subject of several lawsuits and congressional investigations. The White House contended that the content of the meetings and names of the participants, which allegedly included officials from major oil companies such as **Enron Corporation** and Exxon/Mobil, were confidential and protected under **executive privilege**. Critics posited that big oil companies were exercising too much control over government policy and demanded that Bush and Cheney make a full disclosure of participants and decisions. Lawsuits filed by the congressional watchdog General Accounting Office, as well as by watchdog group Judicial Watch under the Freedom of Information Act, were ultimately dismissed by the courts. In July 2007, the newspaper *Washington Post* reported the names of supposed participants in the Task Force, which included **Kenneth Lay**, the deceased ex-chairman of Enron Corporation who was convicted of fraud in 2005 in connection with the company's bankruptcy.

ENRON CORPORATION. With a workforce of 22,000 employees, Enron was one of the leading worldwide energy corporations. Despite earnings of more than $100 billion in 2000, Enron filed bankruptcy in late 2001. Tens of thousands of investors lost millions in retirement and mutual fund accounts when Enron stock tumbled from $90 per share to less than a dollar in 2001. The precipitous decline was in large measure a product of revelations that Enron's leaders—namely **Kenneth Lay**, **Andrew Fastow**, and **Jeffrey Skilling**—had engaged in wide-ranging accounting fraud. The accounting firm **Arthur Andersen** was implicated in the scandal and ultimately went out of business because its employees had obstructed justice by destroying Enron financial documents. By 2007, Enron continued to sell its remaining assets to repay creditors. The company's collapse raised further questions about the **Energy Task Force** headed by Vice President **Richard B. (Dick) Cheney**, as the *Washington Post* alleged in July 2007 that Lay had been a participant in high-level meetings with government officials and others from the energy industry.

ENVIRONMENTAL PROTECTION AGENCY (EPA). Established by Congress in 1970, during the presidency of Richard Nixon, the EPA is an independent federal agency that oversees the regulation of air and water quality, treatment and disposal of land-based pollutants and hazardous waste, and the protection of endangered species.

The EPA under the administration of President **George W. Bush** was involved in several controversies concerning the regulation of clean air and so-called "global warming." Critics of the Bush administration were angry that the EPA refused to allow state governments to require the automobile industry to improve fuel efficiency beyond federal standards. In 2007, the **Supreme Court** ruled in *Massachusetts v. Environmental Protection Agency* that the EPA has the authority to regulate the emission of greenhouse gases in automobile emissions and must do so, notwithstanding some scientific rationale for failing to take action. During the administration of George W. Bush, the EPA was directed by **Stephen Johnson** (2005–2008), **Michael Leavitt** (2003–2004), and **Christine Todd Whitman** (2001–2003).

ESTONIA. This former Soviet Republic in the Baltics became a member of the **North Atlantic Treaty Organization** (NATO) in March 2004. Just over a month later, on 1 May 2004, Estonia became a member of the **European Union.**

EURO. The "Euro" (symbol: €) replaced the European Currency Unit (ECU) in 1999. Banknotes and coins replaced national currencies in select countries in the **European Union** (EU) on 1 January 2002. As of 2008, 20 of the 27 countries of the EU use the currency. The European Central Bank (ECB), based in Frankfurt, **Germany**, controls the Euro's monetary policy. When the Euro was first adopted in 2002, the currency was on par with the US dollar. However, during the presidency of **George W. Bush**, the combination of the US budget deficit and tight monetary policy in the EU pushed the Euro to record heights, reaching $1.60 to 1 Euro in summer 2008, making European products much more expensive to American consumers.

EUROPEAN UNION (EU). Originating with the European Coal and Steel Community following World War II and subsequently the European Economic Community (EEC), the European Union (EU) is a political and economic union among 27 member states with 495 million residents. The EU boasts a single market based on the idea of free movement of labor, goods, and capital across member states. The EU adopted a single currency, the **Euro**, in January 2002. The political institutions of the EU include the Commission (executive) and Parliament (legislature), as well as the European Council and European Court of Justice. Twenty-one of the 27 EU countries are members of the **North Atlantic Treaty Organization** (NATO), which has complicated the EU's efforts to construct a common **foreign policy**.

Nations of the European Union were divided on elements of President **George W. Bush**'s **foreign policy** generally and the US-led **War in Iraq** specifically. French President **Jacques Chirac** threatened to veto any **United Nations** Security Council resolution authorizing the use of force in **Iraq** in early 2003. **Germany's** chancellor **Gerhard Schröder** was a particularly vocal critic of Bush. Yet other EU nations, including **Bulgaria**, the Netherlands, Italy, and **Great Britain**, sent troops to **Iraq** as part of the **Coalition of the Willing**.

Relations between the United States and **France** and Germany improved in Bush's second term. French President **Nicolas Sarkozy** sought closer ties with Bush and made it a point to visit the United States shortly after his election in 2007. Bush enjoyed a closer working relationship with Germany's **Angela Merkel**, who replaced Schröder in 2005.

EVANGELICAL CHRISTIANS. While there is no single, accepted definition, the term Evangelical Christian is most closely linked with Protestantism in the United States. The self-defined characteristics of Evangelical Christians may include "evangelizing" or spreading their faith to others, personal conversion (being "born again"), or emphasizing the New Testament of the Bible and the teachings of Jesus Christ over the Old Testament. On policy issues, Evangelical Christians typically oppose **gay marriage** and **abortion** and support school prayer.

Evangelical Christians comprised an increasingly important source of support for the Republican Party, beginning in the 1980s with the election of President **Ronald Reagan**. President **George W. Bush** became the Evangelicals' candidate of choice in December 1999 at a primary debate in which he stated that Jesus had had the greatest impact on his life. Exit polls suggested that Bush won between 75 and 85 percent of the evangelical vote in 2000 and 2004. Bush never described himself as "born again," and his evangelism is linked innately to his personal conversion. He accentuated his own personal, spiritual journey, which began with a meeting in 1985 with the Reverend Billy Graham, in his 1999 campaign autobiography entitled *A Charge to Keep*. Bush attributes his decision to stop drinking alcohol and focus on his family as a direct result of his personal faith.

Many observers connected elements of Bush's faith with his domestic and **foreign policies**. Bush described himself as a **compassionate conservative** who attempted to balance notions of limited government and self-help with Christian ideals. He founded the **Office of Faith-Based and Community Initiatives** in the White House to facilitate religious organizations' community outreach and private charity programs. Other observers suggest that Bush's **neoconservative** foreign policy, which calls for moral clarity in international affairs and views the United States as a force for good in the world, stems from his faith. *See also* FALWELL, JERRY L.

EVANS, DONALD LOUIS (1946–). Born in Houston, Texas, Evans graduated from the University of Texas at Austin with a bachelor's degree in mechanical engineering (1969) and a master's degree in business administration (1973). He worked in the oil business in the 1970s and 1980s, becoming chief executive officer of Tom Brown, Inc., in 1985.

Evans had extensive connections to President **George W. Bush**. When he was governor of Texas, Bush appointed Evans to the University of Texas Board of Regents (1995). Evans worked on Bush's gubernatorial campaigns in 1994 and 1998. He served as chair of the Bush presidential campaign in 2000. Bush appointed Evans secretary of commerce in 2001. He announced his resignation in November 2004, and was succeeded by **Carlos M. Gutierrez** in February 2005.

EXECUTIVE OFFICE OF THE PRESIDENT (EOP). The Executive Office of the President comprises White House offices and agencies, including the Office of Management and Budget (OMB). These offices are largely staffed by career civil servants and select appointees. The various EOP offices help develop and implement the policy and programs of the president.

President **George W. Bush** used his latitude to create an **Office of Homeland Security** in the EOP in October 2001, following the **terrorist** attacks of **11 September 2001** on New York and Washington, D.C. *See also* DEPARTMENT OF HOMELAND SECURITY; RIDGE, TOM.

EXECUTIVE PRIVILEGE. While not specifically mentioned in the US Constitution, the doctrine of executive privilege has been established through **Supreme Court** cases dating to the early Republic. Under the doctrine, presidents claim confidentiality vis-à-vis Congress or the courts with respect to advisors' counsel. Presidents may also refuse to comply with legal instruments, such as search warrants, that name them or their advisors.

President **George W. Bush** invoked executive privilege on several polemical matters. He invoked executive privilege on the inner workings of and participants in the **Energy Task Force**, to which he appointed Vice President **Richard B. (Dick) Cheney** as chair in 2001. Bush invoked executive privilege in July 2007, when congressional investigators subpoenaed White House documents from **Harriet Miers** connected to the controversial firing of US attorneys in the Department of Justice. The president also invoked executive privilege concerning the 2004 "friendly fire" death of an Army Ranger, Pat Tillman, in **Iraq**.

– F –

FALLON, WILLIAM JOSEPH (1944–). A New Jersey native, Fallon graduated from Villanova University (1967), where he was enrolled in the Navy ROTC. He entered the Navy that year, and his military career spanned four decades. He is also a graduate of the Naval War College and holds a master's degree in international studies from Old Dominion University.

A naval aviator, Fallon was deployed to Vietnam in 1974. His subsequent commands included the **Persian Gulf War** and the **North Atlantic Treaty Organization** (NATO) operations battle group fleet in Bosnia. He was vice chief of Naval Operations from 2000 to 2003. He held the command of US Fleet Forces Command and the US Atlantic Fleet from October 2003 to February 2005. From February 2005 until March 2007, he held the Pacific command.

In early January 2007, President **George W. Bush** appointed Admiral Fallon as commander of **CENTCOM** (US Central Command) to replace **John Abizaid**. CENTCOM was responsible for operations concerning the **War in Iraq**. Fallon held the position until 31 October

2008, at which time he resigned and was replaced by **David Petraeus**. Fallon's resignation stirred controversy. Secretary of Defense **Robert Gates** publicly stated that Fallon chose to resign because of an article in *Esquire* magazine that contended Fallon opposed the Bush administration on potential military action in **Iran**. Other reports suggested that Fallon had been forced to resign by his superiors because he had failed to stop the flow of weapons and **insurgents** crossing into **Iraq**.

FALWELL, JERRY LAMON, SR. (1933–2007). A self-described **Evangelical Christian**, Falwell was born in Lynchburg, Virginia. He graduated from Bible Baptist College in 1956. That same year, he founded the Thomas Road Baptist Church in Lynchburg. In 1971, he founded Liberty University, a Christian-based institution of higher **education**. A nationally known televangelist, Falwell founded the organization Moral Majority in 1979. He was deeply involved and influential in Republican politics, aiding the victory of **Ronald Reagan** in 1980 with the support of evangelicals.

Falwell's legacy of advocating for social conservatism is decidedly mixed. His supporters lauded his emphasis on family values; opposition to **abortion**, **gay marriage**, and pornography; and support of **Israel**. His detractors contended Falwell was a racist for his opposition to civil rights in the 1960s, his hostility to gay rights, and his opposition to Islam.

Falwell died on 15 May 2007 following a viral infection. He was a prolific author. His works include *Achieving Your Dreams* (2006) and *Building Dynamic Faith* (2005).

FASTOW, ANDREW STUART (1961–). A native of Washington, D.C., Fastow earned a master's of business administration degree from Northwestern University and worked for a Chicago-based bank. In 1990, he took a position with the **Enron Corporation**, an energy company, which declared bankruptcy in late 2001. In 1998, he was appointed chief financial officer of Enron.

Fastow, like Enron executives **Kenneth Lay** and Jeffrey Skilling, was implicated in a financial accounting scandal surrounding Enron's bankruptcy that was investigated by the **Securities and Exchange Commission** beginning in 2001. The scandal also involved the accounting firm **Arthur Andersen**, whose employees had obstructed justice by destroying documents. Fastow was convicted in 2004 on fraud and conspiracy charges. He paid a $23 million fine and was sentenced to six years in federal prison.

FATAH. Growing out of the **Palestine Liberation Organization** (PLO), Fatah is a political party cofounded by **Yasser Arafat** and **Mahmoud Abbas**. Although nationalist in orientation, the United States considers Fatah "moderate" and secular compared to its main rival, the Islamist party **Hamas**. Fatah lost the Palestinian parliamentary elections in 2006. In 2007, Abbas, the president of the **Palestinian National Authority**, declared a state of emergency, dismissed the Hamas government of **Ismail Haniya**, and appointed **Salam Fayyad** prime minister. Subsequent fighting between Fatah and Hamas forces left the former in charge of the **West Bank** and the latter in control of the **Gaza Strip**.

FAYYAD, SALAM (1952–). Born in Deir al-Ghosoon, **West Bank**, Palestinian Territories, Fayyad completed a master's degree in business administration from St. Edward's University and a doctorate in economics at the University of Texas (1986). He worked for the International Monetary Fund (IMF) from 1987 to 1995 and as the Palestinian representative to the IMF from 1995 to 2001. **Yasser Arafat** appointed him finance minister for the Palestinian authority in 2001. A member of the **Fatah** party, Fayyad was appointed prime minister of the **Palestinian National Authority** by **Mahmoud Abbas** in 2007. Fayyad replaced **Ismail Haniya**, whom Abbas replaced following a declaration of a state of emergency as violence escalated between Fatah and its rival party, **Hamas**, which effectively controlled the **Gaza Strip** following a de facto civil war.

FEDAYEEN SADDAM. Iraqi dictator **Saddam Hussein** formed the Fedayeen Saddam (which means "Saddam's Men of Sacrifice" in Arabic) as a paramilitary organization. The organization was headed by **Uday Hussein**, Saddam's son, in 1995. The Fedayeen were not part of the Republican Guard or Iraqi Army under Hussein. The Fedayeen pledged personal loyalty to Saddam Hussein and reported directly to him. It is estimated that the ranks of the Fedayeen stood at between

30,000 and 40,000 men prior to the US-led invasion of **Iraq** in March 2003. While the Republican Guard fell to US and other forces of the **Coalition of the Willing** by April 2003, remnants of the Fedayeen were responsible for elements of the **insurgency** that followed the **War in Iraq**. *See also* BA'ATH PARTY.

FEDERAL BUREAU OF INVESTIGATION (FBI). The FBI was formed in 1908 as a force of special federal agents called the Bureau of Investigation. Its name was changed in 1935, and it is housed as an agency within the Department of Justice, headed by the attorney general. The bureau's primary responsibility includes investigating federal crimes and cases of espionage, and providing assistance to state and local law enforcement authorities.

Following the **terrorist** attacks of **11 September 2001**, more than 3,000 of the bureau's approximately 11,000 employees were redirected to counterterrorism and counterespionage activities. Critics contended that the FBI failed to interpret intelligence from field offices in advance of the 9/11 attacks that might have thwarted the hijackings of commercial aircraft. **Robert Mueller**, who replaced Thomas J. Pickard as director of the FBI less than a week before the terrorist attacks, fell under intense congressional and media scrutiny. The agency had suffered a number of public relations fiascos in the 1990s, including incidents in Waco, Texas, and Ruby Ridge, Idaho. In February 2001, Robert Hanssen, a former FBI employee, had been convicted of selling intelligence to **Russia**.

Mueller embarked on a large-scale reorganization of the agency, which is also subject to oversight by the **Director of National Intelligence** (DNI). The FBI's budget grew substantially during the presidency of **George W. Bush**, accounting for nearly a third of the overall budget of the Department of Justice by 2007. Some critics posit that the FBI's greater focus on counterterrorism has distracted the agency from its traditional law enforcement role, placing greater burdens on state and local governments.

FEDERAL EMERGENCY MANAGEMENT AGENCY (FEMA). FEMA is the federal agency that coordinates disaster relief efforts between federal, state, and local governments. FEMA was folded into the new **Department of Homeland Security** (DHS) in March 2003, in the wake of the **11 September 2001 terrorist** attacks on New York and the **Pentagon**. Its role was changed to include responding to disasters and disaster preparedness.

FEMA came under intense congressional and public criticism for the agency's handling of federal disaster relief efforts following **Hurricane Katrina**, which made landfall near New Orleans, Louisiana, on 29 August 2005. New Orleans Mayor **Ray Nagin** and Louisiana Governor **Kathleen Babineaux Blanco** were among the most vocal critics of FEMA's director, **Michael D. Brown**. Brown's detractors contended that he had no experience in emergency management and failed to coordinate an adequate response to the Category 3 storm (using the Saffir-Simpson scale) that devastated New Orleans and the Gulf Coast, killing hundreds and leaving thousands homeless and stranded. Brown was replaced by Coast Guard Vice Admiral Thad Allen on 7 September, and resigned on 12 September. President **George W. Bush** appointed R. David Paulson, former chief of the US Fire Administration, director of FEMA in mid-September 2005.

FEMA was far more successful in managing **Hurricane Rita**, another Category 3 storm that struck the Houston, Texas, area less than a month after Katrina. The impact of Rita was not as grave as anticipated. FEMA's assistance teams helped rehabilitate the agency's reputation somewhat in the aftermath of the storm thanks to better preparation. FEMA won greater acclaim for the agency's disaster preparedness plans and early evacuation of the Houston–Galveston, Texas, area ahead of **Hurricane Ike** in September 2008.

FEDERAL HOME LOAN MORTGAGE CORPORATION. Known as "Freddie Mac," the Federal Home Loan Mortgage Corporation was created in 1970 as a government-sponsored enterprise. Freddie Mac focuses on the secondary mortgage market. The company buys mortgages, packages them into securities, and sells the mortgage-backed securities on the open market. By purchasing mortgages from lenders, Freddie Mac's goal is to ensure that funds are continuously available for mortgage financing in the primary market.

Freddie Mac's investment grade tumbled due to the **sub-prime mortgage** crisis, beginning in September 2008 with increased foreclosures on housing mortgages. As for the **Federal National Mortgage Association**, on 7 September 2008 the Federal Housing Finance

Agency (FHFA) placed Freddie Mac into conservatorship. The US Department of the Treasury invested $1 billion in Freddie Mac securities to shore up the corporation.

FEDERAL NATIONAL MORTGAGE ASSOCIATION. Often referred to as "Fannie Mae," the Federal National Mortgage Association was created in 1938. Congress chartered the agency as a private shareholder company in 1968; its status is that of a government corporation or government-sponsored enterprise. Fannie Mae focuses on three areas of housing: single-family homes, community development, and capital markets. Fannie Mae is not a direct lender. Instead, the agency ensures that funds are available to mortgage brokers and bankers, who can then lend to consumers at affordable rates.

Fannie Mae was at the center of the firestorm of the **sub-prime mortgage** crisis that began in September 2008. Like its analogue the **Federal Home Loan Mortgage Corporation** (Freddie Mac), Fannie Mae pursued programs aimed at enabling low- and middle-income families to purchase homes. Many lenders offered adjustable rate mortgages (ARMs) that provided initial repayments at interest rates below the prime rate. When the interest rate and repayment terms subsequently increased, many homeowners were unable to make the payments and faced foreclosure. As the foreclosure rate mounted, property values in the United States dropped—in some cases by 10–15 percent. Banks responded by tightening loan criteria, resulting in a shortage of credit and a glut of homes for sale.

On 7 September 2008, the Federal Housing Finance Agency (FHFA) placed Fannie Mae into conservatorship. Because Fannie Mae guaranteed approximately $6 trillion of the $12 trillion mortgage market in the United States, the Department of Treasury freed up $100 billion in capital to ensure available funds to mortgage lenders.

FEDERAL PROSECUTORS (SCANDAL). This controversy stemmed from the decision by the administration of **George W. Bush** to fire seven US attorneys in the Department of Justice in December 2006 following the **mid-term elections**. They were replaced by interim appointments at the discretion of the president. Critics of Bush and his attorney general, **Alberto Gonzales**, charged that the federal prosecutors were fired for partisan reasons. The Democratic-controlled Congress launched an investigation into the dismissals in early 2007. Bush advisor **Karl Rove** and counsel **Harriet Miers** were implicated in the probe. Bush invoked **executive privilege**, refused to turn over most of the documents connected to the firings to Congress, and contended that the prosecutors, like other appointed officials in the executive branch, serve at the pleasure of the president. The Department of Justice completed its own internal investigation of the firings in September 2008 and concluded that they were unjustified. Attorney General **Michael Mukasey**, who replaced Gonzales in November 2007, named a special prosecutor, Nora Dannehy, to determine whether criminal charges were warranted against Gonzales and others. None was filed. However, the Democratic majority in Congress altered the **PATRIOT Act** legislation to limit interim presidential appointments in the Department of Justice.

FEDERAL RESERVE. The Federal Reserve, often referred to by the media simply as the "Fed," is the central bank of the United States. The system was created in 1913 by the Federal Reserve Act. The Fed's primary directive is to control national monetary policy, or the supply of money available to banks for consumer and corporate lending. The Fed manages the federal funds rate, which is the rate banks charge one another for overnight loans of federal funds held by the Fed. The Fed also sets the discount rate, which is the amount that banks pay for direct borrowing from the federal government. Lower federal funds and discount rates typically provide larger sums of money for banks to lend. When the Fed is concerned with inflation, raising these key indexes is aimed at slowing consumer and corporate borrowing and spending.

The Fed has branches in 12 districts. Seven members of the Federal Reserve's board of governors direct the bank's operations and are appointed by the president for 14-year terms. The president is legally mandated to make those appointments with an eye to ensuring "fair representation of the financial, agricultural, industrial, and commercial interests and geographical divisions of the country." The president also appoints the chair of the Fed, who serves a four-year term. All appointments require Senate confirmation. *See also* BERNANKE,

BEN SHALOM; GREENSPAN, ALAN; TROUBLED ASSETS RE-LIEF PROGRAM (TARP).

FIELDING, FRED FISHER (1939–). A native of Philadelphia and a graduate of the University of Virginia Law School, Fielding was associate White House counsel for President Richard Nixon from 1970 to 1972. He also practiced law in Washington, D.C., for the firm of Wiley Rein. Fielding was counsel to President **Ronald Reagan** from 1981 to 1986. He was also one of ten members of the **9/11 Commission**, which was charged in 2002 with analyzing the **terrorist** attacks on New York and the **Pentagon** on **11 September 2001**. Fielding also had connections to **Blackwater Worldwide**, for which he was legal counsel, and had a close relationship with Vice President **Richard B. (Dick) Cheney**. Fielding replaced **Harriet Miers** as White House counsel to President **George W. Bush** in January 2007.

FITZGERALD, PATRICK J. (1960–). A native of the New York City borough of Brooklyn, Fitzgerald is a graduate of Amherst College and Harvard Law School (1985). In 1988, he became a US attorney for New York City. He prosecuted Mafia figures in the Gambino crime family, including John Gotti. He subsequently built up an extensive repertoire on **terrorism** issues. He prosecuted Sheikh Omar Abdel Rahman, accused of the 1993 bombing of the **World Trade Center**. He served for 13 years as assistant US attorney for the southern district of New York, acting as chief of the organized crime–terrorism unit. He investigated and prosecuted **Osama bin Laden** (in absentia) and others suspected of the 1998 bombings of US embassies in Nairobi, Kenya, and Dar-es-Salaam, Tanzania. In 2001, he became assistant US attorney for northern Illinois and headed investigations into bribery and corruption allegations against state officials. He concurrently chaired the attorney general's sub-committee on terrorism.

In December 2003, Fitzgerald was appointed special counsel to investigate the disclosure of **Valerie Plame** as a covert agent in the **Central Intelligence Agency**. The alleged leak of Plame's status led to White House officials, including **Karl Rove**, **Ari Fleischer**, Vice President **Richard B. (Dick) Cheney**, and Cheney's chief of staff,

Lewis (Scooter) Libby. Fitzgerald successfully prosecuted Libby, who was found guilty of obstruction of justice and three other counts, was fined, and sentenced to two and a half years in prison—a sentence commuted by President **George W. Bush**, who judged the sentence "excessive." No charges were filed against other White House figures in the scandal, including **Richard Armitage**, who revealed he was the source of the leak in September 2006.

In 2008, Fitzgerald began investigations into allegations that Illinois Governor **Rod Blagojevich** had attempted to sell President-elect **Barack Obama**'s US Senate seat to the "highest bidder."

FLEISCHER, LAWRENCE ARI (1960–). Born in Pound Ridge, New York, Fleischer graduated from Middlebury College (1982). Following his graduation he worked as press secretary for three members of the House of Representatives, and as a field director for the National Republican Congressional Committee. From 1989 to 1994, he worked as press secretary for New Mexico Senator Pete Domenici, and later as spokesperson for the House Committee on Ways and Means. Fleisher was President **George H.W. Bush**'s deputy communications director during the 1992 presidential campaign. Fleisher served as President **George W. Bush**'s press secretary from January 2001 through July 2003. He was succeeded by **Scott McClellan**.

Fleischer was implicated in the **Valerie Plame** affair. In 2004, he was granted immunity by prosecutor **Patrick Fitzgerald** in the trial of **I. Lewis (Scooter) Libby**, who was accused of compromising Plame's status as a covert agent in the **Central Intelligence Agency**. Plame was the spouse of Ambassador **Joseph Wilson**, a critic of the **War in Iraq**. Fleischer testified that he had discussed Plame with the news media and other White House officials after Libby had revealed her position. After leaving the White House, Fleischer took a position as a media consultant for the National Football League (NFL). *See also* ARMITAGE, RICHARD; CHENEY, RICHARD B. (DICK); ROVE, KARL.

FLIGHT 93 (UNITED AIRLINES). United Airlines Flight 93 left Newark, New Jersey, en route to San Francisco, California, on **11 September 2001**. The flight was hijacked 45 minutes after takeoff by four **al-Qaeda terrorist** operatives linked to the so-called "Hamburg Cell" based in **Germany**. After overpowering the crew and pilots, the terrorists steered the flight off its course and directed the aircraft to the southeast; the anticipated target was Washington, D.C., where the hijackers were thought to have planned to use the aircraft as a missile against either the White House or the Capitol.

When the crew and passengers of Flight 93 learned that two other commercial aircraft had been hijacked and flown into the **World Trade Center** in New York City, they revolted. The exact details of the revolt are unclear; some accounts suggest passengers and crew members regained control of the cockpit, while other accounts dispute this suggestion. Regardless, control of the aircraft was lost near rural Shanksville, Pennsylvania. Flight 93 crashed into a field, killing all 44 persons on board, including the terrorists. A permanent memorial at the crash site is scheduled to open in 2011.

FLORIDA RECOUNT. The winner of the 2000 presidential election between **George W. Bush** and **Al Gore** depended on Florida's 25 Electoral College votes. Controversy first erupted over the use of the so-called **butterfly ballot** in **Palm Beach County**, which many voters—particularly the elderly—found confusing and caused them to vote for the wrong candidate. Early results from Florida's 67 counties on 8 November showed that Bush had defeated Gore by a margin of less than a half percent, which triggered an automatic machine recount of ballots under state law. By 10 November, the statewide machine recount showed that Bush's lead had fallen to just over 300 votes. Using the discretion afforded him under Florida law, Gore petitioned four counties to conduct manual recounts: Broward, Miami-Dade, Palm Beach, and Volusia. Local election boards subsequently engaged in a painstaking recount of ballots, during which they attempted to determine voters' intentions when ballots were not completely punched through, leaving so-called "chads."

Florida law requires that counties submit their completed returns to the secretary of state no later than seven days following the election. Three of the four counties believed they could not meet that deadline. A state court ruled that the counties could later amend their returns, and the secretary of state had the discretion to amend the final results. Florida Secretary of State **Katherine Harris** noted on 14 November that she was in receipt of the results from all 67 counties, but since recounts in Broward, Miami-Dade, and Palm Beach continued, she would not certify the results until 26 November.

On 26 November, Harris certified that Bush had won Florida by 537 votes. The certification of Florida's 25 Electoral College votes put Bush over the necessary threshold of 270 to win the election. In a highly controversial move, Harris determined that there was no basis to amend the results of the disputed counties. Litigation ensued, and on 8 December the Florida Supreme Court, in a 4–3 decision, ordered a statewide manual recount of all votes. On 9 December, the US **Supreme Court** halted the recount on a 5–4 decision and scheduled oral arguments in the court case known as ***Bush v. Gore***. On 12 December, the Court made an expedited decision, and in a 7–2 vote, contended that the lack of uniform standards in the county-level recounts violated the Equal Protection Clause (Fourteenth Amendment) of the Constitution, thereby halting the recount. *See also* BAKER, JAMES ADDISON; BUSH, JOHN ELLIS (JEB); GINSBURG, BENJAMIN; LEPORE, THERESA; OLSON, THEODORE BEVRY.

FOLEY, MARK ADAM (1954–). Born in Newton, Massachusetts, Foley entered Florida politics as a city commissioner for Lake Worth in 1977. He served as vice mayor of the city from 1983 to 1984. He served in the Florida House of Representatives from 1990 to 1992, and was elected to the Florida Senate in 1993. A Republican, Foley ran successfully for Congress in 1994, when the Grand Old Party (GOP) won a majority in the House of Representatives for the first time in 40 years. He was re-elected five times from his Orlando-area constituency. He served as deputy Republican whip in 2006. While in Congress, Foley led the charge against child pornography. He was a presumptive candidate for the US Senate in both 2004 and 2006. However, rumors that he was homosexual impeded his campaigns— rumors he argued were false.

On 29 September 2006, ABC News broke a story that Foley had sent "instant messages" and e-mails to underage congressional pages that were of an explicitly sexual and inappropriate nature. Foley resigned his seat in Congress the day the news story broke. Through his attorney, Foley admitted publicly that he was gay. He alleged that he had been molested by a priest as a young man—allegations confirmed partially by the priest in question.

Foley contended that he had sent the improper computer messages while inebriated. In early October 2006, he voluntarily admitted himself to a rehabilitation clinic for alcoholism. Federal and state authorities launched criminal investigations into Foley's actions. State officials announced in September 2008 that there was insufficient evidence to charge Foley criminally. Nevertheless, the House Ethics Committee investigated a potential "cover-up" by Republican leaders, who were alleged to have known about Foley's relationships with adolescent pages for three to four years. The scandal enabled the Democrats to regain Foley's seat in Congress. **Tim Mahoney** defeated the Republican candidate in the 2006 **mid-term elections**—but faced his own scandal two years later over allegations that he had an affair with a campaign worker whom he had paid money to keep the affair quiet.

FORBES, MALCOLM STEVENSON (STEVE), JR. (1947–). Born in Morristown, New Jersey, Steve Forbes is the son of the late millionaire Malcolm Forbes and publisher of *Forbes* magazine. A graduate of Princeton University (1970), Forbes ran for the Republican presidential nomination unsuccessfully in 1996 and 2000, using his family fortune to finance his campaigns. He was a signatory of the **neoconservative Project for the New American Century** (PNAC) in 1997; the centerpiece of his presidential bids was the proposal to replace the Internal Revenue Service with a flat tax (national sales tax).

Forbes supported former New York City Mayor **Rudolph Giuliani**'s bid for the 2008 Republican presidential nomination and served as his campaign cochair. Forbes is a trustee on the board of the conservative Heritage Foundation think tank. He appears frequently on the Fox News Channel show *Forbes on Fox*, which features him and staff from *Forbes* magazine on economic and political matters.

FOREIGN INTELLIGENCE SURVEILLANCE ACT (FISA). Passed by Congress in 1978, the FISA regulates governmental surveillance and intelligence-gathering programs. It was inspired over concerns of domestic spying during the presidency of Richard Nixon.

The legislation limits governmental electronic surveillance activities and physical searches to foreign governments or their agents. Without a court order, the president may authorize surveillance for up to one year, provided there is no likelihood that a US citizen is involved. The president may also petition the FISA court for a warrant; the court must find probable cause for the surveillance, and the government must justify the petition if a US citizen is involved.

FISA was thrown into the spotlight in 2005, when media reports surfaced that the administration of **George W. Bush** had authorized the **National Security Agency** to engage in warrantless **wiretapping** of suspected **terrorists** in the United States as part of the **War on Terror**. The controversy forced Bush to request that Congress ease restrictions on domestic intelligence-gathering prohibited by FISA. In July 2007, Congress passed the Protect America Act, which enables electronic surveillance of communications in which one party is believed to be outside the United States. Congress subsequently amended FISA in 2008. Key provisions included indemnifying telecommunications companies from lawsuits stemming from government surveillance and requiring warrants for wiretapping American citizens abroad. However, the amendments allowed the government to engage in warrantless surveillance for up to seven days without court approval.

FOREIGN POLICY. The **11 September 2001 terrorist** attacks on the **World Trade Center** in New York City and the **Pentagon** in Washington, D.C., had a profound impact on the direction of US foreign policy during the administration of **George W. Bush**. The attacks, perpetrated by the terror group **al-Qaeda**, heralded the beginning of the **War on Terror**. Shortly after the attacks, Bush made it his top priority to punish those responsible for the attacks, as well as those responsible for aiding and abetting the terrorist organization. Seven days after the attacks, Congress passed the **Authorization for the Use of Military Force Against Terrorists** (AUMF) bill, which gave formal authority for the president to pursue the attackers.

On 7 October 2001, the United States, along with a coalition that included **Great Britain**, invaded **Afghanistan**. President Bush contended that intelligence showed that the **Taliban** regime, which had gained power in 1996, had allowed al-Qaeda operatives to train in Afghanistan and otherwise gave material support and succor to supporters of the suspected mastermind of the 9/11 attacks, **Osama bin Laden**. Initially, some 20,000 coalition troops battled the Taliban, aided by the **Northern Alliance**. Some of the heaviest fighting occurred in the **Tora Bora** region in eastern Afghanistan, where bin Laden was thought to have been hiding. The capital of **Kabul** fell to coalition troops in November 2001. Upon their capture, many Taliban prisoners, labeled **enemy combatants** by the president, were relocated by US forces to **Guantanamo Bay, Cuba**, for indefinite detention or eventual trial by **military tribunals**. By 2003, US and coalition forces faced a significant **insurgency** by remnants of the Taliban regime under leader **Mullah Omar**. Many insurgents, who used **improvised explosive devices** (IEDs) to battle coalition forces, crossed the border from **Pakistan** into Afghanistan. By January 2006, **North Atlantic Treaty Organization** (NATO) troops, as part of the **International Security Assistance Force** (ISAF), began replacing US troops to secure and engage in reconstruction of the country.

The invasion of Afghanistan, followed by the president's clarifications in his 2002 State of the Union address, solidified several cornerstones in the so-called **Bush Doctrine** in foreign policy. First, the United States would take diplomatic as well as military action against terrorist organizations that threatened the country. Second, the United States would also take action against any regime that aided, abetted, or harbored terrorist organizations. The Bush Doctrine is widely regarded as a **neoconservative** foreign policy inasmuch as its tenets are grounded in notions of "moral clarity" in international relations, interventionism when it is in the United States' perceived national interest, staunch support for the state of **Israel**, and suspicion of international institutions such as the **United Nations** (UN). Members of the **Project for the New American Century** (PNAC) think-tank, including members of the president's closest advisors such as Vice President **Richard B. (Dick) Cheney**, vice presidential Chief of Staff **I. Lewis (Scooter) Libby**, Secretary of Defense **Donald Rumsfeld**, and Undersecretary of Defense **Paul Wolfowitz**, articulated these themes throughout the 1990s.

The third element to the Bush Doctrine in foreign policy concerned the right of the United States to engage in **preemptive warfare**, unilaterally if necessary, were an attack imminent. In his 2002 State of the Union address, Bush called the regimes of **Iran, Iraq**, and **North Korea** an **axis of evil** for their pursuit of **weapons of mass destruction** (WMDs), whether chemical, biological, or nuclear. The United States subsequently pursued diplomatic sanctions against Iran and North Korea, while the administration increasingly contemplated military action against Iraq.

The policy of preemption was boldly asserted by the Bush administration in the buildup to the **War in Iraq**, which commenced in March 2003. Under the terms of the post-**Persian Gulf War** settlement of 1991, Iraqi dictator **Saddam Hussein** was to allow UN weapons inspectors unfettered access to military and other installations to ensure that Iraq was not stockpiling WMDs that could threaten its neighbors. Moreover, the United States and **Great Britain** imposed "no-fly" zones on Hussein's regime in a bid to contain any potential militarism. By Fall 2002 Hussein stopped complying with UN weapons inspectors and expelled them from the country. Although Chief Weapons Inspector **Hans Blix** doubted that Hussein had stockpiled WMDs, the United States—led by Secretary of State **Colin Powell**—began pushing the UN for military action. Critics charged that Bush's key advisors hoped to accomplish what President **George H.W. Bush** had not accomplished in the Persian Gulf War—regime change in Iraq and a toppling of Hussein's government—even though the elder Bush and the international coalition he assembled had no such mandate.

In October 2002, Congress passed the **Iraq War Resolution** giving Bush authority to take decisive military action against Iraq as the president pursued the issue in the UN. Controversy centered on **United Nations Resolution 1441**, which called for "serious consequences" if Hussein refused to comply with weapons inspectors. Disagreement among UN Security Council members, most notably between the United States and **France** and **Russia**, focused on the precise consequences. French President **Jacques Chirac** advocated greater economic sanctions against Hussein's regime, while Bush was determined to take military action. Chirac ultimately threatened to veto any UN resolution mandating military force, causing a rift not only between the United States and France but within members of NATO. As a result, Bush assembled a **Coalition of the Willing** nations, including Australia, Denmark, Great Britain, the Netherlands, and **Poland**, to invade Iraq on 20 March 2003 in the absence of a UN authorization.

Within six weeks of the invasion, US and coalition forces crushed Iraq's **Republican Guard** and drove Hussein from power. As in Afghanistan, however, a protracted insurgency followed that drove the death toll to more than 4,000 US troops by the end of 2008. Progress in establishing a new democratic regime in Iraq was halting, beginning with the **Coalition Provisional Authority** led by **Jay Garner** and then **L. Paul Bremer**, which was eventually replaced by an **Iraq Governing Council**. Of paramount concern was the reconciliation of Sunni, Shi'ite, and **Kurd**ish factions within the new governmental structures. Regardless, in 2004, the Iraq Survey Group headed by **David Kay** found no evidence of stockpiles of WMDs in Iraq, nor did **Mohammed ElBaradei**, the head of the UN's **International Atomic Energy Agency** (IAEA). Critics charged that the rush to war in Iraq was unnecessary and unfounded, bolstered as they were by the **Downing Street Memo**, leaked in 2005. The memo, penned by the British secret service, alleged that Bush had fixed intelligence to match his desire to force regime change in Iraq.

One notable element of unilateralism in foreign policy in the Bush administration included the United States' withdrawal from the **Anti-Ballistic Missile (ABM) Treaty**, originally signed with the **Soviet Union** in the 1970s. Bush announced the termination of US compliance with the treaty in 2001 and his plans to place a missile defense system in the **Czech Republic** and **Poland**. Russian Presidents **Vladimir Putin** and **Dmitri Medvedev** bitterly opposed the plans, and Putin suggested that Russia might retarget European cities with nuclear missiles if the plan were implemented. A summit between Bush and Putin in April 2008 did not yield any agreement.

Bilateral relations between the United States and Russia became increasingly strained over the course of Bush's two terms. Russia's invasion of **Georgia** in August 2008 drew scathing condemnations from the president. Moreover, the Russian navy's joint exercises with Venezuelan leader **Hugo Chávez**'s military forces in 2008 raised speculation of a new **Cold War** between the United States and Russia despite Secretary of State **Condoleezza Rice**'s dismissal of such allegations. Still, in 2003, Bush and Russian President Putin signed the **Strategic Offensive Reduction Treaty**, which limited the United States and Russia to no more than 2,200 offensive nuclear warheads. The treaty came into effect in July 2003, and represented one of the most important bilateral treaties on nuclear weapons since the end of Cold War.

Apart from conflict surrounding the War in Iraq, relations between the United States and countries of the **European Union** (EU) were generally positive—and improved over the course of Bush's second term. Great Britain remained a steadfast ally of the United States throughout Bush's two terms, and the president enjoyed a particularly deep friendship with Prime Minister **Tony Blair**. While German Chancellor **Gerhard Schröder** and French President Jacques Chirac were outspoken critics of the US-led invasion of Iraq, their successors set out to improve relations with the United States and were ideologically more compatible with Bush. **Angela Merkel** became chancellor of Germany in November 2005, and her concerns about the detention camp at Guantanamo Bay notwithstanding, actively supported the War on Terror. In June 2007, **Nicolas Sarkozy** won the French presidential election and made a special trip to the Bush family compound in Kennebunkport, Maine, to repair bilateral relations. Many newer members of the EU and NATO, including **Poland** and Denmark, sent troops to Iraq. Moreover, NATO witnessed an impressive expansion into countries that were former Soviet satellites and members of the **Warsaw Pact**—much to the chagrin of Russian President Vladimir Putin. **Bulgaria**, **Estonia**, **Latvia**, **Lithuania**, **Romania**, **Slovakia**, and **Slovenia** joined NATO in 2004. Two years earlier, NATO and the EU negotiated a pivotal agreement to allow the EU to use NATO resources separately in an international crisis if the entire organization did not wish to act. Finally, Bush lent support for ongoing efforts to bring peace to **Northern Ireland**, which had embarked on a power-sharing agreement between Catholics and Protestants. He visited Northern Ireland in June 2008 to meet with key political leaders, and called the political progress over the last decade "unimaginable."

Relations between the United States and its North American neighbors were also generally positive. On 11 September 2001, **Canada** allowed US commercial jets to land there, and many Canadians opened their homes to stranded Americans as US airspace remained closed for several days. Although Canadian Prime Minister **Jean Chrétien** opposed the War in Iraq, Canada sent a considerable contingent of forces to Afghanistan. Canadian forces remained following the ouster of the Taliban as part of the ISAF. Trade relations also improved between the United States and Canada as US Trade Representative **Susan Schwab** finalized an agreement with her Canadian counterpart that ended a five-year dispute over softwood lumber exports to the United States in 2006. Bush enjoyed a cordial relationship with Chrétien's successor, **Paul Martin**. Although Bush could not convince him to join a missile defense system for North America, Martin pledged $200 million in aid for the reconstruction of Iraq and undertook measures to bolster border security. In the closing years of his presidency, Bush also enjoyed a strong relationship Prime Minister **Stephen Harper**. Harper's Conservative Party was the only Canadian Party to support the US-led invasion of Iraq.

With the exception of Cuba and **Venezuela**, relations between the United States and Latin America were also largely positive. Venezuelan leader Hugo Chávez's incendiary rhetoric against the United States and personal invectives against Bush, as well as his attempt to maintain high oil prices in the midst of a slowing global economy, contributed to a marked deterioration in bilateral cooperation. Despite **Fidel Castro**'s decision to step down as leader, his successor and brother, Raul, exhibited little signs of progressive change, and the United States maintained its restrictive trade and travel policies towards Cuba. Relations with Mexico, however, were far more positive. Bush enjoyed a solid working relationship with Mexican Presidents **Vicente Fox** and Felipe Calderón. Although Bush and his Mexican counterparts frequently disagreed on US **immigration** policy, enhanced cooperation on drug enforcement and border security was notable.

Humanitarian crises and civil war dominated relations with Africa. Critics charged that the Bush administration did too little to halt widespread murder of civilians in the troubled region of **Darfur** in **Sudan**. Secretary of State **Colin Powell** argued that the Sudanese government's support of *janjaweed* militias that killed and maimed tens of thousands was tantamount to genocide. Bush eschewed direct military action by the United States but supported UN efforts to send peacekeepers as it became evident that troops from the **African Union**—which received considerable aid from the US Congress— were insufficiently trained to quell the violence. In the Democratic Republic of the Congo, a civil war that began in 1998 continued unabated despite the signing of peace agreements in 2003. In January 2008, the International Rescue Committee reported that the conflict had killed more than 5 million people. On a more positive note, the Bush administration's efforts to halt the spread of **acquired immune deficiency syndrome** (AIDS) in Africa won international acclaim. Bush's Emergency Plan for AIDS relief in Africa, begun in 2003, pledged $15 billion over five years to stem the tide of the pandemic largely through new antiretroviral treatments now available. The number of Africans receiving treatment rose from 50,000 in 2003 to 1.3 million by 2007. The program was widely hailed as saving thousands of lives. Detractors, however, noted that the program did not include **abortion** or contraception as a means of AIDS prevention.

Relations between the United States and countries in Asia were, on balance, positive. The United States solidified its trading partnership with India, cooperating to halt the proliferation of nuclear weapons, and India strongly supported the War on Terror. Relations with **Pakistan** were at times more problematic. Pakistani President **Pervez Musharraf** would not allow the United States to hunt for suspected terrorists on Pakistani territory, and military incursions by the United States into the region of **Waziristan** in northern Pakistan strained bilateral rapport. Relations with **China** appeared problematic at the outset of Bush's first term, when a US military plane collided with a Chinese aircraft. The US crew was detained by the Chinese, who claimed that the United States had invaded their airspace; the crew was not released until the State Department issued an apology over the incident. Bush also criticized China for continually devaluing its currency, which added significantly to the US trade deficit, and remained critical over China's human rights policies. Nonetheless, Bush forged strong working relationships with China's leaders, attended the 2008 Summer Olympics in Beijing, and both countries opened new embassies in each other's capitals in an effort to strengthen bilateral relations. Throughout his two terms, Bush emphasized the need for solid trade relations with Japan. And he looked to Japan, as well as China and South Korea, to pressure the **North Korean** regime of **Kim Jong Il** to halt its WMD program as part of "six-party talks" that included Russia. Progress on North Korea was halting, but the support of Asian allies proved vital. On 9 October 2006, North Korea tested a nuclear weapon underground that caused international alarm. Just four months later, however, the talks yielded an agreement whereby North Korea agreed to suspend its nuclear weapons program and allow inspectors from the IAEA to verify dismantling of the facility at Yongbyon. Relations between the United States and North Korea were normalized, and in October 2008, North Korea was removed from the Department of State's list of state sponsors of terrorism.

The search for a broad peace in the Middle East proved elusive over Bush's two terms. Diplomatic efforts failed regarding Iran's nuclear program, and Iranian President **Mahmoud Ahmadinejad**'s fiery anti-American rhetoric did little to improve bilateral relations. Perhaps Bush's greatest failure was the **Road Map for Peace**—an attempt to reconcile the Israeli–Palestinian conflict that did not gain traction. Parliamentary elections in the Palestinian Territories in 2006 left the terrorist organization **Hamas** in control of the **Gaza Strip** and the moderate **Fatah** party in control of the **West Bank**, all but ensuring the plan's failure. The Bush administration's support for **Israel**'s war against **Lebanon** in 2006 further derailed support for the peace plan among Arab countries. Relations with **Syria** reached a nadir as the Bush administration accused Syria of enabling terrorist groups such as al-Qaeda to cross the border into Iraq to join the insurgency against US and coalition troops. One bright spot, however, was **Libya**. In 2003, the Libyan government announced that it was suspending its pursuit of WMDs. In 2006, the United States removed Libya from the Department of State list of state sponsors of terrorism and sought to restore full diplomatic relations.

Although Bush could not gain support for a UN mandate to invade Iraq, the relationship between the United States and the UN was more cooperative in a host of other ways. Following the US- and NATO-led invasion of Afghanistan in October 2001, the UN quickly approved the ISAF, which was charged with rebuilding the country. The UN also coordinated an international disaster relief program to aid victims of the 2004 **tsunami** that devastated countries in Southeast Asia. The

World Health Organization played an important role in coordinating an international response to outbreaks of Asian Bird Flu and Severe Acute Respiratory Syndrome (SARS) in Asia. The IAEA monitored WMD programs in Iran and provided vital information. In addition, Secretary General **Kofi Annan** emphasized programs of UNICEF, the UN's agency concerned with **women**, children, and poverty and targeting the plight of individuals in the developing world, including the AIDS pandemic; for this, he received strong US support. The **International Criminal Court** (ICC) and the International Criminal Tribunal for the former Yugoslavia pursued alleged war criminals from conflicts spanning Africa to the war in **Yugoslavia** in the 1990s.

The United States dominated the World Bank, which was headed by two key **neoconservatives** in the Bush administration, **Paul Wolfowitz** and **Robert Zoellick**, who focused on trade and the indebtedness of developing countries. Finally, whatever the reservations some in the Bush administration had about Kofi Annan, relations with his successor, **Ban Ki-moon** of South Korea, were smooth.

The Bush administration was acutely involved in matters of international trade. In 2001, the United States participated in the so-called "Doha Round" of the World Trade Organization, which sought to address trade difficulties and agricultural practices in developing countries. Bush also spearheaded a significant effort to enhance free trade in the Northern Hemisphere. The president negotiated, and in 2005 Congress approved, the **Central American Free Trade Agreement** (CAFTA) between the United States and Costa Rica, the Dominican Republic, El Salvador, Guatemala, Honduras, and Nicaragua. The agreement reduced tariff and nontariff barriers to trade among member countries. *See also* ARMED FORCES; BROWN, GORDON; HU JINTAO; KYOTO PROTOCOL; NUCLEAR NON-PROLIFERATION TREATY; OLMERT, EHUD; SHARON, ARIEL.

FOX QUESADA, VICENTE (1942–). Born in Mexico City, **Mexico**, Fox studied business at the Universidad Iberoamericana and Harvard University. Fox was president of Coca-Cola Corporation in Mexico and eventually for all Latin American operations. He entered politics in 1988, forming a political party and winning a seat in the legislature. In 1991, he unsuccessfully ran for the governorship of Guanajuato state in Mexico's central highlands. He won his second attempt for governor in 1995 in a landslide vote.

Fox used his position as governor to launch his bid for the presidency in 2000. His center-left political coalition was successful in ousting Ernesto Zedillo. Fox's victory was the first time that a party in opposition to the Institutional Revolutionary Party had carried a presidential election since 1920. He served as president until December 2006, when he was succeeded by Felipe Calderón.

President **George W. Bush** angered Canadian Prime Minister **Jean Chrétien** by making his first trip abroad to visit Fox in Mexico. Traditionally, US presidents visit **Canada** first. Bush attempted to work with Fox to reduce illegal **immigration** into the United States, but a comprehensive solution was never reached by the US Congress. Although Bush and Fox were thought to have enjoyed a cordial relationship with one another, when appointed to the **United Nations** Security Council, Mexico did not support the **War in Iraq**. Fox also made controversial comments about Bush in his book *Revolution of Hope* (2007), suggesting that Bush was a "windshield cowboy" afraid of Fox's horse. Fox also revealed that he and Bush discussed plans to extend the North American Free Trade Agreement (NAFTA) into a single-currency zone akin to the **European Union**.

FRANCE. Relations between France, a leader of the **European Union**, and the United States were exceedingly volatile during President **George W. Bush**'s two terms. **Jacques Chirac**, a neo-Gaullist, won election in 1997 and was president of France when Bush took office in 2000. Chirac won re-election for a five-year term in 2002. Chirac was at the forefront of international sympathy for the United States following the **terrorist** attacks of **11 September 2001** on New York and the **Pentagon**. He also supported the invasion of **Afghanistan**, and sent troops to support the **North Atlantic Treaty Organization** (NATO) contingent, although France is not part of NATO's unified command structure.

However, relations between Bush and Chirac soured in the months leading up to the US-led invasion of **Iraq** in March 2003. Chirac opposed military action against the regime of **Saddam Hussein** for the dictator's failure to comply with **United Nations** (UN) weapons inspectors, who had been expelled from Iraq in 2002. Instead, Chirac proposed greater economic sanctions. Disagreement between France and the United States centered on interpretations of the "serious consequences" contemplated by **United Nations Resolution 1441** if Hussein continued hindering international efforts to verify that Iraq was not stockpiling **weapons of mass destruction** (WMDs). In March 2003, Chirac threatened to veto any UN security council resolution authorizing the use of force. As a result, Bush assembled a **Coalition of the Willing** nations to invade Iraq without a UN mandate. Chirac became a strong critic of the **War in Iraq**, and was particularly taken aback by the Bush administration's refusal to award contracts to France in the rebuilding of postwar Iraq. Anti-French sentiment reached staggering proportions in the United States, as evidenced by some individuals promising not to buy French products and pouring French wine into the gutters.

Chirac did not run for a third term in 2007. His successor, **Nicolas Sarkozy**, pledged to rebuild the US–French relationship. One of Sarkozy's first trips abroad was to visit Bush at his family's compound in Kennebunkport, Maine. Both leaders affirmed the two countries' traditional alliance and promised greater economic and **foreign policy** cooperation in the future. Sarkozy appointed Bernard Kouchner as his foreign minister, which aided in improving foreign relations between France and the United States. Kouchner had supported ousting Hussein from Iraq, albeit for reasons of the Iraqi dictator's brutality. *See also* DE VILLEPIN, DOMINIQUE MARIE FRANCOIS RENÉ GALOUZEAU; GISCARD D'ESTAING, VALÉRY MARIE RENÉ GEORGES; KOUCHNER, BERNARD.

FRANKS, TOMMY RAY (1945–). A native of Wynnewood, Oklahoma, Franks attended the University of Texas at Austin before joining the Army in 1965. He finished a degree at the University of Texas at Arlington (1971) and later graduated from the Armed Forces Staff College. He attended the Army War College and graduated with a master's degree in public administration from Shippensburg University (Pennsylvania). In the 1970s and 1980s, he was stationed in West **Germany**, the **Pentagon**, and Fort Hood, Texas. Franks was a commander in the **Persian Gulf War** (1991) and was later stationed in South Korea, where he commanded an infantry division.

From July 2000 to July 2003 Franks was commander of **CENTCOM**. Following the **terrorist** attacks of **11 September 2001**, he commanded the US-led invasion of **Afghanistan** that toppled the **Taliban** regime. Franks then headed the invasion of **Iraq** in 2003, which ousted dictator **Saddam Hussein**. Franks was criticized for elements of the execution of the **War in Iraq**. Some critics contended that he had not anticipated how the "irregulars" of the **Fedayeen Saddam** would generate the **insurgency** in **Baghdad** and elsewhere following the collapse of the Iraqi Army. Others posited that Franks did not have enough troops for the mission in Iraq because Secretary of Defense **Donald Rumsfeld** wanted troop levels to remain low.

Franks retired as commander of CENTCOM in 2003 and was succeeded by **John Abizaid**. He started a consulting business, and he sits on several boards, including Bank of America.

FRIST, WILLIAM HARRISON (BILL) SR. (1952–). Born in Nashville, Tennessee, Frist graduated from Princeton University (1974) and earned a medical degree from Harvard University (1978). He is a specialist in cardiology, and worked at hospitals in Massachusetts, England, and California before establishing the Vanderbilt Transplant Center in his native Tennessee in 1989.

Frist entered politics in the early 1990s, working for the re-election of **George H.W. Bush** in 1992. In 1994, Frist rode the Republican wave in the **mid-term elections** and successfully challenged Democratic incumbent Senator Jim Sasser in Tennessee. Frist was re-elected with more than 60 percent of the statewide vote in 2000.

Frist chaired the National Republican Senatorial Committee from 2001 to 2003 and was credited with aiding the Republicans to regain a majority in the upper chamber in the mid-term elections of 2002. Frist first gained national attention in 1998, when he gave medical aid to two US Capitol Police officers who were shot. He was the principal spokesman for the Senate after letters containing **anthrax** were sent to the offices of **Tom Daschle** and **Patrick Leahy**.

Frist became majority leader of the Senate in 2003, succeeding **Trent Lott**, who made controversial statements about fellow Senator Strom Thurmond's 1948 presidential bid that forced him to step down. Frist was a strong supporter of President **George W. Bush**'s agenda and helped marshal bills ranging from **tax cuts** to the **Partial-Birth Abortion Ban**, although he parted ways with the president over issues surrounding **stem-cell research**.

Frist limited his service in Congress to two terms and did not stand for re-election in 2006. He returned to the practice of medicine. He was rumored to have been a possible candidate for the presidency in 2008 but did not run. He is also rumored as a gubernatorial candidate in Tennessee in 2010. Frist is author of several books, including *Transplant: A Heart Surgeon's Account of the Life-and-Death Dramas of the New Medicine* (1989), *When Every Moment Counts: What You Need to Know About Bioterrorism from the Senate's Only Doctor* (2002), and coauthor of *Tennessee Senators, 1911–2001: Portraits of Leadership in a Century of Change* (1999).

FRUM, DAVID. *See* AXIS OF EVIL.

– G –

GADHAFI, MU'AMMAR (1942–). *See* LIBYA.

GADHAN, ADAM YAHIYE (1978–). Born in Orange County, California, as Adam Pearlman, Gadhan is also known as "Azzam the American" or in Arabic "Azzam al-Amriki." At age 17, he converted to Islam. He later renounced his American citizenship and supported **jihad** or holy war against the United States. A suspected **terrorist** who joined **al-Qaeda** sometime after 2000, Gadhan is believed to have met with **Khalid Sheikh Mohammed** and is thought to be hiding in **Afghanistan**. Through 2008, he appeared in five different al-Qaeda English-language video messages in which he threatened and/or chastised the United States. In 2006, Gadhan was indicted on charges of treason by a federal court in Southern California. He is the first American charged with treason since 1952. Rumors of his death following US military operations in Afghanistan circulated in 2007 but were never confirmed. *See also* LINDH, JOHN WALKER; WAR ON TERROR.

GARNER, JAY MONTGOMERY (1938–). A native of Arcadia, Florida, Garner earned an undergraduate degree from Florida State University and a master's degree in public administration from Shippensburg University in Pennsylvania. Garner joined the Army in 1962 and is a Vietnam War veteran. He also served in the **Persian Gulf War** as a missile battalion commander. Following the military operations in **Iraq**, Garner headed operations to aid displaced **Kurds** in northern Iraq. He later worked on **anti-ballistic missile** defense issues before retiring as a lieutenant general in 1997. Garner worked for defense contractors for several years and served on a presidential panel on missile defense chaired by **Donald Rumsfeld**.

In April 2003, President **George W. Bush** appointed Garner to head reconstruction efforts following the **War in Iraq** (formally known as the Office of Reconstruction and Humanitarian Assistance). Garner was succeeded by **L. Paul Bremer** less than a month after his appointment. Critics charged that Garner had not done enough to halt the looting of antiquities in **Baghdad** in the immediate aftermath of the war. Others suggested that President George W. Bush replaced him because Garner wanted speedy elections and a more limited US role in the administration of Iraq—a charge denied by Secretary of Defense Donald Rumsfeld.

GATES, ROBERT MICHAEL (1943–). A Kansas native, Gates earned a doctoral degree in Russian and Soviet history from Georgetown University (1974). He joined the **Central Intelligence Agency** (CIA) in 1966. He served on the **National Security Council** from 1974 to 1979 under presidents Gerald Ford and Jimmy Carter before returning to the CIA. He became deputy director of the CIA under President **Ronald Reagan** in 1986. President **George H.W. Bush** named Gates deputy **national security advisor** in 1989, and he remained in that post during the **Persian Gulf War**. Bush nominated him to direct the CIA in 1991. Gates remained at the CIA until President **William Clinton** took office in January 1993. He taught at several universities before being named interim dean, and later president, of Texas A&M University.

Gates served as a member of the **9/11 Commission** that was charged with studying the **terrorist** attacks on New York and the **Pentagon** on **11 September 2001**. He was mentioned as a candidate for secretary of the **Department of Homeland Security** when the agency began operations in 2003, and rumors surfaced in 2005 that he would become the **Director of National Intelligence**.

President **George W. Bush** appointed Gates secretary of defense in November 2006, succeeding **Donald Rumsfeld**, whose handling of the **War in Iraq** had been widely criticized. In early 2007, Gates became caught up in a scandal surrounding treatment of veterans at the **Walter Reed Army Medical Center** in Bethesda, Maryland, and he fired the director. Gates recommended **Mike Mullen** to succeed **Peter Pace** as chair of the **Joint Chiefs of Staff** in 2007; Pace was expected to face intense pressure in reconfirmation in the Senate over the **insurgency** in **Iraq**. In February 2008, Gates attempted to persuade **Turkey** to halt military operations in northern Iraq, where **Kurdish** rebels had set up camp.

Gates is the recipient of numerous medals, including the Presidential Citizens Medal and the National Security Medal. He is author of *From the Shadows: The Ultimate Insider's Story of Five Presidents and How They Won the Cold War* (1996).

GAY MARRIAGE. Also known as same-sex or homosexual marriage, the term refers to the legal recognition of marriage between two individuals of the same gender. In 1996, the Congress passed, and President **William Clinton** signed, the Defense of Marriage Act, which was a response to the possibility that Hawaii would legalize same-sex marriages. The act provided that states are under no obligation to recognize gay marriages performed in other states (as would otherwise be the case under the Full Faith and Credit Clause of the Constitution), and the federal government would not recognize gay marriages performed in states that allowed them.

Opponents of gay marriage posit that a redefinition of marriage to allow for same-sex unions opens up the possibility of other nontraditional marriages, including polygamy. Some of the most vocal critics of gay marriage are opposed on religious grounds, including many **Evangelical Christians**. President **George W. Bush** opposed gay marriage and, in October 2003, suggested that marriage needed to be "codified" as the union between one man and one woman. In 2004, Bush advocated an amendment to the US Constitution that barred gay marriages. In 2006, the House and Senate failed to pass the Federal Marriage Amendment Act by the two-thirds vote necessary. As a result, more than 30 states have adopted state-level defense-of-marriage acts that do not allow same-sex unions. In 2008, Arizona, California, and Florida voters approved ballot measures banning gay marriage.

GAZA STRIP. An area of only 139 square miles, the Gaza Strip has a population of approximately 1.4 million. It is bordered by the Mediterranean Sea and surrounded by **Israel**. Political control of the Gaza Strip was transferred from Israel to the **Palestinian National Authority** in 1994 as part of a peace agreement (Oslo Accords). The other territory controlled by the Palestinian National Authority is the **West Bank**, which is entirely cut off from the Gaza Strip and also surrounded on all sides by Israel.

In 2006, the radical Islamist party **Hamas** won legislative elections in the Palestinian Territories. The United States, **Canada**, and the **European Union** considered Hamas a **terrorist** organization and rescinded all international aid. A centerpiece of Hamas's ideology is the call for the destruction of the Israeli state. The president of the Palestinian Authority, **Mahmoud Abbas**—a member of the moderate **Fatah** party who was supported by President **George W. Bush**—declared a state of emergency in 2007 and dismissed Hamas leader **Ismail Haniya**, who many Palestinians believed was the legitimate prime minister. Months of fighting in what amounted to a civil war between Hamas and Fatah militias eventually left Haniya in control of the Gaza Strip and Fatah in control of the West Bank. *See also* FAYYAD, SALAM; ROAD MAP FOR PEACE.

GEMAYEL, PIERRE AMINE (1972–2006). Educated in law, Gemayel was a Lebanese politician of the pro-Western parliamentary group "the March 14 Alliance" who opposed **Syria**'s occupation of war-torn **Lebanon**. He was assassinated on 21 November 2006 by three armed gunmen in Beirut a day before Lebanon's independence day celebration. The gunmen stated that Gemayel's assassination stemmed from his opposition to Syria and the radical Islamist group **Hezbollah**. The **United Nations** and the United States condemned his killing. The Syrian government was suspected of involvement, which it categorically denied. Gemayel's killing was preceded by the assassination of Lebanese Prime Minister **Rafik Hariri** in February 2005.

GENEVA CONVENTION(S). Last revised in 1949, the Geneva Conventions constitute four treaties that together govern nations' treatment of the wounded, prisoners of war, and civilians in a time of armed conflict. The United States, along with 150 other countries, is a signatory.

Following the **11 September 2001 terrorist** attacks and the subsequent **War on Terror**, the administration of **George W. Bush** contended that suspected **Taliban** and **al-Qaeda** terrorists captured in **Afghanistan, Iraq**, and elsewhere were unlawful **enemy combatants** who were not protected by the Third Geneva Convention, which provides prisoner-of-war protections. The Bush administration used the naval base at **Guantanamo Bay, Cuba**, as a holding facility and planned to try the suspected terrorists using **military tribunals**. In successive cases, the **Supreme Court** ruled against the White House with respect to enemy combatants' rights of **habeas corpus** in US civilian courts.

International human rights groups such as Amnesty International and the International Red Cross were critical of the conditions at Guantanamo Bay and demanded permission to inspect the facility, which the Bush administration denied. These and other groups also demanded information on the practice of **rendition**, or sending prisoners to countries without paramount civil liberties protections, where they might be tortured in the pursuit of intelligence information. *See also* ABU GHRAIB; ARMED FORCES; ASHCROFT, JOHN; *BOUMEDIENE V. BUSH*; GONZALES, ALBERTO; *HAMDAN V. RUMSFELD*; IRELAND; MCCAIN, JOHN; MILITARY COMMISSIONS ACT; *RASUL V. BUSH*; WATERBOARDING.

GEOGHAN, JOHN J. (1935–2003). A Catholic priest in the Boston, Massachusetts, archdiocese, Geoghan was sentenced in 2002 to 10 years in prison for assault and battery of a child. Although he was defrocked in 1998, during his trial many new victims stepped forward with allegations of sexual abuse. Geoghan was suspected of molesting as many as 130 children over several decades. The Boston archdiocese, and Cardinal **Bernard Law**, came under intense scrutiny when reports surfaced that throughout Geoghan's career he had been relocated to different parishes after allegations of child molestation were made. Law resigned in December 2002 as the archdiocese sought to settle victim lawsuits on the order of $10 million. Geoghan was murdered in a Shirley, Massachusetts, correctional facility on 23 August 2003.

GEORGIA. Situated at the intersection of the European and Asian continents in the Caucasus Mountains, Georgia was a republic of the **Soviet Union** after 1917; it gained independence in 1991. In August 2008, open military confrontation erupted between Georgia and **Russia** over the disputed territories of South Ossetia and Abkhazia. Both territories have substantial numbers of ethnic Russians. The Georgian military engaged separatist groups in South Ossetia, prompting the Russian government to make claims of genocide against ethnic Russians. Russia sent troops to Georgia, expelling the Georgian military from South Ossetia and eventually occupying a third of Georgian territory. French President and acting **European Union** President **Nicolas Sarkozy** met with Russian President **Dmitri Medvedev** to broker a peace accord less than two weeks after hostilities began. The agreement called for the withdrawal of Russian troops to the status quo that existed before hostilities began, and was accepted by Medvedev and Georgian President **Mikhail Saakashvili**. President **George W. Bush** called the Russian military invasion of Georgia unacceptable and contended that Russia had damaged its credibility in world affairs. Russia withdrew most of its troops from Georgia by October 2008, although military contingents remained in South Ossetia and Abkhazia.

GEPHARDT, RICHARD (DICK) ANDREW (1941–). A native of St. Louis, Missouri, Gephardt earned a bachelor's degree from Northwestern University (1962) and a law degree from the University of Michigan (1965). He entered private practice and served in the Missouri Air National Guard. Active in St. Louis Democratic Party politics after law school, Gephardt won a seat in the House of Representatives in 1976. He retired in 2004 after winning re-election 13 times. A Democrat with strong ties to labor unions and an opponent of free trade, including the North American Free Trade Agreement (NAFTA), Gephardt was majority leader from 1989 to 1994. He served as minority leader from 1995 to 2002.

Gephardt ran unsuccessfully for the Democratic presidential nomination in 1988 and 2004. He dropped out of the 1988 race due to lagging finances after early wins against the eventual nominee, Michael Dukakis. In 2004, he entered the crowded race for the Democratic nomination against contenders **John Kerry**, **John Edwards**, **Howard Dean**, and **Joe Lieberman**. Despite significant labor union support, Gephardt's campaign failed to gain momentum, suffered from a lack of funding, and was harmed by his initial support of the **War in Iraq**.

Upon his retirement in 2004, Gephardt returned to law practice and served as a consultant to the financial firm of Goldman Sachs.

GERMANY. Reunified in 1990, Germany held two elections and had two different chancellors during the presidency of **George W. Bush**.

Left-wing leader **Gerhard Schröder** of the Social Democratic Party (SDP) became chancellor in 1998 after forming an alliance with the Green Party. The election marked a watershed as the first "red–green" coalition and the first left-of-center government since the end of World War II. Schröder led the coalition to another victory in September 2002 and was a staunch opponent of the **War in Iraq**. In 2005, a center-right coalition of Christian Democrats under the leadership of **Angela Merkel** performed better than Schröder's party, but was compelled to gain SDP support for a working majority—but Merkel was able nevertheless to secure the chancellorship for herself. Merkel enjoyed much warmer relations with Bush; in 2003, she ran afoul of Schröder and many other European leaders, including French President **Jacques Chirac**, by supporting the US invasion of **Iraq**. Bush visited Germany in February 2005 and July 2006. Both visits were aimed at improving bilateral ties. *See also* ATTA, MOHAMED.

GINSBURG, BENJAMIN (1953?–). A graduate of the University of Pennsylvania (1974) and of the Georgetown University School of Law (1982), Ginsburg worked for the Republican National Committee in the 1980s. In 1993, he joined the Washington, D.C., law firm of Patton Boggs. In the 2000 and 2004 elections, Ginsburg served as legal counsel to **George W. Bush**. He played a central role in the 2000 election and the **Florida recount** controversy, including the **Supreme Court** case *Bush v. Gore* (2000), which ended the recount. In the 2004 election, Ginsburg became mired in controversy when it was revealed that he gave legal counsel to the independent group **Swift Boat Veterans for Truth**, which challenged the Vietnam War service record of Democratic presidential nominee **John Kerry** and ran hundreds of televised advertisements nationally against Kerry. Following the revelation, Ginsburg resigned as legal counsel for Bush.

GISCARD D'ESTAING, VALÉRY MARIE RENÉ GEORGES (1926–). Born in Koblenz, **Germany**, Giscard d'Estaing entered politics in **France** in 1956, when he was elected to the National Assembly (parliament) from a center-right party. In 1974, he became the third president of the French Fifth Republic, established in 1958. He was defeated in his re-election bid in 1981 by socialist François Mitterrand. During his single term as president, Giscard d'Estaing was lauded by many for his social progressivism but criticized on matters of economic management.

Although active in local politics in the region of Auvergne, France, Giscard became a major spokesman for greater integration in the countries of the **European Union** during the last several decades. However, French voters rejected his calls to approve a European Constitution in May 2005, which he helped draft. Giscard also supported the **Lisbon Treaty**, which would have streamlined the institutions of the European Union. Voters in Ireland rejected the treaty in June 2008.

GIULIANI, RUDOLPH WILLIAM LOUIS (1944–). A native of the borough of Brooklyn, New York City, Giuliani graduated from Manhattan College (1965) and earned a law degree from New York University (1968). After clerking for a federal judge, he joined the Justice Department in the southern district of New York in 1970. In 1973, he was appointed chief of the narcotics unit and was appointed as a US attorney. He served as an associate deputy attorney general in the administration of Gerald Ford. In the late 1970s, he entered private law practice. Having switched his political party affiliation to Republican with the election of **Ronald Reagan** in 1980, Giuliani returned to Washington in 1981 to become associate attorney general. In 1983, he returned to New York as a US attorney, where he prosecuted high-profile cases including insider trading on Wall Street and Mafia "families" connected to organized crime.

In 1989, Giuliani ran for the mayorship of New York City and lost in an extremely close race. He ran again in 1993 and successfully unseated the incumbent, David Dinkins, on campaign promises to cut taxes and reform city services. He was the first Republican to win the mayorship in nearly 30 years. He campaigned successfully for reelection in 1997, culling almost 60 percent of the citywide vote. He briefly considered a run for the US Senate in 2000 but withdrew as a result of prostate cancer and controversies over his personal life.

Giuliani was mayor of New York City when **al-Qaeda terrorist**s flew two commercial aircraft into the **World Trade Center** on **11 September 2001**. He was lauded for his calmness in the immediate aftermath of the attacks, his coordination with state and federal officials, and his measured security responses. Limited to two terms as mayor, he left office on 31 December 2001. A week earlier, *Time* magazine named him "person of the year," and he was frequently referred to as "America's mayor."

Giuliani started his own consulting business and supported President **George W. Bush** in 2004. He was rumored as a possibility to head the **Department of Homeland Security** when **Tom Ridge** resigned as secretary. In 2006, he was appointed as one of ten members of the **Iraq Study Group** mandated by Congress to study the **War in Iraq** and make recommendations, but resigned shortly thereafter.

In February 2007, he formally announced his candidacy for the Republican nomination for president in the 2008 election. Giuliani was highly favored in polls leading up to the Republican primaries in early 2008. However, he placed fourth in the **New Hampshire Primary** and sixth in the **Iowa Caucuses** behind the winners, **John McCain** and Mike Huckabee, respectively. After finishing third in Florida, Giuliani withdrew from the race on 30 January 2008 and endorsed McCain.

GONZALES, ALBERTO R. (1955–). Born in San Antonio, Texas, Gonzales was raised in Houston. He served in the United States Air Force between 1973 and 1975, and attended the United States Air Force Academy between 1975 and 1977. He earned a bachelor's degree from Rice University in 1979. After completing a law degree at Harvard University in 1982, Gonzales entered private law practice in Houston. In 1994, **George W. Bush**, then governor of Texas, appointed him as his counsel. In 1997, Bush appointed him secretary of state and, in 1999, to the Texas Supreme Court.

Following the 2000 presidential election, Gonzales served as Bush's White House counsel from 2001 to 2005. He succeeded **John Ashcroft** as attorney general in 2005—and was the first Hispanic ever appointed to that position. He was rumored as a possible nomination to the US **Supreme Court** to replace **Sandra Day O'Connor** or Chief Justice **William Rehnquist** in 2005. Conservative groups opposed him given his moderate stances on **abortion**, and Bush nominated **John Roberts** and **Samuel Alito** to the High Court.

Gonzales's tenure as attorney general was controversial. During his Senate confirmation hearings it was revealed that he had authored a memo in 2002 in which he posited that the **Geneva Conventions** on prisoner-of-war protections were outdated and should not be applied to captured **al-Qaeda** and **Taliban** fighters held as **enemy combatant**s in **Guantanamo Bay, Cuba**. He is alleged to have authored a secret memo exploring the use of **torture** by the **Central Intelligence Agency**, including the technique of "**waterboarding**" or simulated drowning, to extract information from captured **terrorists**. Gonzales defended President Bush's claims of **executive privilege** on several issues, including the **Energy Task Force** headed by Vice President **Richard B. (Dick) Cheney**. He was implicated in the **federal prosecutors** scandal in 2006, and was accused of using provisions of the **PATRIOT Act**, which he supported, to improperly gather personal information on US citizens by warrantless **wiretapping**. Gonzales's testimony before Senate investigatory committees, under control of Democrats following the **mid-term elections** of 2006, proved unconvincing and by Spring 2007 calls for his resignation mounted. He ultimately resigned in September 2007 and was succeeded by **Michael Mukasey** in November 2007.

GONZALES V. CARHART **(2007).** This **Supreme Court** case centered on the **Partial-Birth Abortion Ban Act**, which prohibited late-term (third-trimester) **abortion**s. The legislation, signed by President **George W. Bush** in 2003, made no exception for the life of the mother. Two federal courts found the legislation unconstitutional. Attorney General **Alberto Gonzales** appealed to the Supreme Court, which held in a 5–4 decision that the law did not impose an "undue burden" on **women**. Both **John Roberts** and **Samuel Alito**, who were appointed by Bush to the High Court, voted to uphold the ban. Abortion rights groups, including Planned Parenthood, which argued the case in front of the Supreme Court, contended that the ruling was a major setback for women's reproductive rights.

GORE, ALBERT ARNOLD, JR. (1948–). A native of Carthage, Tennessee, Gore grew up in Washington, D.C., and is the son of veteran US senator Albert Gore, Sr. He served as the 45th vice president from 1993 to 2001 during the presidency of **William Clinton**. A graduate of Harvard (1969), Gore was a military journalist briefly during the Vietnam War. Upon his return to Tennessee, he was a reporter for the Nashville-based *Tennessean*. Gore began his political career in 1976, when he was elected to represent the fourth district for

Tennessee in the House of Representatives. He was re-elected three times, and in 1984 won the Senate seat held by Republican Howard Baker. Gore was re-elected to the Senate in 1990 but resigned in 1992 when he was elected vice president.

Early in his candidacy for the vice presidency, Gore debated **Reform Party** candidate H. Ross Perot on the Cable News Network (CNN). The memorable exchanges over the potential economic impact of the North American Free Trade Agreement (NAFTA) accentuated Gore's dispassionate, academic style. As vice president, Gore headed the National Performance Review, or "Reinventing Government" initiative aimed at making the federal bureaucracy more efficient. He was also heavily involved in Internet and technology issues during Clinton's second term.

In 2000, after beating back a primary challenge from former professional basketball player Senator **Bill Bradley**, Gore won the Democrat Party nomination. He chose as his running mate Connecticut Senator **Joseph Lieberman**. The general election pitted the Gore–Lieberman ticket against Republican standard-bearer Texas Governor **George W. Bush** and running mate **Richard B. (Dick) Cheney**. Gore was criticized for running a lackluster campaign that failed to energize the Democratic base despite a strong economy during Clinton's administration. For months, the polls showed the race too close to call.

The 2000 election ultimately hinged on the outcome in Florida. The vote in **Palm Beach County** was disputed on the basis of so-called **butterfly ballots** that left many voters confused. The statewide vote was so narrow that, under state law, an automatic machine recount was triggered—and ultimately showed Bush's lead had narrowed to fewer than 300 votes across Florida's 67 counties. Gore then asked for a manual recount in four Florida counties. The subsequent controversy over the **Florida recount** lasted 36 days. The **Supreme Court** ultimately intervened in the case of *Bush v. Gore* and halted the recount of ballots. Florida secretary of state **Katherine Harris** certified that Bush had won the state by 537 votes—which gave him an Electoral College victory despite Gore's having won a half-million more votes nationwide. Some disgruntled Democrats suggested that Bush had "stolen" the election, as his brother, **John Ellis (Jeb) Bush** was governor of Florida and had appointed Harris.

Following his electoral defeat, Gore taught journalism at Columbia University and, in 2005, launched his own television network, Current TV. He produced a documentary on climate change, *An Inconvenient Truth*, in 2006 and won an Academy Award. In 2007, he was awarded a Nobel Peace Prize for his international role in climate-change issues.

GOSS, PORTER JOHNSTON (1938–). Born in Waterbury, Connecticut, Goss is a graduate of Yale University (1960). He served several years in the US Army after graduation, and then a decade at the **Central Intelligence Agency** (CIA). Goss was engaged in clandestine operations in the Caribbean, Europe, and Latin America. After his retirement from the CIA, he moved to Florida and was elected mayor of Sanibel, and later served on the Lee County Commission. A Republican, he ran successfully for Congress in 1988 in a district in southwestern Florida and was re-elected seven times. In the House of Representatives, he served as chair of the Permanent Select Committee on Intelligence from 1996 to 2004. He was a prominent member of the joint House–Senate Committee that investigated intelligence failings surrounding the **11 September 2001 terrorist** attacks on New York and the **Pentagon**. He was a cosponsor of the **PATRIOT Act** adopted by Congress in 2001.

Goss resigned his seat in the House of Representatives when President **George W. Bush** appointed him to direct the Central Intelligence Agency in September 2004. Goss succeeded **George Tenet**. Goss attempted to implement sweeping operational changes in the agency, which came under heavy criticism for failing to prevent the 9/11 attacks, but he met substantive resistance. Following congressional legislation adopted in 2004, Goss, as director of the CIA, reported to the new **Director of National Intelligence** (DNI). Goss announced his retirement suddenly in May 2006. Media reports suggested that Goss had clashed with DNI **John Negroponte** over organizational structure and human resources in intelligence gathering. He was succeeded as director of the CIA by Air Force General **Michael Hayden**.

GRAHAM, DANIEL ROBERT (BOB) (1936–). A native of south Florida, Graham graduated from the University of Florida with a degree in political science in 1959. He earned a law degree from Harvard University in 1962. He entered politics in 1966, when he won a seat in the Florida House of Representatives; he served two terms. He won a seat in the Florida Senate in 1970 and was re-elected in 1974. A moderate Democrat, Graham ran successfully for the governorship of Florida in 1978, and was re-elected with nearly two-thirds of the statewide vote in 1982. He used his gubernatorial popularity to launch a successful bid for the US Senate in 1986, unseating incumbent Republican Paula Hawkins. He won re-election twice. While in the Senate, he chaired on the Democratic Senatorial Congressional Committee (1993–1994) and served on the Select Committee on Intelligence.

Considered a possibility for the vice presidency through the 1980s, 1990s, and the 2000 election, Graham campaigned unsuccessfully for the Democratic presidential nomination in 2004. Graham was a supporter of the **War on Terror** but had opposed the **War in Iraq**. His presidential campaign began late and suffered from financing setbacks. Perhaps the most memorable component of Graham's presidential bid was his comment "Osama been forgotten," a reference to President **George W. Bush**'s failure to find **al-Qaeda terrorist** leader **Osama bin Laden**, in an early primary debate. Graham dropped out of the presidential race in October 2003, and did not contest any primaries. Graham did not seek re-election to the Senate in 2004, and has since devoted his time to building the Graham Center for Public Service at the University of Florida.

GRANER, CHARLES. *See* ABU GHRAIB.

GRATZ V. BOLLINGER **(2003).** *See* AFFIRMATIVE ACTION.

GREAT BRITAIN. Also known as the United Kingdom, Great Britain comprises England, Scotland, Wales, and **Northern Ireland**. Great Britain is a constitutional monarchy. The head of state is the monarch, the Queen of England, while de facto political authority lies with the Westminster Parliament located in **London**.

During the administration of **George W. Bush**, Great Britain had two prime ministers. **Tony Blair** had been first elected in 1997 and was prime minister when Bush assumed office in January 2001. Blair and his Labour Party won re-election in June 2001, and election to a third mandate in May 2005.

Prime Minister Blair was a staunch supporter of the **War on Terror**. Along with Bush, Blair urged the **United Nations** to take swift action against the regime of **Saddam Hussein**. When the UN Security Council became deadlocked over **United Nations Resolution 1441**, Blair committed 45,000 British troops to the **War in Iraq**, which commenced in March 2003, as part of the **Coalition of the Willing**. Blair was also prime minister in July 2007 when the London subway system was attacked by **al-Qaeda terrorists**.

The War in Iraq became increasingly unpopular in Great Britain, and Blair stepped down as prime minister in June 2007. **Gordon Brown**, former chancellor of the Exchequer, succeeded Blair, who became a special envoy to the Middle East and worked to save remnants of the **Road Map for Peace** between **Israel** and the **Palestinian National Authority**. Brown was more critical of mistakes made in the War in Iraq and remained committed to the effort to secure peace, but he did not enjoy the level of friendship with Bush that prevailed under Blair's tenure.

Bush visited his British counterparts several times over his two terms. His November 2003 trip to Great Britain was an official state visit, during which he met with Blair. In June 2008, Bush returned to Great Britain to meet with Brown. Both British prime ministers also visited the United States. Blair was the first foreign leader to visit Bush in Washington in 2004. He returned again in 2006 and 2007. Gordon Brown visited Bush in April 2008 to discuss **Iran**'s nuclear program, which the United States and Great Britain charged was for the development of **weapons of mass destruction** (WMDs). *See also* DOWNING STREET MEMO; STRAW, JACK.

GREEN ZONE. This four-square-mile area in the heart of **Baghdad, Iraq**, contained the headquarters of the **Coalition Provisional Authority** between April 2003 and June 2004. The Green Zone was established following the ouster of **Saddam Hussein** by a US-led **Coalition of the Willing** that invaded Iraq in March 2003. The area, also known as the International Zone, was heavily fortified by troops and a high wall to ensure security. The area was nonetheless the frequent target of **insurgents** who used **improvised explosive devices** (IEDs) or engaged in suicide bombings against civilian and military installations. *See also* WAR IN IRAQ.

GREENSPAN, ALAN (1926–). A New York City native, Greenspan earned bachelor's, master's, and doctoral degrees (1977) from New York University. He served an unprecedented five terms as chair of the **Federal Reserve** (the Fed). First appointed by President **Ronald Reagan** in 1987, Greenspan was reappointed by presidents **George H.W. Bush**, **William Clinton**, and **George W. Bush**. He retired as Fed chair in January 2006 and was succeeded by **Ben Bernanke**.

Greenspan began his career as an economic consultant in the 1940s. He served as chair of President Gerald Ford's Council of Economic Advisors from 1974 to 1977. He later took directorship positions for various private corporations, including Alcoa, General Foods, and the investment firm J.P. Morgan.

As Fed chair, Greenspan was known for his steadfast commitment to managing the money supply to promote economic growth. He successfully handled the stock market crash of 9 October 1987 by reassuring investors. In the 1990s, however, some observers contended that he wielded too much influence. In December 1996, he suggested that some stocks were inflated due to "irrational exuberance," and the **Dow Jones Industrial Average** closed sharply lower. Upon his retirement, Greenspan was awarded an honorary position on the Treasury of **Great Britain**. He is married to National Broadcasting Corporation (NBC) journalist Andrea Mitchell. *See also* SUBPRIME MORTGAGE; TROUBLED ASSETS RELIEF PROGRAM (TARP).

GRILES, J. STEVEN (1947–). A native of Clover, Virginia, Griles graduated with a bachelor's degree from the University of Richmond in 1970. He worked as a coal lobbyist and later in the administration of **Ronald Reagan** in the Department of the Interior in surface mining and lands and minerals management. He was appointed by President **George W. Bush** as deputy to Secretary of the Interior **Gale Norton** in 2001 and served in that post until 2004. He liaised with the **Energy Task Force** headed by Vice President **Richard B. (Dick) Cheney** as the representative from the Interior Department.

Griles was the top official in the Bush administration implicated in the **Jack Abramoff** scandal that shook Congress. He had testified before the Senate Indian Affairs Committee about his relationship with Abramoff in 2005. In 2007, he faced charges of obstruction of justice for making false statements. He pleaded guilty, was fined $30,000, and sentenced to 10 months in prison.

GRUTTER V. BOLLINGER (2003). *See* AFFIRMATIVE ACTION.

GUANTANAMO BAY, CUBA. This harbor area in southeastern Cuba has been under the control of the US military pursuant to a 1903 treaty, which the Cuban government contends is illegal. The US Navy base covers approximately 45 square miles and is sometimes referred to as "Gitmo." As part of the **War on Terror** following the **11 September 2001 terrorist** attacks on New York and the **Pentagon**, suspected **al-Qaeda** and **Taliban** operatives captured in the US-led invasion of **Afghanistan** were relocated to various "camps" (e.g., "X-Ray," "Delta," etc.) on the naval base and were indefinitely detained. The administration of **George W. Bush** contended that the detainees were unlawful **enemy combatants** who were not subject to the **Geneva Conventions**, did not enjoy the constitutional protection of **habeas corpus** in US civil courts, and were to be tried by **military tribunals**. International watchdog groups, the **European Union**, and the Latin American-based Organization of American States (OAS) criticized the conditions at the detention facilities and the failure to apply the Geneva Conventions to the prisoners. The US military and the Bush administration argued that the detainees were well treated, nourished, and had access to the Koran. A number of European leaders generally supportive of the Bush administration's **War on Terror**, including **Germany**'s **Angela Merkel** and **Tony Blair** of **Great Britain**, called for the closure of the detention facility, as did international human rights groups.

In August 2008, an Algerian detainee claimed that he had been subject to "**waterboarding**," a simulated drowning technique used by the **Central Intelligence Agency** to extract intelligence and information from prisoners. Other prisoners alleged forms of physical and psychological torture. Red Cross inspectors who visited the facility claimed techniques they considered torture had been used on the detainees, including sleep deprivation and beatings. Secretary of Defense **Donald Rumsfeld** issued an order in early 2003 suspending interrogation techniques at the detention facility until a new set of guidelines could be assembled. Allegations of prisoner abuse were investigated internally by the military, as well as by the Armed Services Committee of the House of Representatives. In October 2005, Congress passed the **Detainee Treatment Act**, signed by President Bush, which prohibited the abuse of detainees from rape, torture, or other "cruel and inhumane" treatment, but did not allow prisoners legal counsel and barred them from habeas corpus petitions to US civil courts. Senator **John McCain**, the Republican nominee for the presidency in 2008, was a major proponent of the bill.

A number of detainees challenged the Bush administration's policies in cases that reached the **Supreme Court**. In *Hamdi v. Rumsfeld* (2004), the High Court ruled that the president did not have the power to detain US citizens indefinitely; a plurality of justices issued an opinion that detainees should have the ability to challenge their imprisonment. In *Rasul v. Bush* (2004), the justices decided that US courts could hear habeas corpus petitions from detainees and dismissed the Bush administration's claim that the detention facility at Guantanamo Bay was beyond the reach of US law. In *Hamdan v. Rumsfeld* (2006), the Court found that the military commissions the Bush administration set up were unconstitutional, and that only Congress had the authority to found such commissions. As a result, Congress passed the **Military Commissions Act**. In *Boumediene v. Bush* (2008), the Court ruled that those commissions violated detainees' rights of habeas corpus as well, and prisoners could challenge their detention in US courts. *See also* ZUBAYDAH, ABU.

GULF COAST. *See* HURRICANE IKE; HURRICANE KATRINA; HURRICANE RITA.

GULF WAR. *See* PERSIAN GULF WAR.

GUTIERREZ, CARLOS MIGUEL (1954–). Born in Havana, Cuba, Gutierrez fled the regime of **Fidel Castro** in 1960 and relocated to Miami, Florida. He lived in **Mexico** and studied at the Monterrey Institute of Technology. He began work for Kellogg's Corporation and rose through the ranks over the course of several decades to become chief executive officer. In November 2004, President **George W. Bush** announced Gutierrez's appointment as secretary of the Department of Commerce to replace **Donald Evans**. He was confirmed by the Senate in January 2005 and remained in the post through the end of Bush's second term.

– H –

HABEAS CORPUS. From the Latin "you have the body," the principle of habeas corpus dates to England of the 14th century and is a summons or writ that an individual be brought before a court, which may then decide whether the state authority has the right to detain the individual. This critical civil liberty—that individuals may not be indefinitely detained without cause—is enshrined in the US Constitution in Article I, Section 9, which states that "The privilege of the writ of habeas corpus shall not be suspended, unless when in cases of rebellion or invasion, the public safety may require it." Only once, during the Civil War, has habeas corpus been formally suspended. President Abraham Lincoln did so in 1861.

The controversy over habeas corpus in the administration of **George W. Bush** focused on the rights of prisoners the president defined as unlawful **enemy combatant**s. As part of the **War on Terror**, suspected **al-Qaeda** and **Taliban terrorist**s captured following the US-led invasion of **Afghanistan** were detained at the US naval facility in **Guantanamo Bay, Cuba**. The Bush administration posited that the detainees were not subject either to the **Geneva Conventions** or to habeas corpus in US civil courts. The Bush administration wanted to try the detainees via **military tribunals**. Successive **Supreme Court** rulings confirmed the rights of detainees to habeas corpus. *See also BOUMEDIENE V. BUSH* (2008); DETAINEE TREATMENT ACT (2005); GONZALES, ALBERTO; *HAMDAN V. RUMSFELD* (2006); *HAMDI V. RUMSFELD* (2004); MATERIAL WITNESS; MCCAIN, JOHN; MILITARY COMMISSIONS ACT; MILITARY TRIBUNALS; *RASUL V. BUSH* (2004); RUMSFELD, DONALD; TORTURE; WATERBOARDING.

HADLEY, STEPHEN JOHN (1947–). Born in Toledo, Ohio, Hadley earned a bachelor's degree from Cornell University (1969) and a law degree from Yale University (1972). He served in the US Navy from 1972 to 1975. He later worked for the Department of Defense and on the **National Security Council** staff for President Gerald Ford. In the administration of **Ronald Reagan**, Hadley was council to the Tower Commission, which investigated the Iran–Contra affair. Under President **George H.W. Bush,** he was assistant secretary of defense and was heavily involved in negotiations to reduce nuclear weapons in the United States and **Soviet Union.**

Hadley was deputy national security advisor to President **George W. Bush** from 2001 to 2005. He was at the center of controversy in 2003 when he allowed Bush to reference Iraqi dictator **Saddam Hussein**'s apparent attempt to procure material from the country of Niger in pursuit of **weapons of mass destruction** (WMDs) in a State of the Union address. The intelligence on which that claim was based was later found to be forged. Hadley offered to resign, but Bush refused his request. Hadley replaced **Condoleezza Rice** as national security advisor when she became secretary of state in January 2005.

HALLIBURTON CORPORATION. This firm, headquartered in Dallas, Texas, is an energy corporation involved in oil and gas exploration. Vice President **Richard B. (Dick) Cheney** was an executive with Halliburton, and resigned his position in 2000. Nonetheless, he received nearly $400,000 in deferred compensation, prompting critics to charge that he had a conflict of interest with respect to his chairmanship of the **Energy Task Force**. Further, critics charge that Cheney had ulterior motives in his support for the **War in Iraq**, as Halliburton obtained lucrative contracts for the rebuilding of **Iraq**'s oil field following the US-led invasion of that country in March 2003. Other companies in countries of the **European Union** that did not support the War in Iraq, including **France**—which had extensive ties to Iraq's oil industry—were denied reconstruction contracts by the administration of **George W. Bush**.

Halliburton was widely criticized for its reconstruction efforts in Iraq. The firm had contended that oil revenues to be tapped following the invasion would pay for the war. However, the firm failed in its efforts to tap oil fields in the north of Iraq at great taxpayer expense. As of late 2008, Halliburton remained under federal investigation for having received special consideration for postwar reconstruction contracts.

HALLUMS, ROY (1948–). Born in Memphis, Tennessee, Hallums was working for a Saudi Arabian contracting company in **Iraq** that supplied food to the Iraqi Army when he was kidnapped by insurgents in **Baghdad** on 1 November 2004. He was held for 311 days. In January 2005, Hallums appeared in a videotape begging for his life but did not indicate any demands made by his captors. US troops rescued him at a farmhouse south of Baghdad on 7 September 2005. Hallums' assailants were not apprehended.

HAMAS. *Hamas* is the Arabic acronym for *Harakat al-Muqawamah al-Islamiyyah*, or "Islamic Resistance Movement." The movement was founded in 1987 during the "intifada," or uprising, in the Palestinian Territories of the **West Bank** and **Gaza Strip** against **Israel**, which occupied the territories. Hamas is regarded by the United States as a **terrorist** organization. The movement is known for its suicide bombings in Israel and is considered more radical than the **Palestine Liberation Organization** (PLO), since it calls for the destruction of the Jewish state of Israel.

Hamas defeated its principal rival, the moderate **Fatah** party, in parliamentary elections in the Palestinian Territories in January 2006. Following a state of emergency and **Palestinian National Authority** President **Mahmoud Abbas**'s removal of Hamas leader **Ismail Haniya** and appointment of **Salam Fayyad** as prime minister in June 2007, violent clashes between the two rival parties left Fatah in control of the West Bank and Hamas in control of the Gaza Strip. *See also* ROAD MAP FOR PEACE.

HAMDAN V. RUMSFELD **(2006).** This **Supreme Court** case concerned **military tribunals** that the administration of **George W. Bush** set up to try suspected **enemy combatants** in the **War on Terror**. Salim Ahmed Hamdan, a Yemeni national captured in **Afghanistan** who was **al-Qaeda terrorist Osama bin Laden**'s driver, was detained as an enemy combatant at the naval base at **Guantanamo Bay, Cuba**. He filed a **habeas corpus** petition to the High Court, contending that his detention violated protections afforded by the **Geneva Conventions** and also challenged the constitutionality of the military tribunals.

In a 5–3 decision, the Supreme Court held that the president did not have the authority to set up military commissions unilaterally and that such commissions required congressional legislation. Further, the decision held that the Bush administration could not try detainees via the military commissions because they too violated the Geneva Conventions, as well as the Uniform Code of Military Justice. Chief Justice **John Roberts** recused himself from the case, while another

Bush appointee to the Court, **Samuel Alito**, dissented from the majority. *See also BOUMEDIENE V. BUSH* (2008); DETAINEE TREATMENT ACT (2005); *HAMDI V. RUMSFELD* (2004); MILITARY COMMISSIONS ACT (2006); *RASUL V. BUSH* (2004).

HAMDI V. RUMSFELD **(2004).** This **Supreme Court** case involved a **habeas corpus** petition by Yaser Esam Hamdi, who was captured in **Afghanistan** and suspected of being a **Taliban** fighter. Hamdi was detained at **Guantanamo Bay, Cuba**, as an **enemy combatant** when the military learned that he had dual citizenship in the United States and Saudi Arabia.

A federal court in the Fourth Circuit overturned a district court ruling and posited that Hamdi did not have the right to challenge his indefinite detention. The federal court contended that his detention was constitutional under the Second Article of the Constitution, which gives the president broad latitude in times of war. Hamdi subsequently petitioned the High Court for relief. A majority of justices contended that President **George W. Bush** had the authority to detain unlawful enemy combatants, but that US citizens have the fundamental right to challenge their detention before a civil court judge. *See also RASUL V. BUSH* (2004).

HANIYA, ISMAIL (1962–). Born in a refugee camp in the **Gaza Strip**, Palestinian Territories, Haniya is a political leader in **Hamas**, which the United States regards as a **terrorist** organization. Hamas calls for the destruction of the state of **Israel**. Israel deported him to **Lebanon** in 1992 for his involvement in protests. When Hamas won the parliamentary elections in the **Palestinian National Authority** in 2006, Haniya was appointed prime minister by **Mahmoud Abbas**. Violence in Gaza prompted Abbas to declare a state of emergency and replace Haniya with **Salam Fayyad** in June 2007. The move was of questionable constitutionality, and many Palestinians regarded Haniya as the duly elected prime minister. Continued violence between rival **Fatah** party and Hamas factions left Haniya in control of the Gaza Strip and Fatah in control of the **West Bank**. *See also* ROAD MAP FOR PEACE.

HARIRI, RAFIK BAHAA EL DEEN (1944–2005). Born in Sidon, **Lebanon**, Hariri was the reformist, post-civil war prime minister of

Lebanon from 1992 to 1998 and from 2000 to 2004. He was assassinated on 14 February 2005 when an explosion rocked his motorcade in the capitol of Beirut. The **Syria**n government, which had occupied Lebanon, was suspected of involvement. The outcry over Hariri's assassination led to massive protests, known as the "Cedar Revolution," that ultimately drove Syria to withdraw its troops from the country. *See also* GEMAYEL, PIERRE AMINE.

HARPER, STEPHEN (1959–). Born in Toronto and a graduate of the University of Calgary, Harper was first elected to the parliament of **Canada** in 1993 as a member of the Reform Party. In 2002, he became the leader of the Alliance Party, which supplanted the Reform Party as the major center-right party in Canadian politics. The following year, under Harper's leadership, the Alliance Party and the Progressive Conservative Party merged to form a new Conservative Party. Based in the west of Canada, the party reflects policy stances closer to that of Republicans in the United States insofar as it is opposed to **abortion** and **gay marriage** and draws support from many **Evangelical Christians**. The party also supports less centralization of policy in the federal government and more latitude for provinces to administer their own affairs. The Conservatives under Harper were the only Canadian Party to support the US-led invasion of **Iraq** in 2003. In 2004, the Conservatives won enough seats for Harper to lead the opposition in parliament to the minority government of Liberal **Paul Martin**.

Harper became prime minister following the 24 January 2006 federal election, which turned on a finance scandal in Martin's government. Although Harper's Conservatives swept the west and made significant progress in Ontario and Québec, he led a minority government with only 123 of 308 parliamentary seats—because the other three parties in government could not form a coalition government themselves. On 14 October 2008, Harper held a "snap" election following an impasse on government legislation. Although the Conservatives' share of the national vote declined slightly, Harper's party carried the election with 143 seats and formed a second minority government.

While the governments of Harper's predecessors, Liberals **Jean Chrétien** and Paul Martin, were critical of President **George W. Bush** and sometimes viewed as anti-American, Harper was widely regarded as much more supportive of a close relationship between Canada and the United States in the realm of **foreign policy**. Harper sought to downplay trade disputes under the North American Free Trade Agreement (NAFTA), more readily supported **Israel**, and extended Canada's presence in **Afghanistan** as part of the **International Security Assistance Force** (ISAF).

HARRIS, KATHERINE (1957–). Born in Key West, Florida, Harris is the granddaughter of Ben Hill Griffin, Jr., a prominent cattle rancher and state legislator who built a family fortune. She graduated from Agnes Scott College in Georgia, studied in both Spain and Switzerland, and completed a master's degree in business administration from Harvard in 1997.

Following a career in marketing and real estate, Harris entered politics as a Republican in 1994, when she won a seat to the Florida Senate. In 1998, she defeated the incumbent secretary of state. Following the 2000 presidential election between **George W. Bush** and **Al Gore**, Harris stood at the vortex of the **Florida recount** controversy. After a mandatory statewide machine recount of the vote, Harris certified on 26 November 2000 that Bush had won Florida by 537 votes. The certification of Florida's 25 Electoral College votes put Bush over the necessary threshold of 270 to win the election. She determined that there was no basis to amend results in those disputed counties in which Gore had asked to conduct a manual recount. The state supreme court ordered a manual recount, which the US **Supreme Court** effectively terminated on 9 December in the case *Bush v. Gore*.

Harris successfully ran for the House of Representatives in 2002 from a district around Sarasota. She was re-elected in 2004. In 2005, she and her campaign staff were investigated in the bribery scandal surrounding **Randall (Duke) Cunningham**. In 2006, Harris ran for an open Senate seat in Florida but lost to incumbent Democrat Bill Nelson in a campaign noted for staff resignations and lukewarm support from many Republicans, including Florida Governor **John Ellis (Jeb) Bush**.

HASSAN ABT AL-MAJID AL-TIKRITI, ALI (1941–). Known as "Chemical Ali," Hassan was born in **Tikrit, Iraq**. A member of the

Ba'ath Party and a cousin of dictator **Saddam Hussein**, he earned his sobriquet from the use of chemical weapons against minority **Kurds** in the north of Iraq. He was Hussein's defense minister, interior minister, and governor of Kuwait after Iraq's invasion of that country in 1990, which precipitated the **Persian Gulf War**. Following the US-led invasion of Iraq in 2003, Hassan was captured and charged by the Iraqi government with genocide. He was convicted in June 2007, and was sentenced to be hanged. As of late 2008, his appeals had been rejected but his death sentence had yet to be carried out.

HASTERT, JOHN DENNIS (DENNY) (1942–). Born in Aurora, Illinois, Hastert graduated from Wheaton College (1964) and earned a master's degree in education from Northern Illinois University (1967). He worked as a high school teacher before entering politics in 1980. A Republican, he won a seat in the Illinois House of Representatives, to which he was re-elected twice. He ran for Congress in 1986 in a district that encompassed his hometown and won narrowly. He was re-elected to the House of Representatives ten times. In 1995, when Republicans captured the majority, Hastert was appointed chief deputy whip to work under majority whip **Tom DeLay**. In 1998, when Newt Gingrich stood down from the speakership, Hastert was elected Speaker of the House. He held that position until Democrats won a majority in the **mid-term elections** in 2006, at which time Hastert retired.

HATCH, ORRIN GRANT (1934–). Born in Pittsburgh, Pennsylvania, Hatch earned a bachelor's degree from Brigham Young University (1959) and a law degree from the University of Pittsburgh (1962). He worked in private law practice until 1976, when he launched a successful campaign to unseat the Democratic incumbent senator from Utah, Frank Moss. He won re-election five times through 2006. In the Senate, he chaired the Labor and Human Resources Committee from 1981 to 1986 and the Judiciary Committee from 1995 to 2000.

In 2000, Hatch made an unsuccessful run for the Republican nomination for president on a socially conservative platform, but lost to **George W. Bush**. He withdrew from the campaign after placing sixth in the Iowa Caucuses and polling only 1 percent of the vote. He was rumored as a possible replacement for Attorney General **Alberto Gonzales** and as a potential **Supreme Court** appointee in the Bush administration. Hatch is author of *Square Peg: Confessions of a Citizen Senator* (2002).

HATFILL, STEVEN JAY (1953–). A native of St. Louis, Missouri, Hatfill was a virologist at Fort Detrick, Maryland. The Department of Justice identified him as a "person of interest" in the investigation of the **anthrax** attacks of 2001. He was exonerated in 2008 when authorities believed that **Bruce Ivins**, another researcher at Fort Detrick, who died in August 2008, had perpetrated the attacks. Hatfill eventually settled a lawsuit against the Justice Department, in which he alleged his privacy had been violated, for $5.8 million.

HAYDEN, MICHAEL VINCENT (1947–). Born in Pittsburgh, Pennsylvania, Hayden graduated from Duquesne University with a bachelor's and master's degree in history. He joined the Air Force in 1969 after completing the Reserve Office Training Corps (ROTC) program. His 41-year career in the Air Force includes service as commander of the Air Intelligence Agency, director of the Joint Command and Control Warfare Center, and senior staff positions in the Pentagon, the **National Security Council**, the US European Command in Stuttgart, **Germany**, and the US Embassy in **Bulgaria**. He also served as deputy chief of staff for the **United Nations** command in Korea. From 1999 to 2005, he was director of the National Security Agency (NSA).

President **George W. Bush** appointed Hayden director of the **Central Intelligence Agency** (CIA) in May 2006, following the resignation of **Porter Goss**. His confirmation hearings in the Senate centered on his leadership at the NSA, which had created a domestic telephone call database to monitor calls between US citizens and suspected international **terrorists** after **11 September 2001**. Warrantless **wiretapping** violated the **Foreign Intelligence Surveillance Act** (FISA) legislation passed by Congress, but Hayden argued that he took the action based on advice from the White House and his belief that the president's commander-in-chief authority under the Constitution trumped the congressional statute. He was ultimately confirmed by a vote of 78–15. He resigned his Air Force command on 1 July 2008, in part over concerns about a military officer leading a civilian agency—another point of contention during his confirmation hearings. *See also* ARMED FORCES.

HERSH, SEYMOUR MYRON (1937–). A native of Chicago, Illinois, and a graduate of the University of Chicago, Hersh began his career in journalism in 1959. He worked for United Press International, the Associated Press, and the *New York Times* over the next three decades and was press secretary to Democrat Eugene McCarthy, who ran for president in 1968. In 1970, he won a Pulitzer Prize for investigative journalism that uncovered the My Lai Massacre during the Vietnam War.

A regular contributing author to the *New Yorker* magazine, Hersh was a leading investigative journalist and staunch critic of the administration of **George W. Bush**, the **War in Iraq**, and the **War on Terror**. In 2003, he authored articles that suggested Vice President **Richard B. (Dick) Cheney** and Secretary of Defense **Donald Rumsfeld** had not used standard **Central Intelligence Agency** (CIA) information and analysis in making the case that Iraqi dictator **Saddam Hussein** had acquired **weapons of mass destruction** (WMDs). His reports in early 2004 about abuse of prisoners at **Abu Ghraib** received worldwide attention and earned him an award for magazine reporting. Hersh alleged that the abuses at Abu Ghraib were not isolated incidents, but rather part of a government-wide effort to gain information from suspected **terrorist**s through interrogation methods that included torture at the naval base in **Guantanamo Bay, Cuba**, and in **Afghanistan**. In 2006, Hersh contended that the US military had plans to use nuclear weapons on **Iran**, but in 2008 argued that Bush had changed strategies to "contain" Iran and President **Mahmoud Ahmadinejad** by bolstering Sunni groups with interests inimical to the Bush administration's War on Terror.

HEZBOLLAH. *Hezbollah* means "party of God" in Arabic and is a Shi'ite Muslim fundamentalist organization founded in **Lebanon** to combat the 1982 Israeli invasion of that country. The United States considers Hezbollah a **terrorist** organization. In the 1980s, the organization received financial support from **Iran**, whose aim was to spread the Iranian Revolution to other countries in the Middle East.

Israel attacked Hezbollah targets inside Lebanon in July and August 2006. Israeli defense forces alleged that **Syria** and Iran were behind the Hezbollah militants who launched rockets into Israeli territory, killing and injuring several soldiers and kidnapping several others.

Hezbollah's connections to Iran became a point of contention in the **War in Iraq**. In 2008, General **David Petraeus** contended that Iran, with support from Hezbollah, was aiding **insurgents** in **Iraq** and engaging in attacks on troops.

HOMELAND SECURITY PRESIDENTIAL DIRECTIVE (HSPD). HSPDs govern homeland security policy and are akin to executive orders or National Security Policy Directives (NSPDs). HSPDs are unilateral presidential decisions under existing statutes that instruct the **Department of Homeland Security** to undertake certain actions. Through the end of 2008, President **George W. Bush** issued 24 HSPDs, ranging from the establishment of a Homeland Security Council to coordinate national antiterrorism programs to the use of biometrics for the identification and screening of suspected **terrorist**s.

HOUSING AND ECONOMIC RECOVERY ACT (2008). This legislation, signed by President **George W. Bush** on 30 July 2008, addressed the **sub-prime mortgage** crisis by authorizing the Federal Housing Administration to guarantee $300 billion in new fixed-rate mortgages so long as lenders lowered the principal on new loans to 90 percent of the appraised value. The bill did not avert a major crisis in financial markets in mid-September 2008, which prompted the FHA to place the **Federal National Mortgage Association** (Fannie Mae) and the **Federal Home Loan Mortgage Corporation** (Freddie Mac) in conservatorship as Congress mulled a much larger financial bailout for struggling banks.

HOWARD, JOHN WINSTON (1939–). A native of Sydney, Australia, Howard first won a seat in the Australian parliament in 1974 as a member of the Liberal Party. He was treasurer from 1977 to 1983 in the government of Malcolm Fraser. Following 13 years in opposition to the Labor Party, Howard became prime minister in 1996. He held the premiership for 11 years. In 2007, Howard lost his seat in parliament, and **Kevin Rudd** and the Labor Party regained the majority.

Howard was a close ally to President **George W. Bush** and a vocal supporter of the **War on Terror**. Howard's and the Liberal Party's defeat in 2007 turned on support for the **War in Iraq**. Under Howard's leadership Australia was part of the **Coalition of the Willing** in the March 2003 invasion of **Iraq** that ousted dictator **Saddam Hussein**. Australia's participation in the War in Iraq was highly unpopular, and when no **weapons of mass destruction** (WMDs) were found, Howard's political capital fell further.

HU, JINTAO (1942–). Born in Jiangyan, Jiangsu, **China**, Hu Jintao succeeded Jiang Zemin as general secretary of the Chinese Communist Party in November 2002. Educated as an engineer, he began his political career in the 1970s, holding positions including provincial secretary of the Communist Party in Guizhou, and later in Tibet, before ascending to the Politburo in 1992 and to secretary of the central committee in 1993. Hu is widely credited with fostering China's dramatic economic development. Hu enjoyed generally good relations with President **George W. Bush**, whom he met in 2006 in Vietnam to solidify economic ties between the United States and China. Bush also met with Hu in July 2008, just prior to the Olympic Games hosted by the Chinese in Beijing. Nonetheless, Bush expressed general concern on human rights issues, including Chinese repression in Tibet, and China's devaluation of the *yuan* (Chinese currency), which aggravated the US trade deficit with China.

HUGHES, KAREN PARFITT (1956–). Born in Paris, France, Hughes graduated from Southern Methodist University (1977). After a brief career in journalism, she worked as President **Ronald Reagan**'s press liaison in the 1984 presidential election, after which she became executive director of the Republican Party of Texas. She became a key advisor to **George W. Bush** during the 1990s, serving as his director of communications during his governorship. From 2001 to 2002 she served in the White House as a counselor to and trusted confident of the president. Although she left the White House in 2002, she continued to remain in close contact with Bush and returned to aid his re-election victory in 2004. In 2005, Bush nominated her to the post of undersecretary of state for diplomacy, and she held that position until 2007 before returning to private life.

HUMAN GENOME. The Human Genome Project, begun in 1990 by the National Institutes of Health, completed its mapping of the genes that make up the human species in 2003. The immediate benefits of the research included genetic tests that allow individuals to evaluate their predisposition for a variety of illnesses.

HUNGARY. This central European nation was a member of the **Warsaw Pact** during the **Cold War** and a satellite of the **Soviet Union**. Hungary regained its independence in 1989, when it became a republic. It joined the **North Atlantic Treaty Organization** (NATO) in 1999, and became a member of the **European Union** in 2004. In June 2006, President **George W. Bush** visited Hungary to mark the 50th anniversary of the country's 1956 uprising against the Soviets.

HURRICANE IKE. Making landfall in Galveston, Texas, with winds to 110 miles per hour on 13 September 2008, Ike was a Category 2 hurricane on the Saffir-Simpson scale that caused an estimated $27 billion in damages. The storm was responsible for 164 deaths in the United States, Cuba, and Haiti. It was the third most costly hurricane in US history. Early preparations and mandatory evacuations in the Galveston and Houston, Texas, areas were credited with saving countless lives. As the storm moved inland, it created widespread flooding as far north as **Canada** before moving back into the eastern Atlantic Ocean.

HURRICANE KATRINA. This mammoth storm formed over the Bahamas, passed Florida, moved into the Gulf of Mexico, and struck New Orleans, Louisiana, on 29 August 2005 as a Category 3 storm on the Saffir-Simpson scale with winds of 125 miles per hour. The storm killed 1,839 people and left more than 700 missing. At an estimated $81 billion, damage from the storm made it the costliest natural disaster in US history. The storm surge broke three key levees built by the Army Corps of Engineers to protect the city of New Orleans, which sits several feet below sea level. Flooding devastated St. Bernard Parish, to the southeast of the city; a year after the storm, the parish's population had dwindled from more than 65,000 residents to only 25,000.

The abject failure of federal, state, and local governments to prepare for the storm and to meet the challenges of its aftermath caused national outrage. Prior to the storm, state and local agencies failed to implement adequate evacuation plans. The stunning loss of life was exacerbated by the number of homeless and stranded residents in and around New Orleans. As search and rescue efforts were hampered by a lack of intergovernmental coordination, many victims made their way to Interstate 10 to avoid flood waters or to the New Orleans Superdome, which served as a makeshift shelter that had insufficient facilities to house thousands of victims.

Blame for the inadequate relief effort fell on New Orleans Mayor **Ray Nagin**, Louisiana Governor **Kathleen Babineaux Blanco**, and **Federal Emergency Management Agency** (FEMA) Director **Michael D. Brown**. Nagin, who was criticized for waiting too long to order a mandatory evacuation of the city before the storm hit, was visibly angry at press conferences after the storm, blaming Governor Blanco and President **George W. Bush** for failing to send adequate resources to the city. Blanco was in turn criticized for turning attention to issues of law and order, including the widespread looting that occurred in the city, instead of focusing on rescue efforts. FEMA director Brown, whom President Bush praised for "doing a heck of a job" was relieved of his duties 10 days into the relief effort after charges of incompetence were leveled against him. The aftermath of Hurricane Katrina has been featured in several documentary films, including *When the Levees Broke* (2006) by Spike Lee and *Hellp* (2006) by Darren Martinez.

HURRICANE RITA. Rita made landfall on 24 September 2005 between Sabine Pass, Texas, and Johnson's Bayou, Louisiana, as a Category 3 storm on the Saffir-Simpson scale with winds of 115 miles per hour. One hundred and twenty deaths were reported from the storm, which caused widespread flooding and wind damage along coastal areas in southeastern Texas and Louisiana resulting in an estimated $10 billion in damages.

HUSSEIN AL-TIKRITI, QUSAY SADDAM (1966–2003). The youngest of Iraqi dictator **Saddam Hussein**'s two sons, Qusay Hussein was in charge of elements of internal security and the Republican Guard in his father's regime prior to the US-led invasion of **Iraq** in 2003. He was responsible for mass prison executions in the late 1980s, retribution against Shi'ites who rose up against his father's regime after the **Persian Gulf War**, and the destruction of marshlands in southern Iraq that displaced so-called "Marsh Arabs" who lived there. Qusay and his brother, **Uday Hussein**, were killed by US forces in **Mosul**, Iraq, after a gunfight on 22 July 2003.

HUSSEIN AL-TIKRITI, SADDAM ABD AL-MAJID (1937–2006). A native of **Tikrit, Iraq**, Hussein acceded to the presidency of that country in 1979 under the banner of the secular, pan-Arab **Ba'ath Party**. During a war with **Iran** that lasted from 1980 to 1988, Hussein used chemical weapons against separatist **Kurds** in the north of Iraq. In 1990, he ordered the Iraqi Army to invade the tiny but oil-rich country of Kuwait, which brought about the **Persian Gulf War** in early 1991. The impressive international coalition assembled by President **George H.W. Bush** with the support of the **United Nations** (UN) pushed Iraqi forces out of Kuwait but stopped short of removing Hussein from power. Critics charge that Bush failed to take advantage of a key opportunity to bring greater stability to the Middle East by ousting Hussein. However, the UN mandate to the international coalition did not include Hussein's capture or removal from power. For more than a decade following the Persian Gulf War, the United States and **Great Britain** enforced "no-fly" zones in the north and in the south of Iraq to contain Hussein's military. The **neoconservative Project for the New American Century** wrote to President **William Clinton** in 1998, urging him to take military action to remove Hussein. Clinton demurred.

The Iraqi dictator was ultimately ousted by the US-led **Coalition of the Willing** that invaded Iraq in March 2003. The administration of **George W. Bush** attempted to link Hussein to **al-Qaeda terrorist**s that perpetrated the **11 September 2001** attacks on New York and the **Pentagon**. Bush and Vice President **Richard B. (Dick) Cheney** led the charge against Hussein by arguing he was attempting to procure **weapons of mass destruction** (WMDs) after ejecting UN arms inspectors from the country. While no WMDs were ever located, Hussein's regime—which Bush called part of an **axis of evil**—collapsed within a month of the start of the war, and Hussein was captured by US forces in December 2003. He was turned over to the interim Iraqi government in June 2004 to stand trial on charges of murder and torture. He was convicted of "crimes against humanity" by an Iraqi court in November 2006 and sentenced to be hanged to death. His sentence, which was carried out on 30 December 2006 at an Iraqi army base near **Baghdad**, was captured on video by a mobile cell phone and distributed on the Internet, raising worldwide controversy. *See also* BLIX, HANS; HASSAN AL-MAJID, ALI; WAR IN IRAQ.

HUSSEIN AL-TIKRITI, UDAY SADDAM (1964–2003). The eldest of Iraqi dictator **Saddam Hussein**'s two sons, Uday Hussein controlled the state media in **Iraq** during his father's regime and headed a small security force. He was known for his exuberant lifestyle, including expensive cars and clothes, and was once considered his father's heir apparent until a falling out in the mid-1990s. Uday struck fear in the hearts of many Iraqis for his murderous thuggery and establishment of "rape rooms" used to brutalize **women**. In 1988, he clubbed his father's food taster to death for having introduced him to a woman who would later become his father's wife; Uday reportedly viewed the marriage as an insult to his mother. His father imprisoned him briefly. In 1996, he survived an assassination attempt that left him in poor health. In 2001, he headed the Iraqi Olympic Committee and reportedly beat athletes who did not perform to his expectations. Uday, along with his brother, **Qusay Hussein**, was killed in a gun battle with US troops in **Mosul**, Iraq, on 22 July 2003.

– I –

IMCLONE. A pharmaceutical company established in 1984, ImClone's founder, Samuel Waksal, was arrested in 2002 on charges from the **Securities Exchange Commission** (SEC) that he had engaged in insider trading with friends and family. Waksal pleaded guilty to the charges, was sentenced to more than seven years in prison, and ordered to pay $4 million in fines. At issue was the timing of Waksal and others' sell-off of the company's stock prior to the Food and Drug Administration's (FDA) decision not to approve a new cancer drug. Also caught up in the scandal was television celebrity Martha Stewart, who sold nearly a quarter million dollars in ImClone stock a day before the FDA announcement. Stewart, who maintained her innocence, was sentenced to five months in prison and another five months of house arrest.

IMMIGRATION. Immigration issues were prominent during the presidency of **George W. Bush**. Front and center was the policy response to illegal immigration. Analyses estimate that nearly three-quarters of illegal immigrants to the United States are from **Mexico** or countries of Latin America. As a presidential candidate in 2000, George W. Bush called for a fence along the Mexican border and an end to the so-called "catch and release" of illegal immigrants who had been apprehended by authorities but were not deported if they had committed no other crime. However, Bush also sought to reach out to Hispanic voters and build inroads among a traditionally Democratic voting block. He appointed the first Hispanic attorney general in **Alberto Gonzales**. He also proposed a temporary guest worker program for illegal immigrants in January 2004. Bush's share of the Hispanic vote rose from approximately 35 percent in 2000 to 44 percent in 2004.

Bush's proposal for a guest worker program for immigrants, which many employers supported, became embroiled in greater controversy during his second term. Democrat Ted Kennedy of Massachusetts and Republican **John McCain** produced a Senate bill in 2005 (S. 1033, the Secure America and Orderly Immigration Act) that would have provided a path to legalization for illegal immigrants residing in the United States, guest worker programs, and various border security measures. Critics derided the bill as "amnesty" for illegal immigrants, and the legislation stalled. The last amnesty bill passed in Congress was in 1986, under President **Ronald Reagan**.

In 2005, Congress did pass the "Real ID Act," which mandated certain security and authentication measures by state authorities for the issuance of drivers' licenses and state forms of identification that would be accepted by the federal government. The bill was cast not only as an attempt to preclude illegal immigrants from obtaining drivers' licenses easily but also as a tool in the **War on Terror**.

In 2006, massive protests were sparked by a House bill introduced by Republican Representative James Sensenbrenner (The Border Protection, Antiterrorism, and Illegal Immigration Control Act of 2005) that would have, inter alia, provided minimum penalties on illegal immigrants and prohibited citizens from aiding undocumented aliens. The bill would have also mandated that the federal government take custody of illegal immigrants detained by local authorities—and that so-called "sanctuary cities" that failed to cooperate with federal authorities on immigration issues would lose federal grants. Critics charged that the bill's provisions were draconian and would have negative impacts on individuals seeking asylum or refugee status, as well as on community policing. The protests by many Hispanics, particularly in California, in April 2006, evoked controversy when they took to the streets waving Mexican and other nations' flags. Sensenbrenner's bill passed the House of Representatives but not the Senate.

By the end of 2006, comprehensive immigration reform had failed, in large measure due to the pending **mid-term elections**. In October 2006, Bush signed into law the Secure Fence Act, which provided for an additional 700 miles of fencing along the border with Mexico in Texas, New Mexico, Arizona, and California and other measures to impede illegal immigration. Several other bills, including the Comprehensive Immigration Reform Act of 2007, were discussed by the Democratic majority from 2007 to 2008 but failed to pass.

In August 2008, the US Immigration and Customs Enforcement (under the **Department of Homeland Security**) launched "Operation Scheduled Departure." The program was an attempt to convince an estimated 457,000 illegal immigrants without criminal convictions to leave the country voluntarily — in other words, "deport themselves" within 90 days of contacting the authorities. In the several weeks the operation was in place, only eight illegal immigrants came forward.

IMPROVISED EXPLOSIVE DEVICE (IED). The weapon of choice by **insurgents** in **Iraq** and **Afghanistan**, IEDs include bombs placed in cars; grenades, artillery rounds, or other explosives placed along roadsides; and types of rocket-propelled grenades and munitions that were used against US and coalition forces. Forty percent of the deaths of US troops in the **War in Iraq** were attributable to IEDs. *See also* ARMED FORCES.

INSURGENT, INSURGENCY. In the context of the **War in Iraq** and the US-led invasion of **Afghanistan**, the terms insurgent and insurgency refer to individuals and various rebel factions acting independently or with the support of the **terrorist** organization **al-Qaeda** or the **Taliban** to battle US and coalition forces using nonconventional methods, including **improvised explosive devices** or guerrilla tactics.

INTELLIGENCE REFORM AND TERRORISM PREVENTION ACT (2004). Passed by Congress and signed into law by President **George W. Bush**, this bill mandated sweeping reform of intelligence and security measures by the federal government in the wake of the **11 September 2001 terrorist** attacks. The centerpiece of the legislation was the establishment of a new **Director of National Intelligence** (DNI), to which the **Central Intelligence Agency** (CIA) reports, and a **National Counterterrorism Center**.

INTERNATIONAL ATOMIC ENERGY AGENCY (IAEA). Located in Vienna, Austria, the IAEA was founded as an independent agency of the **United Nations** (UN) in 1957. Its mission is to promote the safe, secure, and peaceful use of nuclear technology and multilateral cooperation. The IAEA played a significant role in the buildup to the **War in Iraq** in 2003. The director of the IAEA, **Mohammed ElBaradei**, along with UN chief weapons inspector **Hans Blix**, searched for evidence, posited by the United States and **Great Britain**, that Iraqi dictator **Saddam Hussein** had violated the terms of the **Persian Gulf War** settlement by producing **weapons of mass destruction** (WMDs). Their search did not uncover any such program in **Iraq** prior to the March 2003 US-led invasion. ElBaradei was particularly critical of the US justification for military action based on independent intelligence. *See also* DOWNING STREET MEMO; KAY, DAVID.

INTERNATIONAL CRIMINAL COURT (ICC). The ICC was established in 2002 in The Hague, Netherlands. Its mission is to investigate and prosecute allegations of genocide and war crimes. By the end of 2008, 108 countries had ratified the Rome Statute that established the court. President **William Clinton** signed the Rome Statute in 2000. However, the treaty was not ratified under the administration of **George W. Bush**. **United Nations** (UN) Ambassador **John Bolton** outlined the administration's opposition to the court, citing concerns over national sovereignty. In 2005, the United States nonetheless supported a UN resolution mandating that charges of genocide in the **Darfur** region of **Sudan** be investigated by the ICC. Other countries that have not ratified the ICC include **China**, India, and **Russia**. *See also* MORENO-OCAMPO, LUIS.

INTERNATIONAL SECURITY ASSISTANCE FORCE (ISAF). In December 2001, the **United Nations** (UN) authorized a security and reconstruction mission in **Afghanistan** led by the **North Atlantic Treaty Organization** (NATO). ISAF was established following the October 2001 US invasion of Afghanistan, which toppled the **Taliban** regime and targeted **al-Qaeda terrorist**s. ISAF troops numbered approximately 43,000 by the end of 2008, and included 26 NATO countries and five other nonmember countries. The contingent of US forces numbered approximately 32,000. ISAF was originally tasked with solidifying security gains in Afghanistan's capital, **Kabul**. In December 2003, the UN expanded ISAF's mission to cover the entire country, with the objective of achieving security and stability in the war-torn nation. Beginning in 2006, however, ISAF forces increasingly faced resistance from Taliban **insurgents**. US and Canadian troops suffered a disproportionate number of casualties. General Dan McNeill, the US general who headed ISAF, contended in 2008 that the insurgency was not worsening. However, during the 2008 election Democratic presidential candidate **Barack Obama** posited that the insurgency made Afghanistan, not **Iraq**, the front line in the **War on Terror**. *See also* ARMED FORCES; CANADA; KARZAI, HAMID.

INTERNET. A global communications exchange system preceded by the World Wide Web in the 1990s, the Internet became a staple of life in the United States from 2000 to 2008. The number of Internet users worldwide nearly quadrupled during this period. The Internet allows users to exchange and access vast amounts of information using personal computers that are connected virtually around the globe by servers. Search engines, such as Google and Yahoo, enable users to easily research subjects and find scores of websites, from shopping to scholarly research and publications.

The Internet had a profound impact on politics during the presidency of **George W. Bush**. Bush followed the lead of his predecessor, **William Clinton**, by making White House documents, details on the president's policies, speeches, and other governmental information available on the Internet—so called "e-government."

The Internet also had a profound effect on political organizations. In 2000, Democratic presidential hopeful **Howard Dean** used the

Internet to raise record amounts of funds—mostly from individual donors making contributions of $100 or less. In 2008, Democratic presidential nominee **Barack Obama** used the Internet similarly for fund-raising. Obama also used digital technology to keep supporters apprised of his campaign appearances, policy stances, and grassroots efforts by sending frequent electronic messages (e-mail) via the Internet and to cell phones.

Web logs or "blogs" on the Internet revolutionized political dialogue during Bush's two terms. Blogs are message strings, freely accessible by all on the Internet, in which ideas may be exchanged and virtual debates held. The explosion in the number of blogs on the Internet spanned not only presidential campaigns but also opponents and proponents of the **War in Iraq** and the **War on Terror**.

While many support the Internet's potential for e-government, "e-commerce," and civic dialogue, detractors point to the medium's drawbacks. Online shopping has damaged local retail sales as many consumers prefer to purchase goods through their computers. State governments and Congress continue to wrestle with issues surrounding the taxation of goods purchased on the Internet. The Internet has also contributed to a significant decline in newspaper readership and print news sales as individuals can read newspapers selectively for free online. Others lament the ubiquity of pornography on the Internet and its possible access by children. Finally, some question the quality of civic dialogue in blogs or Internet chatrooms as individuals exchange information and ideas virtually, rather than make the person-to-person connections required to build community solidarity and trust—elements vital to "social capital" according to some scholars. That many blog sites contain inaccurate or untruthful information may also have further negative ramifications, including the undermining of political parties.

INTERSTATE 35 (I-35 BRIDGE COLLAPSE). This highway runs in a north–south direction, beginning in Duluth, Minnesota, and terminating in Laredo, Texas. On the evening of 1 August 2007, a bridge over the Mississippi River on I-35 in Minneapolis, Minnesota, collapsed at the height of rush-hour traffic. Thirteen people were killed and another 145 injured when the center span of 40-year-old bridge failed and approximately 100 vehicles fell into the river. The incident accentuated growing concerns about the overall state of aging infrastructure of the nation's bridges and roads.

IOWA CAUCUSES. The Iowa Caucuses are central in US presidential elections. The caucuses are, along with the **New Hampshire Primary**, a major electoral test for presidential candidates in the primary season and a bellwether of potential support in a general election campaign. The caucuses are meetings of individuals and party activists across Iowa's 99 counties that ultimately select delegates for the presidential nominating conventions in the Democratic and Republican parties. **George W. Bush** won the Iowa Caucuses with 41 percent of the vote in 2000 (he did not face a Republican challenger in 2004). Democrat **Al Gore** won the Iowa Caucuses with 63 percent of the vote in 2000; **John Kerry** received 38 percent in 2004, ranking 6 percent higher than **John Edwards** and outpacing **Howard Dean** by 20 percent.

IRAN. With a population of 70 million and significant oil and natural gas reserves, Iran borders **Russia, Afghanistan, Pakistan,** and **Iraq** (as well as Armenia, Azerbaijan, Turkmenistan, Kazakhstan, **Turkey**, and the Caspian Sea) and has been of enormous geopolitical importance to the **foreign policy** of the United States, including that of President **George W. Bush**. The bilateral relationship between the United States and Iran has been troubled since the presidency of Jimmy Carter.

The capital of Iran, Tehran, was the locus of the revolution in 1979 that forced the Shah into exile and facilitated the return of Ayahtollah Ruhollah Khomeini. Khomeini achieved an Islamic Republic that made him supreme leader. That same year, students raided the US embassy and held more than 50 Americans hostage for 444 days. The hostages were released the evening that **Ronald Reagan** was inaugurated in January 1981.

From 1980 to 1988, Iran and **Iraq** engaged in a protracted military conflict. The United States gave measured support to the secular **Ba'ath Party** regime of **Saddam Hussein**. Nonetheless, it is estimated that between a half million and a million Iranians and Iraqis perished in a war that was reminiscent of the atrocities of World War I. The **United Nations** (UN), which brokered a cease-fire, confirmed that Iraq used chemical weapons against Iranians, as well as against **Kurds** in the north of Iraq.

In the wake of the Iran–Iraq War, in the late 1980s and 1990s, reformist Presidents Akbar Hashemi Rafsanjani and Mohammad Khatami focused on economic reconstruction. Nonetheless, Iran had been listed by the US Department of State as a state sponsor of **terrorism** since 1984. Relations between the United States and Iran became aggravated anew during the presidency of George W. Bush. In his State of the Union address in 2002, Bush identified Iran, along with Iraq and **North Korea**, as part of an **axis of evil** for allegedly seeking **weapons of mass destruction** (WMDs). Moreover, Bush accused Iran of supporting **terrorist** groups, such as **Hezbollah**. The Bush administration further accused Iran of providing safe haven for **al-Qaeda** terrorists crossing the border with Iraq and aiding the **insurgency** against US and coalition troops in the **War in Iraq**.

In 2005, bilateral relations between the United States and Iran worsened when conservative **Mahmoud Ahmadinejad** won the Iranian presidency. Ahmadinejad called for the destruction of **Israel** and sought close relationships with traditional adversaries of the United States, including **Fidel Castro** of Cuba and **Hugo Chávez** of **Venezuela**, and with **Syria** and **Russia**. The greatest controversy centered on Ahmadinejad's pursuit of nuclear technology, which he claimed was for peaceful purposes only but which the United States and UN contend violate provisions of the **Nuclear Non-Proliferation Treaty**. In December 2006, led by the United States, the UN imposed sanctions on Iran for failing to terminate the enrichment of nuclear material. Although Iran enabled inspectors from the **International Atomic Energy Agency** (IAEA) to review its nuclear program, successive reports in 2007 and 2008 showed that Iran continued its enrichment of uranium and prompted the UN to impose wider economic sanctions. Nonetheless, experts estimate that Iran's first nuclear power plant could be operational in 2009.

IRAQ. The country of Iraq has borders with Kuwait, Saudi Arabia, Jordan, **Syria**, **Iran**, and **Turkey** and has limited access to the Persian Gulf. Its capital is the ancient city of **Baghdad**. Given its geographic location and oil reserves, Iraq, like Iran, is of vital importance to United States **foreign policy**.

Saddam Hussein and his **Ba'ath Party** seized power in Iraq in 1979. Opposed to the Islamic Revolution in Iran, Hussein claimed that Iran had attempted to overthrow his regime. In 1980, hostilities between the two countries sparked the Iran–Iraq War, which lasted until 1988. The United States had given measured support for Iraq, but had placed troops in Saudia Arabia as a hedge against a widening of the war that might also threaten **Israel**.

Iraq provoked a major international crisis when Hussein invaded the tiny, oil-rich emirate of Kuwait in August 1990. President **George H.W. Bush** sought and won approval for military action sanctioned by the **United Nations** (UN). He assembled a multinational coalition for the **Persian Gulf War**, which forced Hussein's eventual retreat from Kuwait in 1991. The UN mandate called for the restoration of a sovereign Kuwait, but not the ouster of Hussein. As part of the postwar settlement, Hussein had to accede to weapons inspections by the UN and the imposition of "no-fly" zones patrolled by the United States and **Great Britain** to ensure that his regime did not threaten neighboring countries. In 1998, the **Project for the New American Century** (PNAC), a prominent **neoconservative** foreign policy think tank, urged President **William Clinton** to take action to remove Hussein from power for allegedly violating the terms of the post-Persian Gulf War settlement. Clinton demurred, but did authorize numerous military engagements that shot down Iraqi military planes that violated the no-fly zones.

Following the **terrorist** attacks on New York and the **Pentagon** on **11 September 2001**, President **George W. Bush** contended that Hussein and his regime had connections with the **al-Qaeda** operatives who carried out the attacks. Moreover, in his 2002 State of the Union address, Bush posited that Iraq was part of an **axis of evil** that included Iran and **North Korea**. He argued that these regimes were doggedly pursuing **weapons of mass destruction** (WMDs). With respect to Iraq, Bush defended his claims by contending that Hussein's regime had attempted to purchase nuclear material from **Niger** and pointed to Hussein's decision to expel UN weapons inspectors from Iraq, in violation of the post-Persian Gulf War agreement.

In October 2002, the US Congress authorized Bush to take military action against Iraq (the **Iraq War Resolution**). The resolution cited Hussein's violation of UN mandates, including the pursuit of WMDs. Bush and Secretary of State **Colin Powell** urged the UN to sanction multilateral action, but French President **Jacques Chirac** led opposition on the Security Council and threatened to veto any resolution that called for military options in Iraq. As a result, Bush assembled a

Coalition of the Willing—countries that included Great Britain—and invaded Iraq in March 2003. The immediate military action was successful. US and coalition forces captured Baghdad and other major cities within four to six weeks; Hussein fled, was ultimately captured nine months later, and was hanged by Iraqi authorities in December 2006. The subsequent **War in Iraq**, however, pitted US and coalition forces against a growing number of **insurgents** beginning in 2006 that complicated efforts to secure peace for the new Iraqi government led by Prime Minister **Nouri al-Maliki** and President **Jalal Talabani**.

IRAQ GOVERNING COUNCIL (IGC). The IGC was the provisional government of **Iraq** from July 2003 through June 2004. The majority of members (13) on the IGC were Shi'ite Muslims. The 25 members of the IGC were appointed by the **Coalition Provisional Authority** (CPA) under administrator **L. Paul Bremer**, and included notable leaders **Ahmed Chalabi**, **Jalal Talabani**, **Ibrahim al-Jaafari**, Ghazi Mashal Ajil al-Yawer, and **Iyad Allawi**. The IGC was to provide leadership and input to the CPA prior to the transfer of authority to the interim and transitional governments that reestablished Iraq's sovereignty following the US-led invasion in March 2003.

IRAQ STUDY GROUP. Congress appointed the bipartisan Iraq Study Group, charged with evaluating the **War in Iraq** and making recommendations, on 14 March 2006. Cochaired by former Secretary of State **James Baker** (Republican) and former Representative Lee Hamilton (Democrat), the Iraq Study Group's other four Republican members included former **Supreme Court** justice **Sandra Day O'Connor**, former Secretary of State Lawrence Eagleburger, former Attorney General Edwin Meese, and former Wyoming Senator Alan Simpson; the other four Democrats included Vernon Jordan, former White House Chief of Staff Leon Panetta, former Secretary of Defense William Perry, and former Virginia Senator Charles Robb. Former New York Mayor **Rudolph Giuliani** resigned from the group on 24 May 2006; **Robert Gates** resigned on 8 November 2006 when he was nominated to be secretary of defense.

The group issued a final report on 6 December 2006. The report alleged that the **Pentagon** had underestimated the **insurgency** in **Iraq**, and that US troop commitments elsewhere impeded strengthening troop levels in Iraq. Moreover, the report suggested that the war in Iraq had diverted critical resources from **Afghanistan**, where **Taliban insurgents** had begun to step up attacks on US and coalition troops. Finally, the report recommended diplomatic engagement with **Iran** and **Syria** to obtain a sustainable peace in Iraq and that significant power should be shifted to Iraqi authorities. *See also* ARMED FORCES.

IRAQ WAR. *See* WAR IN IRAQ.

IRAQ WAR RESOLUTION. Known formally as the Authorization for the Use of Military Force Against Iraq Resolution of 2002, this bill was signed into law by President **George W. Bush** on 16 October 2002. It passed the House of Representatives by a vote of 296–133 on 10 October 2002. Only six Republicans voted against the resolution; 126 of 208 Democrats voted against the bill. The bill passed the Senate by a vote of 77–23 on 11 October 2002. It passed with the support of 48 of 49 Republicans and 29 of 50 Democrats. Arizona Senator **John McCain**, the 2008 Republican presidential nominee, voted in favor of the bill; 2004 Democratic presidential candidate **John Kerry** also voted for the bill; New York Senator **Hillary Clinton**, a contender for the 2008 Democratic presidential nomination, also voted in favor of the bill. The eventual 2008 Democratic presidential nominee, **Barack Obama**, was not in the Senate at the time of the vote but later criticized the **War in Iraq** as a mistake.

The resolution authorized the president to take military action against **Iraq** and the regime of dictator **Saddam Hussein**, which he did in March 2003. Among the most serious allegations contained in the bill was that Hussein was actively pursuing **weapons of mass destruction** (WMDs) and had violated the terms of the cease-fire from the **Persian Gulf War** in 1991 by expelling **United Nations** (UN) weapons inspectors and violating "no-fly" zones in the north and south of Iraq. Further, the bill alleged that Hussein had tried to assassinate President **George H.W. Bush** in 1993, harbored **terror**ists, and that **al-Qaeda** operatives were known to be in Iraq.

Although the bill called for the removal of Saddam Hussein, it also encouraged President George W. Bush to employ diplomacy and work through the UN. Bush and Secretary of State **Colin Powell** attempted to convince the UN not only that Hussein was connected to al-Qaeda and the **11 September 2001** attacks on New York and the **Pentagon** but also that he had been stockpiling WMDs. When French President **Jacques Chirac** made it clear that **France** would block any UN authorization for military force against Iraq, Bush assembled an international coalition, the **Coalition of the Willing**, that acted unilaterally without a UN mandate. *See also* WAR ON TERROR.

IRELAND. *See* LISBON TREATY; NORTHERN IRELAND.

IRISH REPUBLICAN ARMY. *See* NORTHERN IRELAND.

ISLAMIC DAWA PARTY. This conservative Islamic political party was formed to combat secularism and socialism in **Iraq**. The party's founder, Mohammad Baqir al-Sadran, opposed the **Ba'ath Party** of **Saddam Hussein**, who imprisoned him in 1980. The Islamic Dawa Party supported the revolution in **Iran** and had launched an insurgency against Iraq in 1979–1980. A split between al-Sadran and Dawa supporters in **Lebanon**, who looked to the Iranian Ayatollah Ruhollah Khomeini for leadership, effectively divided the party. Following the US-led invasion of Iraq in March 2003 and Hussein's ouster, many exiled members of the Dawa Party returned to their homeland. The Dawa Party drew the most votes as part of the United Iraqi Alliance in the elections of January and December 2005. Both post-invasion prime ministers—**Ibrahim al-Jaafari** and his successor, **Nouri al-Maliki**—belonged to Dawa.

ISLAMIC JIHAD. Also known as Egyptian Islamic Jihad, this **terrorist** group was formed in the 1970s out of the Muslim Brotherhood, which sought to overthrow the Egyptian government. The group was responsible for the assassination of President Anwar Sadat in 1981 and made an attempt on the life of President Hosni Mubarak in 1995. **Ayman al-Zawahiri** took over leadership of the group in 1995, merging it with **al-Qaeda** in **Afghanistan** just prior to the **11 September 2001** attacks on New York and the **Pentagon**. *See also* BIN LADEN, OSAMA; TALIBAN; TERRORISM; TERRORIST.

ISOLATIONISM. *See* FOREIGN POLICY; NEOCONSERVATIVE.

ISRAEL. Israel was founded on 15 May 1948 as a Jewish state. Partition of the former British Mandate of Palestine into Arab and Jewish components had been approved by the **United Nations** a year earlier. An ensuing civil war between Palestinian Arabs and Jews in 1948 prompted military intervention from Israel's Arab Neighbors. Following a cease-fire in 1949, Jordan occupied what became known as the **West Bank**, Egypt the area known as the **Gaza Strip**, and Israel expanded the reaches of its western borders. The West Bank and Gaza Strip became a refuge for Palestinians within the Jewish state and a bone of contention between Israel and its Arab neighbors for decades to come.

President **George W. Bush** was a strong supporter of a peaceful resolution to the conflict between Israelis and Palestinians. He visited Israel in 1998 before he became president. During the 2000 election, he publicly stated that the United States should be a better friend to Israel. He was critical of **Palestine Liberation Organization** (PLO) leader **Yasser Arafat**, who died in 2004. In 2003, he favored talks between Israeli Prime Minister **Ariel Sharon** and Palestinian Prime Minister **Mahmoud Abbas**, which were made possible by the **Road Map for Peace**. The Road Map for Peace, agreed upon by the United States, the **United Nations**, the **European Union**, and **Russia**, called for an independent Palestinian state. Bush supported Sharon's decision to withdraw unilaterally and relocate Jewish settlers from the **Gaza Strip** in 2005.

Bush also supported Israel's military action in **Lebanon** in July and August 2006, calling it part of the **War on Terror**. After rocket attacks launched from inside Lebanon killed and wounded several Israeli soldiers and resulted in the capture of several more, Prime Minister **Ehud Olmert** ordered retaliatory strikes against the **terrorist** group **Hezbollah**, which is supported by **Iran** and **Syria**. The ensuing 33-day war ended with a cease-fire brokered by the United Nations; estimates of deaths in the conflict range from a few hundred civilians and Hezbollah fighters to more than a thousand. Bush made his first visit to Israel as president in January 2008 to promote peace in the Middle East.

IVINS, BRUCE EDWARDS (1946–2008). *See* ANTHRAX (ATTACKS).

– J –

JACKSON, ALPHONSO ROY (1945–). A Texas native who grew up in Dallas, Jackson graduated with bachelor's and master's degrees from Truman State University in Missouri. He earned a law degree from Washington University (St. Louis) in 1973. In the 1970s, he worked for the St. Louis, Missouri, Housing Authority. From 1989 to 1996 he was chief executive officer of the Dallas, Texas, Housing Authority. **George W. Bush**, then governor of Texas, appointed Jackson to the Board of Regents of Texas Southern University in 1995.

Jackson joined the administration of George W. Bush in 2001, when he became deputy secretary at the Department of Housing and Urban Development (HUD). He became acting secretary of HUD when **Mel Martinez** resigned to campaign for a Senate seat from Florida in 2004. Bush nominated Jackson as secretary, and he was confirmed in March 2004. Jackson tendered his resignation as HUD secretary in March 2008 and was succeeded by **Steven C. Preston** in April 2008.

JEFFERSON, WILLIAM JENNINGS (1947–). Born in Lake Providence, Louisiana, Jefferson earned a bachelor's degree from Southern University (1969), a law degree from Harvard University (1972), and a master of laws degree in taxation from Georgetown University (1996). He was a law clerk for Judge Alvin B. Rubin of the US District Court for the eastern district of Louisiana from 1972 to 1973. From 1973 to 1975, he was a legislative assistant to veteran Democratic Senator J. Bennett Johnson of Louisiana.

Jefferson entered politics in 1980, when he was elected to the Louisiana Senate from New Orleans, and was re-elected four times through 1990. He ran unsuccessfully for the mayorship of New Orleans in 1982 and in 1986. In 1990, he launched a successful bid for a seat in the House of Representatives, winning Louisiana's second congressional district. He was the first African-American elected to the House from Louisiana since Reconstruction. In the House, he joined the Black Caucus, served on the powerful Ways and Means Committee, and was a staunch supporter of **William Clinton**'s presidential campaign in 1992. He was re-elected nine times through 2008.

Jefferson received national and international attention when he was investigated by the **Federal Bureau of Investigation** (FBI) on suspicion of corruption. At issue were alleged bribes Jefferson took to facilitate a Louisville, Kentucky-based technology company's relations with several African nations and the Export-Import Bank. The FBI caught Jefferson on videotape taking the alleged bribes and uncovered $90,000 in his freezer when law enforcement officials raided his home in August 2005.

In an unprecedented move, the FBI also raided Jefferson's offices on Capitol Hill in May 2006, which prompted members of Congress—including Republican **Dennis Hastert** and Speaker **Nancy Pelosi**—to demand that the FBI return the material taken from Jefferson's office. Hastert, Pelosi, and others suggested that the FBI had breached the constitutional separation of powers between the executive and legislative branches. A legal battle ensued, which ultimately entitled Jefferson to review the documents taken by law enforcement to determine if the files were subject to privilege. In 2006, several of Jefferson's aides pleaded guilty to charges concerning the bribery allegations. House leaders forced Jefferson to step down from his committee assignment on Ways and Means as a federal investigation continued. Jefferson nonetheless prevailed in his re-election bid in 2006, aided by strong African-American support in his New Orleans district in the wake of the federal mishandling of relief efforts following **Hurricane Katrina** a year earlier. In June 2007, he was indicted on seven counts, including bribery, to which he pleaded not guilty. He lost his 2008 re-election bid to Republican Joseph Cao.

JEFFORDS, JAMES MERRILL (1934–). A native of Rutland, Vermont, Jeffords graduated from Yale University (1956) and from Harvard Law School (1962). He served in the US Navy from 1956 to 1959, and remained in the reserves until 1990, when he retired at the rank of captain.

Jeffords began his political career in politics in 1966, when he won a seat to the Vermont Senate. Two years later, he won the statewide race for attorney general. A Republican, he ran successfully for the Vermont seat in the House of Representatives in 1974. He won re-election to the House six times and served on the Education and Labor Committee. In 1988, Jeffords won election to the US Senate from Vermont and was re-elected twice. He retired in 2006 and was succeeded by socialist Bernie Sanders, who caucuses with the Democratic Party. While in the Senate, Jeffords served as chair of the Committee on Labor and Human Resources, and was a member of the Health, Education, Labor, and Pensions and Environment and Public Works Committees.

Jeffords stirred ample controversy in the 107th Congress (2001–2002). On 24 May 2001, he switched his affiliation from the Republican Party to Independent, and threw his support to the Democrats. The move was allegedly due to disagreements with Republicans over an educational bill. However, many observers noted that Jeffords had one of the most liberal voting records among Republicans. Regardless, Jeffords' defection enabled the Democrats to organize the Senate with majority status just five months into the legislative session. Following the 2000 elections, party control was divided evenly, 50–50, in the upper chamber. Vice President **Richard (Dick) Cheney**, who would cast a tie-breaking vote, had previously enabled the Republicans to hold a majority. Jeffords' defection had palpable consequences for President **George W. Bush**, particularly on the reorganization of federal agencies into the **Department of Homeland Security**. Republicans regained the majority in the Senate in the 2002 **mid-term elections**.

JIHAD, JIHADIST. Typically translated as "holy war," the word jihad in Arabic connotes a struggle or crusade. The English-language press usually refers to anyone engaged in jihad as a "jihadist," although in Arabic the term used is "mujahid" (singular) or **mujahideen** (plural). Jihad may be called for by Muslim spiritual leaders, is a religious obligation for Muslims, and the Koran teaches that soldiers who die in jihad go to heaven immediately. Muslim scholars disagree whether jihad should be interpreted as an internal struggle of the soul, or as a battle against "infidels" (non-Muslims).

Following the **Soviet Union**'s invasion of **Afghanistan** in the late 1970s, spiritual leaders called for jihad, and mujahideen fighters battled Soviet forces with the support of the United States and other countries. President **Ronald Reagan** called the mujahideen "freedom fighters." Importantly, **Osama bin Laden**, who masterminded the **11 September 2001** terror attacks on New York and the **Pentagon**, led the mujahideen effort. Jihad has since been promoted by various Islamic **terrorist** groups, including **al-Qaeda**, **Hezbollah**, and **Hamas**, which call for the destruction of **Israel**. During the 1980–1988 war between **Iran** and **Iraq**, Ayatollah Khomeini of Iran declared jihad against the secular **Ba'ath Party** regime of **Saddam Hussein**.

During the presidency of **George W. Bush** jihad became increasingly connected to the **War on Terror**. Following the US-led invasion of Afghanistan in October 2001, remnants of the **Taliban** regime declared jihad against the "forces of oppression." The call to jihad was taken up by **insurgents**, including al-Qaeda terrorists, who engaged in guerrilla warfare against US and coalition troops as part of the **International Security Assistance Force** (ISAF).

"JOE THE PLUMBER." *See* WURZELBACHER, SAMUEL JO-SEPH.

JOHANNS, MICHAEL OWEN (1950–). Johanns was born in Osage, Iowa. He attended St. Mary's College and earned a law degree from Creighton University. He practiced law in O'Neill and Lincoln, Nebraska, before seeking public office in 1982, when he won a four-year term on the Lancaster County Board of Commissioners. He was elected to the Lincoln city council in 1989, and became Lincoln mayor in 1991. He was re-elected mayor in 1995. He was elected governor of Nebraska in 1998 and won re-election easily in 2002.

Johanns succeeded **Ann Veneman** as secretary of agriculture under President **George W. Bush** in January 2005. In September 2007, he resigned as secretary to run for the open Senate seat vacated by Republican Chuck Hagel. He was succeeded as secretary of agriculture by **Edward Schafer**. Johanns won election to the Senate in 2008 with 58 percent of the vote.

JOHN PAUL II (1920–2004). Born Karol Jozef Wojtyla in Poland, John Paul became pope of the Catholic Church in October 1978. He was the first non-Italian to reign as pope in more than 400 years. He survived two assassination attempts in the early 1980s—one in May 1981 and another in May 1982. He died in 2004 of natural causes. In 2005, his successor, Pope **Benedict XVI**, initiated the process to have John Paul II beatified. He was one of the most widely venerated popes of the 20th century.

JOHNSON, STEPHEN L. (1951–). A native of Washington, D.C., Johnson graduated with a bachelor's degree from Taylor University in Indiana and a master's degree in pathology from George Washington University. He was director of operations at Hazelton Laboratories Corporation and Litton Bionetics, Inc., before joining the Environmental Protection Agency (EPA) in the 1970s. At the EPA, he was acting administrator, deputy administrator, acting deputy administrator, and assistant administrator of the Office of Prevention, Pesticides, and Toxic Substances. Johnson succeeded **Michael Leavitt** as acting administrator of the EPA in January 2005. President **George W. Bush** nominated him to fill the vacancy permanently in March 2005.

In May 2008, Johnson testified before Congress concerning allegations that the White House had interfered with his decision to grant the State of California a waiver to limit the so-called "greenhouse gases" that are putatively one of the major causes of climate change and global warming. Johnson had allegedly been ready to grant California a waiver to enact special restrictions, but rescinded the waiver when President Bush disagreed. Democrats on the Senate Environment and Publics Work Committee called for Johnson's resignation. Johnson had refused to turn over documents that the House Oversight and Government Reform Committee subpoenaed.

JOINT CHIEFS OF STAFF. The heads of each of the armed services — the Air Force, Army, Marines, and Navy — comprise the Joint Chiefs, which is headed by a chairman and a vice chairman for a total of six members. Their charge is to advise the president on military operations, planning, and intelligence. The advisory role of the Joint Chiefs is statutory under the National Security Act of 1947, which also created the **National Security Council** (NSC). *See also* ARMED FORCES; MULLEN, MICHAEL; MYERS, RICHARD; PACE, PETER; SHELTON, HUGH.

– **K** –

KABUL, AFGHANISTAN. The capital of **Afghanistan**, Kabul has a population of approximately 3 million. The city was occupied by

Soviet troops in the 1980s, and fell under the control of the **Taliban** in 1996. With the aid of **mujahideen** fighters of the **Northern Alliance**, US troops captured Kabul quickly following the invasion of Afghanistan in October 2001. Kabul is the location of the Afghan government, both during the transitional administration and under President **Hamid Karzai**.

KARADŽIĆ, RADOVAN (1945–). Educated as a psychiatrist, Karadžić was president of the Serbian Republic of the former **Yugoslavia** (1992–96). He was indicted as a war criminal for alleged crimes against Bosnian Muslims and Croats in the Bosnian War from 1992 to 1995. He went into hiding in 1996. He was arrested in Belgrade on 18 July 2008 and extradited to the International Criminal Tribunal for the former Yugoslavia in The Hague, Netherlands. As of early 2009, he awaited trial.

KARPINSKI, JANIS LEIGH, COL. (1953–). A member of the Army since 1977, Karpinski served in the **Persian Gulf War**. She became a reservist in 1987. Following the invasion of **Iraq** in March 2003, Karpinski was charged with overseeing 15 military detention facilities, one of which was **Abu Ghraib**. Journalist **Seymour Hersh** detailed allegations of abuse of prisoners at Abu Ghraib in April 2004. More than two dozen personnel were implicated in the abuse, including Lynndie England and Charles Graner, who were photographed in the act. Lieutenant General **Ricardo Sanchez** had suspended Karpinski in January 2004. In April 2005, she was relieved of command, and in May 2005 she was demoted from brigadier general to colonel. She is author of *One Woman's Army: The Commanding General of Abu Ghraib Tells Her Story* (2005), in which she contends her demotion was political retribution and that she was not cognizant of the abuse. She argued that prisoner abuse was perpetuated in **Afghanistan** and **Guantanamo Bay, Cuba**, by contract employees at the behest of Secretary of Defense **Donald Rumsfeld**.

KARZAI, HAMID (1957–). Born in Kandahar, **Afghanistan**, Karzai studied politics in India. He actively supported and raised money for the **mujahadeen** fighters following the **Soviet Union**'s invasion of Afghanistan in 1979 and liaised with the **Central Intelligence Agency** (CIA), which clandestinely provided financial aid and arms to anti-Soviet, Afghan **insurgent**s. When Soviet troops eventually withdrew, Karzai became deputy foreign minister from 1992 to 1996 in the government of Burhanuddin Rabbani. Four years of civil war chased Rabbani from power when the **Taliban** clerics gained control of **Kabul**, the Afghan capital, in 1996.

Karzai supported **Northern Alliance** and mujahadeen fighters against the Taliban regime, which had given aid and succor to **Osama bin Laden**, mastermind of the **11 September 2001 terrorist** attacks on New York and the **Pentagon**. The Taliban was toppled by the US-led invasion of Afghanistan in October 2001. In 2001, Karzai was wounded in a "friendly-fire" incident with US troops.

Karzai became chair of the interim transitional government in December 2001. In June 2002, the Afghan *Loya Jirga*, an assembly of tribal leaders, appointed him president of the transitional government. On 9 October 2004, he won a national election for the presidency and became the first democratically elected president in Afghan history. Between 2002 and 2008, he survived four assassination attempts.

Karzai enjoyed good relations with President **George W. Bush**, who endorsed him for the presidency in 2004. Nonetheless, as the Taliban and **al-Qaeda insurgency** stiffened in 2006 he rebuffed notions that **Iran** was supporting the terrorists. Karzai came under some criticism for his willingness to negotiate with the Taliban, which he had briefly supported in the early 1990s.

KASICH, JOHN RICHARD (1952–). Kasich is a native of McKees Rocks, Pennsylvania. He earned an undergraduate degree from Ohio State University in 1974. After serving as an assistant to a state senator, Kasich ran successfully for the Ohio Senate in 1978. He first won a seat to the US House of Representatives in 1982. He was re-elected eight times. A fiscal conservative, Kasich served on the Budget Committee and was chair from 1995 to 2000. He formed an exploratory committee for the Republican presidential nomination in 1999 but withdrew without contesting any races and supported **George W. Bush**. Kasich did not stand for re-election to the House in 2000. He took a position with the financial firm of **Lehman Brothers** and hosted a television program on Fox News Channel, which was canceled in April 2007.

KAY, DAVID A. (1940–). A graduate of the University of Texas at Austin, Kay holds master's and doctoral degrees from Columbia

University in international affairs. Following the **Persian Gulf War**, Kay was the chief **United Nations** weapons inspector in **Iraq** from 1991 to 1992, charged with identifying and destroying potential **weapons of mass destruction** (WMDs). From 1993 to 2001, he worked for Science Applications International Corporation on weapons development issues.

Kay was appointed by the **Director of National Intelligence** (DNI) to head the Iraq Survey Group following the US-led invasion of **Iraq** in March 2003. The Group's mandate was to search for WMDs stockpiled by the regime of **Saddam Hussein**. In January 2004, Kay concluded that no such stockpiles existed, and he subsequently resigned his post. The findings called into question the intelligence and rationale used by President **George W. Bush** to justify the invasion, and Kay was questioned by Congress about the putative prewar intelligence failures. Kay later took a position as senior fellow at the Potomac Institute for Policy Studies, where he concentrated on matters of counterterrorism and weapons proliferation.

KEMPTHORNE, DIRK ARTHUR (1951–). A native of San Bernardino, California, Kempthorne earned a degree in political science from the University of Idaho (1975). He first began a career in public service with the Idaho Department of Lands. He entered politics in 1985 by winning the mayorship of Boise, Idaho, and won re-election in 1989. In 1992, he successfully ran for a Senate seat in Idaho. After one term in the Senate, he ran for governor of Idaho and won the election with 68 percent of the vote. He was re-elected in 2002. In March 2006, President **George W. Bush** nominated Kempthorne to secretary of the interior to replace **Gale Norton**. He was approved unanimously in May 2006. Critics of Kempthorne contended that he did not support protection of endangered species and was opposed to stricter environmental regulations.

KERIK, BERNARD BAILEY (1955–). A career law enforcement officer, Kerik was born in Newark, New Jersey. He served as police commissioner in New York City from 2000 to 2001 under Mayor **Rudolph Giuliani**. President **George W. Bush** nominated Kerik to replace **Tom Ridge** as secretary of the **Department of Homeland Security** in December 2004. Within a week Kerik withdrew his nomination over allegations that he had hired an illegal immigrant to care for his children. Bush subsequently nominated **Michael Cher-toff**, who was confirmed as secretary in early 2005. In 2006, Kerik pleaded guilty to ethics charges brought about by authorities in New York City; in 2007, he was indicted on charges relating to the Internal Revenue Service.

KERRY, JOHN FORBES (1943–). Born in Colorado, Kerry attended boarding schools in Massachusetts as a child. He graduated from Yale University with a major in political science in 1966. Having joined the Naval Reserve in 1965, Kerry entered military service in 1966 as a lieutenant and was sent to Vietnam. He was the recipient of a Silver Star, a Bronze Star, and three Purple Hearts for valor, and he served until 1970. A vocal critic of the war in Vietnam, he was the first veteran to testify before Congress. Still a reservist, he joined the group Vietnam Veterans Against the War, which staged protests around the country. He was one of the organizers for Operation POW, a series of antiwar protests that sought to bring attention to the plight of prisoners of war, for which he was arrested and detained briefly in May 1971.

Kerry entered politics in 1972 as a Democrat in an abortive attempt to win a congressional seat in Lowell, Massachusetts. He subsequently returned to law school and graduated from Boston College in 1976, then worked as an assistant district attorney for Middlesex County, Massachusetts, until 1982—at which time he successfully ran for lieutenant governor of Massachusetts. Two years later, he launched a successful campaign for the US Senate, replacing retiring Senator Paul Tsongas. He was re-elected four times through 2008, and served as chair of the Democratic Senatorial Campaign Committee (1989–1990) and the Committee on Small Business and Entrepreneurship (2001–2002). He has also served as a member of the Foreign Relations, Finance, and Commerce, Science, and Transportation Committees and was a central congressional figure in the investigation of the Iran–Contra Scandal under President **Ronald Reagan**.

In December 2002, Kerry announced his intention to form an exploratory committee to run for the Democratic nomination for president in 2004. He faced a crowded field of Democratic hopefuls, including **Wesley Clark**, **Howard Dean**, **John Edwards**, **Richard**

Gephardt, Robert (Bob) Graham, Dennis Kucinich, Joseph Lieberman, and Al Sharpton. He won strong victories in the **Iowa Caucuses** and the **New Hampshire Primary** to take a quick lead. By mid-February 2004, the race was essentially between Kerry and Edwards. Kerry locked up the nomination by dominating the March "**Super Tuesday**" states, at which time Edwards suspended his campaign.

Kerry chose Edwards as his vice presidential running mate. His general campaign against incumbent President **George W. Bush** focused on the **War in Iraq**, which Kerry voted to authorize in 2002, but later opposed. His campaign suffered a number of setbacks, including the notion that he had "flip-flopped" on **Iraq**. He made an infamous comment on the campaign trail that he had "voted *for* the war in Iraq before he voted *against* it" in reference to several Senate resolutions, yet he had also contended in 2003 that **Saddam Hussein** had to be disarmed and must not be allowed to pursue **weapons of mass destruction** (WMDs). He was also criticized by Vietnam veterans who formed the group **Swift Boat Veterans for Truth**. The group challenged Kerry's service on fast water craft, or "swift boats," and his medals of valor for injuries he sustained while commanding them in Vietnam. A Roman Catholic, Kerry also stirred controversy for his support of **abortion**, which placed him at odds with the church.

Kerry lost the 2004 election to George W. Bush by 3 percent nationally (51–48). He returned to the Senate and formed a political action committee that aided Democratic candidates in the 2006 **mid-term elections**. Kerry did not seek the Democratic presidential nomination in 2008 and threw his support to Illinois Senator **Barack Obama**. Following Obama's defeat of **John McCain**, Kerry was rumored to be on Obama's list of possibilities for secretary of state.

KHALILZAD, ZALMAY MAMOZY (1951–). Born in Mazar-i-Sharif, **Afghanistan**, Khalilzad emigrated to the United States as a teenager. He attended the American University in Beirut before completing a doctoral degree at the University of Chicago. Khalilzad taught political science at Columbia University from 1979 to 1986, and worked at the RAND Corporation from 1989 to 1991. From 1991 to 1992, he was assistant deputy undersecretary of defense for policy planning. He returned to the RAND Corporation until 1999 as director of the strategy, doctrine, and force structure for Project Air Force.

After serving in various positions in the administration of **George W. Bush**, including the **National Security Council** and special assistant to the president for Islamic Outreach, Khalilzad was appointed ambassador to Afghanistan in 2003 and remained in the post until 2005. In June 2005, he replaced **John Negroponte** as ambassador to **Iraq**. Khalilzad was succeeded by **Ryan Crocker** in March 2007, when he was confirmed by the Senate as ambassador to the **United Nations** (UN), replacing **John Bolton**, a recess appointment. As UN ambassador, Khalilzad focused his efforts on **Iran**'s nuclear program and was a leading voice in opposition to **Russia**'s invasion of **Georgia** in August 2008.

KHAN, ABDUL QADEER (AQ) (1936–). Born in Bhopal, India, Khan resettled in **Pakistan** with his family as a teenager. He holds an undergraduate degree from the University of Karachi, a master's degree in engineering from the Technische Universiteit Delft (Netherlands), and a doctoral degree in engineering from the Katholieke Universiteit Leuven (Belgium). In the early 1970s, he worked at an Amsterdam laboratory that provided fuel for European nuclear reactors. He returned to Pakistan in 1976 to head the country's nuclear program, and was accused by the Dutch of having stolen nuclear secrets. It is believed that Pakistan acquired nuclear weapons capabilities a decade later under Khan's leadership and with the aid of **China**. The confirmation came in 1998, when Pakistan successfully tested a nuclear weapon.

Khan was subsequently suspected of attempting to proliferate nuclear weapons to several regimes that President **George W. Bush** would call an **axis of evil** in 2002—**Iran** and **North Korea**, as well as Libya. He came under increased scrutiny following the US-led invasion of **Afghanistan** in October 2001, when intelligence suggested the **terrorist** group **al-Qaeda** had made repeated efforts to procure a nuclear or radiological weapon and Pakistani scientists were implicated. In January 2004, Khan admitted his involvement with the Iranian, North Korean, and Libyan nuclear programs, signed a confession, and was pardoned a month later by President **Pervez Musharraf**. In May 2008, Khan recanted his confession and contended that his confession was forced by authorities and that he had never traveled to **Libya** or Iran.

KIM, JONG IL (1941–). The son of Kim Il Sung, who established and became leader of **North Korea** in 1948, Kim was born in the **Soviet Union**, where his father was serving during World War II. After completing studies in economics, he worked his way up the ranks of the communist apparatus of North Korea during the 1980s. In 1991, he became supreme commander of the army. When his father died in 1994, Kim took the reins of power as general secretary of the Workers' Party.

An enigmatic and secretive leader, Kim's regime admitted in 2002 that it had produced nuclear weapons in violation of an agreement with the United States eight years earlier to dismantle North Korea's **weapons of mass destruction** (WMD) program. In his 2002 State of the Union address, President **George W. Bush** contended that North Korea was part of an **axis of evil** along with **Iran** and **Iraq** and a state sponsor of **terrorism**. The Bush administration used diplomacy and sanctions on Kim's regime in an effort to halt its WMD program. However, North Korea withdrew from the **Nuclear Non-Proliferation Treaty** in 2003, and successfully tested a nuclear weapon underground in October 2006. The test prompted international talks that ultimately led to the normalization of relations between North Korea and the United States. In October 2008, North Korea was removed from the State Department's list of state sponsors of terror.

In 2008, rumors abounded that Kim was ill or had suffered a stroke or heart attack. None of the reports was confirmed, although his lack of public appearances fueled intense speculation about his possible infirmity or imminent death.

KIRKUK, IRAQ. This city of approximately 750,000 is located in northern **Iraq** and is situated in some of the country's richest oil fields. Historically, the city's population has been mixed between **Kurds**, Turkmen, Assyrians, and Arabs. Under the regime of **Saddam Hussein**, however, the city was subject to an "Arabization" policy that included expelling individuals of ethnic groups not of Arab origin. Following the US-led invasion of Iraq in March 2003 Kirkuk's status was the subject of great controversy. Kurds in the north of the country wish to annex it to Kurdistan, while other ethnic groups also lay claim to the city. **Turkey**, which borders Kurdistan, fears any move toward an independent Kurdish state that might place into question the status of Kurds within its borders. Some observers feared that the situation in Kirkuk, coupled with the **insurgency** and **War in Iraq**, might lead to a civil war.

The Iraqi Constitution of 2005 provided for a referendum to decide the city's future in November 2007—but only once Hussein's "Arabization" policy had been reversed and displaced ethnic Kurds had a chance to return. The referendum was delayed several times through 2008 in anticipation of recommendations by the **United Nations**.

KOSOVO. More than 90 percent of the population of this disputed territory of the former Yugoslavia is ethnic Albanian. Kosovo fell under the control of a **United Nations** (UN) interim administration in 1999, following the war in Kosovo and military action taken by the **North Atlantic Treaty Organization** (NATO) to halt the violence of the civil war between Kosovar Albanians and Serbians. In February 2008, Kosovo's parliamentary assembly declared the territory a republic. The United States, as well as **Great Britain** and **France**, recognized the declaration, while other members, notably **Russia**, rejected it. *See also* KOUCHNER, BERNARD.

KOUCHNER, BERNARD (1939–). A native of Avignon, France, Kouchner is cofounder of the organization Doctors without Borders. He served in various governments of the Left in **France** in the 1980s and 1990s, holding the portfolio for the ministry of health twice. Between June 1999 and January 2001, Kouchner was the **United Nations** special representative in **Kosovo**, where he focused efforts on constructing a civil administration in the war-torn territory of the former **Yugoslavia**. Kouchner became the French foreign minister following **Nicolas Sarkozy**'s victory in the French presidential elections of June 2007. His appointment was welcomed by the administration of **George W. Bush**. Although he opposed the **War in Iraq**, Kouchner favored the removal of **Saddam Hussein** from power and doggedly opposed **Iran**'s nuclear program in the last two years of Bush's second term. *See also* CHIRAC, JACQUES; DE VILLEPIN, DOMINIQUE.

KOZLOWSKI, L. DENNIS (1946–). A native of Newark, New Jersey, Kozlowski was the chief executive officer (CEO) of **Tyco Corporation**, a global manufacturing firm. He joined the firm in the 1975, became chief executive office in 1992, and resigned in 2002.

Kozlowski, who enjoyed an extravagantly lavish lifestyle, was indicted on charges of grand larceny and convicted in 2005 after two trials (the first was a mistrial). He had misappropriated $400 million in the corporation's profits to support his New York apartment and costly parties. He was sentenced to a minimum of more than eight years and a maximum of 25 years in prison.

KUCINICH, DENNIS JOHN (1946–). Born in Cleveland, Ohio, Kucinich earned bachelor's and master's degrees in communications from Case Western Reserve University in 1973. He entered politics in 1969, successfully winning a seat on the Cleveland City Council. In 1972 and 1974, he ran unsuccessfully for the US House of Representatives. He was elected mayor of Cleveland in 1977 at just 31 years of age, but lost his re-election bid two years later when the city fell into financial default. He returned to politics in 1983, when he won a seat on the Cleveland City Council. In 1994, he won a seat in the Ohio Senate.

Kucinich entered the House of Representatives in 1996 after narrowly winning the tenth district of Ohio, which comprises Cuyahoga County. He was re-elected seven times through 2008. An advocate of national health insurance, he served on the Education and Labor Committee as well as the Government Reform Committee.

Kucinich was a candidate for the Democratic presidential nomination in 2004 and 2008. In both campaigns, he was an indefatigable critic of President **George W. Bush** and the **War in Iraq**. His pro-choice stance on **abortion** and support for environmentalism, including his call for the passage of the **Kyoto Protocol** on global warming, won praise from liberal activists. In neither primary campaign, however, was Kucinich able to establish the momentum necessary to overtake his rivals. In 2004, he placed well behind front-runners **John Kerry** and **John Edwards** in the **Iowa Caucuses** and the **New Hampshire Primary**, but remained in the race until just a month before the Democratic Convention. He ultimately endorsed Kerry in July 2004.

Kucinich announced his intention to seek the 2008 Democratic nomination for the presidency nearly two years before the election, in December 2006. His campaign was decidedly left-of-center, with proposals to legalize **gay marriage**, implement universal health care, remove all troops from **Iraq**, and withdraw the United States from the North American Free Trade Agreement (NAFTA). In the Iowa Caucuses, Kucinich asked voters to throw their support to **Barack Obama** if his own candidacy did not appear viable; Obama won the Iowa Caucuses with 38 percent, and Kucinich gained no significant support. In the New Hampshire Primary, Kucinich gained just over 1 percent of the statewide vote. Despite endorsements from a number of Hollywood celebrities he dropped his presidential bid on 24 January 2008 after culling less than 1 percent in the Nevada Caucuses.

KURD(S). The Kurdish people live predominantly in western **Turkey**, northern **Iraq**, **Iran**, and **Syria**. They speak a language that is similar to Iranian. Under the regime of **Saddam Hussein**, Kurds in Iraq were subject to forced relocation under a policy of "Arabization" in the northern part of the country. In what the Hussein regime called the "Anfal" campaign following the 1991 **Persian Gulf War**, the Iraqi army murdered thousands of Kurds, destroyed villages, and used chemical weapons against the civilian population. The campaign was retribution for Kurdish demands for independence.

The US-led invasion of Iraq in March 2003, and the subsequent fall of Hussein's regime, allowed many Kurds to return to their ancestral region, which includes the cities of **Kirkuk** and **Mosul**. Under the Iraqi Constitution of 2005, Kurds were to hold a referendum to determine the status of the region's governance by November 2007. As of 2008, the referendum was postponed in anticipation of **United Nations** recommendations. One of the key concern in granting the region greater autonomy is Turkey's concerns that an independent Kurdish state in Iraq might cause unrest among Kurds living within Turkey's borders. *See also* HASSAN AL-MAJID, ALI; WAR IN IRAQ.

KYOTO PROTOCOL. This protocol to the **United Nations** Framework Convention on Climate Change was written at the so-called "Earth Summit" in Rio de Janeiro, Brazil, in June 1992. The goal of the treaty is to reduce "greenhouse gases" that some scientists and observers, including Nobel Laureate **Al Gore**, believe cause climate change, most notably in the form of global warming. The protocol was adopted in December 1997, in Kyoto, Japan, and entered into effect by February 2005. The protocol requires nations to reduce pollutants, such as carbon dioxide, by a specified amount over time. As of 2008, 183 nations had ratified the Kyoto Protocol. The administration of **William Clinton** signed the protocol in November 1998. However, the US Senate refused to ratify it. One concern was that the protocol was asymmetric, exempting polluting countries such as India and **China** from emission standards. President **George W. Bush** withdrew support for the protocol in 2001, contending the standards were too costly to the US economy.

– L –

LATVIA. This Baltic country with a population of just over 2 million was dominated by the **Soviet Union** during the **Cold War**. Latvia gained independence in 1991. The country joined the **North Atlantic Treaty Organization** (NATO) in March 2004, and the **European Union** in May 2004. President **George W. Bush** visited Latvia in May 2005 to mark the 60th anniversary of the defeat of the Nazis in World War II.

LAW, BERNARD FRANCIS (1931–). Born in Mexico, where his father was stationed with the US Air Force, Law earned a degree from Harvard College and attended the St. Joseph Seminary in Louisiana and the Pontifical College Josephinum in Ohio. He was ordained a priest in the Catholic Church in 1961. He became a bishop in Missouri in 1973, and was appointed archbishop of Boston, Massachusetts, in 1983. Law resigned as archbishop in December 2002, following the worst sex abuse scandal in the church's history in the United States. Law had knowingly relocated priests, including **John Geoghan**, suspected of repeatedly abusing children. The result was a panoply of lawsuits that cost the Boston archdiocese $120 million, which Law's successor, Seán O'Malley, was forced to settle by selling church assets and closing parishes.

LAY, KENNETH LEE (1942–2006). A native of Missouri, Lay became chief executive officer of the energy giant **Enron Corporation** in 1986. He resigned in January 2002, amid the company's bankruptcy, which cost hundreds of thousands of investors their retirement accounts. It was later revealed that the accounting firm **Arthur Andersen** had destroyed documents in connection with an investigation of the corporation's finances. A grand jury indicted Lay on 11 counts of securities fraud and false testimony; he was convicted on 10 counts. He died of a heart attack in July 2006, while on vacation in Colorado several months before he was scheduled for sentencing by a federal judge. *See also* CHENEY, RICHARD BRUCE; ENERGY TASK FORCE; SKILLING, JEFFREY.

LEAHY, PATRICK JOSEPH (1940–). Born in Montpelier, Vermont, Leahy earned an undergraduate degree from St. Michael's College (1961) and a law degree from Georgetown University (1964). He entered politics in 1966, when he was elected as a state attorney. He ran successfully for the US Senate in 1974 as a Democrat, and has been re-elected five times through 2004. He chaired the Agriculture, Nutrition, and Forestry Committee from 1987 to 1995 and the Judiciary Committee in the 110th Congress (2007–2008). Leahy, along with **Tom Daschle**, received **anthrax**-tainted letters just a week following the **11 September 2001 terrorist** attacks on New York and the **Pentagon**. Neither Leahy nor his staff was harmed. *See also* HATFILL, STEPHEN JAY; IVINS, BRUCE EDWARDS.

LEAVITT, MICHAEL OKERLUND (1951–). Born in Cedar City, Utah, Leavitt graduated from Southern Utah University. He started his own insurance business before running successfully for the governorship of Utah in 1992. He is the only Utah governor to have been re-elected twice. President **George W. Bush** appointed Leavitt to head the **Environmental Protection Agency** (EPA) in October 2003 to replace acting administrator Marianne Horinko. In December 2004, Leavitt was succeeded by **Stephen Johnson** at EPA and became secretary of Health and Human Services and remained in the post through the end of Bush's second term.

LEBANON. Bordered by **Syria** to the North, **Israel** to the South, and the Mediterranean Sea to the East, Lebanon has a population of approximately 4 million. A French colony that gained independence in 1943, the country descended into civil war between 1975 and 1990. Syria originally sent troops to Lebanon as a peacekeeping force in 1976. Syrian troops remained until 2005 and the so-called "Cedar Revolution" that followed the assassination of Prime Minister **Rafik Hariri**. During the revolution, hundreds of thousands of protestors went to the streets of Beirut demanding that Syria end the occupation of Lebanon. Under regional and international pressure, the last Syrian troops departed at the end of April 2005.

LEHMAN BROTHERS. This global financial services corporation declared bankruptcy in September 2008. The bankruptcy filing—the largest in US history at the time—marked the beginning of financial market turmoil resulting from the **sub-prime mortgage** crisis. Lehman Brothers was sold off to several international corporations, including Barclays (**Great Britain**), which purchased much of the company's holding at a price of more than $1 billion. *See also* AMERICAN INTERNATIONAL GROUP; BEAR STEARNS; HOUSING AND ECONOMIC RECOVERY ACT (2008); TROUBLED ASSETS RELIEF PROGRAM (TARP).

LEPORE, THERESA (n.d.). A native of **Palm Beach County**, Florida, LePore was supervisor of elections in that county during the 2000 presidential election. She was responsible for the so-called **butterfly ballot** that confused many voters and was at the center of controversy during the **Florida recount** between **Al Gore** and **George W. Bush**. Nicknamed "Madame Butterfly" by the press, she was widely blamed by Democrats for Gore's loss in the state. LePore lost her re-election bid for supervisor of elections in 2004.

LIBBY, I. LEWIS (SCOOTER) (1950–). Born in New Haven, Connecticut, Libby graduated with a bachelor's degree from Yale University (1972) and a law degree from Columbia (1975). He joined a private law practice before moving to the Department of State in 1981 at the behest of his former professor and mentor, **Paul Wolfowitz**. In 1985, Libby returned to the prominent Washington, D.C., law firm of Mudge Rose. He served as deputy undersecretary of defense for policy from 1992 to 1993 under President **George H.W. Bush**. In 1997, he was a signatory to the "Statement of Principles" of the **neoconservative Project for the New American Century** (PNAC). In 2001, he became chief of staff and assistant for national security affairs to Vice President **Richard B. (Dick) Cheney**.

Libby was implicated in the "outing" of **Central Intelligence Agency** (CIA) covert agent **Valerie Plame**, spouse of former ambassador **Joseph Wilson**, a critic of the **War in Iraq**. He was ultimately indicted and convicted on four counts of perjury, obstruction of justice, and making false statements during the investigation of the matter. He resigned as Cheney's chief of staff in October 2005. He was convicted in March 2007, and in June 2007, was sentenced to 30 months in prison and ordered to pay a fine in the amount of $250,000. President **George W. Bush** intervened and commuted the imprisonment portion of his sentence but not the fine. Bush cited Libby's public service and work in the legal field as justifications for his decision. Libby was nonetheless disbarred in Pennsylvania and the District of Columbia due to his felony conviction.

LIBERIA. This western African nation of approximately 3.5 million fell into chaos and civil war beginning in 1999. Liberia's brutal dictator, Charles Taylor, ultimately fled the country in 2003 to seek exile in Nigeria. About 100 US Marines participated in peacekeeping activities with other African nations in August 2003 in the capital city of Monrovia.

LIBYA. This North African country has been ruled by Colonel Mu'ammar Gadhafi, widely viewed as a dictator, since his successful coup in 1969 against the Libyan monarchy. In May 1981, President **Ronald Reagan** accused Libya of being a state sponsor of international **terrorism**. Diplomatic relations between the United States and Libya were subsequently suspended. In 1986, Reagan ordered air raids on Tripoli and Benghazi, where **terrorist** training camps were thought to be located, and in retribution for the bombing of a night club frequented by US service personnel in West Berlin, **Germany**. Libyan terrorists were also suspected of bombing Pan Am Flight 103, which exploded over Lockerbie, Scotland, in December 1988, killing

275. President **George H.W. Bush** obtained economic sanctions by the **United Nations** against Libya in 1992.

Relations between the United States and Libya improved markedly during the administration of **George W. Bush**. In 2003, the Libyan government announced that it was suspending its pursuit of **weapons of mass destruction** (WMDs) and had decided to compensate the families of Pan Am Flight 103. In 2006, the United States removed Libya from the Department of State list of state sponsors of terrorism and sought to restore full diplomatic relations.

LIEBERMAN, JOSEPH ISADORE (1942–). Born in Stamford, Connecticut, Lieberman is a graduate of Yale University in economics (1964) and law (1967). He entered politics in 1970 as a state senator in Connecticut, where he was majority leader from 1974 to 1980. In 1980, he ran unsuccessfully for a seat in the House of Representatives. He was elected Connecticut state attorney in 1982. In 1988, he mounted a campaign for the US Senate and defeated incumbent Republican Lowell Weicker. Lieberman was re-elected in 1994 and 2000 as a Democrat. In 2006, he lost the Democratic primary due to his support for President **George W. Bush** and the **War in Iraq**. He subsequently won his seat by running as an Independent in the general election. In the Senate, Lieberman chaired the Governmental Affairs Committee (2001–2002) and the Homeland Security and Governmental Affairs Committee (2007–2008).

In 2000, Democratic presidential nominee **Al Gore** chose Lieberman as his vice presidential running mate. Lieberman became the first Jew in American history to be on any party's presidential ticket.

In 2004, Lieberman ran unsuccessfully for the Democratic presidential nomination. A moderate, Lieberman failed to attract substantial support in the crowded Democratic field, which included fellow senator and eventual nominee, **John Kerry**, as well as **John Edwards**. Lieberman's former running mate, Al Gore, backed **Howard Dean**. Lieberman suspended his campaign in early February 2004 after failing to win any of the early contests, including the **New Hampshire Primary** and the **Iowa Caucuses**.

Lieberman drew the ire of his fellow Democratic senators in 2008 when he not only publicly supported Republican presidential nominee **John McCain** but also actively campaigned on his behalf and spoke at the Republican Convention in Minneapolis, Minnesota. He cited his long friendship with McCain in the Senate, as well as McCain's stances on the **War on Terror** as reasons why he supported the Arizona senator rather than the Democratic nominee, **Barack Obama**. Following the presidential election, it was rumored that Lieberman, an "Independent Democrat," might lose his chairmanship in the 111th Congress (2009–2010). It was also rumored that Lieberman might join the Republican Party. Although Senate Majority Leader **Harry Reid** of Nevada contended that he was very angry at Lieberman's support of McCain, following a leadership meeting in November 2008, Lieberman was not substantially sanctioned.

LIMBAUGH, RUSH HUDSON III (1951–). A native of Cape Girardeau, Missouri, Limbaugh is a conservative political commentator with his own nationally syndicated radio show. An implacable critic of President **William Clinton**, Limbaugh was credited with aiding Republicans in their **mid-term election** victory in 1994. Between 2003 and 2006, he was the subject of an investigation by the **Palm Beach County**, Florida, authorities for so-called "doctor shopping" for prescription drugs to which he was addicted. Limbaugh ultimately struck a deal to have the charges dropped after investigators tried to gain access to his medical records.

In the 2008 presidential election, Limbaugh launched "Operation Chaos." On his radio show he advocated that Republicans vote in Democratic primaries where they were able in order to ensure a protracted primary contest between front-runners **Hillary Clinton** and **Barack Obama**. Limbaugh was also highly critical of the Republican nominee, **John McCain**, whose credentials he considered insufficient as a conservative. Limbaugh criticized the choice of McCain by centrists in the Republican camp as the source of the Party's defeat in the 2008 election. *See also* SUPER TUESDAY.

LINDH, JOHN PHILLIP WALKER (1981–). Born in Washington, D.C., Lindh was raised in California. Originally a Catholic, Lindh converted to Islam in 1997 and traveled to Yemen to learn Arabic. After a brief return to the United States, he left again for Yemen and traveled on to **Pakistan** to study at a religious school. In November 2001, he was captured by **Northern Alliance** forces in **Afghanistan**, where he was serving among **Taliban** fighters near the city of Mazar-i-Sharif. Lindh was eventually questioned by the **Central Intelligence Agency** (CIA) and the **Federal Bureau of Investigation** (FBI) and returned to the United States to face trial on conspiracy to kill Americans, providing material support to **terrorist**s, and a number of other charges stemming from his participation in the Taliban.

Lindh, who had been shot in the leg during an uprising immediately after his capture, contended that he had been mistreated by US authorities and not given proper medical care. The Justice Department subsequently offered Lindh a plea bargain, which he accepted. In exchange for pleading guilty to serving in the Taliban army and carrying weapons, he received 20 years in prison without parole and was prohibited from discussing his case while incarcerated. His sentence was handed down in October 2002.

LISBON TREATY. This treaty, signed on 13 December 2007, was aimed at reforming elements of governance of the member states of the **European Union**, including the executive, the legislature, and in foreign affairs. The treaty was to come into force in 2009. However, in June 2008, voters in the Republic of Ireland rejected the treaty in a referendum. Irish *Taoiseach* (prime minister) Brian Cowan was blamed for the defeat, as he claimed publicly that he had not read the entire document. The defeat of the Lisbon Treaty followed the demise of efforts to ratify a European Union Constitution several years earlier under the leadership of former French President **Valéry Giscard d'Estaing**.

LITHUANIA. This Baltic Republic of the former **Soviet Union** gained independence in 1990—the first to do so when the Soviet Union began to collapse. In March 2004, Lithuania became a member of the **North Atlantic Treaty Organization** (NATO), and in May 2004, joined the **European Union**. President **George W. Bush** visited Lithuania in May 2005.

LONDON, ENGLAND (BOMBINGS). On 7 July 2005, at the height of morning commuter traffic, the London Underground (subway) was attacked by three separate but coordinated bombs. A double-decker bus was also bombed. Fifty-six people were killed and more than 700 injured. The attack was the single deadliest on the London transportation system. In September 2005, the **terrorist** group **al-Qaeda** claimed responsibility for the attack, which the British government disputed. All four of the bombers, who died in the blasts, were Muslim. All four were also British nationals and dubbed "home-grown terrorists."

LOTT, CHESTER TRENT, SR. (1941–). Born in Grenada, Mississippi, Lott graduated with an undergraduate degree (1963) and a law degree (1967) from the University of Mississippi. He entered politics in 1972, when he won Mississippi's fifth district seat in the House of Representatives as a Republican. He was re-elected seven times. In the House, he served on the Judiciary Committee, and was the minority whip from 1981 to 1989. In 1988, Lott launched a successful run for the US Senate and was re-elected in 1994, 2000, and 2006. In the Senate, he served as whip (1995–1996, 2007), majority leader (1996–2001), and minority leader (2001–2002).

Although Republicans regained control of the Senate following the 2002 **mid-term elections**, Lott resigned his leadership position in December 2002, and **Bill Frist** of Tennessee became majority leader in the 108th Congress (2003–2004). Lott made controversial comments at a birthday party for South Carolina Senator Strom Thurmond, who had run for the presidency on a racial segregation platform in 1948. In expressing his support for Thurmond, Lott stated, "When Strom Thurmond ran for president, we voted for him. We're proud of it. And if the rest of the country had followed our lead, we wouldn't have had all these problems over the years, either." Lott's comments caused a firestorm of controversy in the press, and President **George W. Bush** withdrew his support of Lott in the Senate.

Despite his re-election in 2006, Lott resigned from the Senate in December 2007. Although he posited that he wanted to spend more time with his family, the announcement came just days before his brother-in-law, Richard Scruggs, was indicted for bribing a state judge in Mississippi by promising to elicit Lott's assistance in procuring him a seat on the federal bench. Lott returned to Washington as a lobbyist. He is also author of *Herding Cats: A Life in Politics* (2005).

LYNCH, JESSICA DAWN (1983–). A West Virginia native, Lynch was a private in the Army during the US-led invasion of **Iraq** in

March 2003. On 23 March 2003, Lynch's truck convoy was ambushed near the city of **Basra**. During the attack, Lynch suffered a broken arm and hip and was captured. On 1 April 2003, the Marines rescued Lynch after an Iraqi who knew of her whereabouts supplied them with information.

Controversy over Lynch's capture and rescue, as well as her injuries, ensued upon her return to the United States. She argued that media stories contending she had fought back during the ambush were false—she claimed her gun jammed. Further, she disputed claims that she had been mistreated while a prisoner of war. She contended that the filming of her rescue was part of a larger propaganda campaign by the **Pentagon** to build support for the **War in Iraq**.

– M –

MADOFF, BERNARD LAWRENCE (BERNIE) (1938–). *See* SECURITIES AND EXCHANGE COMMISSION.

MADRID, SPAIN (BOMBINGS). On 11 March 2004, just three days before scheduled elections in Spain, a **terrorist** cell carried out a series of coordinated bombings on the Madrid commuter rail line. The explosions killed 191 people and injured more than 1,700. The bombings had signature traits of the terrorist organization **al-Qaeda**, although a definitive link was never established by Spanish authorities. Controversy surrounded the investigation of the attacks, as the ruling party of **José María Aznar** contended that the attacks were carried out by Basque terrorists and opined that the attacks were part of a plot to drive him from power. Aznar's government, which had supported President **George W. Bush** and the **War in Iraq**, lost the elections on 14 March.

MAHDI ARMY. This paramilitary organization was created and headed by Shi'ite **Muslim** cleric **Muqtada al-Sadr** following the US-led invasion of **Iraq** in 2003. Described by US authorities as part of the **insurgency** in the **War in Iraq**, the militia targeted US forces through such tactics as roadside bombs and **improvised explosive devices** (IEDs). The Mahdi Army battled coalition forces in the city of Najaf in August 2004, until **Ayatollah Ali al-Sistani** successfully persuaded members to turn in their arms. Skirmishes between the militia and US troops and Iraqi security forces continued until 2008, when al-Sadr declared a cease-fire, which proved pivotal in decreasing violence in Iraq.

MAHONEY, TIMOTHY EDWARD (1956–). Born in Illinois, Mahoney was a successful computer business and finance entrepreneur who was recruited by the Democratic Party to run against **Mark Foley** in Florida's 16th congressional district in the **mid-term elections** of 2006. When it was revealed that Foley had engaged in inappropriate, sexual computer conversations with congressional pages, Mahoney easily won the district.

During the 2008 congressional election, reports surfaced that Mahoney had an extramarital affair with a woman on his staff and paid her to remain silent, allegedly with campaign funds. Mahoney lost the election to Republican Tim Rooney.

MAJOR LEAGUE BASEBALL (MLB). Controversy first rocked Major League Baseball in March 2005, when the US Congress launched a hearing into steroid use in the sport. Following dramatic and contentious testimony from players, the House Government Reform Committee argued that MLB policies were insufficient and threatened to legislate on the matter. In Spring 2006, baseball commissioner Bud Selig appointed former Democratic Senator **George Mitchell** to investigate steroid use by players. Mitchell produced a detailed report in December 2007, in which he outlined alleged use of steroids and other illegal substances by nearly 90 players, including Major League All-Stars. Fans of the New York Yankees, whose players figured disproportionately in the report, posited that Mitchell's report showed a conflict of interest, as no Boston Red Sox players appeared on the list—and Mitchell was a director for the team. Mitchell flatly denied the allegation.

MANSFIELD, GORDON H. (n.d.). An Army Vietnam veteran, Mansfield was executive director of the Paralyzed Veterans of America in the 1990s. In the administration of **George W. Bush**, he became deputy secretary of veterans affairs in 2004 after serving as assistant secretary for congressional and legislative affairs since 2001. He became acting secretary of the Department of Veterans Affairs from October to December 2007, succeeding **Jim Nicholson**, who resigned from the cabinet. **James Peake** replaced Mansfield as secretary on 20 December 2007.

MARTIN, PAUL EDGAR PHILIPPE (1938–). A native of Ontario, **Canada**, Martin first entered politics in 1988, when he was elected from the Liberal Party to the House of Commons for a constituency in Montréal, Québec. In 1993, Prime Minister **Jean Chrétien** appointed him minister of finance, and he remained in that post until 2002. Martin won the leadership of the Liberal Party in November 2003 and became prime minister a month later. In 2004, Martin faced a federal election, which was fought amid a scandal concerning federal contracts in his home province of Québec. The Liberals lost 35 seats and were forced into a situation of minority government for the first time since 1979. In January 2006, Martin faced a second federal election, forced by opposition parties that passed a motion of no confidence over issues surrounding the contracts scandal. Martin's Liberal Party lost 32 seats. The Conservative Party of **Stephen Harper** won a plurality of seats in the House of Commons and formed a minority government. Harper then succeeded Martin as prime minister.

Known for his pragmatic approach to budgeting, Martin endeavored to reduce Canada's debt. He generally enjoyed cordial relations with President **George W. Bush** on trade and security issues. Bush visited Martin in Canada in December 2004. However, Martin opposed Bush's plans for an **anti-ballistic missile** defense system and contended Canada would not participate in the program. After leaving politics, Martin became heavily involved in international development and finance.

MARTINEZ, MELQUIADES RAFAEL (MEL) (1946–). A Cuban native, Martinez emigrated to the United States in 1962. As an orphan, he was cared for by Catholic charities and foster parents. He earned a law degree from Florida State University (1973) and worked in private law practice for a quarter century. He entered politics in 1994 as a Republican in an unsuccessful bid for lieutenant governor. After serving as chair of the Orlando Housing Authority, he became

George W. Bush's campaign manager for Florida in the 2000 presidential election. From 2001 to 2003, he served as Bush's secretary of the Department of Housing and Urban Development. He was succeeded by **Alphonso Jackson**.

Martinez ran successfully in 2004 for an open US Senate seat in Florida, defeating his Democratic opponent, Betty Castor in a very close election. In 2005, Martinez was one of several Republican senators who sought to intervene on behalf of **Terry Schiavo**. Schiavo was a brain-dead woman on life support, whose husband ultimately terminated her medical assistance after a US federal court ruled in his favor. Martinez served on the Armed Services, Housing and Urban Development, and Energy and Natural Resources Committees in the Senate. He also chaired the Republican Party for the 2007–2008 election cycle.

MATERIAL WITNESS. A material witness is an individual who may have information regarding a criminal act, but who is not charged with a crime. Following the **11 September 2001 terrorist** attacks on New York City and the **Pentagon**, the administration of **George W. Bush** held individuals suspected of having information regarding **terrorism**. The administration held material witnesses indefinitely, allegedly to guarantee testimony before a grand jury. Civil libertarians staunchly opposed the practice of indefinite detention, which they argued was tantamount to suspending the right of **habeas corpus** (the right to go before a judge). The Bush administration contended that habeas corpus did not apply to material witnesses, nor were they privy to the Sixth Amendment right to counsel since they were not charged with any crime. The most dramatic case involved **José Padilla**, a US citizen implicated in a plot to detonate a radiological bomb. *See also* AL-QAEDA; TERRORIST; WAR ON TERROR.

MAZEN, ABU. *See* ABBAS, MAHMOUD.

MCCAIN, JOHN SIDNEY III (1936–). The son of a naval officer, McCain was born in the Panama Canal Zone. He graduated from the Naval Academy in 1958 and finished aviator training several years later. His first combat assignment was on the aircraft carrier USS *Forrestal* in 1967. A fire aboard the ship nearly cost McCain his life.

In October 1967, while on a bombing mission over North Vietnam, McCain's plane was shot down and he was captured. He spent five and a half years, two of which were in solitary confinement, in North Vietnamese prisons, including the infamous "Hanoi Hilton." As a prisoner of war (POW) McCain's limbs were broken repeatedly, leaving his arms permanently handicapped. He refused early release from his captors to remain with fellow American POWs. He was ultimately released in March 1973.

Following his rehabilitation McCain commanded a flight training squadron in Florida and then served as the Navy's liaison to the US Senate. He retired from the Navy with the rank of captain in 1981. His commendations include the Bronze Star, Distinguished Flying Cross, Legion of Merit, Purple Heart, and Silver Star.

McCain settled in Phoenix, Arizona, with his second wife, Cindy Lou (née Hensley), and worked in her father's distribution company. His father-in-law introduced him to many prominent businessmen in the community, who urged him to run for Congress. In 1982, after fighting off a Republican primary challenge, McCain won election from the first congressional district of Arizona. He won re-election by a wide margin in 1984, having established a strong record in support of President **Ronald Reagan**'s conservative domestic and **foreign policy** agenda. In 1986, he ran successfully for the Arizona Senate seat vacated by the retiring Barry Goldwater. He was elected three times through 2004. While in the Senate, he chaired the Committee on Indian Affairs (1995–1996, 2003–2004) and the Committee on Commerce (1995–2000).

McCain was thrown into the national spotlight in 1987 in a scandal known as the "Keating Five." He was acquainted with Charles Keating, a banker who attempted to halt a federal takeover of Lincoln Savings and Loan, which he owned, by soliciting aid from McCain and four other senators. McCain had received campaign contributions from Keating, raising the appearance of impropriety. A Senate Ethics Committee investigation eventually cleared McCain of any wrongdoing, although he was chastised for exercising poor judgment. Three other senators, Alan Cranston (D-CA), Dennis DeConcini (R-AZ), and Donald Riegle (D-MI) were rebuked.

In September 1999, McCain announced his candidacy for the Republican nomination for president in 2000. His self-styled "maverick" image targeted independent and swing voters. His principal rival, Texas Governor **George W. Bush**, appealed to the Republican base, including **Evangelical Christians**, and had raised much more in campaign funds. Engaging in substantial "retail politics," including chats with voters in restaurants and the "town hall" meeting format for his campaign, McCain prevailed in the **New Hampshire Primary** by 19 points. What ensued was a vicious campaign in which McCain accused Bush of lying about his record. Bush accused McCain of "crossing the line" in calling him similar to **William Clinton** in terms of ethics. The smear campaign against McCain was even more palpable, with independent groups challenging McCain's Vietnam service record. McCain's momentum was broken in the February South Carolina primary, which Bush won. On **Super Tuesday** 7 March 2000, Bush won a majority of states, and McCain withdrew from the race a few days later, throwing his full support to his rival.

Returning to the Senate, McCain's policy positions frequently put him at odds with many Republicans. One prime example included his bipartisan effort to pass campaign finance legislation. The **Bipartisan Campaign Reform Act** (2002), which McCain coauthored with Democrat Russell Feingold, endured a **Supreme Court** challenge launched by fellow Republican Senator Mitch McConnell. Although he supported the **War in Iraq**, McCain became an indefatigable critic of Secretary of Defense **Donald Rumsfeld** over the conduct of post-invasion strategy in **Iraq** and efforts to deal with the **insurgency**. He also parted ways with the Bush administration over **torture**, opposing the controversial tactic of **waterboarding** to extract information from suspected **terrorists**. In 2005, he sponsored an amendment, **Detainee Treatment Act** (2005), that prohibited torture or inhumane treatment of detainees at **Guantanamo Bay, Cuba**, and elsewhere.

In April 2007, McCain announced his candidacy for the Republican nomination for president in the 2008 election. Throughout much of the pre-primary season he trailed Republican front-runners **Rudolph Giuliani** and **Mitt Romney**. His campaign was hindered by his previous efforts to deal with illegal **immigration**, which drew criticism from some Republicans. He sponsored an unsuccessful bill in 2007, which included temporary worker visas. His detractors labeled the bill as "amnesty." Shunning the **Iowa Caucuses**, which were won by Arkansas Governor **Mike Huckabee**, McCain nevertheless prevailed in the **New Hampshire Primary** over Mitt Romney, whom he also defeated in South Carolina. On Super Tuesday in March 2000, McCain won a majority of states and essentially racked up enough delegates to secure the nomination.

McCain faced Democratic standard-bearer **Barack Obama** in the general election campaign. Shortly after the Republican convention in St. Paul, Minnesota, he announced his selection of Alaska Governor **Sarah Palin** as his vice presidential running mate. Palin was the first woman to appear on a Republican presidential ticket. The youthful and conservative Palin immediately energized the Republican base, which remained skeptical about McCain both in terms of his policy positions and his age—at 72, he would have been the oldest candidate to attain the presidency. Further, he had survived several bouts with skin cancer. Nonetheless, Palin's popularity fell in the weeks to follow, in part due to her lackluster media interviews.

The **sub-prime mortgage** crisis that began to rock the economy in September 2008 placed the McCain–Palin ticket increasingly behind Barack Obama and his running mate **Joe Biden**, and McCain's campaign never recovered. Although President George W. Bush and Vice President **Richard B. (Dick) Cheney** were conspicuously absent on the campaign trail, the economy dominated the last six weeks of the general election. McCain tried to use a memorable exchange between Barack Obama and **Samuel Joseph Wurzelbacher** ("Joe the Plumber") in Ohio to raise doubts about Obama's economic policy. Obama indicated he wanted to raise taxes on the top 5 percent of wage earners as a means of "spreading the wealth." Regardless, McCain culled 45.9 percent of the national vote for only 173 Electoral College votes. Barack Obama prevailed with 52.8 percent of the vote and 365 Electoral College votes. McCain lost critical swing states that Bush had won in 2004, including Ohio and Florida, which tipped the balance to Obama. He returned to the Senate, vowing to work with President-elect Obama on the challenges of the financial crisis confronting the nation.

MCCLELLAN, SCOTT (1968–). Born in Austin, Texas, McClellan is a graduate of the University of Texas at Austin. He worked as campaign manager to his mother, Carole Keeton Strayhorn, who was Texas state comptroller and ran unsuccessfully for the Texas governorship in 1996. McClellan traveled with President **George W. Bush**

during the 2000 presidential election and acted as his press secretary. In 2003, he was hired as deputy White House press secretary. He succeeded **Ari Fleischer** as press secretary in 2003 and served in that position until 2006, when **Tony Snow** replaced him.

McClellan was at the center of controversy in 2008 when he published his memoir entitled *What Happened?* In the book, he contended that the Bush administration had engaged in a propaganda campaign to persuade the American public to support the **War in Iraq**. In the 2008 presidential election, he supported the candidacy of Democrat **Barack Obama**.

MCCONNELL, JOHN MICHAEL (MIKE) (1943–). A native of Greenville, South Carolina, McConnell is a graduate of Furman University with a degree in economics, and he holds a master's degree in public administration from George Washington University. An expert in intelligence affairs and a career naval officer, he commanded Middle East operations in the 1970s, served as an assistant to the director of Naval Intelligence in the 1980s, and was intelligence director to the **Joint Chiefs of Staff** from 1990 to 1992 during the **Persian Gulf War**. He served as the director of the **National Security Agency** from 1992 to 1997.

In 2007, McConnell succeeded **John Negroponte** as **Director of National Intelligence** (DNI), where he continued efforts to reform the intelligence community and the embattled **Central Intelligence Agency** (CIA). McConnell was an advocate of easing intelligence-gathering activities in the updated **Foreign Intelligence Surveillance Act** (FISA) legislation (**Protect America Act**). In congressional testimony, he contended that he had not engaged in illegal **wiretapping** of US citizens.

MCVEIGH, TIMOTHY JAMES (1968–2001). The architect of the bombing of the Murrah Federal Building in Oklahoma City, Oklahoma, in 1995 that claimed 168 lives, McVeigh was convicted in federal court and sentenced to death in 1997. It was the worst incident of **terrorism** on US soil until the attacks of **11 September 2001**. His sentence was carried out on 11 June 2001 by lethal injection in Terre Haute, Indiana.

MEDICARE PRESCRIPTION DRUGS. Formally known as the Medicare Prescription Drug, Improvement, and Modernization Act, this major bill became law in 2003. Backed by President **George W. Bush**, the bill marked the most significant change in Medicare since its inception in the 1960s. The entitlement program for senior citizens known as "Part D" was changed to include a prescription drug benefit, and through federal subsidies encouraged private companies to retain prescription drug benefits for retirees, who are required to make co-payments. The major provisions of the bill took effect in 2006. Controversy over the bill centered on its costs. Initial estimates of the cost to the federal budget were in the order of $500 billion. The Bush administration did not make a clear case about how the program would be funded, and fiscal conservatives—particularly Republicans—were concerned with the ramifications for an ever-expanding federal deficit that was aggravated by the costs of the **War in Iraq**. By 2005, the White House augmented the program's annual cost estimate to more than $1 trillion.

MEDVEDEV, DMITRI ANATOLYEVICH (1965–). A native of Leningrad, **Russia**, Medvedev holds a doctoral degree in law from Leningrad State University (1990). In the 1990s, he worked as a consultant for the St. Petersburg Mayor's Office and engaged in private business in the lumber industry. In 2000, he headed **Vladimir Putin**'s presidential campaign. Following Putin's victory, Medvedev became chair of Gazprom, Russia's nationalized natural gas company. In 2005, he became prime minister under Putin. In March 2008, he won the presidential election by a wide margin, succeeding Putin, who had served the maximum of two consecutive terms under the Constitution. Medvedev was widely regarded as Putin's heir apparent. Putin became prime minister following Medvedev's victory, spurring observers to posit that Putin remained in de facto control of the Kremlin.

Only three months after becoming president, Medvedev sent Russian troops to **Georgia** in a conflict over the regions of Abkhazia and South Ossetia. Both regions were claimed by Georgia but have significant ethnic Russian populations. Russia's invasion of Georgia, and subsequent recognition of the two regions as independent entities, severely strained relations between Medvedev's government and

President **George W. Bush**. In late August 2008, French President **Nicolas Sarkozy** brokered a negotiated agreement with Medvedev to withdraw Russian troops from Georgia.

Medvedev also opposed Bush's plan for an **anti-ballistic missile** system in **Poland** and the **Czech Republic**. He claimed that Russia would counter US plans with missiles targeted on Europe.

MEHLMAN, KENNETH BRIAN (1966–). A graduate of Franklin and Marshall College (1988) and Harvard University Law School (1991), Mehlman worked at the Washington, D.C., law firm of Akin Gump and was heavily involved in state and congressional elections for Republicans in the 1990s. He served as field director for **George W. Bush**'s 2000 presidential campaign, became White House political director following the election, and managed Bush's 2004 re-election campaign. He served as chair of the Republican National Committee from 2005 to 2006. In 2008, he managed New York City Mayor **Rudolph Giuliani**'s unsuccessful bid to secure the Republican nomination for president.

MEREDITH V. JEFFERSON COUNTY BOARD OF EDUCATION (2007). *See* AFFIRMATIVE ACTION.

MERKEL, ANGELA DOROTHEA (1954–). Born in Hamburg, **Germany**, Merkel first won election to the German Bundestag (legislature) as a member of the center-right Christian Democratic Union (CDU) in 1990. She succeeded **Gerhard Schröder** as chancellor of Germany in November 2005, following an election that yielded a grand coalition between the CDU and rival Social Democratic Party (SDP). She is the first female chancellor in German history.

Merkel enjoyed a close relationship with President **George W. Bush**. She met with Bush at his Crawford, Texas, ranch in November 2007. She worked to repair damaged relations between the United States and Germany in light of her predecessor's staunch opposition to the **War in Iraq**. She contended that Schröder's opposition weakened Germany's role in pressuring the regime of **Saddam Hussein** on **weapons of mass destruction** (WMDs). She was also supportive of finding a diplomatic solution to **Iran**'s quest for nuclear technology, and was critical of Iranian President **Mahmoud Ahmadinejad** for his anti-**Israel** rhetoric.

She showed her support for Israel by visiting that country in March 2007, when she met with Israeli Prime Minister Ehud Olmert and addressed the Knesset (Israeli Parliament). Nonetheless, Merkel criticized the Bush administration's detention of suspected **terrorists** as **enemy combatants** at the **Guantanamo Bay, Cuba**, facility.

MEXICO. President **George W. Bush** parted with tradition in his first year of office by visiting Mexico, a member of the North American Free Trade Agreement (NAFTA), for his first trip abroad. Traditionally, American presidents have visited **Canada**—the United States' largest trading partner—on their first official trip out of the country. The move did not go unnoticed by Canadian Prime Minister **Jean Chrétien**, who was displeased. Between 2000 and 2006, Bush met with Mexican President **Vicente Fox** on several occasions, and the search for a solution to illegal **immigration** from Mexico figured prominently into their relationship. Fox lost the 2006 election to Felipe Calderón, who objected to the US Congress's decision to build a 700-mile wall along the southwest border to prevent Mexicans from illegally entering the United States. Calderón also supported the comprehensive immigration bill, sponsored by **John McCain**, that ultimately failed. Nonetheless, it is with Calderón that Bush found agreement on an initiative to promote joint security and halt the international drug smuggling trade, and to facilitate the extradition of Mexican drug cartel operatives for trial in the United States.

MID-TERM ELECTIONS. Also referred to as "off-year" elections, mid-term elections for Congress occur two years following the presidential election. At stake are all seats for the House of Representative (435) and one-third of the 100 seats in the Senate. Historically, mid-term elections entail a loss of seats for the president's party in the House, and often in the Senate. In every election between 1938 and 1994, the president's party suffered losses in the House. In four cases—1946, 1954, 1994, and 2006—the losses in the House were so great that the president's party lost control of the lower chamber in a stunning reversal. In the Senate, the losses have been less easy to predict, and somewhat more moderate, in light of fewer contested seats. Nonetheless, in 1946, 1954, 1986, 1994, and 2006 the president's party also lost control of the upper chamber.

In the mid-term elections of 2002, President **George W. Bush** took to the campaign trail over the issue of creating a new **Department of Homeland Security**. Republicans controlled the House and passed the bill swiftly. However, the Senate was controlled by Democrats following Vermont Senator **James Jeffords**'s decision to leave the Republican Party and throw his support behind the Democratic leadership, which consequently organized a majority in the Senate in May 2001. The bill languished in the Senate as Bush and Democrats sparred over labor protections for employees in the new department. Bush used this issue, as part of the larger **War on Terror**, to rally support for Senate Republicans in the mid-term campaign. Republicans regained the majority in November 2002 by picking up two seats, and the "lame-duck" session of the Senate passed the bill on the president's terms.

In 2006, Republicans lost control of both chambers of Congress. A key factor was the lack of popularity of the **War in Iraq** due to the growing **insurgency** that contributed to a mounting death toll among US troops. Democrats picked up 31 seats to gain a 233–202 advantage in the House of Representatives. Senate Democrats defeated six Republican incumbents, leaving them with 49 seats. Two independent members, **Joseph Lieberman** of Connecticut and Bernie Sanders of Vermont, caucused with the Democrats and allowed them to form a majority. House Speaker **Nancy Pelosi** had vowed to restrict funding for the War in Iraq as part of the Democrats' campaign strategy. However, attempts to "de-fund" the war failed as Bush vetoed appropriations bills with such provisions, and neither House nor Senate Democrats had the votes to override the president's objections.

MIERS, HARRIET ELLAN (1945–). A native of Dallas, Texas, Miers graduated from Southern Methodist University with degrees in mathematics (1967) and law (1970). She subsequently clerked for Joe Estes, the chief judge of the US District Court for the northern district of Texas. She entered private law practice in 1972, making partner in the firm of Locke, Liddel, and Sapp. She worked in the administration of **George W. Bush** as staff secretary before becoming White House counsel in 2004. She remained in that position until 2007.

In October 2005, President Bush nominated her to the **Supreme Court** to fill the vacancy created by the retirement of Justice **Sandra**

Day O'Connor. In initial meetings with Senators, Miers alleged lack of legal knowledge stirred opposition, and members of the Judiciary Committee demanded internal White House legal documents that she had drafted. Bush refused to provide them, citing **executive privilege**. Miers asked Bush to withdraw her nomination in late October, and he agreed. He then nominated **Samuel Alito**, who was confirmed in January 2006.

Miers was implicated in the controversy over the firing of **federal prosecutors** working in the Department of Justice in 2006. When the Senate Judiciary Committee investigated the firings, members demanded that Miers testify and turn over documents. The president invoked executive privilege and ordered Miers not to appear before the committee. She was cited for contempt—a charge with which Senate Republicans disagreed—but was not legally sanctioned.

MILITARY COMMISSIONS ACT (2006). This bill was passed in October 2006 and was a direct result of the **Supreme Court**'s ruling in *Hamdan v. Rumsfeld* (2006) that the **military tribunals** created by President **George W. Bush** were unconstitutional. The High Court held that the president did not have the authority to create the tribunals, per se. The Military Commissions Act therefore gave the president a statutory framework from which to try suspected **terrorists** and **enemy combatants** held at **Guantanamo Bay, Cuba**, in military courts. The law was struck down in *Boumediene v. Bush* (2008) when the Supreme Court found that the Military Commissions Act violated **habeas corpus** and that enemy combatants had recourse to civil courts.

MILITARY TRIBUNALS. As part of the **War on Terror** following the US-led invasion of **Afghanistan** in October 2001, President **George W. Bush** intended to try suspected **al-Qaeda** and **Taliban** **terrorist**s, many of whom were detained in **Guantanamo Bay, Cuba**, in military rather than civilian courts. The Bush administration drew upon the historical precedent of the military tribunals used to try Nazis captured off the US coast in World War II. The key difference between the World War II experience and the War on Terror, however, was that in the latter case detainees were unlawful **enemy combatants** who did not belong to a national army. The Bush administration contended not only that they were ineligible for protections under the US Constitution but also that the **Geneva Conventions** on prisoner-of-war treatment were inapplicable.

Detainees challenged the constitutionality of the military tribunals, or commissions, by filing **habeas corpus** petitions to have their cases heard before a civil judge. In *Rasul v. Bush* (2004), the **Supreme Court** held that US courts had the authority to determine whether detainees were unlawfully imprisoned and dismissed the argument that the facility in Cuba was beyond the reach of US law. In *Hamdan v. Rumsfeld* (2006), the Court had also decided a habeas corpus petition by a detainee, concluding that the military commissions set up by the Bush administration were unconstitutional and could only be founded by an act of Congress. As a result, Congress passed the **Military Commissions Act** of 2006. In *Boumediene v. Bush* and *Al Odah v. Bush* (2008), the High Court found that this Act of Congress also violated detainees' rights to habeas corpus and ruled the Military Commissions Act unconstitutional.

MILOŠEVIĆ, SLOBODAN (1941–2006). Milošević served as president of Serbia from 1989 to 1997, and president of the Federal Republic of **Yugoslavia**, which consisted of Serbia and Montenegro (of the former Yugoslavia) from 1997 to 2000. In the presidential election of September 2000, he initially refused to accept a first-round defeat to Vojislav Koštunica. Mass protests forced him from office several weeks later.

Milošević had been indicted by the International Criminal Tribunal for the former Yugoslavia, located in The Hague, Netherlands, in 1999. He was accused of genocide against Bosnian Muslims, crimes against humanity, and violating the **Geneva Conventions**. Prime Minister Zoran Djindjic had Milošević arrested. When Serbian authorities were unable to make a convincing legal case against Milošević, Djindjic had him sent to The Hague in 2001 to face criminal proceedings by the international court for the former Yugoslavia. Milošević maintained his innocence and represented himself in court. He died of a heart attack during his trial on 11 March 2006.

MINETA, NORMAN YOSHIO (1931–). A native of San Jose, California, Mineta and his family were interned during World War II, as his Japanese-born parents were not US citizens. He graduated from the University of California, Berkeley, with a degree in business in 1953. He served in Korea and Japan as an intelligence officer in the Army before he was appointed to a seat on the San Jose City council in 1967. In 1971, he won a single term as mayor of San Jose. A Democrat, Mineta ran successfully for the House of Representatives in 1974 and was re-elected 10 times. He chaired the Committee on Public Works and Transportation from 1993 to 1994. After leaving Congress for defense contractor Lockheed Martin in 1995, President **William Clinton** tapped Mineta as his secretary of commerce in 2000. President **George W. Bush** appointed Mineta as secretary of transportation in 2001, and he was the only Democrat to serve in Bush's cabinet. Following the **terrorist** attacks of **11 September 2001** on New York and the **Pentagon**, Mineta ordered all civil aviation grounded—a historical first. Mineta resigned in June 2006 and was succeeded by **Mary Peters**. He later joined the public relations firm of Hill & Knowlton. In December 2006, Bush awarded him the Presidential Medal of Freedom.

MITCHELL, GEORGE JOHN (1933–). A native of Waterville, Maine, Mitchell is a graduate of Bowdoin College (1954) and Georgetown University Law School (1961). He ran successfully for a US Senate seat as a Democrat in Maine in 1982 and was re-elected in 1988. From 1985 to 1994, he served as Senate majority leader and was an implacable critic both of President **Ronald Reagan** and President **George H.W. Bush**. He did not run for re-election in 1994, and returned briefly to private law practice. In 1995, President **William Clinton** appointed him as a special envoy to **Northern Ireland**. In 2006, he headed the investigation into the use of steroids in **Major League Baseball** (MLB). His report, issued a year later, found widespread steroid use among top athletes in the profession.

MOHAMMED, KHALID SHEIKH (1965–). Born in Kuwait, Mohammed is the **al-Qaeda terrorist** operative alleged by the **9/11 Commission** to have masterminded the **11 September 2001** terror attacks on New York and the **Pentagon**. He is a close associate of **Osama bin Laden**. He is also believed responsible for many other acts of terror, including the bombing of the **World Trade Center** in 1993, an aborted terror attack planned for Los Angeles, California, in 2002, and the murder of journalist **Daniel Pearl**, as well as aiding shoe-bomber **Richard Reid** and planning the bombings of hotels in **Bali**, Indonesia.

Mohammed was apprehended in March 2003 in Rawalpindi, **Pakistan**, by Pakistani authorities, who turned him over to the United States. After reportedly being sent to **Poland** for interrogation, he was eventually transferred to the detainee holding facility in **Guantanamo Bay, Cuba**. He alleged that he was tortured while in custody and subjected to the controversial method of **waterboarding** to extract information from suspected terrorists. In February 2008, he was charged with murder and war crimes. As of 2009, his fate remained uncertain. The **Supreme Court** ruled that **military tribunals** to be used to try suspected terrorists were unconstitutional in the case of *Boumediene v. Bush*. *See also* MILITARY COMMISSIONS ACT (2006); RENDITION.

MONSOOR, MICHAEL (1981–2006). A native of Garden Grove, California, Monsoor was a Navy SEAL who was shot and killed in Ramadi, **Iraq**, under heavy enemy fire while attempting to save a member of his team. President **George W. Bush** posthumously awarded Monsoor the Bronze Star and the Purple Heart for his courage.

MONTENEGRO. In a referendum held on 21 May 2006, this region of the former **Yugoslavia** voted in favor of independence from Serbia. The Montenegrin government declared formal independence on 3 June. Serbia, the **European Union**, and the United States all recognized Montenegro's sovereignty.

MOORE, ROY STEWART (1947–). Moore, the Republican chief justice of the Alabama Supreme Court, made national headlines in November 2003 when he refused to comply with a federal court order that mandated the removal of the Biblical Ten Commandments from the state courthouse. He was ultimately removed as chief justice by the Alabama Court of the Judiciary. In 2006, he ran unsuccessfully for the Alabama governorship.

MORENO–OCAMPO, LUIS (1952–). A native of Buenos Aires, Argentina, Moreno-Ocampo is the chief prosecutor of the **International Criminal Court** (ICC), which was established by the Rome Statute via the **United Nations** in 1998. The United States voted against the treaty. In 2006, Moreno-Ocampo was thrown into the international spotlight as opponents of the US-led **War in Iraq** alleged war crimes by the United States and troops from Australia, **Poland**, and the **Great Britain**. The latter three countries are signatories of the Rome Statute. Moreno-Ocampo contended that the ICC did not have jurisdiction to prosecute alleged crimes under the Rome Statute, and that none of the more than 200 complaints was sufficient to try in the court.

MOSELEY-BRAUN, CAROL ELIZABETH (1947–). Moseley-Braun graduated from the University of Illinois at Chicago (1969) and earned a law degree from the University of Chicago (1972). From 1973 to 1977, she served as a US attorney in Chicago. She entered politics as a Democrat in 1978, winning a seat in the Illinois House of Representatives, and served through 1986. In 1992, she won a US Senate seat from Illinois and became the first African-American woman to serve in the upper chamber. In February 2003, she announced her candidacy for the Democratic presidential nomination in 2004. Her campaign failed to gain momentum, however, and just days before the **Iowa Caucuses** she withdrew from the race and threw her support to Vermont Governor **Howard Dean**.

MOSUL, IRAQ. This city is located in northern **Iraq**, along the Tigris River, and has a population of approximately 1.8 million. Mosul is the third largest city in Iraq behind **Baghdad** and **Basra**. Mosul fell quickly to US forces following the March 2003 invasion of Iraq. On 22 July 2003, Iraqi dictator **Saddam Hussein**'s sons, **Uday Hussein** and **Qusay Hussein**, were killed in a gunfight with US troops in the city. Beginning in 2004, Mosul was the locus of the **insurgency** against US and coalition forces, which forced thousands to flee the city. In May 2008, in conjunction with US forces, the Iraqi Army launched a major military effort to restore security to the city.

MOUSSAOUI, ZACARIAS (1968–). A French citizen born to Moroccan parents, Moussaoui is also known under the name Abu

Khaled al Sahrawi. He was dubbed the "twentieth hijacker" by the media and US law enforcement for allegedly conspiring to commit the **11 September 2001 terrorist** attacks on New York and the **Pentagon**. He is thought to have been a possible replacement for several other **al-Qaeda** operatives who were to join the other 19 terrorists who perpetrated the worst terror attack on US soil.

Moussaoui attended business school in **London**, England, in the 1990s. He apparently met shoe-bomber **Richard Reid** while in London and became increasingly interested in **jihad**. He traveled to **Afghanistan** to take part in a terror training camp, and then later to Malaysia, where he received financial and other support from radical Islamists. In 2001, Moussaoui attended a flight training school in Norman, Oklahoma. During this time, he allegedly received financial support from the **al-Qaeda** Hamburg Cell. Three weeks before the 11 September 2001 terrorist attacks, Moussaoui was arrested by the **Federal Bureau of Investigation** (FBI) on an immigration violation.

Moussaoui was indicted in December 2001 on charges relating to conspiracy to commit acts of **terrorism**. At his trial he refused to enter a plea and shunned legal counsel. He later convinced the judge, who had entered a not guilty plea on his behalf, that he could represent himself. Although he admitted connections with al-Qaeda, Moussaoui contended that he was not involved in the 11 September 2001 attacks—and that he was instead planning a separate operation. At his trial no direct evidence linked him to the 11 September 2001 attacks. Nonetheless, in April 2005, after much wrangling over Moussaoui's right to gain access to government documents and call suspected terror suspects (including **Khalid Sheikh Mohammed**) to his defense, he shocked the court by pleading guilty to all charges. He contended that his plan was not to participate in the 11 September 2001 attacks, but rather to hijack a Boeing jet and fly it to Afghanistan to free a fellow al-Qaeda operative. He remained defiant at sentencing, positing that he had "won" and America had lost. In May 2006, a jury decided against the death penalty and Moussaoui was sentenced to life in prison. He was transported to the federal maximum security prison in Florence, Colorado, where he is incarcerated.

MUELLER, ROBERT SWAN III (1944–). A native of New York City who grew up in Philadelphia, Pennsylvania, Mueller holds a bachelor's degree from Princeton University (1966), a master's degree in international relations from New York University (1967), and a law degree from the University of Virginia (1973). He joined the Marine Corps before law school and earned a Purple Heart and a Bronze Star for his service during the Vietnam War. Following law school, he worked in private practice and in the US attorney's office in San Francisco, California. He moved to Boston in 1982, working as a federal prosecutor and in private practice. In 1989, he joined the Department of Justice and oversaw criminal cases, including organized crime.

President **George W. Bush** nominated Mueller as director of the **Federal Bureau of Investigation** (FBI) in July 2001 to succeed the acting director, Thomas Pickard. Mueller was confirmed unanimously by the US Senate, and took up his position just one week before the **11 September 2001 terrorist** attacks on the **World Trade Center** in New York and the **Pentagon**. In the aftermath of the attacks, Mueller faced intense congressional and media scrutiny for the failure of the FBI to prevent the attacks. In 2004, he was also implicated in the controversy over warrantless **wiretapping**, which was later resolved with changes to the **Foreign Intelligence Surveillance Act** (FISA). *See also* ASHCROFT, JOHN; GONZALES, ALBERTO; PROTECT AMERICA ACT (2007).

MUGABE, ROBERT GABRIEL (1924–). A Marxist revolutionary who fought white rule in Zimbabwe in the 1960s and 1970s, Mugabe rose to power in 1980, when he became prime minister. He became president in 1987. In the 1990s, he embarked on a controversial land reform policy to forcibly claim farms owned by the white minority.

In March 2008, Mugabe faced opposition in the presidential election but would not concede that he lost the first round of the election. Morgan Tsvangirai, Mugabe's opponent, withdrew from the runoff after sustained violence by Mugabe's regime. International condemnation of the election dynamics ultimately resulted in a power-sharing agreement between Mugabe, who remained president, and Tsvangirai, who became prime minister in 2008. In 2003, President **George W. Bush** imposed sanctions on Mugabe's regime for human rights violations, and the **European Union** leveled a travel ban on Mugabe's Zimbabwe.

MUHAMMAD, JOHN ALLEN (1960–). An Army veteran who was born in New Orleans, Louisiana, Muhammad was the mastermind of the **Beltway Sniper** shootings around the Washington, D.C., metropolitan area in October 2002. He and his 17-year-old accomplice, Lee Boyd Malvo (1985–), used a modified passenger vehicle to shoot ten individuals and injure three others. Ten of the 12 victims of random shootings perpetrated by Muhammad and Malvo died.

Muhammad and Malvo were arrested on 24 October 2002. In November 2003, Muhammad was convicted on murder charges and sentenced to death by a Virginia court. He was also convicted in Maryland and sentenced to multiple life terms in prison. At the end of 2008, his death sentence had not been carried out. Malvo was tried in Virginia in 2003. He was convicted of murder and was sentenced to life without the possibility of parole in March 2003.

MUJAHIDEEN. A derivative of the Arabic word for "struggle," the term *mujahideen* was used in the 1980s primarily to describe Muslim resistors engaged in guerrilla warfare against forces of the **Soviet Union** that invaded **Afghanistan** in 1980. Following the US-led invasion of Afghanistan in October 2001, which toppled the **Taliban** regime, the term referred to **insurgents** who battled US forces. Similarly, the term was used to describe **al-Qaeda** and other insurgent groups in the **War in Iraq** following the US invasion in March 2003.

MULLEN, MICHAEL GLENN (MIKE) (1947–). A native of Los Angeles, California, Mullen graduated from the US Naval Academy (1968), the Naval Postgraduate School (1991), and the Harvard Business School of Advanced Management (1991). His commands include three Navy ships, several battle groups, and the US Second Fleet for the **North Atlantic Treaty Organization** (NATO). He was commander of US Naval Operations in Europe, and became chief of naval operations in 2004. In October 2007, he succeeded General **Peter Pace** as chairman of the **Joint Chiefs of Staff**. In his Senate confirmation hearings, Mullen expressed dissatisfaction with political progress in **Iraq**, vowed to exert pressure on Iraqi politicians toward the withdrawal of US troops, and contended that the presence of US troops in Iraq would not constitute an open-ended commitment. *See also* ARMED FORCES.

MULTILATERALISM. In international relations, multilateralism refers to nations seeking resolution of problems in concert with one another instead of taking unilateral action. Examples include international institutions such as the **United Nations** (UN); organizations under treaties such as the **North American Free Trade Agreement** that provide resolution of trade disputes between the United States, **Canada**, and **Mexico**; and the **International Criminal Court**.

Critics charged that the **neoconservative foreign policy** of the administration of **George W. Bush** violated essential tenets of multilateralism by challenging the efficacy and legitimacy of the UN. Moreover, critics pointed to the Bush administration's rejection of the **Kyoto Protocol** on global warming and the **War in Iraq**, led by the United States and a **Coalition of the Willing**, rather than by UN mandate, as further examples.

MUMBAI, INDIA. Also known historically as Bombay, this coastal Indian city boasts a population of more than 13 million and is India's major financial center. Mumbai was the subject of several **terrorist** attacks over the course of **George W. Bush**'s presidency. On 11 July 2006, a series of bombs exploded on commuter rail lines around Mumbai, killing 209 people and injuring more than 700. Police suspected that radical Islamist groups with connections to **al-Qaeda** were responsible for the attack. On 26 November 2008, radical Islamist groups carried out a series of attacks and kidnappings across Mumbai, killing more than 150 and injuring another 300 people.

MURTHA, JOHN PATRICK, JR. (1932–). A native of New Martinsville, West Virginia, Murtha was raised in western Pennsylvania. He joined the Marine Corps in 1952 and served in Vietnam from 1966 to 1967, having sought active duty after serving in the reserves. During his tour of duty, he received two Purple Hearts and a Bronze Star. He retired from the Marine Corps reserves as a colonel in 1990. He entered politics in 1969, when he won a seat to the Pennsylvania statehouse. In 1974, he became the first Vietnam veteran elected to the US House of Representatives. A Democrat, he won re-election 17 times through 2008.

Although he voted for the **Iraq War Resolution** in 2002, Murtha became a steadfast critic of the **War in Iraq** and the **foreign policy** of President **George W. Bush**. In 2005, he offered an unsuccessful resolution to withdraw US troops from **Iraq**. He also led an inquiry into the deaths of civilians by US Marines in Haditha, Iraq, that resulted in lawsuits against him. He stirred further controversy during the 2008 presidential election. A supporter of Democratic candidate **Barack Obama**, Murtha suggested that voters in his western Pennsylvania district might not vote for an African-American candidate because they feared change and were "racist." When he attempted to clarify his comments, he suggested his constituents were "rednecks." Murtha nevertheless won the district in 2008 with 58 percent of the vote.

MUSHARRAF, PERVEZ (1943–). This former general seized power in **Pakistan** in a coup in 1999, ousting Nawiz Sharif and proclaiming himself chief executive. He appointed himself president in 2001. He actively cultivated the support of the United States and other Western governments by announcing his intention to combat international **terrorism**. Following the **11 September 2001 terrorist** attacks on New York and the **Pentagon**, Musharraf offered the use of airbases by the United States to combat the **Taliban** regime in **Afghanistan**. He nonetheless frustrated the administration of **George W. Bush** in the search for **al-Qaeda** operatives, including **Osama bin Laden**, by refusing to allow US forces into remote areas of Pakistan where terrorists were thought to be hiding. He also faced increasing civil violence stemming from dissatisfaction with his leadership among Pakistani Islamists—as well as opposition from those seeking greater democracy. In August 2008, Musharraf resigned in the wake of an effort to impeach him from office following June elections in which his party came in third behind the party of **Benazir Bhutto**. He was succeeded in September 2008 by President **Asif Ali Zardari**. *See also* WAZIRISTAN.

MYERS, RICHARD BOWMAN (1942–). A native of Kansas City, Missouri, Myers is a graduate in mechanical engineering from Kansas State University (1965) and earned a master's degree in business administration from Auburn University (1977). He joined the Air Force in 1965 as an officer and attended flight school in Oklahoma. A Vietnam War veteran who flew combat missions, his later commands included US forces in Japan and Pacific forces in Hawaii, as well as the North American Aerospace Defense Command and Air Force Space Command before he became vice chairman of the **Joint Chiefs of Staff** under President **George W. Bush** in March 2000. He succeeded General **Hugh Shelton** as chairman of the Joint Chiefs of Staff on 1 October 2005 and remained in the post until 30 September 2005. He was succeeded by General **Peter Pace**. Myers took up a part-time teaching position at Kansas State University upon his retirement, and he became a member of several boards, including the military contractor Northrup Grumman. *See also* ARMED FORCES.

– N –

NADER, RALPH (1934–). A native of Winsted, Connecticut, Nader is a graduate of Princeton University (1955) and Harvard Law School (1958). In the 1960s, he was an assistant to New York Senator Daniel Moynihan and worked on public safety issues. While holding several academic positions, Nader became a strong advocate for consumer safety matters. In 1971, he founded the nonprofit group Public Citizen that championed causes ranging from automobile safety to opposition to nuclear power. He first ran for president in 1972 as a write-in candidate.

In 2000, Nader ran for the White House on the Green Party ticket. His platform centered on environmental issues and frustration with the two-party system. He contended that there were few policy differences between the Republican and Democratic parties or between **George W. Bush** and **Al Gore**. Nader culled 2.8 million votes in the 2000 election. Most critical, however, was his base of support in Florida. Nader received more than 97,000 votes in Florida. Presumably, many of those votes were from more liberal Democrats disgruntled with Gore, a moderate. Democrats were furious, suggesting that had Nader's supporters thrown their votes to Gore, the **Florida recount** would have been unnecessary. Florida's 25 electoral votes were certified for Bush by just 537 popular votes. On this basis, Democratic critics of Nader suggest that his candidacy helped elect Bush by siphoning off critical Democratic support. Nader ran as an independent candidate for the presidency in 2004 and 2008, winning just .38 and .56 percent of the popular vote, respectively.

NAGIN, CLARENCE RAY, JR. (1956–). Born in New Orleans, Louisiana, Nagin earned a bachelor's degree in accounting from Tuskegee University (1978) and a master's in business administration from Tulane University (1994). He was vice president of Cox Communications before he ran successfully for the mayorship of New Orleans in 2002 to succeeded Marc Morial.

Nagin was mayor in 2005 when **Hurricane Katrina** devastated New Orleans and the Gulf Coast. He quickly found himself at the center of controversy over the lack of preparations for the storm at the local level. Critics of Nagin charged that he did not take the appropriate action to evacuate residents inland with available school buses. For his part, Nagin blamed Governor **Kathleen Babineaux Blanco** and the **Federal Emergency Management Agency** (FEMA) director **Michael D. Brown** for the unacceptably slow rescue-and-recovery response. In January 2006, he stirred further controversy by positing that New Orleans would be a "chocolate city" once again—a reference to his belief that despite the fact that many African-American residents had moved to Houston, Texas, or other cities in the wake of the storm, the city would once again have a majority black population in the future. Nagin won re-election in May 2006 in a close race against the lieutenant governor. His term expires in 2010.

NATIONAL COUNTERTERRORISM CENTER (NCTC). The National Counterterrorism Center was established by the **Intelligence Reform and Terrorism Prevention Act** in 2004. The center is located in Washington, D.C., and is charged with planning and coordinating counterterrorism programs across the federal government. The NCTC falls under the supervision of the **Director of National Intelligence** (DNI). The establishment of the NCTC was one of the key recommendations of the **9/11 Commission**.

NATIONAL ENERGY POLICY DEVELOPMENT GROUP. *See* CHENEY, RICHARD B.; ENERGY TASK FORCE.

NATIONAL SECURITY ADVISOR. Also known as the assistant to the president for national security affairs, the national security advisor is appointed at the president's discretion and does not require Senate approval. He or she serves at the president's pleasure, is a member of the **National Security Counsel**, and is the president's principal advisor on national security matters. During the administration of President **George W. Bush**, the national security advisors were **Condoleezza Rice** and **Stephen Hadley**.

NATIONAL SECURITY AGENCY (NSA). Created in 1952 under President Harry Truman within the Department of Defense, the National Security Agency is responsible for foreign intelligence gathering. Following passage of the **Intelligence Reform and Terrorism Prevention Act** (2004), the NSA reported to the **Director of National Intelligence** (DNI) and focuses on foreign communications and surveillance.

In the administration of **George W. Bush**, the NSA was at the center of controversy concerning warrantless **wiretapping**. The *New York Times* reported in 2005 that the NSA had surveilled foreign communications—including those taking place with US citizens—and had circumvented court orders in compliance with the **Foreign Intelligence Surveillance Act** (FISA) Court. One member of the FISA Court resigned in protest. Bush contended that the **Authorization for the Use of Military Force** to battle **terrorism** trumped the FISA Court requirements. In 2007, Congress passed the **Protect America Act**, which eliminated the provision for court orders for foreign communications and enabled the NSA to conduct domestic surveillance as long as one individual involved in the communications was believed to be abroad. The FISA Amendments passed by Congress in 2008 renewed the major provisions in the Protect America Act, which concerned civil libertarians worried about domestic wiretapping in the open-ended **War on Terror**. *See also* AMERICAN CIVIL LIBERTIES UNION (ACLU).

NATIONAL SECURITY COUNCIL. The National Security Council was established by Congress in the National Security Act of 1947. The purpose of the council is to provide **foreign policy** and military advice to the president, who chairs the proceedings, and to coordinate policy with other departments and agencies. Current members include the vice president; secretaries of state, treasury, and defense; the president's **national security advisor**; chairman of the **Joint Chiefs of Staff**; and the **Director of National Intelligence** (DNI).

NEGROPONTE, JOHN DMITRI (1939–). Born in London, England, Negroponte graduated from Yale University (1960). He left Harvard Law School to join the foreign service that same year. His distinguished State Department career spanned four decades and included service in Asia, Europe, and Latin America. He was ambassador to Honduras (1981–1985), assistant secretary of state for oceans and international environmental and scientific affairs (1985–1987), deputy assistant to the president for national security affairs under **Ronald Reagan** (1987–1989), ambassador to **Mexico** under **George H.W. Bush** (1989–1993), and ambassador to the Philippines under **William Clinton** (1993–1996).

Negroponte served as ambassador to the **United Nations** from 2001 to 2004 and as ambassador to **Iraq** from 2004 to 2005 under President **George W. Bush**. He became the first **Director of National Intelligence** (DNI) in April 2005, and held that post until February 2007. As DNI, Negroponte worked to streamline counterintelligence operations and reform the **Central Intelligence Agency** (CIA). He was succeeded by **John Michael McConnell**. Negroponte moved back to the State Department in February 2007. He was confirmed as deputy secretary of state and reported to **Condoleezza Rice**. *See also* INTELLIGENCE REFORM AND TERRORISM PREVENTION ACT (2004).

NEOCONSERVATIVE, NEOCONSERVATISM. The terms, first coined in the 1970s, had a negative connotation in the description of former Democrats who had lost faith in liberalism and espoused a more conservative viewpoint on domestic affairs as a result of Lyndon Johnson and the Great Society agenda of the 1960s. Its contemporary incarnation is best known in the realm of **foreign**

policy, as articulated by the signatories to the **Project for the New American Century** (PNAC), founded by conservative writer and news commentator William Kristol. The tenets of neoconservatism in foreign policy include notions of "moral clarity," interventionism relative to the United States' national interest, a suspicion of **multilateralism** and international institutions such as the **United Nations** (UN), and staunch support for the state of **Israel**. In 1998, PNAC wrote to President **William Clinton** and urged him to take decisive action against Iraqi dictator **Saddam Hussein**, who the signatories alleged had continually defied the internationally sanctioned settlement following the **Persian Gulf War**. Many neoconservatives were frustrated that President **George H.W. Bush** did not remove Hussein from power in the 1991 conflict, although the UN mandate fell short of that objective.

The neoconservative philosophy in foreign affairs buttressed the so-called **Bush Doctrine**, which President **George W. Bush** outlined in a State of the Union address in 2002: The United States would act decisively against nations that harbored **terrorist**s, and would act unilaterally against such regimes as well as state sponsors of **terrorism** without UN approval, if necessary. The **War in Iraq**, led by the United States in March 2003 with an international "**Coalition of the Willing**" absent a UN mandate, is a prime example of the administration's neoconservative foreign policy stance. Bush's decision to go forward with an **anti-ballistic missile** defense system in **Poland** and the **Czech Republic**, over the objections of **Russia**, is another example.

Critics charge that the Bush administration's rejection of multilaterialism in foreign affairs, and its objection to the **Kyoto Protocol** and the **Comprehensive Test Ban Treaty** relative to arguments about US national interests, damaged America's international reputation and leadership. *See also* PREEMPTION.

NEW HAMPSHIRE PRIMARY. Under its state constitution, New Hampshire must hold the first-in-the-nation primary election for the presidency. As a bellwether for presidential hopefuls, the primary has taken on nearly mythical proportions: No Republican or Democratic candidate won either party's nomination without first carrying New Hampshire between 1952 and 1992. The trend was broken in 1992, when **William Clinton** lost New Hampshire but ultimately triumphed in later races to secure the Democratic nomination. In 2000, **George W. Bush** lost New Hampshire to **John McCain** but won enough delegates in subsequent races to lock up the Republican nomination. In 2004, Democratic candidate **John Kerry** placed first in the New Hampshire primary, defeating **Howard Dean**, **Wesley Clark**, and **John Edwards**. In 2008, Democratic candidate **Hillary Clinton** defeated rival **Barack Obama** but lost the nomination in a protracted primary battle in other states. **John McCain**, however, prevailed over his rivals **Mitt Romney** and **Rudolph Giuliani** in 2008.

NEW ORLEANS, LOUISIANA. *See* BLANCO, KATHLEEN BABINEAUX; BROWN, MICHAEL D.; FEDERAL EMERGENCY MANAGEMENT AGENCY (FEMA); HURRICANE KATRINA; NAGIN, CLARENCE RAY, JR.

NEY, ROBERT WILLIAM (1954–). A native of West Virginia, Ney was raised in Ohio. He graduated from Ohio State University (1976) and entered politics in 1980, winning a seat in the Ohio statehouse. He was appointed to the Ohio Senate in 1984, and won re-election twice. He won election to the US House of Representatives as a Republican in 1994, and was re-elected five times through 2004. He withdrew from his re-election bid in August 2006 and resigned his seat in Congress over allegations that he had received gifts from lobbyist **Jack Abramoff**. Ney later pleaded guilty to charges of conspiracy, was sentenced to 30 months in prison, and served 17 months. *See also* DELAY, TOM; SCANLON, MICHAEL.

NICHOLSON, ROBERT JAMES (JIM) (1938–). A native of Iowa, Nicholson graduated from West Point (1961), holds a master's degree in public policy from Columbia University, and earned a law degree from the University of Denver (1972). A Vietnam War veteran, Nicholson won a Bronze Star and several other medals, and retired from the Army as a colonel in 1991. He served as the Republican Party's chairman from 1997 to 2000. President **George W. Bush** appointed him ambassador to the Holy See (the Vatican) in 2001. He became secretary of veterans affairs in January 2005, replacing **Anthony Principi**, and held the position until October 2007. He was succeeded by **James Peake**.

NIGER. A former French colony in the Sahara Desert that gained independence in 1960, Niger was thrown into the spotlight in President **George W. Bush**'s State of the Union address in January 2003. Bush cited documents, later determined by the International Atomic Energy Agency and the **Central Intelligence Agency (CIA)** to be forged, that referenced attempts by Iraqi dictator **Saddam Hussein** to procure "yellowcake" uranium in the pursuit of **weapons of mass destruction** (WMDs). Ambassador **Joseph Wilson** had gone to Niger in 2002 to verify the allegations and reported that there was no evidence Hussein had attempted to purchase yellowcake. Doubts about the intelligence notwithstanding, the White House retained the reference in the State of the Union address, which foreshadowed the US-led invasion of **Iraq** two months later. *See also* AXIS OF EVIL; PLAME, VALERIE ELISE; WAR IN IRAQ.

9/11/2001. *See* 11 SEPTEMBER 2001; PENTAGON; WORLD TRADE CENTER.

9/11 COMMISSION. Formally known as the National Commission on Terrorist Attacks Upon the United States, Congress mandated this commission in November 2002 to investigate the **terrorist** attacks on the **World Trade Center** in New York and the **Pentagon** in Washington, D.C., on **11 September 2001**. The Commission's mandate included an assessment of emergency preparedness and crisis management following the attacks. The Commission was divided equally among Democrats and Republicans. New Jersey Governor Thomas Kean, a Republican, chaired the commission. Other Republicans included former White House counsel **Fred Fielding**, former Senator Slade Gorton, former Secretary of the Navy John Lehman, and former Illinois Governor James Thompson. Democrats included former Congressman Lee Hamilton, Richard Ben-Veniste, Jamie Gorelick, former Senator Bob Kerry, and US Representative Timothy Roemer.

The Commission issued its final report in July 2004. The report called for a comprehensive counterterrorism strategy. Some of the key recommendations included efforts to preclude **al-Qaeda** and other terrorist organizations from procuring funding, shoring up democracy in **Afghanistan** and other Muslim countries, bolstering border and transportation security measures implemented by the **Department of Homeland Security**, and the creation of a new **Director of National Intelligence** to coordinate intelligence gathering by the **Central Intelligence Agency** (CIA) and other federal agencies. *See also* DIRECTOR OF NATIONAL INTELLIGENCE (DNI); INTELLIGENCE REFORM AND TERRORISM PREVENTION ACT (2004); NATIONAL COUNTERTERORISM CENTER (NCTC).

NO CHILD LEFT BEHIND. Championed by President **George W. Bush**, this **education** legislation was signed into law in 2001. The legislation reauthorized federal funding for schools under the Elementary and Secondary Education Act of 1965. The reauthorization included performance-based standards to be used in the assessment of schools and students' academic progress. Parents of children attending "failing" schools were allowed greater school choice. Bush and supporters of the bill argued that it would provide greater accountability for teachers and schools. Critics charged that the bill's sharp focus on measuring children's performance would lead to an overemphasis on testing.

The National Education Association sued the Department of Education in 2005 over funding provisions in the law. In January 2008, a US appellate court agreed that states and local school districts could not be forced to pay with their own funds to comply with the federal law's testing and other requirements.

NORTH ATLANTIC TREATY ORGANIZATION (NATO). The North Atlantic Treaty Organization was founded in 1949 to promote military cooperation among North American and European countries in the aftermath of World War II. The initial signatories included Belgium, **Canada**, Denmark, **France**, Iceland, Italy, Luxembourg, Netherlands, Norway, Portugal, **Great Britain**, and the United States. France withdrew from the organization in 1966, but remained committed to the defensive posture of NATO. **Germany**, Greece, and **Turkey** became members in the 1950s; Spain joined in 1982. The organization played a particularly important role during the **Cold War**, as member states pledged that if any other member state were attacked, they would come to that member's defense. The framework is similar to that of the **Warsaw Pact** nations. With the fall of the **Soviet Union** in 1991, many former **Warsaw Pact** nations have since joined NATO, including the **Czech Republic**, **Hungary**, and **Poland** (1999); and **Bulgaria**, **Estonia**, **Latvia**, **Lithuania**, **Romania**, **Slovakia**, and **Slovenia** (2004).

Following the US-led invasion of **Afghanistan** in October 2001, NATO forces acted outside Europe for the first time when they took control of the **International Security Assistance Force** (ISAF).

NORTH KOREA. Divided from South Korea by a demilitarized zone at the 38th Parallel following World War II, North Korea is a one-party communist state with a population of 23 million. Its official name is the Democratic People's Republic of Korea. The capital is Pyongyang. From 1948 until his death in 1994, Kim Il Sung ruled the country and remains a mythical personage in the totalitarian state's symbolism. His son, **Kim Jong Il**, acceded to power upon his father's death.

In his 2002 State of the Union address, President **George W. Bush** named North Korea, along with **Iran** and **Iraq**, as an **axis of evil** for allegedly sponsoring international **terrorism** and attempting to procure **weapons of mass destruction** (WMDs). North Korea withdrew from the **Nuclear Non-Proliferation Treaty** in 2003. "Six-party talks" between North Korea and **Russia**, **China**, South Korea, Japan, and the United States ensued but made little progress on North Korea's nuclear weapons program. On 9 October 2006, North Korea tested a nuclear weapon underground.

In February 2007, the six-party talks yielded a pivotal agreement. North Korea agreed to suspend its nuclear weapons program and allow inspectors from the **International Atomic Energy Agency** (IAEA) to verify dismantling of the facility at Yongbyon. North Korea gained energy assistance from the countries involved, as well as a commitment to normalize relations with the United States. On 11 October 2008, North Korea was removed from the Department of State's list of state sponsors of terrorism.

NORTHERN ALLIANCE. Known also as the United Islamic Front for the Salvation of **Afghanistan**, the **mujahideen** militias of the Northern Alliance unsuccessfully battled the **Taliban**, which seized control of the country in 1996. The Northern Alliance did, however, retain de facto control of the north of the country.

With the US-led invasion of Afghanistan in October 2001, Northern Alliance fighters joined forces with US and coalition troops to oust the Taliban regime. The transitional government of **Hamid Karzai** was notably comprised of several key Northern Alliance leaders. Most Northern Alliance fighters were either absorbed into the Afghan army or disarmed.

NORTHERN IRELAND. This statelet or province, often referred to as "Ulster," is part of **Great Britain** and has a population of just over 1.5 million. The statelet was created as a result of the Government of Ireland Act of 1920, which partitioned Ireland between the 26 counties of the Free State (which would become the Republic of Ireland in 1949) and Northern Ireland, which would be administered by Great Britain. Beginning in the 1960s, in what is referred to as the "Troubles," Northern Irish nationalists—predominantly Catholic—rallied for civil rights against successive Unionist governments controlled by Protestants loyal to the British crown. The situation degenerated into de facto civil war in the 1970s, 1980s, and early 1990s as the nationalist Irish Republican Army (IRA) battled loyalist paramilitaries, British troops, and the Northern Ireland police force, the Royal Ulster Constabulary, using guerrilla military operations and bombings in Ulster and on the British mainland. Great Britain considered the IRA **terrorist**s.

The United States played a pivotal role in the search for peace and reconciliation in Northern Ireland. In 1998, President **William Clinton** and his special envoy to Northern Ireland, **George Mitchell**, secured an agreement between nationalists and loyalists, the British government, and the government of the Republic of Ireland, called the Good Friday Agreement. The Accord provided for a path to self-determination for Ulster. Partisans loyal to the Unionist leader Reverend Ian Paisley, however, balked at the agreement. Home rule in Northern Ireland was suspended in 2002. An election in 2003 failed to yield any further progress on a power-sharing executive envisioned in the Good Friday Agreement.

In 2005, the IRA declared that it would end all paramilitary operations and decommissioned its arms. Following the election of March 2007, a power-sharing executive was established and home rule was reinstituted. Sinn Féin (nationalist) leader Gerry Adams stepped aside from the government. Democratic Unionist Party leader Reverend Ian Paisley became first minister, while Sinn Féin's Martin McGuinness became deputy first minister. The watershed event was a major step in Northern Ireland's quest for self-governance within Great Britain and improved relations between the Catholic (nationalist) and Protestant (loyalist) communities in the troubled province. President **George W. Bush** visited Northern Ireland in June 2008 and called the political progress over the past decade "unimaginable." He met with Northern Ireland's political leaders to discuss policing, justice, and investment issues.

NORTON, GALE ANN (1954–). A native of Wichita, Kansas, Norton graduated with undergraduate and law degrees from the University of Denver (1975 and 1978, respectively). She entered politics in 1991, when she won election as attorney general of Colorado. A Republican, Norton ran unsuccessfully for a US Senate seat from Colorado in 1996. In 2001, President **George W. Bush** appointed her secretary of the interior. She remained in that post until March 2006, when she was succeeded by **Dirk Kempthorne**. Norton's tenure as secretary of the interior was notable for the criticism she received from environmentalists, who disagreed with her pro-business and pro-development stances on energy and natural resources. After leaving public service she took a position as legal counsel for Shell Oil Company.

NOVAK, ROBERT DAVID SANDERS (1931–2009). A native of Joliet, Illinois, Novak graduated from the University of Illinois at Urbana-Champaign (1952) and subsequently served in the army during the Korean War. His journalism career spanned six decades. His influential conservative column, syndicated by the *Chicago Sun-Times* newspaper, is the longest in US history—45 years through 2008. A traditional conservative with libertarian tendencies, Novak was a critic of **neoconservatism** and the **War in Iraq** during the administration of **George W. Bush**. In early August 2008, Novak announced he had a brain tumor and would suspend his column. However, he reprised writing his column for a different syndicate just three weeks later.

NUCLEAR NONPROLIFERATION TREATY. This international treaty, signed by the United States, went into effect in 1970. It is aimed at precluding the spread of nuclear weapons to nonnuclear powers and promoting the peaceful use of nuclear technology. Four other countries known to have nuclear weapons are also signatories: **China**, **Russia**, **France**, and **Great Britain**. Only four nations that are known to have nuclear weapons or nuclear weapons technology are not signatories to the treaty—India, **Israel**, **North Korea**, and **Pakistan**.

President **George W. Bush** supported the treaty and criticized North Korea, **Iran**, and **Iraq** (the **axis of evil**) in his 2003 State of the Union address for attempting to procure **weapons of mass destruction** (WMDs) in violation of the treaty's tenets. North Korea, which signed the treaty in 1985, withdrew from it in January 2003. Investigations by the **International Atomic Energy Agency** (IAEA) in Fall 2003 showed that Iran, a signatory to the treaty, had begun enriching uranium. Iranian President **Mahmoud Ahmadinejad** claimed the enrichment was for peaceful civilian use, not for nuclear weapons. **Libya** complied with the treaty in December 2003 when Mu'ammar Gadhafi suspended the pursuit of WMDs and allowed international observers to enter the country for verification.

NUSSLE, JAMES ALLEN (1960–). A native of Des Moines, Iowa, Nussle earned a bachelor's degree from Luther College (1983) and a law degree from Drake University (1985). After working in private law practice, he ran successfully for Congress from Iowa in 1990. He was re-elected seven times. He chaired the House Committee on the Budget from 2001 to 2006. In 2006, he ran unsuccessfully for the governorship of Iowa. In September 2007, President **George W. Bush** tapped Nussle to succeed **Rob Portman** as head of the **Office of Management and Budget** (OMB). He served as a senior advisor to Republican presidential candidate **Rudy Giuliani** in 2008.

– O –

OBAMA, BARACK HUSSEIN (1961–). Born in Honolulu, Hawaii, Obama was raised by his maternal grandparents. His parents separated when he was two years old, and his father, a Kenyan national whom he saw only once thereafter, died in a car accident in 1982. His mother, an anthropologist who traveled frequently, passed away from ovarian cancer in 1995. Obama graduated from Columbia University with a degree in political science (1983) and became a community organizer in Chicago, working for several educational foundations. He graduated from Harvard Law School in 1991—becoming Harvard's first African-American president of the law review—after which time he taught law at the University of Chicago.

A Democrat, Obama entered politics in 1996, when he won a seat to the Illinois State Senate and was re-elected in 1998. Controversy developed over Obama's start in politics, which was supported by former domestic terrorist **William Ayers**. In 2000, Obama ran unsuccessfully for a seat in the US House of Representatives for a district in Chicago. In 2004, he won election to the junior US Senate seat from Illinois. He joined the Congressional Black Caucus and established the most liberal voting record in the upper chamber according to the *National Journal*. In the Senate, he served on the Foreign Relations, Energy and Commerce, and Veterans Affairs Committees. His legislative accomplishments included supporting border security and weapons nonproliferation legislation. He sponsored a bill, signed by President **George W. Bush**, which provided aid to the Democratic Republic of the **Congo**. Although he was not elected to the Senate at the time of the vote for the **War in Iraq**, he publicly opposed the action.

In February 2007, Obama announced his candidacy for the Democratic nomination for the presidency. A relative unknown in the crowded Democratic primary and caucuses that followed in 2008, he lost the **New Hampshire Primary** to rival **Hillary Clinton** by three percentage points to place second. He placed first in the **Iowa Caucuses**, with **John Edwards** and Hillary Clinton ranking second and third, respectively. The trend that ensued was one in which Obama tended to prevail in caucus states while Clinton won primary states with more heterogeneous voting populations.

Controversy erupted when the Democratic National Committee (DNC) decided initially not to seat the convention delegations of Florida and Michigan because both states had moved their primary dates up on the calendar in violation of party rules. Obama was not on the ballot in Michigan, and neither candidate campaigned in Florida. Clinton prevailed in the Sunshine State. In May, the DNC reversed its decision and seated half of each state's delegation. In early June, Obama secured enough delegates to clinch the nomination. Clinton suspended her campaign on 7 June and endorsed her former rival. Obama became the first African-American nominee of either major party in American history.

Obama chose fellow Delaware Senator **Joe Biden** as his vice presidential running mate in August 2008. In the general election campaign, the Obama–Biden ticket squared off against Republican presidential nominee **John McCain** and his running mate, Alaska Governor **Sarah Palin**. Obama and McCain were virtually tied in opinion polls in the early days of the general campaign. By mid-September, however, Obama's lead widened with the effects of the **sub-prime mortgage** crisis that helped plunge the economy into recession. Obama astutely attempted to tie McCain to allegedly failed economic policies of George W. Bush. He also vowed to end the War in Iraq, while bolstering the **War on Terror** by dealing with the **insurgency** in **Afghanistan** as a top priority.

In October 2008, Obama had an exchange in Ohio with **Samuel Joseph Wurzelbacher** ("Joe the Plumber"), an Ohio resident who questioned his economic and tax increase proposals on top wage earners. Obama famously remarked that he wished to "spread the wealth," and the McCain campaign seized upon the comment to argue that Obama would engage in a socialist-style redistribution of wealth. Discussions of Joe the Plumber figured prominently in the final debate of the campaign on 15 October. Regardless, polls showed that McCain trailed Obama by 7–10 points in the run-up to the election. On 4 November, Obama won 53 percent of the national vote and 365 Electoral College votes. His popular vote exceeded McCain's by 9.4 million ballots.

Following his electoral victory, as the economic situation worsened, President-elect Obama swiftly began to name members of his cabinet. In December 2008, he asked Secretary of Defense **Robert Gates**, a Republican named by George W. Bush, to remain in his position. He also announced that he would nominate Hillary Clinton as secretary of state. *See also* BLAGOJEVICH, MILORAD (ROD) R.

OBAMA, MICHELLE LAVAUGHN (1964–). Née Robinson, Michelle Obama is the wife of President **Barack Hussein Obama**. She is the first African-American first lady. She married Obama in 1992, and has two daughters by him, Malia and Natasha (Sasha). She graduated with a degree in sociology from Princeton University in 1985. She received a law degree from Harvard Law School in 1988. She has worked in private law practice, as well as for the mayor of Chicago, Illinois, and for community service organizations.

O'CONNOR, SANDRA DAY (1930–). Born in El Paso, Texas, and raised in Arizona, O'Connor received her law degree at Stanford University (1952), where she served on the law review and graduated in only two years. She worked as a deputy attorney for San Mateo County, California, and was in private practice in Phoenix, Arizona, in the 1950s. She served as assistant attorney general for the state of Arizona from 1965 to 1969 before being appointed to fill a vacancy in the Arizona senate. She was subsequently elected twice in her own right. She successfully ran for a judgeship in Maricopa County before being appointed to the Arizona Court of Appeals in 1979. President **Ronald Reagan** chose her as his first appointment to the **Supreme Court** of the United States in 1981 to fill the vacancy left by retiring justice Potter Stewart. O'Connor became the first woman in US history to serve on the High Court, and was unanimously confirmed by the Senate.

Regarded as a moderate justice, O'Connor's was the pivotal vote on many cases to come before the Supreme Court, including controversial decisions about **abortion**. In 2005, she retired. President **George W. Bush** named **Samuel Alito** to take her seat in October 2005; Alito was confirmed by the Senate in January 2006.

ODIERNO, RAYMOND T. (1954–). A native of Rockaway, New Jersey, Odierno is a graduate of West Point (1976) and earned dual master's degrees from the Army War College. He is a veteran of the **Persian Gulf War**, served under the secretary of defense, and from 2004 to 2006 was assistant chairman to the **Joint Chiefs of Staff**. He became commander of the multinational forces in **Iraq** in 2006 and was responsible for implementing the "surge" strategy advocated by President **George W. Bush** to quell the ongoing **insurgency** in that country through early 2008. He was promoted to the rank of general in September 2008. *See also* WAR IN IRAQ.

OFFICE OF FAITH-BASED AND COMMUNITY INITIATIVES. President **George W. Bush** established this White House office by executive order in January 2001, shortly after taking office. The office is charged with aiding faith-based organizations, such as churches and synagogues, to use federal grants to provide social services. As such, the office was a reflection of Bush's 2000 campaign, in which he referenced his **compassionate conservatism**. The White House implemented a number of directives to faith-based organizations receiving federal funds, including nondiscrimination on the basis of religion and restrictions on the use of funds for any religious purpose.

Critics charged that the office violated the Establishment Clause (First Amendment) of the Constitution mandating separation of church and state. Moreover, they contended that many of the grants went to churches with pastors who supported the Bush administration. In June 2006, a federal court struck down one program at a prison in Iowa for using federal funds that established an **Evangelical Christian** education program for inmates. In June 2007, however, the US **Supreme Court** ruled that citizens—solely because they are taxpayers—did not have standing to challenge executive orders that they contended were in violation of the First Amendment of the Constitution.

OFFICE OF HOMELAND SECURITY (OHS). Following the **11 September 2001 terrorist** attacks on New York and the **Pentagon**, President **George W. Bush** established by executive order the Office of Homeland Security in the **Executive Office of the President**. He appointed former Pennsylvania Governor **Tom Ridge** to head the office, which was charged with coordinating counterterrorism policies across federal agencies. In March 2002, OHS devised a color-coded terrorist threat level scheme that critics and the media called confusing.

Many in Congress contended that in his "czar" role Ridge did not have the adequate human or financial resources to adequately carry out a comprehensive counterterrorism strategy. Congress ultimately passed legislation in late 2002 that created the **Department of Homeland Security**, which subsumed most of the functions of the OHS in March 2003. OHS remains in the EOP primarily as a coordinating mechanism for homeland security matters, much as the **National Security Council** performs a similar function in matters of **foreign policy** and defense. *See also* CHERTOFF, MICHAEL.

OFFICE OF MANAGEMENT AND BUDGET (OMB). Housed in the **Executive Office of the President**, OMB boasts a staff nearly as large as the White House—more than 500. Among its many functions, OMB provides economic analysis and forecasts to the president and oversees regulations in the departments and agencies of the federal government. The office plays a pivotal role in the budget process. All departments and agencies must first submit their budget requests to OMB for review to ensure priorities are consistent with the president's agenda—a process known as "central clearance"—before appropriations requests are sent to Congress. Formerly known as the Bureau of the Budget, OMB takes its current name from the 1970 reorganization of its functions, spearheaded by President Richard Nixon. During the administration of **George W. Bush**, the heads of the OMB were **Jim Nussle** and **Rob Portman**.

OFFICE OF NATIONAL DRUG CONTROL POLICY (ONDCP). This White House agency, housed in the **Executive Office of the President**, was created by Congress in the Anti-Drug Abuse Act of 1988. The office sets national policies on illegal drug control, drug trafficking, and interdiction efforts. The office was established under President **George H.W. Bush** on 29 January 1989. Bush had vowed a "war on drugs." The first director of the office, often referred to as the "drug czar," was William J. Bennett. The office was raised to cabinet-level status under President **William Clinton** in 1993. In the administration of **George W. Bush**, drug czar **John P. Walters** focused efforts on the interdiction of drugs from **Mexico** and South America.

OIL FOR FOOD SCANDAL. The Oil for Food Program was implemented by a **United Nations** (UN) resolution in 1995 and supported by President **William Clinton**. The objective of the program was to allow the Iraqi regime of **Saddam Hussein**, which was under stiff economic sanctions following the **Persian Gulf War**, to sell a limited amount of oil in exchange for food and medicine. Upon the termination of the program in November 2003, following the US-led **War in Iraq**, allegations of corruption in the administration of the program surfaced. Former **Federal Reserve** chairman **Paul Volcker** began an independent inquiry into the charges, which implicated the French Banque Nationale de Paris (BNP-Parisbas), as well as UN Secretary General **Kofi Annan**. Volcker's interim report on the matter, issued in 2005, stopped short of criminal allegations against the UN official responsible for the program, Benon Sevan, who negotiated improper sales of Iraqi oil. The interim report also contended that the company charged with inspecting products sent to Iraq under the program, Cotecna Inc., for which Annan's son worked, had not conducted adequate inspections. The scandal provoked additional investigations by the US Congress, the **Iraq Governing Council**, and the French government, and also implicated a member of the British parliament, George Galloway, who was accused of taking kickbacks from the program.

OLMERT, EHUD (1945–). Born in Palestine, Olmert is a graduate of the Hebrew University of Jerusalem and a veteran of the **Israeli** Defense Forces. He entered the Israeli legislature, the Knesset, in 1973. He won re-election seven times, and served in several ministries. In 1993, he won election as the mayor of Jerusalem and served two terms. Elected to the Knesset again in 2003, Olmert assumed the duties of acting prime minister when **Ariel Sharon** suffered an incapacitating stroke that left him in a coma in January 2006.

Olmert was widely criticized for the conflict with **Lebanon** in September 2006. In December 2006, he did not publicly rule out a unilateral strike on **Iran** following Iranian President **Mahmoud Ahmadinejad**'s anti-Israeli comments and planned pursuit of **weapons of mass destruction** (WMDs). Olmert was nonetheless committed to working with Palestinian leader **Mahmoud Abbas** and the unilateral disengagement of Israeli settlers in Palestinian territory, a policy legacy of his predecessor.

In 2007, Olmert faced several investigations, one concerning allegations of criminal behavior as former finance minister and another regarding his handling of the conflict with Lebanon. In May 2008, he was the subject of bribery allegations and two months later decided he would not contest the Kadima Party's leadership. He nonetheless remained prime minister until scheduled elections in February 2009 due to the inability of his successor, Tzipi Livni, to form an interim government.

OLSON, THEODORE BEVRY (1940–). Born in Chicago, Illinois, Olson was raised in northern California. He earned an undergraduate degree from the University of the Pacific and a law degree from the

University of California, Berkeley. He served as assistant attorney general under President **Ronald Reagan**, after which time he returned to private law practice.

Olson successfully represented **George W. Bush** in the **Supreme Court** case *Bush v. Gore* during the controversy over the **Florida recount** in the 2000 presidential election. The High Court's termination of the recount awarded Bush all of Florida's Electoral College votes and the election.

Olson's wife, Barbara, was aboard the hijacked American Airlines jet that **al-Qaeda terrorist**s crashed into the **Pentagon** on **11 September 2001**. She perished along with 124 passengers and crew.

President Bush appointed Olson as solicitor general—the number-three position in the Department of Justice—in June 2001. He remained in the post until his resignation in July 2004. He was succeeded by Paul Clement. Olson returned to private law practice with the Washington firm of Gibson Dunn. In 2005, he was rumored as a potential Supreme Court nominee to replace **Sandra Day O'Connor**. Bush, however, nominated **Samuel Alito**, who was confirmed in January 2006.

OMAR, MULLAH MUHAMMED (1959–). Omar was the leader of the **Taliban** regime that acceded to power in **Afghanistan** in 1996. The regime was toppled in 2001 by the US-led invasion following the **11 September 2001 terrorist** attacks on New York and the **Pentagon**. Omar is thought to have fled to **Pakistan** in 2001. Omar's persona is cloaked in mystery. Little is known about him, and even his appearance is a subject of debate as few photos of him exist. He was a **mujahideen** fighter during the Soviet occupation of Afghanistan in the 1980s, during which he lost one eye from shrapnel. As of 2009, he remained on the US government's "most wanted" list for aiding the **al-Qaeda** terrorist organization.

O'NEILL, PAUL HENRY (1935–). A native of St. Louis, Missouri, O'Neill holds an undergraduate degree in economics from California State University, Fresno, and graduate degrees from Claremont Graduate School and Indiana University. His private-sector career includes executive positions at International Paper and Alcoa, where he was chairman and chief executive officer from 1987 to 1999. In the 1960s and 1970s, he worked for the Department of Veterans Affairs and in the **Office of Management and Budget** (OMB).

O'Neill was President **George W. Bush**'s first secretary of treasury and took office in January 2001. He resigned in December 2002 and was succeeded by **John Snow**. O'Neill's tenure was replete with disagreements over the president's policies, including **tax cuts**. He also disagreed with the **War in Iraq**. O'Neill's perspectives were the basis of *Wall Street Journal* writer and author Ron Suskind's 2004 book entitled *The Price of Loyalty: George W. Bush, the White House, and the Education of Paul O'Neill*. One of O'Neill's chief criticisms was that **neoconservative**s in the Bush administration planned to invade **Iraq** even before the **terrorist** attacks of **11 September 2001**. *See also* DOWNING STREET MEMO.

OPERATION ANACONDA. *See* AFGHANISTAN.

OPERATION CHAOS. *See* LIMBAUGH, RUSH.

OPERATION ENDURING FREEDOM. *See* AFGHANISTAN.

– P –

PACE, PETER (1945–). Born in Teaneck, New Jersey, Pace is a graduate of the US Naval Academy and holds a master's degree from George Washington University. A Marine, he is a Vietnam veteran whose commands have included posts in Japan, Korea, Thailand, and Somalia. He became vice chairman of the **Joint Chiefs of Staff** in 2005. In June of that year, he replaced **Richard Myers** as chair of the Joint Chiefs. In June 2007, Secretary of Defense **Robert Gates** indicated publicly that he counseled President **George W. Bush** not to renominate Pace as head of the Joint Chiefs. Following the **mid-term elections** of 2006, which yielded Democratic control of the House and Senate, Gates was concerned about Pace's probability of confirmation. Pace made controversial comments several years earlier in which he disagreed with Defense Secretary **Donald Rumsfeld** on alleged **torture** of **enemy combatants** suspected of **terrorism**, and further disagreed with the Bush administration's claims about **Iran**'s involvement in supporting the **insurgency** in **Iraq**. Pace was succeeded by Admiral **Michael Mullen** and retired as a general. *See also* ARMED FORCES.

PADILLA, JOSÉ (1970–). Also known by the name of Abdullah al-Muhajir, Padilla is an American citizen, born in New York, and later a resident of Chicago, Illinois. He was accused of plotting a radiological attack within the United States and suspected of having connections to the **terrorist** group **al-Qaeda**. He was arrested in 2002 and held as an **enemy combatant**. His detention set off a series of lawsuits by civil liberties groups, since Padilla was a US citizen. The question was whether President **George W. Bush** had the ability to detain a US citizen as an enemy combatant. A federal court argued that he did, and the **Supreme Court** dismissed Padilla's **habeas corpus** petition. Nevertheless, in 2005, Attorney General **Alberto Gonzales** transferred Padilla's case from military to civilian courts. He was indicted and convicted of counts relating to **terrorism** and planning to kill Americans overseas in 2007, and sentenced to just over 17 years in prison in 2008. He is serving his sentence at the federal maximum security prison in Florence, Colorado. *See also* BIOTERRORISM; WEAPONS OF MASS DESTRUCTION (WMDs).

PAIGE, RODERICK RAYNOR (1933–). A native of Monticello, Mississippi, Paige graduated with an undergraduate degree from Jackson State University (Mississippi) and master's and doctoral degrees from Indiana University. He worked as a schoolteacher, then as dean of the college of education at Texas Southern University. In 1989, he was elected as a trustee of the Houston, Texas, Independent School District.

Paige served as secretary of **education** in President **George W. Bush**'s first term. He was an indefatigable supporter of the president's **No Child Left Behind** legislation, which passed in 2001. It was later revealed that Paige had enlisted the support of conservative commentator Armstrong Williams, who illegally engaged in propaganda for the legislation, and was fined $75,000. Paige resigned in November 2004, and was succeeded as secretary of education by **Margaret Spellings**.

PAKISTAN. Bordered by **Afghanistan**, **China**, India, and **Iran**, Pakistan is an Islamic republic with a population of 172 million. The seat of government is located in Islamabad. The former British colony gained its independence in 1947.

Pakistan became an increasingly important ally in the **War on Terror** during the presidency of **George W. Bush** following the **11 September 2001 terrorist** attacks on New York and the **Pentagon**, but also sustained political change and instability. Reformist politician **Benazir Bhutto** returned to Pakistan in 2007, only to be assassinated in an apparent bombing by **al-Qaeda** in December of that year. In August 2008, **Pervez Musharraf**, who had come to power in a military coup in 1999, resigned under mounting political pressure. He was succeeded by **Asif Ali Zardari**, the spouse of slain leader Benazir Bhutto. One point of tension in the US–Pakistani relationship was the hunt for suspected **al-Qaeda** and **Taliban** terrorists hiding in Pakistan. The Pakistani government would not allow US troops to conduct military operations on its territory. Bilateral relations became strained when the United States bombed suspected **terrorist** strongholds in the **Waziristan** region that borders Afghanistan in June 2008.

In November 2008, Indian authorities suspected Pakistani terrorists of carrying out the bombings in **Mumbai** that killed almost 200 people. Secretary of State **Condoleezza Rice** worked to decrease tensions between India and Pakistan, both of which have nuclear weapons.

PALESTINE LIBERATION ORGANIZATION (PLO). Founded in 1964, the Palestine Liberation Organization is a secular movement devoted to the establishment of a sovereign Palestinian state. It was long considered a **terrorist** organization by the United States. **Yasser Arafat** headed the PLO from 1969 until his death in 2004. Basing many of its paramilitary operations in **Lebanon**, the PLO used guerrilla warfare tactics to challenge **Israel**'s dominance in the occupied territories in the **West Bank** and **Gaza Strip**. The PLO was driven from Lebanon in 1982, following the Israeli occupation of that country. From 1985 to 1988, during the Lebanese civil war, Syrian-backed troops drove Palestinian refugees out of the country and caused mass suffering and death. In a watershed development in 1993, Arafat accepted Israel's right to exist in exchange for Palestinian statehood, as part of secret negotiations between Israel and the PLO (the Oslo Accords). The agreement called for an interim **Palestinian National Authority** to govern the West Bank and Gaza.

Between 2000 and 2004, as progress stalled on a longer-term settlement, Palestinians clamored for self-rule, and the territories descended into unprecedented civil violence in the so-called "second intifada." The violence prompted the administration of **George W. Bush**, along with the **European Union**, **Russia**, and the **United Nations**, to search for a permanent solution to the Israeli–Palestinian conflict through the **Road Map for Peace**. *See also* ABBAS, MAHMOUD; FATAH; HAMAS; HANIYA, ISMAIL; OLMERT, EHUD; SHARON, ARIEL.

PALESTINIAN NATIONAL AUTHORITY. Formed in 1994 following the Oslo Accords between the **Palestine Liberation Organization** and **Israel**, the Palestinian National Authority took administrative control of the **West Bank** and the **Gaza Strip**. Political strife followed the legislative elections in January 2006, when the secular **Fatah** party lost to **Hamas**, which Israel and the United States regard as a **terrorist** organization. President **Mahmoud Abbas** attempted to replace Hamas leader **Ismail Haniya** as prime minister, provoking a civil conflict that ultimately left Fatah in charge of the West Bank and Hamas controlling the Gaza Strip. *See also* ARAFAT, YASSER; FAYYAD, SALAM; ROAD MAP FOR PEACE.

PALIN, SARAH LOUISE (1964–). Born in Sandpoint, Idaho, Palin grew up in Wasilla, Alaska. She graduated from the University of Idaho with a degree in journalism (1987). After graduation, she worked as a television broadcaster in Anchorage, Alaska. In 1992, she was elected to the first of three terms on the Wasilla City Council. In 1996, she was elected mayor, and re-elected twice. She entered statewide politics in 2002, running unsuccessfully for the office of lieutenant governor in Alaska. From 2003 to 2004, she headed the Alaska Oil and Gas Conservation Commission. In 2006, she defeated fellow Republican incumbent Frank Murkowski in the primary contest for governor. She then defeated the Democratic candidate for governor, Tony Knowles, by more than 6 percent of the statewide vote. Palin ran on a platform that included governmental and budget reform. In 2008, she signed a law giving a contract to TransCanada Pipelines to transport natural gas reserves from Alaska's North Slope through **Canada** and to the lower 48 states.

Republican presidential nominee **John McCain** selected Palin as his vice presidential running mate on 29 August 2008, shortly before the Republican national convention. McCain hoped that choosing Palin, who was widely hailed as a social conservative, would help win over the base of the Republican Party, which remained skeptical about his moderate policy stances and independent streak. Palin became only the second woman nominated for the vice presidency — and the first female on a Republican presidential ticket.

Palin was initially well-received by the Republican base following the announcement. Her acceptance speech at the Republican convention several days later won early acclaim and was viewed by an estimated 40 million. Yet, in the weeks that followed, her lackluster media performances raised doubts about the viability of her candidacy. Critics charged that she lacked the necessary experience to be a heartbeat away from the presidency, should McCain prevail. She came under intense media scrutiny for a putative lack of knowledge of foreign affairs. In an interview with the American Broadcasting Company's (ABC) reporter Charles Gibson, Palin struggled to answer a question about the **Bush Doctrine** and the **War on Terror** and received widespread negative attention. Further interviews solidified such concerns, prompting the McCain campaign to limit Palin's unrehearsed comments to media. Some conservatives charged the national media with gender bias, contending that the major networks purposefully set out to undermine Palin's candidacy. Further, late-night comedians mocked her accent and phrases, including her description of the difference between a "soccer mom" (her self-description) and a pit bull: lipstick. Regardless, also at issue were some of Palin's policy positions, including global warming, that conflicted with McCain's views. As McCain's popularity began to dwindle, many Republicans called on him to remove her from the ticket, but he remained steadfast in his decision.

Palin played the traditional role of the vice presidential candidate in her harsh criticism of her opponents, Democratic presidential nominee **Barack Obama** and his vice presidential running mate, **Joe Biden**. In her single debate with Biden, however, the consensus was that her performance was under par and Biden had prevailed. The **sub-prime mortgage** crisis that plunged the American economy into a sudden and deep economic downturn by late September 2008 indubitably crippled the McCain campaign. The McCain–Palin ticket ultimately lost the election by nearly 10 million votes nationwide.

Palin returned to Alaska to finish her gubernatorial term, which expires in 2012. In 2009, she founded a political action committee (PAC) called SarahPAC to aid Republican candidates. Her continued involvement in Republican politics, and her popularity among some in the Republican base, fueled speculation of a possible run for the presidency in 2012. In July 2009, she resigned her position as governor of Alaska but did not indicate whether she would seek the Republican nomination for the presidency in 2012.

PALM BEACH COUNTY, FLORIDA. This county in southeastern Florida north of Miami, with a population of approximately 1.3 million, was at the center of controversy in the presidential election of 2000 between **George W. Bush** and **Al Gore**. At issue was the so-called **butterfly ballot** designed by Democratic supervisor of elections **Theresa LePore**, which confused many voters, particularly the elderly. On election day, many voters believed they had inadvertently voted for a candidate not of their preference—namely independent candidate **Patrick Buchanan**. Gore won the county by a margin of 37 percent, although a media analysis of ballots suggested he may have lost more than 6,000 votes due confusion over the ballot. Palm Beach was one of four disputed counties in which recounts of ballots were conducted. The **Supreme Court** ended the **Florida recount**

in December 2000, when it decided the case ***Bush v. Gore***. *See also* BAKER, JAMES ADDISON; GINSBURG, BENJAMIN; HARRIS, KATHERINE; OLSON, THEODORE BEVRY.

PARENTS V. SEATTLE. *See* AFFIRMATIVE ACTION.

PARHAT V. GATES (2005). *See* DETAINEE TREATMENT ACT.

PARTIAL-BIRTH ABORTION BAN ACT (2003). Adopted by the Republican Congress in 2003 and signed by President **George W. Bush**, this legislation prohibits aborting a fetus when it is partially delivered from a woman's womb, typically in the third trimester. Twice in the 1990s, Congress had passed such a prohibition of the procedure—in 1995 and 1997—but President **William Clinton** vetoed the legislation.

In a major victory for the Bush administration in April 2007, the **Supreme Court** ruled by a 5–4 margin in ***Gonzales v. Carhart*** (2006) that the legislation did not violate the Constitution, despite failing to provide an exception to allow the procedure when the life of the mother is in danger. Significantly, the two justices Bush appointed during his term, **Samuel Alito** and Chief Justice **John Roberts**, voted to uphold the ban.

PATAKI, GEORGE ELMER (1945–). A graduate of Yale (1964) and Columbia Law School (1970), Pataki began his political career in 1981, when he became mayor of Peekskill, New York. He won election to the New York State Assembly in 1984 and was re-elected four times. In 1992, he won election to the New York Senate. In 1994, Pataki won the race for the New York governorship. He was re-elected in 1998 and 2002.

Pataki was governor during the **11 September 2001 terrorist** attacks that destroyed the **World Trade Center**. In concert with New York City Mayor **Rudolph Giuliani**, Pataki commissioned a memorial to be built on "ground zero"—the site of the Twin Towers—at a cost of $10 million. Plans for the memorial, however were mired in controversy about the design of the memorial and construction of new office buildings on the site.

At the end of his third term in 2006, Pataki was succeeded by **Eliot Spitzer** and returned to private law practice. In September 2007, President **George W. Bush** appointed Pataki to serve as a delegate to the **United Nations** (UN) for the duration of the general assembly session.

PATERSON, DAVID ALEXANDER (1954–). A native of Brooklyn, New York, Paterson graduated from Columbia University (1977) and earned a law degree from Hofstra University (1983). He won election to the New York State Senate in 1985 upon the death of the incumbent legislator for the district and served in the seat until 2006, when he was elected lieutenant governor. Upon **Eliot Spitzer**'s resignation as governor in March 2007, Paterson became the first African-American governor of New York and the first legally blind governor of any state.

PATRIOT ACT. Known by its acronym, the USA PATRIOT Act (Uniting and Strengthening America by Providing Appropriate Tools Required to Intercept and Obstruct Terrorism) was passed in 2001 following the **11 September 2001 terrorist** attacks on New York and the **Pentagon**. The law made substantial changes to federal agencies' ability to engage in intelligence-gathering activities both domestically and abroad. Civil libertarians contended that the act violates constitutional protections—in particular the provisions for **wiretapping** and searching private property without court orders, as well as the detention of immigrants. The law also provided the federal government with special measures to deter money laundering and to seize illicit funds and other assets belonging to suspected terrorists.

The Patriot Act was reauthorized by Congress in 2005. The reauthorized bill included the strengthening of provisions to combat **terrorism** at the nation's seaports and included a provision for the death penalty for suspected terrorists. It also made changes to wiretapping provisions regarding electronic surveillance. Key wiretapping provisions were to be "sunset" in 2009. *See also* AMERICAN CIVIL LIBERTIES UNION; FOREIGN INTELLIGENCE SURVEILLANCE ACT; PROTECT AMERICA ACT (2007).

PAULSON, HENRY MERRITT, JR. (1946–). A native of **Palm Beach**, Florida, Paulson graduated from Dartmouth College (1968) and earned a master's of business administration from Harvard University (1970). He worked at the Pentagon and in the administration of Richard Nixon in the early 1970s before joining the Chicago investment firm of Goldman Sachs. He became chief executive of the company in 1998.

In July 2006, Paulson succeeded **John Snow** as secretary of the treasury under President **George W. Bush**. In Fall 2008, Paulson, along with **Federal Reserve** chair **Ben Bernanke**, was thrown into the spotlight by the economic tumult caused by the sub-prime mortgage crisis. Snow was the administration's lead figure in its subsequent efforts to stabilize the economy and banking system, including the bailout of **American International Group** (AIG), providing $700 billion to shore up banks, and placing government corporations **Federal National Mortgage Association** (Fannie Mae) and the **Federal Home Loan Mortgage Corporation** (Freddie Mac) into conservatorship. *See also* BEAR STEARNS; HOUSING AND ECONOMIC RECOVERY ACT (2008); LEHMAN BROTHERS; TROUBLED ASSETS RELIEF PROGRAM (TARP).

PEAKE, JAMES BENJAMIN (1944–). Born in St. Louis, Missouri, Peake graduated from West Point (1966) and served in the Vietnam War, during which he won a Bronze Star, Purple Heart, and a Silver Star. In 1972, he graduated with a medical degree from Cornell University. His extensive medical service to the Army culminated in his appointment as Surgeon General of the Army from 2000 to 2004. He retired in 2004, at the rank of lieutenant general, and earned a number of commendations for his service in the medical profession.

In December 2007, Peake succeeded **Jim Nicholson** as secretary of veterans affairs in the administration of **George W. Bush**. *See also* ARMED FORCES.

PEARL, DANIEL (1963–2002). Pearl was a *Wall Street Journal* journalist who was kidnapped by **al-Qaeda terrorists** in **Pakistan** in January 2002. Pearl was the South Asia bureau chief stationed in **Mumbai**, India. A Jewish American, Pearl's throat was slit and his head was severed a month after his kidnapping. The gruesome incident was captured on video and released by his captors. **Khalid Sheikh Mohammed**, a top al-Qaeda leader captured in **Afghanistan** and detained in **Guantanamo Bay, Cuba**, confessed to Pearl's beheading.

Pearl's ordeal and murder were the subject of a book written by his French wife, Mariane, entitled *A Mighty Heart* (2003), which was transformed into a film produced in 2007.

PELOSI, NANCY PATRICIA D'ALESANDRO (1940–). A native of Baltimore, Maryland, Pelosi graduated from Trinity College in Washington, D.C. (1962). She relocated with her husband to San Francisco, California, in 1969 and became involved in local Democratic politics. She served as chair of the California State Democratic Party from 1981 to 1983 and finance chairman of the Democratic Senatorial Campaign Committee from 1985 to 1986 before running successfully to fill a vacancy in the 8th congressional district of California (San Francisco) in 1987. She was re-elected 10 times through 2008.

Pelosi served as minority whip from 2001 to 2002 and minority leader from 2003 to 2006. When Democrats captured control of the House of Representatives in the **mid-term elections** of 2006, she was elected as the first female speaker of the House in the 110th Congress (2007–2008).

Pelosi was a steadfast opponent of the **War in Iraq** and President **George W. Bush**'s strategy to provide a "surge" in troop strength in **Baghdad** to combat the **insurgency** in 2007. She promised to "defund" the War in Iraq but faced a presidential veto when she and liberal Democrats attempted to do so in 2007. That same year, she took a controversial trip to the Middle East, including **Syria**, the Palestinian Territories, and Saudi Arabia. The White House criticized her meeting with Syria's leaders, who backed **terrorist** groups **Hamas** and **Hezbollah**, and not only maintained troops in **Lebanon** but were suspected of involvement in the assassination of Lebanese leader **Rafik Hariri**.

Although Pelosi is widely considered a liberal in her domestic and **foreign policy** stances on issues spanning **abortion** rights to foreign aid, she faced a 2008 election challenge from **Cindy Shee-han**, the mother of an Iraqi war veteran who died in Iraq in 2004. Sheehan alleged that Pelosi was not "liberal enough" for her San Francisco district and chided Pelosi for not ending military operations in **Iraq**. Nonetheless, Pelosi culled 72 percent of the district's vote in 2008. She is the author, with Amy Hill Hearth, of *Know Your Power: A Message to America's Daughters* (2008).

PENTAGON. This five-sided building located in Arlington County, Virginia, across the Potomac River in Washington, D.C., was built in 1943. It houses the headquarters of the US Department of Defense (originally called the Department of War). Nearly 26,000 military and civilian employees work in the complex.

On **11 September 2001**, **al-Qaeda terrorists** commandeered American Airlines Flight 77 en route from Washington, D.C.'s Dulles International Airport to Los Angeles, California, and crashed the Boeing 757 jetliner into the west side of the building. Sixty-four passengers and crew, including five hijackers, died on impact. The impact of the crash, explosion, and fire caused part of the building to collapse and killed 125 people working in the Pentagon. The conflagration lasted three days.

The damage to the Pentagon was repaired within a year of the attack. On 11 September 2008, a memorial park on the grounds of the Pentagon was opened to honor the victims of the worst terrorist attack on US soil. *See also* ARMED FORCES.

PERINO, DANA MARIE (1972–). Born in Evanston, Wyoming, Perino graduated from the University of Southern Colorado (1994) and earned a graduate degree in public affairs from the University of Illinois at Springfield. She worked as press secretary for former US Representative from Colorado Dan Schaefer before moving to communications posts for the Department of Justice and the **George W. Bush** White House Council on Environmental Quality.

In March 2006, Bush named her deputy White House press secretary. In August 2007, she succeeded **Tony Snow**, who was battling cancer, as White House press secretary. She is only the second female press secretary, following Dee Dee Myers in the administration of William Clinton.

PERLE, RICHARD NORMAN (1941–). Born in New York City, Perle is a graduate of the University of Southern California (1964) and earned a master's degree from Princeton University (1967). From 1969 to 1980, he worked as an assistant to Democratic Senator Henry Jackson from the state of Washington. In the 1980s, he was an assistant secretary of defense under President **Ronald Reagan**.

A prominent **neoconservative**, Perle cosigned the letter from the think tank the **Project for the New American Century** (PNAC) urging President **William Clinton** to take military action against Iraqi dictator **Saddam Hussein** in 1998. Perle was initially a staunch supporter of regime change in **Iraq** and the US-led invasion of that country in March 2003, contending that Hussein had ties to **terrorist**s. He also argued that the United States had overestimated Hussein's military strength and that only a small contingent of forces would be necessary to overthrow the Iraqi regime. In 2006, Perle expressed misgivings about the **War in Iraq** and criticized its handling by the administration of **George W. Bush**. Perle is coauthor, with David Frum, of *An End to Evil: How to Win the War on Terror* (2003).

PERSIAN GULF WAR. The Persian Gulf War began on 16 January 1991. The United States, alongside 33 other nations that comprised an international coalition approved by the **United Nations** (UN), took decisive military action against **Iraq** to liberate the tiny emirate of Kuwait. The action took place after Iraqi dictator **Saddam Hussein** invaded the country on 2 August 1990 and failed to comply with United Nations resolutions that demanded he withdraw troops by 15 January 1991. The military operation, dubbed Operation Desert Storm, included more than 660,000 US troops. General Norman Schwarzkopf oversaw the allied operation.

The conflict stemmed from Hussein's contention that Kuwait was an Iraqi province that had been wrongly separated from the motherland. Moreover, Hussein contended that Kuwait had engaged in "economic warfare" by illegally tapping into Iraqi oilfields by a process known as "slant drilling," a technique that pumps oil from horizontal rather than strictly vertical drilling. Kuwait's coastal access to the Persian Gulf was also highly desirable from the Iraqi perspective.

President **George H.W. Bush** demanded full and unconditional withdrawal of Iraqi troops from Kuwait to reestablish the status quo. Chairman of the Joint Chiefs of Staff **Colin Powell** initially opposed military options. Then Secretary of Defense **Richard B. (Dick) Cheney** worked tirelessly with others in the administration to assemble an unprecedented international coalition against Hussein that included 33 other nations. The initial air campaign component of the war was over within approximately 96 hours. A cease-fire was called on 27 February 1991. Fewer than 400 allied troops were killed in the conflict, while estimates suggest that anywhere from 100,000 to 300,000 Iraqis were killed. On 10 March 1991, US forces began departing from the region.

President George H.W. Bush was criticized for not having removed Saddam Hussein from power—although the UN mandate did not authorize such action. Allied forces instead enforced a "no-fly zone" in the northern and southern areas of Iraq to prohibit Hussein from engaging in aggression against neighboring countries, and international economic sanctions were imposed on Iraq. This policy of "containment" was continued under **William Clinton**.

In 1998, signatories of the **neoconservative Project for the New American Century** (PNAC) wrote to President Clinton recommending Hussein's ouster for allegedly violating the terms of the postwar settlement. Major figures in the subsequent administration of **George W. Bush** were signatories of PNAC's principles—including Vice President Richard Cheney, **I. Lewis (Scooter) Libby**, secretary of defense **Donald Rumsfeld**, and deputy defense secretary **Paul Wolfowitz**—leading critics of the US-led invasion of Iraq in March 2003 to conclude that key Bush advisors had targeted Iraq for military action prior to the **11 September 2001 al-Qaeda terrorist** attacks on New York and the **Pentagon**. No substantive link between Hussein and those attacks was ever proven. Moreover, critics charged that because no **weapons of mass destruction** (WMDs) were ever found following the invasion, the Bush administration had manipulated intelligence to use the 9/11 attacks and putative links to Hussein as a pretext for his removal from power. *See also* ARMED FORCES; ARMITAGE, RICHARD LEE; COALITION OF THE WILLING; FOREIGN POLICY; PERLE, RICHARD NORMAN; POWELL, COLIN LUTHER; WAR IN IRAQ.

PETERS, MARY (1948–). A native of Phoenix, Arizona, Peters earned her bachelor's degree from the University of Phoenix. She began her public service career in the Arizona Department of Transportation, becoming its director in 1998. In the administration of **George W. Bush**, she served as head of the Federal Highway Administration from 2001 to 2005. In October 2006, she succeeded **Norman Mineta** as secretary of transportation. In February 2007, she was the subject of controversy when she used her authority to allow Mexican trucks across the US–**Mexico** border. The Teamsters Union, which alleged that Mexican trucks were unsafe, launched an unsuccessful bid to oust her from her post, but she remained through the end of Bush's second term.

PETRAEUS, DAVID (1952–). Born in Orange County, New York, Petraus is a graduate of West Point. He holds a master's in public affairs and a doctoral degree in international relations from Princeton University. His dissertation dealt with the lessons of the Vietnam War and the implications for the use of military force after that conflict. In the 1970s and 1980s, he developed an expertise for mechanized units and commands. In 1995, he headed the **United Nations** (UN) efforts to stabilize the island nation of Haiti. He served as an assistant to chairman of the **Joint Chiefs of Staff**, **Hugh Shelton**, from 1997 to 1999. Promoted to brigadier general, he was a commanding general in Kuwait in the aftermath of the **Persian Gulf War**. He rose rapidly in the ranks beginning in 2001, and served in the former **Yugoslavia** as an assistant to the chief of operations involving **North Atlantic Treaty Organization** (NATO) forces. He was involved in combat operations in the US-led invasion of **Iraq** and in some of the heavy fighting in **Mosul** and **Baghdad** early in the military operation. In 2004, he assumed responsibilities for training the Iraqi army to handle security in the country as head of the multinational force. He was promoted to general in 2007. He played a particularly important role in outlining the "surge" strategy of sending additional troops to Baghdad to halt the **insurgency** and restore stability in Iraq. He was succeeded by **Raymond Odierno** as head of the multinational force in Iraq in September 2008.

In April 2008, President **George W. Bush** nominated Petraeus to command **CENTCOM** to oversee the **War in Iraq**. He was a steadfast optimist in his belief that stability and peace were being achieved in Iraq, notwithstanding critics' charges that the war had been mishandled in the early phases. Petraeus holds a number of military decorations, including a Bronze Star, for his service. *See also* ARMED FORCES.

PKK. The acronym for *Partiya Karkerên Kurdistan* or Kurdistan Workers Party, the PKK is a Turkish-based leftist party that agitates for an independent, ethnic-based state of Kurdistan comprising parts of Turkey, **Iran**, **Iraq**, and **Syria**. The United States considers the PKK a **terrorist** group for its armed struggle primarily against the Turkish government.

Following the **War in Iraq**, the Turkish military attacked purported PKK strongholds based across the border in northern **Iraq** in 2007, claiming that the rebel group was launching guerrilla attacks into Turkey. The administration of **George W. Bush** cautioned **Turkey** to temper its response to **insurgents** for fear of destabilizing the region.

PLAME (WILSON), VALERIE ELISE (1963–). Plame is the wife of former Ambassador **Joseph Wilson**, a critic of the **War in Iraq**. A career agent with the **Central Intelligence Agency** (CIA), Plame served in covert operations in Europe during the administration of **George W. Bush**. Her status as a covert agent was publicly revealed in an article penned by journalist **Robert Novak** in July 2003. Critics suggested that her "outing" was political retribution by the White House for her husband's criticism of the US-led invasion of **Iraq**, which failed to locate suspected **weapons of mass destruction** (WMDs) allegedly stockpiled by dictator **Saddam Hussein**. A grand jury investigation into the matter, dubbed "Plamegate," revealed that Vice President **Richard B. Dick Cheney**'s chief of staff, **I. Lewis (Scooter) Libby**, had indicated Plame's role in a meeting with *New York Times* reporter Judith Miller in 2002 as part of a discussion meant to refute Wilson's investigation of suspected Iraqi attempts to procure nuclear material from Africa. Libby was ultimately not charged with any crime surrounding Plame, and it was later revealed that the source of Novak's column was Deputy Secretary of State **Richard Armitage**. Plame resigned her position at the CIA in 2006 and is author of *Fair Game: My Life as a Spy, My Betrayal by the White House* (2007). *See also* FITZGERALD, PATRICK J.; NIGER.

POLAND. This central European country, once under the domination of the **Soviet Union** and a member of the **Warsaw Pact**, regained its independence and a return to democratic politics in 1989. In 1999, Poland joined the **North Atlantic Treaty Organization**. In 2004, Poles voted to join the **European Union** (effective 2005).

Poland was a significant member of the **Coalition of the Willing** that militarily supported the US-led invasion of **Iraq** in 2003, and between 900 and 2,000 troops were involved in the **War in Iraq** and the subsequent rebuilding of the country.

A staunch ally of the United States and supporter of President **George W. Bush**'s **foreign policy**, Poland was at the center of controversy over the proposed **anti-ballistic missile** defense system to be stationed within its borders and in the **Czech Republic**. In 2007, Russian President **Vladimir Putin** suggested that missiles might be targeted on Poland if the plan moved forward.

PORTMAN, ROBERT JONES (1955–). Born in Cincinnati, Ohio, Portman is a graduate of Dartmouth College (1979) and earned a law degree from the University of Michigan (1984). He worked in private law practice in international trade before he became associate counsel to President **George H.W. Bush** in 1989. He also served as director of Bush's office of legislative affairs (1989–1991) before returning briefly to private law practice. He won a special election for an Ohio seat to the US House of Representatives in 1993 and was re-elected six times through 2004.

In April 2005, President **George W. Bush** tapped Portman to serve as the United States Trade Representative (USTR). From 2006 to 2007, he served as the head of the **Office of Management and Budget** (OMB), replacing **Joshua Bolten**. He left the administration in June 2007 and returned to practice law in Cincinnati, Ohio.

POWELL, COLIN LUTHER (1937–). A decorated veteran born in New York City, Powell was a central figure in the administrations of **Ronald Reagan**, **George H.W. Bush**, and **George W. Bush**. He graduated from the City College of New York with a degree in geology and later earned a master's of business administration from George Washington University. Powell entered military service in 1958 as a second lieutenant, served in Korea, and during his 35-year military career was promoted to the rank of four-star general. He served as **national security advisor** to President Reagan. He became chairman of the **Joint Chiefs of Staff** to President George H.W. Bush in 1989 and remained in that post until 1993. He was an integral part of Bush's **foreign policy** team during the **Persian Gulf War**. Although Powell generally advocated military solutions as a last resort, he is credited with the success of the strategy to push Iraqi dictator **Saddam Hussein**'s troops out of the emirate of Kuwait, which Hussein had invaded in 1990.

Following George H.W. Bush's defeat in the presidential election of 1992, Powell retired from the Army, returned to private life, and wrote an autobiography entitled *My American Journey* (1995). A popular figure and moderate Republican, Powell was urged by some to run for the presidency in 1996 but declined.

He returned to public service in 2001, when President George W. Bush nominated him to the post of secretary of state. Powell earned the distinction of becoming the highest-ranking African-American in the history of US government. His initial opposition to the **War in Iraq** ran counter to the stances of many **neoconservatives** in Bush's cabinet in 2002–2003. Powell nevertheless led the diplomatic charge in the **United Nations** and in multilateral relations to build support for the eventual invasion of **Iraq** in March 2003, however dubious the evidence that Saddam Hussein had **weapons of mass destruction**

(WMDs). He also articulated the military strategy of **shock and awe** in the US-led invasion of Iraq.

Powell resigned as secretary of state in 2004, and was succeeded by **Condoleezza Rice**. His civilian awards include a Congressional Gold Medal and two Presidential Medals of Freedom. He stunned many in Fall 2008 when he endorsed Democratic presidential nominee **Barack Obama** over Republican Arizona Senator **John McCain**. *See also* ARMED FORCES; COALITION OF THE WILLING.

PREEMPTION, PREEMPTIVE WARFARE. The notion of preemptive warfare is closely related to the so-called **Bush Doctrine** in **foreign policy** articulated by President **George W. Bush**, most notably in his 2002 State of the Union address, following the **11 September 2001 terrorist** attacks on New York and the **Pentagon**. In that address, and in a series of other speeches in 2002 and 2003, Bush posited that the United States had the right to take military action not only against nonstate actors (terrorists) but also against any regime giving safe harbor to terrorist organizations, such as **al-Qaeda**, which may be planning attacks on the United States. This rationale was used to justify the US-led invasion of **Afghanistan**, as the **Taliban** regime had enabled al-Qaeda to operate terrorist training camps on its soil prior to the 9/11 attacks. Further, Bush used the precepts of preemptive warfare theory to justify the **War in Iraq** by arguing that Iraqi dictator **Saddam Hussein** was attempting to procure, or had already stockpiled, **weapons of mass destruction** (WMDs) that could be used against the United States or its allies.

Critics of preemptive warfare charge that the doctrine rejects **multilateralism** in foreign policy and undermines international institutions, such as the **United Nations** (UN), that seek diplomatic resolution of conflicts. Further, critics contend that preemptive warfare violates the intentions of the framers of the US Constitution. The framers gave Congress the right to "declare" war, while providing the president, as commander in chief, the responsibility to "repel sudden attacks"—a defensive, not preemptive posture. Finally, the precepts of preemptive warfare run counter to the defensive doctrine of containment espoused during the **Cold War** with the **Soviet Union**, during which the United States attempted to halt the spread of communism around the world.

PRESTON, STEVEN C. (1960–). A native of Janesville, Wisconsin, Preston earned a bachelor's degree from Northwestern University (1982) and a master's in business administration from the University of Chicago (1985). His private-sector experience includes working as an investment banker for **Lehman Brothers**, where he became vice president, and for First Data Corporation, where he became executive vice president.

In June 2006, Preston became head of the Small Business Administration under President **George W. Bush**. In June 2008, Preston succeeded **Alphonso Jackson** as secretary of housing and urban development.

PRINCIPI, ANTHONY JOSEPH (1944–). A native of New York City, Principi is a graduate of the US Naval Academy (1967) and earned a law degree from Seton Hall University (1975). A Vietnam War veteran, in the 1980s he worked as legislative counsel for the Navy, chief counsel to the Senate Committee on Veterans' Affairs, and assistant deputy administrator for the Veterans Administration. From September 1992 until January 1993, he served as acting secretary of veterans affairs under President **George H.W. Bush**. In January 2001, he became secretary of veterans affairs under President **George W. Bush**. He remained in that post until January 2005, when he was succeeded by **Robert Nicholson**.

PROJECT FOR THE NEW AMERICAN CENTURY (PNAC). Founded' by Robert Kagan and conservative commentator William Kristol in 1997, PNAC is a **neoconservative** think tank with members in academe as well as in government service. Prominent members of the administration of **George W. Bush** were signatories to the group's statements of principles, including **United Nations** (UN) Ambassador **John Bolton**, Vice President **Richard B. (Dick) Cheney**, Ambassador to **Iraq Zalmay Khalilzad**, **I. Lewis (Scooter) Libby**, Secretary of Defense **Donald Rumsfeld**, and Deputy Defense Secretary **Paul Wolfowitz**. Other high-ranking administration officials with connections to PNAC include Deputy Secretary of State **Richard Armitage**, Defense Policy Advisory Board Chair Richard Perle, and US Trade Representative **Robert Zoellick**, as well as **Linda Chavez**, who withdrew her nomination for secretary of labor in 2001.

Known primarily for its **foreign policy** stances, PNAC advocates American global leadership through "moral clarity" and military strength. The organization takes a dim view of international institutions such as the UN and rejects **multilateralism** in foreign affairs when necessary. As such, critics charge that PNAC's stances heavily influenced President Bush's worldview and **foreign policy** in the White House, including his articulation of the **Bush Doctrine**, the invasion of **Afghanistan**, and the **War in Iraq**.

In 1998, prominent members of PNAC wrote an open letter to President **William Clinton** calling for Iraqi dictator **Saddam Hussein**'s ouster. They contended that Hussein had violated the terms of the post-**Persian Gulf War** settlement in 1991 by expelling UN arms inspectors. Clinton did take *selective* military action against Hussein. Critics maintain that the US-led invasion of **Iraq** in March 2003 under President Bush, who claimed Hussein had attempted to obtain **weapons of mass destruction** (WMDs), was a pretext for the war, and that neoconservatives in the administration had considered large-scale military action against Hussein's regime even before the **11 September 2001 terrorist** attacks on New York and the **Pentagon**.

PROTECT AMERICA ACT (2007). This bill, passed by Congress in August 2007, made changes to the **Foreign Intelligence Surveillance Act** (FISA). The legislation specifically altered FISA to allow warrantless **wiretapping** in the **War on Terror**. The **National Security Agency** (NSA) was able to conduct wiretaps of individuals, including US citizens, as long as the agency believed that at least one party in communications was reasonably believed to be abroad. The law also mandated that the NSA report such activities within 72 hours to the FISA Court. Civil libertarians opposed the measure, which they contended violates constitutional protections of privacy and Fourth Amendment search and seizure protections.

PUTIN, VLADIMIR VLADIMIROVICH (1952–). Born in St. Petersburg, **Russia**, Putin graduated in international law from Leningrad

State University (1975). After college, he worked for the **Soviet Union**'s KGB, or internal state security apparatus, where he surveilled foreigners in the Soviet Union as well as in Dresden, East **Germany**, where he was stationed from 1985 to 1990. With the Soviet Union's collapse in 1991, Putin worked for the St. Petersburg mayor's office in various positions until 1998. Following several years of service for the Russian president's office, he was appointed to the FSB, the successor to the KGB in the Russian Federation. In August 1999, after just a few days as deputy prime minister, the Russian *Duma* or parliament elected him as prime minister in the wake of a parliamentary party struggle.

Putin's tough stance toward the breakaway region of **Chechnya** in 1999 positioned him well for his presidential campaign in 2000. He became acting president in December 1999, when his predecessor, Boris Yeltsin, resigned suddenly. Putin won a four-year term as president in 2000, and was re-elected in 2004. He was constitutionally prohibited from seeking a third successive term in 2008. However, his successor, **Dmitri Medvedev**, appointed him prime minister. Many observers contend that Putin remained the most powerful politician in Russia and that Medvedev followed his cues.

Putin's domestic and **foreign policy** drew criticism from President **George W. Bush**, despite Bush's many laudatory comments about his friendship with the Russian leader. In a set of domestic reforms, Putin gained the power to appoint governors of Russian regions and eroded regional autonomy.

In 2003, Putin joined other European leaders, including French President **Jacques Chirac** and German Chancellor **Gerhard Schröder**, in opposing the **War in Iraq** without a **United Nations** (UN) mandate. Putin also opposed Bush's plans for an **anti-ballistic missile** system to be located in **Poland** and the **Czech Republic**, and in 2007 suggested Russia might target its remaining nuclear arsenal on European countries if the project moved forward. In 2008, Russia's invasion of **Georgia**—putatively over the status of ethnic Russians living in the Abkhazia and South Ossetia regions—drew an immediate rebuke from the Bush White House. The combination of dissensus over the missile system in Central Europe and the Georgia invasion created the most tense US–Russian bilateral relations since the **Cold War**. In Fall 2008, Russia's joint naval exercises with **Venezuela**'s **Hugo Chávez** added to speculation of a chill in US–Russian foreign policy cooperation.

– R –

RASUL V. BUSH (2004). Shafiq Rasul, a British national who was captured among **Taliban** operatives during the US-led invasion of **Afghanistan** in 2001, was detained on suspicion of **terrorism** and detained at **Guantanamo Bay, Cuba**, and classified as an **enemy combatant**. He filed a **habeas corpus** petition for his release, which was heard before the **Supreme Court** in 2004. The central issue of the case was whether US civilian courts had jurisdiction over the detention of foreign nations. A federal circuit and appellate court had denied Rasul's petition. By a 6–3 vote, the High Court reversed the lower courts' rulings. Rasul was released into British custody before the Supreme Court made its ruling. The case was nevertheless a setback for the administration of **George W. Bush**, which had planned to try suspected **terrorists** through **military tribunals**. *See also BOUMEDIENE V. BUSH; HAMDI V. RUMSFELD*; WAR ON TERROR.

RATHER, DANIEL IRVIN (DAN) (1931–). A native of Wharton, Texas, Rather studied journalism at Sam Houston State University and graduated in 1953. He began his career in journalism as a reporter for the Associated Press and moved into television in Houston in 1959. He earned notoriety for his coverage of the assassination of President John F. Kennedy in 1963. A regular contributor to the Columbia Broadcasting System's long-running news show *60 Minutes*, Rather moved on to anchor the CBS nightly news from 1981 to 2005.

Rather resigned from CBS in the wake of a story he reported on President **George W. Bush**'s service record in the Texas Air National Guard that ran in September 2004. The documents that were critical of Bush's service, obtained in the personal files of Bush's commanding officer, were later thought to be fraudulent. Rather was criticized for reporting the story without adequate verification of the documents' authenticity, and three other CBS employees were fired. In 2007, Rather sued CBS executives, contending he had been made a scapegoat in the reporting scandal.

REAGAN, RONALD WILSON (1911–2004). The 40th president of the United States was born on 6 February 1911 in Tampico, Illinois, to Nelle and John Reagan. He attended high school in Dixon, Illinois, during which time he worked part-time as a lifeguard. He graduated from Eureka College, a small Christian liberal arts school, in 1932. He was an avid swimmer and football player, and earned degrees in both sociology and economics. Reagan began a broadcasting career shortly thereafter, announcing Chicago Cubs baseball games for WOC (later WHO) radio in Davenport, Iowa. In 1937, Warner Brothers Studios offered him a seven-year movie contract. He starred in *Love Is in the Air* (1938), *Brother Rat* (1938), and *Brother Rat and a Baby* (1940). His heartrending role as Notre Dame football player George "The Gip" Gipper opposite Pat O'Brien won him widespread acclaim—and gave him an unforgettable phrase he would resurrect decades later, as president, when he squared off with Congress: "Win one for the Gipper."

In 1964, as cochair of California Republicans for Barry Goldwater's presidential candidacy, Reagan made one of his most important speeches. In "A Time for Choosing," he lambasted the growth of "big government" and threats to individual liberty. Although Goldwater lost the election to Lyndon Johnson in a landslide, Reagan's stances struck a chord with California voters, who elected him governor in 1966 and again in 1970. In 1969, when rioting students at the University of California, Berkeley, took over a parking lot (the People's Park protests), Reagan ordered National Guard troops to occupy the campus. One student was killed and several injured in scuffles with authorities. Reagan was widely hailed for his fiscal policies while governor of California. He balanced the state budget and turned a record deficit of $200 million into a surplus by trimming government expenditures.

Reagan was elected to the presidency in 1980 and won re-election in 1984. His major initiatives included cutting domestic spending, reforming the tax code, and increasing defense spending—which dramatically ballooned the federal deficit.

He left the Oval Office in January 1989 with a popularity rating of 63 percent—higher than that of any president since Franklin

D. Roosevelt. In February 1994, Reagan announced that he had Alzheimer's disease. He died at the age of 93 on 5 June 2004, at his ranch in Santa Barbara, California. His 1981 autobiography is entitled *Where's the Rest of Me?* The Ronald Reagan Presidential Library opened in 1991 in Simi Valley, California, and houses archival holdings for his administration.

REED, RALPH EUGENE, JR. (1961–). Born in Portsmouth, Virginia, Reed earned a bachelor's degree from the University of Georgia (1985) and a doctorate in history from Emory University (1989). A political activist, Reed worked for the College Republicans in the 1980s and cultivated close ties with lobbyist **Jack Abramoff**. He served as executive director of the Christian Coalition from 1989 to 1997, and also worked on the 1996 campaign of Republican nominee Robert Dole in 1996.

Reed was involved in President **George W. Bush**'s 2000 primary campaign, and was criticized for his role in the attacks on Bush's rival, **John McCain**. In 2001, he became the chairman of the Georgia Republican Party.

Reed was implicated in the Indian casino gambling scandal surrounding Jack Abramoff that surfaced in 2005. Reed was accused of committing fraud along with Abramoff and Michael Scanlon by lobbying against Indian gaming but charging Indian tribes for counsel. Reed contended that he had been misled by Abramoff, and although a central figure in the Senate investigation into the matter, he did not face prosecution.

REID, RICHARD (1973–). Also known as Abdul Raheem, Reid is typically referred to as the "shoe bomber" by the media. A British national, he converted to Islam while in prison in Great Britain. Reid attempted to ignite explosives in his shoes on a flight from Paris, France, to Miami, Florida. He was arrested in December 2001, after the flight was diverted to Boston, Massachusetts. In January 2003, he was sentenced in federal court to life in prison and is serving his term at the federal maximum security facility in Florence, Colorado. Reid's actions prompted federal authorities to mandate the screening of all airline passengers' shoes. **Zacharias Moussaoui**, the so-called "twentieth hijacker," implicated Reid in the **al-Qaeda terrorist** plot of **11 September 2001**. Reid denied any involvement, and no charges were brought against him on that account.

REFORM PARTY. Having run for the presidency in 1992 as an independent who garnered 19 percent of the popular vote, Texas millionaire H. Ross Perot founded the Reform Party in 1994 and announced his second candidacy under the party's banner in 1996. Perot's 1996 campaign was hampered by his late entry into the race against Democratic incumbent **William Clinton** and Republican nominee Robert Dole.

Patrick Buchanan, a conservative Republican who challenged President **George H.W. Bush** in the 1992 primaries, gravitated toward the Reform Party in the late 1990s. Buchanan advocated tougher policies on immigration, **abortion**, and tax reductions—and his social conservatism was at odds with Perot's prior platform. Buchanan attempted to capture the Reform Party's nomination to run against **George W. Bush** in 2000 but was unsuccessful in a clash of forces within the Reform Party. Buchanan attempted to attract voters by running under the "Freedom Party" banner, which he claimed was the "real" party of rank-and-file Reform Party activists. Buchanan won 2.8 million votes (2.7 percent of the popular vote) and no Electoral College votes. Buchanan's support was particularly controversial in **Palm Beach County**, Florida, which used a **butterfly ballot** that confused many elderly voters and was a precipitating factor in the **Florida recount**.

The Reform Party remained in disarray through the 2004 presidential elections, throwing its support to **Ralph Nader** rather than fielding a candidate of its own. Infighting continued into the 2008 election, and the Reform Party garnered only 470 votes in the presidential contest, as its candidates appeared on the ballot solely in Mississippi.

REHNQUIST, WILLIAM HUBBS (1924–2005). A native of Milwaukee, Wisconsin, Rehnquist was a World War II veteran who later received degrees from Harvard University and a law degree from Stanford, where he graduated first in his class. He clerked for **Supreme Court** Justice Robert Jackson before taking up private practice in Arizona from 1953 to 1969. Rehnquist worked in President Richard

Nixon's Office of White House Counsel from 1969 to 1971. Nixon nominated him to associate justice of the Supreme Court to replace John Marshall Harlan in 1971.

Rehnquist evinced a conservative voting record as an associate justice, writing critical opinions on desegregation and opposing the *Roe v. Wade* (1973) decision that legalized **abortion**. When Chief Justice Warren Burger retired in 1986, President **Ronald Reagan** nominated Rehnquist to take his place. Rehnquist was confirmed by a Senate vote of 65–25. Antonin Scalia was later tapped by Reagan to fill the associate justice position created by Rehnquist's vacancy. Rehnquist presided over the impeachment trial of President **William Clinton** in 1999.

Rehnquist died of complications from thyroid cancer on 3 September 2005. His support for states' rights, particularly in reference to the wall separating church from state, is one of his most controversial legacies. President **George W. Bush** nominated **John Roberts** to succeed Rehnquist. Roberts was confirmed on 29 September 2005 by a 78–22 vote in the US Senate.

RENDITION. Rendition is the controversial practice used by the administration of **George W. Bush** following the **11 September 2001 terrorist** attacks of sending suspected terrorists and **enemy combatants** thought to be abetting terrorist groups to other countries for detention, imprisonment, and questioning by the **Central Intelligence Agency** (CIA). Some of the alleged countries involved include **Afghanistan**, **Poland**, Egypt, Jordan, and **Syria**. Several suspected terrorists are alleged to have been kidnapped in Europe and claim to have been tortured. Secretary of State **Condoleezza Rice** stated in 2006 that the United States did not have a policy of transferring suspected terrorists to countries where they are tortured. Nonetheless countries of the **European Union** were particularly critical of the practice, investigated it, and threatened sanctions against any member nation that facilitated so-called "black sites" or clandestine prisons. A 2007 film directed by Gavin Hood entitled "Rendition" closely mimicked the alleged deportation a Canadian national with dual Syrian citizenship who claimed to have been tortured under the practice. *See also* DETAINEE TREATMENT ACT; TORTURE; WATERBOARDING.

RICE, CONDOLEEZZA (1954–). Born in Birmingham, Alabama, Rice earned an undergraduate degree in political science from the University of Denver (1974), a master's degree from the University of Notre Dame (1975), and a doctoral degree from the University of Denver (1981). An expert on the **Soviet Union**, Rice taught at Stanford University from 1981 to 1993. She worked in the administration of President **George H.W. Bush** for the **National Security Council** as an advisor for Soviet affairs from 1989 to 1991. In 1993, she became provost for Stanford University after earning tenure and served on several corporate boards, including Chevron.

Rice served as **foreign policy** advisor to **George W. Bush** during the 2000 presidential election. Following his electoral victory, Bush tapped Rice to serve as his **national security advisor**. She served in that capacity from 2001 to 2005, and was the first woman to hold the position. Rice favored the US-led invasion of **Iraq** in March 2003, and defended the administration's stance on **Saddam Hussein** and his putative quest for **weapons of mass destruction** (WMDs) in a *New York Times* editorial just a few months before the war began.

Rice became secretary of state in January 2005, succeeding **Colin Powell** upon his retirement. She was an advocate of so-called "transformational diplomacy" aimed at spreading democracy throughout the Middle East. She was active in her efforts to streamline the Department of State relative to the **War on Terror**. She was also particularly active in the Israeli–Palestinian conflict and helped broker the **United Nations** cease-fire in the conflict between **Israel** and **Syria** in 2006. She oversaw progress in battling the **insurgency** in Iraq and was a staunch defender of the US military mission in Iraq and **Afghanistan**. Finally, from 2005 to 2008 Rice focused on **Iran** and halting President **Mahmoud Ahmadinejad**'s pursuit of nuclear technology through international sanctions and the United Nations.

RIDGE, THOMAS JOSEPH (1945–). Born in Munhall, Pennsylvania, Ridge graduated from Harvard University (1967). After a year of law school, he was drafted into the Army. He served in Vietnam and earned numerous medals, including the Bronze Star, before returning home in 1970. He finished his law degree at Dickinson University (1972) and worked in private practice before becoming assistant district attorney for Erie County, Pennsylvania, in 1980. In 1982, he ran successfully for the US House of Representatives, and won re-election six times. He became the first Vietnam War veteran to serve in Congress. In 1994, he focused his attention on the Pennsylvania governorship. A Republican, Ridge won convincingly in a state where Democrats outnumber Republicans by a wide margin. He was re-elected in 1998.

Ridge resigned the governorship before his term was up when President **George W. Bush** asked him to head the newly created **Office of Homeland Security** in the wake of the **terrorist** attacks on New York and the **Pentagon** on **11 September 2001**. In January 2003, Ridge became the first secretary of the **Department of Homeland Security**. He supervised the merger of 22 federal agencies into the mammoth new department—which represented the largest governmental reorganization since the Department of Defense was created in the 1940s. Ridge resigned in February 2006 and was succeeded by **Michael Chertoff**. He cited personal and family reasons for his resignation, and returned to the private sector, serving on several boards and starting his own consulting firm. In 2008, Ridge supported Republican presidential nominee **John McCain** and was rumored as a potential vice presidential candidate before McCain chose Alaska Governor **Sarah Palin**.

ROAD MAP FOR PEACE. In June 2002, President **George W. Bush** announced this long-term strategy for ending the conflict between **Israel** and the Palestinians. The United States was joined by **Russia**, the **European Union**, and the **United Nations** (UN) in calling for a halt to violence and the creation of an independent Palestinian state that recognized Israel's right to exist. Early progress was made between the **Palestinian National Authority** leader **Mahmoud Abbas** and his Israeli counterpart, Prime Minister **Ariel Sharon**. However, substantive progress was derailed by an escalation of violence and the victory by **Hamas**—which the United States and Israel consider a **terrorist** organization—in the January 2006 parliamentary elections in the Palestinian Territories. The elections ultimately left the **Fatah**

party of Abbas in charge of the **West Bank** and Hamas in control of the **Gaza Strip**.

ROBERTS, CHARLES PATRICK (PAT) (1936–). Born in Topeka, Kansas, Roberts graduated from Kansas State University with a degree in journalism (1958). A Marine Corps veteran, he worked for several newspapers in Arizona in the 1960s before becoming an assistant to Kansas Congressman Keith Sebelius. He ran successfully for the House of Representatives as a Republican in 1980 and was re-elected seven times. He was elected to the Senate in 1996 to replace retiring Senator Nancy Landon Kassebaum. He was re-elected in both 2002 and 2008. His committee assignments have included the Armed Services Committee, Finance, Agriculture, and Health, Education, Labor and Pensions. In June 2003, he headed the select committee charged with investigation intelligence failures prior to the US-led invasion of **Iraq**, after which no **weapons of mass destruction** (WMDs) were discovered. The report concluded that a lack of human intelligence relative to Iraqi dictator **Saddam Hussein**'s attempts to procure WMDs, as well as failures by intelligence analysts concerning Hussein's alleged links to **terrorist** group **al-Qaeda**, were to blame.

ROBERTS, JOHN GLOVER, JR. (1955–). Born in Buffalo, New York, Roberts grew up in Indiana. He earned both his undergraduate and law degree from Harvard University, where he was law review editor. He clerked for Second Circuit Court of Appeals Judge Henry Friendly and later for **Supreme Court** Justice **William Rehnquist**. From 1981 to 1982, he worked in the administration of **Ronald Reagan** as an assistant to the attorney general, and from 1982 to 1986 in the office of the White House counsel. After several years in private law practice, he served in the administration of **George H.W. Bush** as deputy solicitor general from 1989 to 1992, arguing the government's position before the Supreme Court. He served briefly on the US Court of Appeals for the District of Columbia in 1992 and ruled on the case of ***Hamdan v. Rumsfeld***, which was later appealed to the Supreme Court. His judgeship was never confirmed by Congress, and he returned to private law practice and taught at Georgetown University following Bush's unsuccessful re-election bid. He was ultimately nominated by President **George W. Bush** to the US Court of Appeals for the District of Columbia in 2003, and he served in that position until 2005.

In July 2005, Bush nominated Roberts to replace retiring Supreme Court Justice **Sandra Day O'Connor**. However, when Chief Justice William Rehnquist died in September 2005, Bush rescinded the nomination for O'Connor's seat and nominated Roberts for chief justice. Roberts was confirmed by the Senate by a 78–22 margin in late September. A Catholic, Roberts is widely viewed as a moderate. He supported restrictions on **abortion** and voted to uphold the **Partial-Birth Abortion Ban Act**, but did not support overturning the landmark case of *Roe v. Wade*.

ROMANIA. A former satellite of the **Soviet Union** and **Warsaw Pact** member, Romania regained its independence following a bloody revolution in 1989. Romania joined the **North Atlantic Treaty Organization** (NATO) in March 2004, and the **European Union** in January 2007. President **George W. Bush** visited Romania in November 2002 and again in April 2008.

ROVE, KARL CHRISTIAN (1950–). Born in Colorado and raised in Nevada and Utah, Rove got his start in politics at the University of Utah, where he became chairman of the campus College Republicans in the 1970s. In 1973, he became chairman of the national organization after an intense elections dispute. He later built a career in political consulting and campaigning, working on prominent senatorial and gubernatorial campaigns in Texas and around the nation. He managed **George W. Bush**'s abortive bid for a congressional seat in 1978, as well as **George H.W. Bush**'s run for the White House in 1980. He worked briefly for President George H.W. Bush's re-election campaign in 1992, but was fired after "planting" a story with columnist **Robert Novak** that disparaged Bush's campaign finance director, Robert Mosbacher.

Rove emerged as one of the most powerful and influential advisors to President George W. Bush following his management of Bush's election to the presidency in 2000. He was also a lightning rod for critics of the Bush administration. He served as senior advisor to the president and deputy chief of staff between 2001 and 2007, and he was involved in both domestic and **foreign policy** matters. Rove is thought to have wielded significant influence over Bush's decision to launch the **preemptive**, US-led invasion of **Iraq** in March 2003, which toppled the regime of **Saddam Hussein** in search of **weapons of mass destruction** (WMDs). He was also the principal strategist for Bush's re-election campaign in 2004. Although implicated in the "outing" of covert **Central Intelligence Agency** (CIA) agent **Valerie Plame**, as well as the controversy surrounding the dismissal of seven US attorneys, no formal charges were filed against him nor did evidence of wrongdoing surface in either case.

Rove resigned from his advisory role in the White House in August 2007, following the **mid-term election** losses by Republicans that robbed Bush of party control of the House and Senate. He frequently appeared as a consultant and commentator for various media outlets, including Fox News.

RUDD, KEVIN MICHAEL (1957–). Born in Queensland, Australia, Rudd worked in foreign affairs for the Australian government in the 1980s. He was elected to parliament in 1998, rose to become leader of the opposition, and was elected to head the Labour Party in 2006. In November 2007, he defeated the incumbent government of **John Howard**. An opponent of the **War in Iraq**, in which Australian troops had participated under former Prime Minister Howard, Rudd withdraw Australian combat troops from **Iraq** in June 2008, leaving only a small contingent of Australian forces in the country.

RUMSFELD, DONALD HENRY (1932–). A native of Evanston, Illinois, Rumsfeld graduated with a degree from Princeton University (1954). He attended Georgetown University Law School but did not graduate. From 1954 to 1957, he served as a flight instructor in the US Navy, after which time he worked for members of Congress from Ohio and Michigan. In 1962, Rumsfeld ran successfully for an Illinois congressional district. He was re-elected three times.

In 1969, Rumsfeld resigned his seat in the House of Representatives to work as director of the Office of Economic Opportunity for President Richard Nixon, and later as counsel to the president. In 1973, he became US ambassador to the **North Atlantic Treaty Organization** (NATO). Following Nixon's resignation in August

1974, Rumsfeld oversaw the White House transition to Gerald Ford, subsequently becoming White House **chief of staff**. In 1975, Ford appointed him secretary of defense.

After working in the private sector for a pharmaceutical company in the late 1970s and early 1980s, Rumsfeld was appointed as a special envoy by President **Ronald Reagan** in 1983 to halt the war between **Iran** and **Iraq**. In 1996, he chaired Republican nominee Robert (Bob) Dole's failed presidential campaign. He is a cofounder of the **neoconservative** think tank **Project for the New American Century** (PNAC) and a signatory of the organization's letter to President **William Clinton** in 1998 calling for the ouster of Iraqi dictator **Saddam Hussein**.

President **George W. Bush** appointed Rumsfeld secretary of defense in 2001. Following the **11 September 2001 terrorist** attacks on New York and the **Pentagon**, Rumsfeld oversaw the US-led invasion of **Afghanistan**, which toppled the **Taliban** regime and destroyed **al-Qaeda** training camps.

Rumsfeld was a major proponent of the **War in Iraq** and was responsible for the military strategy from the time of the invasion in March 2003 until his resignation in December 2006. He was often at the center of controversy, calling **France** and **Germany** the "old Europe" when French President **Jacques Chirac** and German Chancellor **Gerhard Schröder** expressed their dissent and withheld approval of a **United Nations** resolution sanctioning an invasion. A steadfast supporter of Bush's policy of detaining suspected **enemy combatants**, Rumsfeld was later caught in the **Abu Ghraib** prison scandal in which Iraqi prisoners were humiliated and forced into homosexual acts. Although Rumsfeld was never charged with any wrongdoing, demoted Brigadier General **Janis Karpinski** alleged that he had authorized civilian contractors to engage in interrogation techniques, including sleep deprivation, that contravened the **Geneva Conventions**.

Most importantly, Rumsfeld was increasingly a lightning rod for critics who charged that the growing **insurgency** in Iraq in 2004 was a product of an inadequate number of troops dating to the invasion. His gruff, often condescending approach to journalists at press conferences did little to endear him to the media. The cacophony of calls for Rumsfeld to resign reached a peak in 2006, when eight retired generals and admirals called on him to step down. Many compared Rumsfeld to Robert McNamara, the unpopular secretary of defense under Lyndon Johnson who was blamed for the quagmire in Vietnam. President Bush, however, continued to express his confidence in Rumsfeld's abilities.

Rumsfeld ultimately decided to resign in November 2006, just prior to the **mid-term elections** that gave Democrats majorities in both the House of Representatives and the Senate. President Bush did not announce the resignation until two days after the elections—a move that some Republicans felt had damaged their fortunes. Rumsfeld was succeeded as secretary of defense by **Robert Gates**. He subsequently began work on a memoir and took an appointment at Stanford University. *See also* ARMED FORCES.

RUSSERT, TIMOTHY JOHN (1950–2008). A native of Buffalo, New York, Russert earned a bachelor's degree from John Carroll University (1972) and a law degree from Cleveland State University (1976). He worked as chief of staff for prominent New York Senator Daniel Patrick Moynihan and later for New York Governor Mario Cuomo before becoming host of the National Broadcasting Corporation's (NBC) Sunday morning news program *Meet the Press* in 1991. Russert served in that capacity for 16 years, and also became senior vice president of NBC news. He earned a strong reputation as a tough but fair interviewer and was lauded for impeccable research and analysis of current events. He was best known for his interminable support of the Buffalo Bills National Football League (NFL) team and his affable demeanor and decency to his interviewees. He was a frequent moderator of election debates, including between Democrats **Barack Obama** and **Hillary Clinton** during the 2008 presidential primary campaign.

Russert testified in the case against **I. Lewis (Scooter) Libby** concerning the "outing" of **Central Intelligence Agency** (CIA) covert agent **Valerie Plame**. Libby had contended that Russert told him of her identity, but Russert denied that anyone had made her identity known to him. Russert further denied having any conversations with Libby, although it was revealed after his death that he had been a source of journalist **Robert Novak**, who originally revealed Plame's identity.

Russert died on 13 June 2008 of a heart attack. His career in journalism drew praise from his colleagues, as well as from **George W. Bush**, **John McCain**, and **Barack Obama**, whom Russert had interviewed.

RUSSIA. Also known as the Russian Federation following the collapse of the **Soviet Union** in 1991, Russia is the largest country in the world as regards landmass. With a population of approximately 140 million, Russia is an important energy producer and remains a pivotal military power in light of its nuclear arsenal.

Relations between the United States and Russia were positive at the beginning of **George W. Bush**'s presidency. Bush portrayed his relationship with Russian President **Vladimir Putin** as close and congenial in his first term, frequently referring to the Russian colloquially as "Vlad." Bush and Putin signed the **Strategic Offensive Reduction Treaty** in May 2002. The treaty was the most important nuclear disarmament agreement in more than a decade. Despite Putin's opposition to the **War in Iraq** and growing American criticism over a resurgence of authoritarianism in Russia, the rapport between Bush and Putin seemed further solidified when Bush visited Russia in May 2005 to commemorate the 60th anniversary of the end of World War II.

The relationship was strained, however, with Bush's announcement of plans to place an **anti-ballistic missile** shield in **Poland** and the **Czech Republic**. Putin opposed the plan, suggesting that European sites might be targeted by Russian nuclear missiles if the plan were implemented. Russian opposition seemingly stemmed more generally from the fact that former **Warsaw Pact** countries had recently joined the **North Atlantic Treaty Organization** and were promoting American **foreign policy** on the country's doorstep.

US-Russia relations reached a nadir in August 2008 when Russian President **Dmitri Medvedev** ordered troops to invade two breakaway regions in **Georgia**, South Ossetia and Abkhazia. Georgia President **Mikhail Saakashvili** appealed to the United States and the international community for help. Bush contended that the invasion was a violation of Russia's commitment to the **United Nations** (UN) charter on the equality of nations, UN ambassador **John Bolton** warned of negative consequences for Russia's relationship with the United

States, and Secretary of State **Condoleezza Rice** claimed Russia would "pay a price" in terms of its international reputation.

The downward turn in US–Russia relations continued toward the end of Bush's term. In 2008, Russian warships arrived in Havana, Cuba, on a tour of the Western hemisphere. Much to American dismay, the flotilla engaged in joint military maneuvers with Venezuela, whose leader, **Hugo Chávez**, was an indefatigable critic of the Bush administration. *See also* BESLAN, RUSSIA; CHECHNYA; WARSAW PACT.

– S –

SAAKASHVILI, MIKHAIL (1967–). Born in Tbilisi, **Georgia** (then part of the **Soviet Union**), Saakashvili graduated with a degree in law, worked for the Georgian government, and received a master of law degree from Columbia University in New York (1994). He built an international reputation on human rights issues, and after a brief period as minister of justice, was elected to the presidency of Georgia in 2004 following the ouster of former President Eduard Shevardnadze. He was re-elected to another four year term in 2008. Saakashvili was president when **Russian** forces invaded Georgia in August 2008 in the dispute over two breakaway regions, South Ossetia and Abknazia, both of which comprise large numbers of ethnic Russians. *See also* MEDVEDEV, DMITRI; PUTIN, VLADIMIR; RUSSIA.

SAFAVIAN, DAVID. *See* ABRAMOFF, JACK.

SANCHEZ, RICARDO (1951–). Born in Rio Grande City, Texas, Sanchez was an Army reserve officer training corps (ROTC) student and graduated from Texas A&M University, Kingsville (1973). He served in Germany, South Korea, and Panama, as well as at Fort Bragg, North Carolina, before commanding a battalion in the **Persian Gulf War** in 1991.

In June 2003, Sanchez became commander of ground forces following the US-led invasion of **Iraq** three months earlier. He was commander when the scandal concerning treatment and alleged torture of

detainees at the **Abu Ghraib** prison outside **Baghdad** was reported
in the media in April 2004. Sanchez gave up his command in Iraq
two months later and transferred to Germany, only to retire two years
later. He was the highest-ranking Hispanic officer in the military at the
time. In media interviews and in his memoir entitled *Wiser in Battle:
A Soldier's Story*, Sanchez contended that he was scapegoated for the
Abu Ghraib scandal, despite the fact that he was not charged with
wrongdoing and a subordinate, **Janis Karpinski**, was demoted due to
the incidents. *See also* ARMED FORCES.

SARKOZY, NICOLAS PAUL STÉPHANE (1955–). Born in Paris,
the son of Hungarian immigrants, Sarkozy earned a law degree from
the Université de Paris Nanterre. In 1977, he became a councilor for
the Parisian suburb of Neuilly-sur-Seine and became minister for
the budget in 1993 in the government of Prime Minister Édouard
Balladur. In 1995, he backed Balladur for the presidency in lieu of
supporting the winning candidate, **Jacques Chirac**, and sparked a
decade-long rivalry between himself and Chirac within the major
party of the right in **France**, the *Rassemblement pour la République*
(RPR or Rally for the Republic, and its successor the *Union pour la
Majorité Presidentielle*, UMP or Union for the Presidential Majority).

Chirac nonetheless appointed Sarkozy as minister of the interior
in 2002 upon his re-election, and he then served as minister of finance from 2004 to 2005. In 2005, he once again became minister
of the interior and stirred ample controversy for his allegedly racist
remarks following the Paris riots in Fall 2005, during which he called
the rioters, many of whom were North African immigrants, "scum."
After securing leadership of the UMP in 2005, he ran successfully for
the presidency in 2007, defeating rival socialist candidate Ségolène
Royal with 53 percent of the popular vote in the runoff election.

Sarkozy's election marked a positive turning point in France's
relations with the United States. He visited **George W. Bush** at
the Bush family compound in Kennebunkport, Maine, in Summer
2007, where he pledged a rapprochement between the two countries
following Bush's confrontation with Chirac in the **United Nations**
(UN) over the **War in Iraq** four years earlier. Chirac had pledged
to veto any UN-sanctioned invasion of the Iraqi regime of **Sad-**

dam Hussein. Sarkozy also appointed **Bernard Kouchner**, who had supported the ouster of Hussein, as his foreign minister and promised continuing French support for the **International Security and Assistance Force** (ISAF) in **Afghanistan**. *See also* ARMED FORCES.

SCANLON, MICHAEL. *See* ABRAMOFF, JACK.

SCHAFER, EDWARD THOMAS (1946–). A native of Bismarck, North Dakota, Schafer became governor of North Dakota in 1992 and was re-elected in 1996. He succeeded **Mike Johanns** as secretary of agriculture in the administration of **George W. Bush** in January 2008.

SCHIAVO, TERRI (1963–2005). Née Theresa Marie Schindler, Schiavo sustained brain damage in Tampa, Florida, in 1990 following cardiac arrest and was placed on artificial life support. Her husband, Michael Schiavo, attempted to have her feeding tube removed in 1998 and was opposed by her parents. The case caused a firestorm of national controversy as it wound its way through the legal system and became a symbol for right-to-life groups. The Florida legislature intervened in 2003, passing a law that allowed Governor **John Ellis (Jeb) Bush** to stay a court decision allowing the removal of her feeding tube. The US Congress ultimately intervened as well, passing a bill that allowed the federal courts jurisdiction in the matter of her life support. **George W. Bush** returned to Washington from a vacation in Texas to sign the emergency legislation. Nonetheless, neither the federal courts nor the **Supreme Court** agreed to hear the case. Schiavo's feeding tube was removed in March 2005 and she died after two weeks. Autopsies revealed that Schiavo was permanently brain-dead.

SCHORI, KATHARINE JEFFERTS (1954–). A native of Pensacola, Florida, Schori earned a doctoral degree in oceanography from Oregon State University (1983). She was ordained a priest in the Episcopal Church in 1994. She became the first female bishop, or primate, of the Episcopal Church of the United States in June 2006.

SCHRÖDER, GERHARD FRITZ KURT (1944–). Born in Nordrhein-Westfalen, **Germany**, Schröder entered politics in 1980 with his election to the Bundestag (lower house of parliament) as a member of the leftist Social Democratic Party (SDP). He became chancellor of Germany in October 1997. Although as chancellor Schröder sent German troops as part of the **North Atlantic Treaty Organization** (NATO) contingent in **Afghanistan**, he was an outspoken critic of the **War in Iraq** and the **foreign policy** of President **George W. Bush**. He also cultivated a strong relationship with **Russian** President **Vladimir Putin**. Christian Democratic leader **Angela Merkl** succeeded Schröder as chancellor following the elections of September 2005. Schröder left politics that year to join a publishing conglomerate. *See also* INTERNATIONAL SECURITY ASSISTANCE FORCE.

SCHWAB, SUSAN C. (1955–). A graduate of George Washington University with a doctoral degree in public administration, Schwab was dean of the school of public policy at the University of Maryland from 1995 to 2003. She succeeded **Rob Portman** as US Trade Representative in June 2006. One of her major accomplishments was ending a long-standing trade dispute with **Canada** over softwood lumber exports to the United States.

SCHWARZENEGGER, ARNOLD ALOIS (1947–). Born in Thal, Austria, Schwarzenegger moved to the United States in 1968. A bodybuilder, he pursued an acting career beginning in the 1970s. He became a Hollywood legend for his roles in films including *Commando*, *The Running Man*, *Predator*, *Total Recall*, and most importantly, the *Terminator* series of films in the 1980s and 1990s.

A moderate Republican, Schwarzenegger campaigned for President **George H.W. Bush** and served as the chair of the President's Council on Physical Fitness from 1990 to 1993. In August 2003, he announced his candidacy for the governorship of California in the election to recall incumbent Democrat **Joseph Graham (Gray) Davis** over his handling of the budget. Davis was removed, and Schwarzenegger culled more than 48 percent of the statewide vote to become governor. He was nicknamed the "Governator," a reference to his role in the film *Terminator*. When legislators in the state assembly refused to take action on his proposed budget, Schwarzenegger called them "girlie men," earning national headlines. Despite some setbacks in his first term, notably the defeat of several ballot measures he supported, Schwarzenegger won re-election in November 2006 with 56 percent of the statewide vote.

Because he is not a natural-born citizen, Schwarzenegger is ineligible to run for the presidency, prompting some of his supporters to clamor for a change to the Constitution. In 2008, he supported and campaigned for Republican nominee **John McCain**.

SECURITIES AND EXCHANGE COMMISSION (SEC). An independent agency of the federal government, the SEC is charged with regulating and overseeing securities and investment markets, including stock trades and broker services. The SEC and its chairman, **Christopher Cox**, were thrown into the national spotlight in Fall 2008 when the effects of the **sub-prime mortgage** crisis caused the economy and stock market to plummet. Critics charge that Cox and the SEC failed to properly regulate financial institutions. The SEC fell under further scrutiny in December 2008 following the arrest of Bernard Madoff. Madoff allegedly bilked investors out of millions with a so-called "Ponzi" scheme and the SEC—although it investigated Madoff for fraud dating to the 1990s—failed to prevent the fraud. *See also* BERNANKE, BEN SHALOM; HOUSING AND ECONOMIC RECOVERY ACT (2008); LEHMAN BROTHERS; PAULSON, HENRY MERRITT; TROUBLED ASSETS RELIEF PROGRAM (TARP); WASHINGTON MUTUAL.

11 SEPTEMBER 2001. The deadliest **terrorist** attacks in the history of the United States were perpetrated by 19 **al-Qaeda** operatives who used boxcutters to hijack a total of four commercial aircraft on the morning of 11 September 2001. Al-Qaeda ringleader **Osama bin Laden** claimed responsibility for the attacks. Bin Laden contended that the death and destruction had exceeded his expectations.

At 8:46 A.M., hijacker **Mohamed Atta** flew American Airlines Flight 11, a Boeing 767 en route from Boston to Los Angeles, into the north tower of the **World Trade Center** in New York City. At 9:03 A.M. the hijackers crashed United Airlines Flight 175, also en route from Boston to Los Angeles, into the south tower of the World Trade Center. All aboard the two aircraft perished instantly. The heat from the subsequent fires, fed by jet fuel, melted the buildings. Both towers collapsed by 10:30 A.M. The death toll reached more than 2,700 as workers from 80 countries died in the inferno. Many jumped to their death from the buildings rather than succumb to the smoke and fire before the buildings caved in.

The al-Qaeda terrorists also commandeered American Airlines Flight 77, en route from Washington, D.C., to Los Angeles, and crashed the Boeing 757 into the **Pentagon** in Arlington, Virginia at 9:37 A.M. 64 passengers on the flight perished, and another 125 workers in the building were killed.

Additionally, the terrorists hijacked United Airlines **Flight 93**, en route from Newark, New Jersey, to San Francisco, California, apparently with the intention of flying the aircraft into the White House. When passengers aboard the flight learned of the hijackers' intentions, and of the attacks on the World Trade Center and the Pentagon, they attempted to wrest control of the aircraft from the terrorists. Control of the aircraft was lost, however, and the Boeing 757 crashed in a field near Shanksville, Pennsylvania, at 10:03 a.m, killing 37 passengers and seven crew on board.

The **Federal Bureau of Investigation** (FBI) came under intense scrutiny for having failed to recognize the al-Qaeda plot. Many of the hijackers had trained at flight schools in the United States, and some expressed an interest only in maneuvering aircraft—not in landing or taking off. Critics contended that the FBI failed to interpret intelligence from field offices in advance of the 9/11 attacks that might have thwarted the hijackings of commercial aircraft.

The 9/11 attacks heralded the beginning of the **War on Terror** and fundamentally altered the course of **George W. Bush**'s presidency. Within weeks, Bush established an **Office of Homeland Security** in the White House to coordinate federal anti-terrorist programs, and he vowed to bring bin Laden to justice. In October 2001, the United States toppled the **Taliban** regime in **Afghanistan**, which had given safe harbor to al-Qaeda operatives believed to be responsible for the 9/11 attacks. Although neither bin Laden nor his close associate **Ayman al-Zawahiri** were captured, the FBI had arrested the so-called "twentieth hijacker"—**Zacarias Moussaoui**—three weeks before the 9/11 attacks. Moussaoui was sentenced to a life term in prison in 2006 for his alleged involvement in the plot. Moreover, US forces captured

Abu Zubaydah in March 2002 and **Khalid Sheikh Mohammed** in March 2003. Both were detained as **enemy combatants** and alleged that they were subjected to **torture**, including the practice of **waterboarding** (simulated drowning). The **9/11 Commission** posited that Mohammed was the mastermind of the 9/11 plot and Zubaydah was thought to have been involved in the planning of the attacks.

The governmental response to the 9/11 attacks included the creation of a range of new institutions as part of the open-ended War on Terror. The establishment of the **Department of Homeland Security** in 2003 represented the largest governmental reorganization since the 1940s. Following the recommendations of the 9/11 Commission, Congress created the position of **Director of National Intelligence** (DNI) to oversee the **Central Intelligence Agency** (CIA) and streamline intelligence gathering. Congress also created a **National Counterterrorism Center** as a clearinghouse for intelligence information. *See also* ARMED FORCES; AUTHORIZATION FOR THE USE OF MILITARY FORCE AGAINST TERRORISTS; BUSH DOCTRINE; FOREIGN POLICY; GUANTANAMO BAY, CUBA; INTELLIGENCE REFORM AND TERRORISM PREVENTION ACT (2004); JIHAD; MUJAHADEEN; PAKISTAN; PREEMTIVE WARFARE.

SERBIA. This central European country, a republic in the former **Yugoslavia**, declared independence in June 2006, ending three years of a confederal arrangement with Montenegro. *See also* KARADŽIĆ, RADOVAN; KOSOVO; MILOŠEVIĆ, SLOBODAN.

SHARON, ARIEL (1928–). Born in the British Mandate of Palestine (now **Israel**) to Russian immigrants, Sharon served in the Israel Defense Forces from 1948 to 1974. He rose through the ranks to general, although allegations of misconduct for a massacre of Palestinians in Gaza in 1953 dogged his military career. He became an aide to Prime Minister Rabin in 1975, and two years later won a seat in the Knesset (legislature) after forming his own elections list. He became defense minister in 1981, but stepped down shortly thereafter following allegations that he had allowed a massacre of civilians in **Beirut** during the 1982 **Lebanon** War. He remained in the Knesset, however, and assumed a number of other ministerial portfolios during the 1980s and 1990s.

Sharon was elected prime minister in 2001. He was best known for his advocacy of the international effort surrounding the **Road Map for Peace** in the Palestinian Territories supported by the United States, **European Union**, and **Russia**. Sharon agreed to a unilateral withdrawal of Israeli settlers from the **Gaza Strip** in 2004, angering many and inciting protests. He suffered a stroke in December 2005, and another in January 2006, that left him in a coma and a permanent vegetative state according to physicians. **Ehud Olmert** became acting prime minister and assumed the premiership fully in May 2006.

SHEEHAN, CINDY LEE MILLER (1957–). A California native, Sheehan drew national and international media attention for her opposition to the administration of **George W. Bush** and the **War in Iraq**. Sheehan's son, Casey, was an Army specialist killed in combat outside **Baghdad, Iraq**, in April 2004. He was posthumously awarded a Bronze Star and Purple Heart.

Sheehan commenced her antiwar effort following her son's death. She questioned the rationale for the invasion of Iraq, as well as the objectives—suggesting the military quest had as much or more to do with oil than with toppling the regime of **Saddam Hussein** to aid Iraqis in establishing democracy. Sheehan camped outside George W. Bush's Crawford, Texas, ranch in August 2005 and demanded a meeting with him. The president demurred, but Sheehan's campaign continued through the United States, Europe, Latin America, and later Cuba—where she demanded that the United States close the detainee detention facility in **Guantanamo Bay, Cuba**.

Sheehan ran for Congress as an independent against incumbent House Speaker **Nancy Pelosi** in the 2008 elections. She ran for the San Francisco district seat on the basis that Pelosi was not "liberal" enough for the constituency and because Pelosi had failed to impeach Bush. Sheehan culled 17 percent of the district vote to Pelosi's 72 percent.

SHELTON, HENRY HUGH (1942–). A native of Tarboro, North Carolina, Shelton earned a bachelor's degree from North Carolina State University and a master's degree from Auburn University. A Green Beret and decorated Vietnam War veteran, Shelton was promoted to brigadier general in 1987 and served as assistant commander of the 101st Airborne during the **Persian Gulf War**. He was promoted to lieutenant general in 1993. He commanded operations in the US-led intervention in Haiti in 1994, and became commander in chief of the US Special Operations Command in 1996.

President **William Clinton** appointed Shelton chairman of the **Joint Chiefs of Staff** in October 1997. He remained in that post through the first year of President **George W. Bush**'s first term. Shelton was en route to England during the **11 September 2001 terrorist** attacks on New York and the **Pentagon**. Air Force General **Richard Myers** assumed the position of acting chairman of the Joint Chiefs during his absence, and replaced Shelton as chair of the Joint Chiefs in October 2001. Shelton joined the boards and directorates of several corporations and served as an advisor to Democrat **John Edwards**' 2004 presidential campaign. *See also* ARMED FORCES.

SHINSEKI, ERIC KEN (1942–). Born in Lihue, Hawaii, Shinseki is a graduate of the United States Military Academy (1965) and holds a master's degree from Duke University. A Vietnam veteran, Shinseki later served in **Germany** and Italy and was commander of **North Atlantic Treaty Organization** (NATO) operations in the former **Yugoslavia** in the 1990s. He became Army chief of staff in 1998 and held that position until 2003. Shinseki publicly disagreed with Secretary of Defense **Donald Rumsfeld** and Deputy Secretary of Defense **Paul Wolfowitz** over the number of troops necessary for the US-led invasion of Iraq in March 2003. Shinseki questioned whether a half-million troops was sufficient for the military operation and advocated a higher number both for the invasion and the postwar reconstruction effort. Shinseki retired as a four-star general in 2003. In 2006, he testified before Congress on troop levels. **CENTCOM** commander **John Abizaid** later testified that he believed Shinseki's earlier assessment that a larger contingent of troops was necessary was, in fact, correct. *See also* ARMED FORCES.

SHOCK AND AWE. A military tactic, shock and awe is the use of massive and rapid force to overwhelm the enemy, devastate its military capabilities, and force capitulation. The notion was formalized by the National Defense University in 1996, but used decades prior in conflicts in World War II (the dropping of the atomic bomb on

Hiroshima and Nagasaki and the Nazi *Blitzkrieg* or "lightning war" are notable examples) and the **Persian Gulf War** in 1991.

Shock and awe formed the basis for the US military strategy for the **War in Iraq** in the early stages of the invasion of that country in March 2003 and was articulated by Secretary of State **Colin Powell**. The objective was to devastate the Iraqi army, the Republican Guard, and **Saddam Hussein**'s paramilitary force, the **Fedayeen Saddam**, if possible. Although **Baghdad** and other major cities fell quickly to US and coalition forces upon the initiation of hostilities, critics—including Arizona Senator and 2008 presidential candidate **John McCain**—charged that insufficient troop levels at the beginning of the conflict precipitated the ease with which a growing **insurgency** was able to inflict increased casualties and necessitated a "surge" in troops by 2007. *See also* ARMED FORCES; BUSH, GEORGE W.; PETRAEUS, DAVID H.

SIGNING STATEMENTS. Signing statements are those written and verbal statements presidents make when signing a bill into law, often to offer criticism of select provisions or to interpret the implementation of provisions. The practice began under President **Ronald Reagan** and continued throughout the administrations of **George H.W. Bush**, **William Clinton**, and **George W. Bush**. The **Supreme Court** has given no legal weight or authority to presidential signing statements.

The Congressional Research Service reported in September 2007 that George W. Bush had made 157 signing statements, of which 118 were to challenge provisions of laws. As one example, when Bush signed the **Detainee Treatment Act** (2005) he indicated he would interpret the provisions of the bill prohibiting inhumane treatment of **enemy combatants** and mandating that interrogations conform to the US Army Field Manual consistent with his role as commander in chief to protect the nation from future **terrorist** attacks.

Critics contend that signing statements are tantamount to a line-item veto. Legislation giving President Clinton a line-item veto in the 1990s was ruled unconstitutional by a federal court. Regardless, the practice is consistent with the Bush administration's articulation of "unitary executive" theory elaborated by Vice President **Richard B. (Dick) Cheney**'s legal counselor **David Addington**. The theory holds that the president controls the entirety of the executive branch, with minimal congressional interference within statutory bounds. Moreover, the theory posits that the president's commander-in-chief role places the legislative and judicial branches in a position inferior to his during times of war. *See also* WAR ON TERROR.

SIMPSON, ORENTHAL JAMES (O.J.) (1947–). A record-setting football player for San Francisco City College and later the University of Southern California in the 1960s, Simpson won the Heisman Trophy in 1969. He entered professional football with the Buffalo Bills that same year, and by the mid-1970s shattered records as a running back. A familiar face on national television in advertisements for Hertz Rent-a-Car, Simpson also appeared in several movies, including *Naked Gun* with costar Leslie Nielsen.

In 1994, Simpson was thrown into the spotlight following the murders of his ex-wife, Nicole Brown Simpson, and her friend Ronald Goldman in Los Angeles. When police set out to arrest Simpson, he engaged them in a slow-speed freeway chase for hours, which was covered live by the media. Simpson stood trial for murder charges amid a veritable media frenzy. He was acquitted in 1995. However, the families of Goldman and Brown filed a civil action against Simpson and won a wrongful death case. Simpson was ordered to pay $33.5 million in damages to the families.

In 2006, Simpson planned to publish a book on the murders. The original book was pulled from publication in November 2006. In 2007, the Goldman family filed a lawsuit, and a Florida bankruptcy court ordered proceeds from the book to go toward settlement of the wrongful death suit. The book was released in 2007 with the title *If I Did It: Confessions of the Killer.* In September 2007, Simpson was placed under arrest in Las Vegas, Nevada, on a host of charges that he and accomplices had entered a casino hotel room and stolen sports memorabilia while holding hostages at gunpoint. Simpson claimed the memorabilia had been stolen from him. In October 2008, he was convicted on gun-related robbery and kidnapping charges and sentenced to no less than nine years in prison.

SKILLING, JEFFREY. *See* ENRON CORPORATION.

SLOVAKIA. Previously part of Czechoslovakia, this republic was a former **Warsaw Pact** member under Soviet domination after World War II. Slovakia peacefully split from its neighbor, the **Czech Republic**, in January 1993 in what has been dubbed the "Velvet Divorce." Slovakia joined both the **North Atlantic Treaty Organization** (NATO) and the **European Union** in 2004.

SLOVENIA. A component of the former **Yugoslavia** until it gained its independence in 1991, this central European country joined the **North Atlantic Treaty Organization** (NATO) and the **European Union** in 2004.

SMITH, ROBERT C. (BOB) (1941–). Born in Trenton, New Jersey, Smith is a graduate of Lafayette College and a veteran of the Vietnam War, in which he served from 1965 to 1967. A teacher and real estate business owner, Smith moved to New Hampshire and ran successfully for the House of Representatives as a Republican in 1984. He was re-elected twice to the House, and was a prominent advocate for Vietnam veterans and prisoners of war. In 1990, he won a Senate seat, replacing retiring Republican Gordon Humphrey. He was re-elected in 1996. Smith served on the Senate Ethics and Environment and Public Works Committees.

Smith announced his candidacy for the Republican nomination for the presidency in 1999, but his campaign failed to gain traction against front-runner **George W. Bush**. He left the Republican Party, unsuccessfully sought the nomination from the US Taxpayers Party, later announced himself as an independent, and ultimately threw his support behind Bush in Fall 1999. He was defeated by John Sununu in the Republican primary contest for the Senate in 2002.

SNOW, JOHN WILLIAM (1939–). A native of Toledo, Ohio, Snow is a graduate of the University of Toledo, and earned his doctoral degree in economics from the University of Virginia (1965). He completed a law degree at George Washington University (1967) and worked briefly in private law practice until 1972. He held several positions in the Department of Transportation under President Richard Nixon, and was appointed Federal Highway Administrator under President Gerald Ford. He worked in the railroad industry in the 1980s and in an advisory capacity on regulatory and economic issues for President **Ronald Reagan** in the 1980s.

President **George W. Bush** tapped Snow as his secretary of the treasury in February 2003, to replace **Paul O'Neill**, who retired. Snow resigned in May 2006 and was replaced by **Henry Paulson**. His tenure as secretary of treasury was troubled, as he was unable to persuade Congress or the public to accept significant social security reform proposed by the president—namely qualified privatization of some savings—and an overhaul of the tax code.

SNOW, ROBERT ANTHONY (TONY) (1955–2008). A native of Kentucky and a graduate of Davidson College and the University of Chicago, Snow worked variously as a columnist and editorial-page editor for the *Washington Times*, *Detroit News*, *The Daily Press* (Newport News, Virginia), the *Virginian Pilot* (Norfolk, Virginia), and the *Greensboro Record* (North Carolina). He served as director of speechwriting in the administration of **George H.W. Bush** from 1992 to 1993. He hosted the Fox News Network from 1996 to 2006. In 2006, President **George W. Bush** tapped Snow as his White House press secretary.

Snow resigned as press secretary in September 2007, announcing that he was battling colon cancer. He died on 12 July 2008.

SOVIET UNION. The Soviet Union, also known as the Union of Soviet Socialist Republics (USSR), was the United States' principal military and ideological rival in the decades following World War II and during the **Cold War**, which spanned the 1940s through 1991. The communist state was founded in 1922 after the 1917 Russian Revolution, spearheaded by Vladimir Ilych Lenin, which ousted Czar Nicholas II. The political structure of the country was a highly centralized federation of republics, most of which could be traced to Imperial **Russia** (Finland and **Poland** notwithstanding). The "command" economy was planned by political leaders, typically through "five-year plans" that dictated manufacturing and agricultural production goals. Private property was abolished for all intents and purposes. The only political party—the Communist Party—maintained a monopoly on power for seven decades.

By the 1980s, the Soviet Union was struggling to keep pace with US technology, and the financial burden of military spending took a heavy toll on the economy. Mikhail Gorbachev became general secretary of the Soviet Union in 1985 and advanced policies of greater openness (*glasnost*) and economic rebuilding (*perestroika*). These reforms arguably paved the way for the eventual dissolution of the Soviet Union, although some suggest that President **Ronald Reagan**'s proposal for a space-based **anti-ballistic missile** system, the Strategic Defense Initiative (SDI), hastened the breakup by convincing Gorbachev that Soviet competition against the project would bankrupt the country's finances. Gorbachev's economic reforms nevertheless caused a deterioration in living standards, particularly because of increased inflation. The openness he championed, paradoxically, encouraged the public to express anger over the effects of the reforms.

By 1989, pressure for greater autonomy in the republics intensified. The Russian Republic held a congress in an attempt to usurp authority from the central government in Moscow. After a coup attempt against Gorbachev in 1991, power in Russia shifted definitively to Boris Yeltsin. The Baltic Republics of **Estonia**, **Latvia**, and **Lithuania** then declared independence. A meeting between Yeltsin and his counterparts from Belarus and Ukraine ultimately produced an agreement to dissolve the Soviet Union, which came to an end on 25 December 1992 when Gorbachev resigned. *See also* GEORGIA; MEDVEDEV, DMITRI ANATOLYEVICH; PUTIN, VLADIMIR VLADIMIROVICH; WARSAW PACT.

SPELLINGS, MARGARET (1957–). Born in Michigan, Spellings grew up in Houston, Texas. She graduated from the University of Houston (1979) with a degree in political science. A former assistant executive director for the Texas Association of School Boards, Spellings directed **George W. Bush**'s 1994 gubernatorial campaign and served as his advisor from 1995 to 2000.

Spellings served as a domestic policy advisor to President George W. Bush from 2001 to 2005, and was the principal architect of the controversial **No Child Left Behind** legislation. She replaced **Rod Paige** as secretary of **education** in January 2005 at the beginning of Bush's second presidential term. Beginning in 2005, she headed the president's Commission on the Future of Higher Education. She served out Bush's second term and was only the second female secretary of education in the department's history.

SPITZER, ELIOT LAURENCE (1959–). A native of the Bronx (New York City), Spitzer earned a bachelor's degree from Princeton University and graduated from Harvard Law School. Following a clerkship and a brief stint in private law practice, he joined the Manhattan District Attorney and won acclaim for his prosecution of organized crime. After an unsuccessful run for attorney general of New York in 1994, he was elected to that position in 1998. He worked indefatigably to enhance the status of the office by focusing on corporate crime, environmental protection, and fraud cases. A rising star in Democratic circles, Spitzer announced his candidacy for the New York governorship more than a year before the 2006 election, and he won handily with more than two-thirds of the statewide vote.

Spitzer's political career came to an abrupt end when the *New York Times* reported a story in March 2008 that he had frequented a high-priced prostitution ring. Spitzer announced his resignation on 12 March 2008, and was succeeded by **David Paterson** five days later. The *Times* later alleged that Spitzer had used campaign money to pay for the hotel rooms and call girls, but federal prosecutors announced they had no evidence and did not intend to prosecute Spitzer.

STEM-CELL RESEARCH. Stem cells come from either adult or embryonic tissue. Many doctors believe that the use of stem cells has the potential to treat a wide array of diseases, including diabetes, Parkinson's disease, cancer, and Alzheimer's, among others. In the administration of **George W. Bush**, the issue of federal funding of stem-cell research was raised several times. In 2001, Bush enabled researchers to use federal funds for stem-cell research derived from fetuses from reproductive purposes that were no longer needed or going to be destroyed. The policy excluded the cloning of embryos or the destruction of viable fetuses.

In September 2006, Bush issued the first veto of his presidency when Congress passed a law liberalizing embryonic stem-cell research to include embryos couples had frozen for future use. The president contended that such research "crossed a moral boundary" that was unacceptable. The House of Representatives attempted, unsuccessfully, to override the veto.

STOP LOSS. This military policy enables the president, as commander in chief, to involuntarily extend the length of service duty of members of the armed forces. The policy was used during the **Persian Gulf War** and several military interventions under President **William Clinton** in the 1990s. Controversy developed over use of the policy for reservists in the **War in Iraq** in the administration of **George W. Bush**. Democratic presidential nominee **John Kerry** labeled the policy a "backdoor draft" during the 2004 campaign, but courts have repeatedly upheld the president's authority when the policy has been challenged legally. Bush's use of the policy stirred a backlash by veterans' groups opposed to the War in Iraq. The policy was also the subject of a March 2008 film entitled *Stop-Loss* directed by Kimberly Peirce that depicted a soldier who deserted the war effort after receiving notice of an extension of his service duties. *See also* SHEEHAN, CINDY LEE MILLER.

STRATEGIC OFFENSIVE REDUCTION TREATY. Also known as the Treaty of Moscow, the Strategic Offensive Reduction Treaty was signed by President **George W. Bush** and Russian President **Vladimir Putin** on 24 May 2002. The treaty is one of the most important post-**Cold War** bilateral agreements, as it limits the United States and **Russia** each to no more than 2,200 offensive nuclear warheads. The treaty came into effect in July 2003 and expires in 2012.

STRAW, JACK (1946–). Born in Essex, England, Straw earned a law degree at the University of Leeds. He was first elected to the British Parliament in 1977 as a Labour Party member for a constituency in Lancashire. When Labour was victorious in 1997 under the leadership of Prime Minister **Tony Blair**, Straw was named home secretary and held that post until 2001. From 2001 to 2006, he held the position of foreign secretary. He supported the US-led invasion of **Iraq** in March 2003 and developed a particularly close relationship with Secretary of State **Condoleezza Rice** in the administration of **George W. Bush**.

Following Labour's lackluster polling in the 2006 elections in **Great Britain**—which were largely connected to a popular backlash against the **War in Iraq**—Blair reorganized his cabinet. In an apparent demotion, Straw became leader of the House of Commons and later lord chancellor and secretary of state for justice. *See also* BROWN, JAMES GORDON; DOWNING STREET MEMO.

SUB-PRIME MORTGAGE (CRISIS). The roots of the sub-prime mortgage crisis, which plunged the US economy into the worst recession in decades by Fall 2007, are traceable to federal government policies and lending practices by banks in the aftermath of the **11 September 2001 terrorist** attacks. As a means of spurring economic growth in the wake of the attacks and an economy attempting to recover from the technology "bubble" that burst in the late 1990s, the **Federal Reserve** (Fed) cut interest rates to banks, thereby freeing up capital made available to finance home and other purchases, as well as investments. The sale of homes increased dramatically, but often with loan terms that included very low interest rates, set below the prime rate, or interest-only loans on which no principal was paid for a set period. Depending on the loan, purchasers would see the interest rates increase (adjustable rate mortgages), need to pay a "balloon" payment, and/or begin making principal payments as time progressed. One result of the practice is that banks lent credit liberally to purchasers with questionable abilities to repay the loans over time. As homeowners began to default on loans, the **Federal National Mortgage Association** (Fannie Mae), which purchases notes from banks to make further funds available for loans, increasingly inherited properties on which homeowners were defaulting.

The crisis came to a head in September 2007 as the default rate skyrocketed and banks were far less willing to make risky loans to homebuyers or others in need of credit. The "credit crunch" further damaged the ailing housing construction and resale markets. The effects were spiraling, as the economy contracted and not only banks, but other corporations such as the automobile industry, saw profits decline and could not procure adequate credit. The US government attempted to deal with the problem piecemeal at first, offering financial aid to firms such as **Bear Stearns** and **American International Group** (AIG). As the crisis worsened, Federal Reserve chairman **Ben Bernanke** infused large amounts of capital into the banking system, and Congress eventually passed a huge "bailout" bill in the amount of $700 billion to aid not only banks but other corporations as part of the **Troubled Assets Relief Program** (TARP).

Some critics of the administration of **George W. Bush** faulted a lack of oversight by the **Securities and Exchange Commission** and its chair, **Christopher Cox**, for failing to supervise the banking industry. Others blamed prior congressional legislation, such as the Community Reinvestment Act, which encourages banks to provide loans to low-income individuals and families who want to purchase homes. Whatever the case, the first installment of half of the $700 billion bailout seemingly had little positive effect on the economy in fall 2008 and many—including members of Congress—were angered by the appearance of corporate greed. Banks did not necessarily use the funds to relieve the credit crunch but instead pursued other ends, such as the purchase of other troubled financial institutions, and did not cut corporate executives' salaries and large bonuses. *See also* FEDERAL HOME LOAN MORTGAGE CORPORATION (FREDDIE MAC); HOUSING AND ECONOMIC RECOVERY ACT (2008); LEHMAN BROTHERS; PAULSON, HENRY MERRITT; WASHINGTON MUTUAL.

SUDAN. This former British colony gained its independence in 1956. It is the largest country on the African continent. Civil war recommenced in 1983, largely between rival factions of Arabs in the north of the country and Christians in the south. Although a peace agreement that included significant autonomy for the southern part of Sudan was reached in 2005, the government pursued rebels in the southern **Darfur** region, and *janjaweed* militias committed atrocities that Secretary of State **Colin Powell** called genocide. The matter was referred to the **International Criminal Court** (ICC). The **United Nations** (UN) was reticent to intervene directly in Darfur, and the administration of **George W. Bush** was criticized by many for an unwillingness to pursue the issue with greater vigor. *See also* MORENO-OCAMPO, LUIS.

SUNNI TRIANGLE (IRAQ). This geographic area in **Iraq** is typically described as the area north of **Baghdad**, with the cities of **Tikrit**, Ramadi, and Bakuba on the north, south, and east sides, respectively, of the "triangle." Sunni Muslims comprise the overwhelming number of residents and were at the heart of the **insurgency** that was mounted against US and coalition forces following the invasion of Iraq in March 2003. Iraqi dictator **Saddam Hussein** was born in Tikrit and derived significant support from this particular region of the country. It was within the Sunni Triangle that Hussein was captured by US forces in December 2003.

SUPER TUESDAY. In presidential election years, Super Tuesday refers to that set of states that hold primary elections simultaneously. In 1988, following the disastrous campaign of Democratic nominee Walter Mondale four years earlier, many southern states decided to hold their primary elections on the same day, in order to hold leverage over the eventual party nominee. Erstwhile typically held in March, recent Super Tuesday contests have been "front-loaded" earlier in the electoral season. In 2000, more than 80 percent of Democratic and 18 percent of Republican delegates were at stake on Super Tuesday (5 February), and the strong showings by **Al Gore** and **George W. Bush** enabled both to secure their nomination at the party conventions later that year. More delegates were available to candidates in both parties in 2008 compared to any previous Super Tuesday—more than half of Democratic delegates and two-fifths of Republican delegates. On 5 February 2008, **John McCain**'s strong showing all but assured his nomination by the Republican Party. **Barack Obama** edged out **Hillary Clinton** only by a few delegates, forcing a protracted race in the Democratic Party that was not settled until some three months later. Conservative radio commentator **Rush Limbaugh** attempted to exploit divisions among Democrats, calling upon Republican and Independent voters to partake in the Democratic primaries that followed in order to extend the Obama–Clinton rivalry.

SUPREME COURT. The Supreme Court is the only court in the United States that is specifically mentioned in the Constitution. Congress created a framework for the federal district and appellate courts in the Judiciary Act of 1789. As its name suggests, the Supreme Court is the court of last appeal and the only court to deal with certain types of cases, including foreign dignitaries, disputes between the states, and disputes between the federal government and the states.

President **George W. Bush** made two appointments to the Supreme Court, both in his second term. In July 2005, Bush nominated **John Roberts** to replace retiring Supreme Court Justice **Sandra Day O'Connor**. However, Chief Justice **William Rehnquist** died in September 2005, and Bush rescinded Robert's nomination for O'Connor's seat and instead nominated him as chief justice. Roberts was confirmed by the Senate by a 78–22 margin in late September. Bush then nominated **Samuel Alito** to the High Court in October 2005 to fill O'Connor's seat. Alito was confirmed by the Senate by a vote of 52–42.

The composition of the Supreme Court during George W. Bush's presidency was decidedly conservative. In social policy, the justices supported the administration's positions by upholding the **Partial-Birth Abortion Ban Act** (2003) in the case *Gonzales v. Carhart* (2007). The Court also generally favored the White House's positions on **affirmative action**. The justices struck down programs in Kentucky and Washington that mandated raced-based criteria in assigning children to schools, as well as admissions policies for minorities at the University of Michigan.

In **foreign policy** and military affairs connected with the **War on Terror**, however, the Court sparred with the Bush administration. The White House lost major cases relating to **habeas corpus** for **terrorist** suspects and **enemy combatants** held at **Guantanamo Bay, Cuba**, and the establishment of **military tribunals** to try the detainees. In *Rasul v. Bush* (2004), the Court ruled enemy combatants were eligible for habeas corpus and could challenge their detention. In *Hamdi v. Rumsfeld* (2004), the Court decided that the detention of a US citizen as an enemy combatant is unconstitutional. In a 5–3 decision in *Hamdan v. Rumsfeld* (2006), the justices contended that President Bush did not have the authority to establish military tribunals for enemy combatants. As a result, Congress passed the **Military Commissions Act** (2006) that accorded Bush that authority. The High Court reviewed that legislation in *Boumediene v. Bush* (2008) and struck down the act, contending that the law violated rights to habeas corpus and reconfirming that detainees were subject to constitutional protections. *See also* GONZALES, ALBERTO.

SURGE. *See* WAR IN IRAQ.

SWIFT BOAT VETERANS FOR TRUTH. This independent group was formed during the 2004 election to oppose Democratic presidential candidate **John Kerry**. Members were former Vietnam Veterans who took issue with Kerry's opposition to the Vietnam War and his allegations of war crimes by US forces there. The group also challenged Kerry's service record and medals. The group ran television advertisements contending that Kerry was not fit to be commander in chief based on the testimony of soldiers who had served with Kerry. Many in the media were skeptical of the group's allegations, and Arizona Republican Senator **John McCain**, himself a prisoner of war in Vietnam, condemned the ads. **George W. Bush**'s campaign refused to condemn the ads, but said it would not challenge Kerry's military service record. The revelation that Bush legal counsel **Benjamin Ginsburg** had advised the group, however, solidified critics' assertion of a connection between the Bush campaign and the Swift Boat Veterans.

SYRIA. Divided from **Iraq** following World War II, Syria fell under French rule and gained its independence in 1946. It was ruled by **Ba'ath Party** leader Hafez al-Assad from 1970 until his death in 2000, at which time his son Bashar al-Assad took over the reins of power and instituted limited political reforms.

Syria is regarded by the United States and **Israel** as a state sponsor of **terrorism**, and the country is known to have given safe haven to **terrorist** organizations including **Hamas**, **Hezbollah**, and **Islamic Jihad**. The United States also implicated Syria in the assassination of Rafik Hariri, the prime minister of **Lebanon** who was slain in March 2005. Further, the administration of **George W. Bush** accused Syria of enabling terrorist groups such as **al-Qaeda** to cross the border into Iraq to join the **insurgency** against US and coalition troops.

– T –

TAGUBA REPORT. *See* ABU GHRAIB PRISON.

TALABANI, JALAL (1933–). A **Kurd** born in northern **Iraq**, Talabani was a major figure in battling the regime of **Saddam Hussein**

for Kurdish autonomy. A member of the interim **Iraq Governing Council** established following the US-led invasion of Iraq in March 2003, Talabani was elected as president of Iraq in April 2005 by the new parliament. Following Iraq's adoption of a new constitution in 2006, he was re-elected to the presidency. *See also* COALITION PROVISIONAL AUTHORITY; WAR IN IRAQ.

TALIBAN. A Pashto word derived from the Arabic for "student," the Taliban is a Sunni Muslim fundamentalist movement formed in 1993 and based in **Afghanistan**. Many Taliban were part of the **mujahideen** resistance to the Soviet occupation of Afghanistan in the 1980s. When Soviet forces withdrew, a civil war ensued, which enabled the Taliban to seize control of governmental institutions in Afghanistan in 1995. Headed by **Mullah Muhammed Omar**, the Taliban regime was notable for its adherence to Sharia law, censorship, and repression of **women**. The regime gave safe harbor to **terrorists**, including **Osama bin Laden**, and provided training camps for the terror group **al-Qaeda**, which was responsible for the **11 September 2001** attacks on the **World Trade Center** in New York and the **Pentagon** in Washington, D.C.

In October 2001, a multinational force led by the United States toppled the Taliban regime. However, remnants of the Taliban joined a growing **insurgency** against the US forces and **International Security Assistance Force** (ISAF) following the invasion, eroding security and jeopardizing the transition to democratic institutions. *See also* KARZAI, HAMID; MOHAMMED, KHALID SHEIKH; NORTH ATLANTIC TREATY ORGANIZATION (NATO); NORTHERN ALLIANCE; PAKISTAN; SOVIET UNION; WAZIRISTAN.

TASK FORCE ON NATIONAL ENERGY POLICY. *See* ENERGY TASK FORCE.

TAX CUTS. A leitmotiv in Republican politics, tax cuts are part of fiscal policy (taxing and spending). As a candidate in 1999 and 2000, **George W. Bush** advocated tax cuts to stimulate the economy. He argued that an apparent surplus at the time should be distributed to taxpayers. His Democratic rival, **Al Gore**, instead argued that the surplus should be used to shore up the ailing Social Security system and proposed that savings from the surplus should be sequestered in a "lockbox."

At Bush's request, Congress passed sweeping tax reform in 2001 known as the Economic Growth and Tax Relief Reconciliation Act. The law provided for a tax rebate, eliminated the so-called "marriage tax penalty" whereby couples filing a joint return could potentially pay higher taxes than if they had filed separately, and lowered marginal rates over a period of nine years.

In 2003, Bush supported a second round of tax cuts codified in the Jobs and Growth Tax Relief Reconciliation Act. The law provided for increased exemptions in the Alternative Minimum Tax and reduced capital gains and other income taxes.

Democrats and some fiscally conservative Republicans opposed the tax cuts, contending that they added to the burgeoning federal deficit, particularly in light of the costs of the **War in Iraq**.

TENET, GEORGE JOHN (1953–). Born in New York City, Tenet earned a bachelor's degree in foreign service from Georgetown University (1976) and a master's degree in international affairs from Columbia University (1978). In the 1980s, he joined the staff of Pennsylvania Senator John Heinz and later worked on the Senate Select Committee on Intelligence. He served on the **National Security Council** (NSC) from 1993 to 1995 under President **William Clinton**. He served as deputy director and then acting director of the **Central Intelligence Agency** (CIA) from 1995 to 1997. He was confirmed as director of the CIA in 1997 and remained in the post following the election of **George W. Bush** in 2000.

Tenet's leadership of the CIA was thrown into question following the **11 September 2001 terrorist** attacks on the **World Trade Center** in New York and the **Pentagon** in Washington, D.C. Critics contended that the CIA had failed to analyze pre-attack intelligence adequately, and Tenet embarked on a significant endeavor to reorganize the agency. He was further criticized for having made a forceful argument to President Bush that Iraqi dictator **Saddam Hussein** had procured **weapons of mass destruction** (WMDs), and when none were located following the US-led invasion of **Iraq** in March 2003, calls for his resignation increased. Tenet ultimately resigned in June 2004 as director of the CIA and was succeeded by **Porter J. Goss**.

Tenet sits on several boards, and in 2007 released his memoir entitled *At the Center of the Storm: My Years at the CIA*. In December 2004, President Bush awarded him the Presidential Medal of Freedom.

TERRORISM. The term *terrorism* originated with the French Revolution (1789), when factions opposed to the monarchy and the Catholic Church used violence, fear, and intimidation to gain political power. Terrorism signifies violent acts perpetrated by groups to instill fear in the general population and coerce political authorities to accede to their demands. By a General Assembly resolution passed in 1999, the **United Nations** (UN) condemned terrorism as "criminal acts intended or calculated to provoke a state of terror in the general public," and found such acts unjustifiable "whatever the considerations of a political, philosophical, ideological, racial, ethnic, religious or other nature that may be invoked to justify them."

During the presidency of **George W. Bush,** terrorism was most often linked to groups in the Middle East that oppose US foreign policy and US support for the state of **Israel**. In the past, the United States considered (and continues to consider) groups such as **al-Qaeda, Hamas, Hezbollah,** the **Palestine Liberation Organization** (PLO), and the **Taliban** as terrorist organizations.

Following the **11 September 2001 terrorist** attacks on the **World Trade Center** in New York and the **Pentagon** in Washington, D.C., President George W. Bush launched an indefinite **War on Terror**. It began with the October 2001 US-led invasion of **Afghanistan**, which toppled the Taliban regime. The Taliban had given safe harbor to **al-Qaeda** terrorists, including **Osama bin Laden**. In his 2002 State of the Union address, Bush argued that **Iran, Iraq,** and **North Korea** constituted an **axis of evil** because the countries were allegedly pursuing **weapons of mass destruction** (WMDs). The address was the harbinger of the **War in Iraq,** which toppled the regime of Iraqi dictator **Saddam Hussein**, as well as diplomatic efforts to halt nuclear weapons programs in Iran and North Korea.

Since 1979, the US Department of State has identified regimes that support terrorist organizations as "state sponsors of terror." As of January 2009, these include **Syria** (since 1979), Cuba (since 1982), **Iran** (since 1984), and **Sudan** (since 1993). Countries that were eventually removed from the list under the administration of George W. Bush include Afghanistan, **Iraq**, **Libya**, and **North Korea**. Libyan leader Mu'ammar Gadahfi denounced terrorism, and full diplomatic relations were reestablished with the United States after he ended the WMD program. In 2008, North Korea was removed from the list when the country announced it would allow international inspections of it nuclear facilities. *See also* BALI, INDONESIA; BESLAN, RUSSIA; BIOTERRORISM; MUMBAI, INDIA; PEARL, DANIEL; TERRORISM INFORMATION AND PREVENTION SYSTEM.

TERRORISM INFORMATION AND PREVENTION SYSTEM (TIPs). This program was first suggested by President **George W. Bush** in 2002, and was supported by Attorney General **John Ashcroft**. The TIPs program was to elicit mail carriers, government employees, and ordinary citizens to report suspicious and potentially **terrorist** activities to the government. The program was roundly criticized by civil libertarians, who were concerned about privacy issues and Fourth Amendment constitutional provisions regarding searches and seizures. The program was specifically banned in the Homeland Security Act of 2002, passed by Congress, which created the **Department of Homeland Security**.

TERRORIST. A terrorist is anyone who engages in acts of **terrorism** or violent actions, individually or as a group, to achieve political goals. Common examples of terrorist acts include kidnapping, torturing, murdering, and raping individuals, as well as bombing civilian or military targets (airplanes, ships, government offices, military bases). In the Middle East, many Islamic extremist groups, such as **al-Qaeda**, justify terrorist acts by invoking an interpretation of the Koran that supports **jihad**, or holy war. *See also* AFGHANISTAN; BIN LADEN, OSAMA; TALIBAN; WAR IN IRAQ; WAR ON TERROR.

THOMPSON, TOMMY GEORGE (1941–). A native of Elroy, Wisconsin, Thompson holds a law degree from the University of Wisconsin. He entered politics in 1966 by winning a seat in the Wisconsin legislature, where he served two decades. He served four terms as governor of Wisconsin from 1987 to 2001, and during his tenure he built a nationwide reputation for welfare reform. Thompson served as President George W. Bush's first secretary of health and human services. He resigned in January 2005 and was succeeded by Mike Leavitt.

Thompson made an unsuccessful bid for the Republican presidential nomination in 2008. He dropped out of the race in August 2007 after placing sixth in the **Iowa Caucuses**. He threw his support to candidate **Rudy Giuliani**, but later supported **John McCain** after Giuliani's exit from the primaries. Thompson serves as president of a health-care company and sits on several boards.

TIKRIT, IRAQ. This town of approximately 250,000 lies to the north of **Baghdad, Iraq,** and is the birthplace of Iraqi dictator **Saddam Hussein**. It is located at the northern point of the so-called **Sunni Triangle**. In the US-led invasion of Iraq in March 2003, the town fell quickly as US and coalition forces overran Hussein's Republican Guard. Hussein was captured not far from Tikrit in December 2003. Following the invasion, however, Tikrit became a base for significant **insurgent** attacks on US and coalition forces and was not secured until late 2005.

TORA BORA. Located in eastern **Afghanistan** near the border with **Pakistan**, Tora Bora is a rugged mountainous area with a series of caves. The caves served as a hiding place and base for offensive military actions by the **Taliban** following the US-led invasion of Afghanistan in October 2001. Intelligence suggested that **al-Qaeda** leader **Osama bin Laden** may have been in hiding there, although he was not captured. The area nonetheless was subject to some of the most intense battles between US forces and remnants of the **Taliban** between October and December 2001. This battle alone claimed an estimated 200 US soldiers' lives. The area remained a hotbed of **insurgency** as Taliban fighters regrouped. US forces took more definitive control of the area following Operation Anaconda in early spring 2002. *See also* INTERNATIONAL SECURITY ASSISTANCE FORCE; NORTHERN ALLIANCE.

TORTURE. The **Geneva Conventions** of the **United Nations** (UN), to which the United States is a signatory, define torture as "any act by which severe pain or suffering, whether physical or mental, is intentionally inflicted on a person for such purposes as obtaining from him or a third person information or a confession, punishing him for an act he or a third person has committed or is suspected of having committed, or intimidating or coercing him or a third person, or for any reason based on discrimination of any kind, when such pain or suffering is inflicted by or at the instigation of or with the consent or acquiescence of a public official or other person acting in an official capacity. It does not include pain or suffering arising only from, inherent in, or incidental to lawful sanctions."

The issue of torture plagued the administration of **George W. Bush** in connection with the **War in Iraq** and the **War on Terror** more generally. Critics charged that suspected **terrorists** and **enemy combatants** captured in **Afghanistan** and **Iraq** and held in Iraq or **Guantanamo Bay, Cuba**, were subject to controversial interrogation techniques that contravened the Geneva Conventions, including sleep deprivation and simulated drowning (**waterboarding**). Suspicions grew as the Bush administration refused to allow international organizations to monitor detainees' conditions at Guantanamo Bay and with revelations of a policy of **rendition**, or sending detainees to so-called "black sites" in Central and Eastern European countries where they were interrogated outside US civilian or military jurisdictional control.

The most dramatic case of torture dominated national and international news in 2003 when stunning video of the degrading treatment of detainees at the prison in **Abu Ghraib**, Iraq, at the hands of private Lynndie England surfaced. England and others who engaged in the mistreatment of prisoners were tried and convicted.

Concerns over Bush administration policy compelled 2008 Republican nominee and Arizona Senator **John McCain** to sponsor the **Detainee Treatment Act**, which passed Congress as an amendment to the 2005 defense appropriations bill. The amendment made inhumane treatment of prisoners illegal and forbade interrogation techniques not in line with the US Army Field Manual on Interrogation. The amendment did not sanction the right to **habeas corpus** by detainees who were non-US citizens. In a **signing statement**, President Bush seemingly challenged the provisions of the amendment, contending that he would interpret the provisions relative to his constitutional obligation as commander in chief to protect the nation from future terrorist attacks. *See also* AMNESTY INTERNATIONAL; *BOUME-DIENE V. BUSH* (2008); *HAMDAN V. RUMSFELD* (2006); *HAMDI V. RUMSFELD* (2004); MILITARY COMMISSIONS ACT (2006); MILITARY TRIBUNALS; ZUBAYDAH, ABU.

TROUBLED ASSETS RELIEF PROGRAM (TARP). The Troubled Assets Relief Program was adopted by Congress in late 2008 to aid failing banks in the wake of the **sub-prime mortgage** crisis. The program grew out of earlier attempts by the federal government to shore up investment firms including **Bear Stearns** and **American International Group** (AIG), among others, as **Federal Reserve** chair **Ben Bernanke** sought to infuse cash into the banking system. TARP authorized the Department of Treasury to secure up to $700 million in assets held by banks — in particular mortgage-backed securities — as homeowners who had purchased adjustable rate mortgages (ARMs) and other types of loans began defaulting on them.

The first half of the $700 billion was made available in 2008. Critics contended that banks did not use the funds in ways contemplated by lawmakers — namely to aid homeowners facing foreclosures and to ease the availability of credit to ensure the stability of financial markets. Moreover, critics charged that the bill did little to halt the economic downturn. *See also* BERNANKE, BEN; HOUSING AND ECONOMIC RECOVERY ACT (2008); LEHMAN BROTHERS; PAULSON, HENRY MERRITT; WASHINGTON MUTUAL.

TSUNAMI. Tsunamis create large waves and are typically generated by earthquakes at the bottom of the ocean. On 26 December 2004, a major tsunami developed in the Indian Ocean. The waves devastated parts of Indonesia and Thailand while also affecting India, Sri Lanka, and other countries bordering the Indian Ocean. Estimates suggest that more than 200,000 people died in the natural disaster. International aid and relief efforts were bolstered by former Presidents **William Clinton** and **George H.W. Bush**, who appeared together on television and in other venues to raise funds for the victims. The disaster also incited the **United Nations** to undertake plans for an Indian Ocean tsunami warning system in 2005. *See also* USA FREEDOM CORPS.

TURKEY. This Eurasian country straddles Asia and Europe across the Bosporus. A moderate Muslim country with a tradition of secular governments, Turkey has been a member of the **North Atlantic Treaty Organization** (NATO) since 1952. In 2005, Turkey opened negotiations to consider joining the **European Union**.

Relations between the United States and Turkey came under some strain with the **War in Iraq**. Turkey feared an independent **Kurdistan** breaking away from **Iraq** that might spur Kurdish separatists within its own borders to clamor for independence. The Turkish military attacked purported strongholds of the **PKK**, or Kurdistan Workers Party, based across the border in northern Iraq in 2007. Turkey contended that the rebel group was launching guerrilla attacks from Iraq into Turkish territory. The administration of **George W. Bush** cautioned Turkey to temper its response to **insurgents** for fear of destabilizing the region.

TYCO CORPORATION. An international corporation based in New Jersey that specializes in fire prevention services, home protection services, and manufacturing, Tyco was front and center of several corporate scandals during the presidency of **George W. Bush**. In 2004, it was revealed that two Tyco executives, **Dennis Kozlowski** and Mark Swartz, stood accused of bilking nearly $600 million from the corporation. Both were convicted on theft charges and were sentenced to prison.

– U –

UNITARY EXECUTIVE THEORY. *See* ADDINGTON, DAVID S.; CHENEY, RICHARD B. (DICK); SIGNING STATEMENTS.

UNITED NATIONS (UN). Established on 24 October 1945, the United Nations (UN) is an international organization originally devoted to preventing conflicts between nations. Its mission has been expanded to include human rights monitoring, and the development and promotion of democracy. As of 2009, 192 countries belong to the UN. **China, France, Russia, Great Britain**, and the United States constitute the five nations with permanent membership on the Security Council. Any one of these countries can veto a resolution on such issues as the imposition of economic sanctions or military action contemplated by the UN.

Conflict between the United States and member nations of the UN was thrown into the spotlight on several occasions during the presidency of **George W. Bush**. The first major conflict was over the eventual **War in Iraq**. Iraqi dictator **Saddam Hussein** had forced UN weapons inspectors out of the country in 2002. Bush considered Hussein an imminent threat, part of an **axis of evil** alongside **Iran** and **North Korea**, insofar as he believed Hussein's regime was pursuing **weapons of mass destruction** (WMDs). In November 2002, the UN did adopt **United Nations Resolution 1441**, which warned that **Iraq** would face "serious consequences" for failing to comply with its obligations under the 1991 cease-fire agreement following the **Persian Gulf War**. But when Hussein continued to balk at allowing weapons inspectors to return to Iraq by early 2003, Bush sought UN approval to take military action. He was unable to secure agreement, however. The United States and France disagreed on which types of action constituted "serious consequences." French President **Jacques Chirac** preferred economic sanctions and vowed to veto any Security Council resolution on military action. Secretary of State **Colin Powell** made a forceful case before the UN—whatever his personal reservations about war with Iraq—but those arguments did not convince some of the United States' long-standing allies in the UN or the **North Atlantic Treaty Organization** (NATO), including **Germany**'s Chancellor **Gerhard Schröder**. Russia and China also opposed military intervention.

Bush subsequently arrayed a **Coalition of the Willing**—countries that included **Australia, Great Britain, Poland**, and a host of others—to invade Iraq **preemptive**ly in March 2003 and oust Hussein. The Bush administration linked Hussein's regime to the **al-Qaeda terrorist**s responsible for the **11 September 2001** attacks on the **World Trade Center** in New York and the **Pentagon** in Washington, D.C. The intelligence suggesting those links was not substantiated, nor were WMDs ever found after the invasion.

Many critics of the Bush administration suggest that the invasion of Iraq without UN approval was part of a larger **neoconservative foreign policy** that denigrated the utility of international organizations. A backlash developed in Congress, which would not confirm **John Bolton** to the position of US ambassador to the UN, forcing Bush to make him a "recess appointment."

The UN's detractors contended that the organization—as well as the Bush administration—did too little to intervene in another major conflict during Bush's presidency, the civil war in **Sudan**. Secretary of State Colin Powell argued that the slaughter of civilians, many **women** and children, in the **Darfur** region of the country at the hands of government-backed *janjaweed* militias constituted genocide.

However, in many other issues that the UN confronted significant international cooperation and consensus were achieved. Following the US and NATO-led invasion of **Afghanistan** in October 2001 that toppled the **Taliban** regime, the UN quickly approved the **International Security Assistance Force** (ISAF), which was charged with rebuilding Afghanistan and ensuring political stability. The UN also coordinated an international disaster relief program to aid victims of the 2004 tsunami that devastated countries that bordered the Indian Ocean, including Indonesia, Thailand, India, and Sri Lanka. In 2006, the UN implemented a tsunami warning system for the region.

International cooperation was also evident in other venues with respect to the UN's specialized agencies. The World Health Organization played an important role in coordinating an international response to outbreaks of Asian bird flu and severe acute respiratory syndrome (SARS) in Asia. Before and after the War in Iraq, the **International Atomic Energy Agency** (IAEA) monitored WMD programs in Iran and provided vital information. In addition, under Secretary General **Kofi Annan**, UNICEF, the UN's agency concerned with women, children, and poverty, targeted the plight of individuals in the developing world, including **acquired immune deficiency syndrome** (AIDS) in Africa. The **International Criminal Court** (ICC) and the International Criminal Tribunal for the former Yugoslavia pursued alleged war criminals from conflicts spanning Africa to the war in **Yugoslavia** in the 1990s. Finally, the United States dominated the World Bank, which was headed by two key **neoconservatives** in the Bush administration, **Paul Wolfowitz** and **Robert Zoellick**.

During Bush's two terms, the US ambassadors to the UN were **John Negroponte** (2001–2004), John Danforth (2004–2005), John Bolton (interim, 2005–2006), and Zalmay Khalilzad (2007–2008).

Ban Ki-moon of South Korea became UN secretary general in January 2007. *See also* BLAIR, TONY; BUSH DOCTRINE; DOWNING STREET MEMO; HOWARD, JOHN; INTERNATIONAL ATOMIC ENERGY AGENCY; INTERNATIONAL CRIMINAL COURT; TORTURE; UNITED NATIONS RESOLUTION 1441; VIERA DE MELLO, SÉRGIO.

UNITED NATIONS RESOLUTION 1441. This resolution, adopted by the **United Nations** (UN) Security Council on 8 November 2002, was an ultimatum to Iraqi dictator **Saddam Hussein** to allow UN weapons inspectors to return to **Iraq** to verify that he was not pursuing **weapons of mass destruction** (WMDs) per the terms of the cease-fire of 1991 following the **Persian Gulf War**. The Resolution also took issue with Hussein's use of the **Oil for Food Program** and his failure to compensate Kuwait for the destruction Iraq's invasion of that country had caused in 1990. The Resolution cited that a further "material breach" of Iraq's obligations would be met with "serious consequences."

A dispute erupted between members of the Security Council. The main controversy centered on the interpretation of "serious consequences." President **George W. Bush** advocated a military invasion of Iraq, a course that was backed by **Great Britain**. **China**, **Russia**, and France opposed military intervention. French President **Jacques Chirac** proposed economic sanctions and vowed to veto any resolution authorizing military action. In the absence of a UN authorization, the United States and Great Britain led an invasion of Iraq with a **Coalition of the Willing** in March 2003 that ultimately toppled Hussein's regime. No WMDs were found following the invasion.

USA FREEDOM CORPS. Housed within the **Executive Office of the President** (EOP), the USA Freedom Corps was created by **George W. Bush** on 30 January 2002 through an executive order. The organization, which included a council chaired by the president and a director responsible for day-to-day affairs, was charged with identifying and promoting volunteer opportunities. It was through the USA Freedom Corps that President Bush used his father, former President **George H.W. Bush**, and former President **William Clinton**, to raise awareness of and funds for the victims of the **tsunami**

that devastated Indonesia and other countries in the Indian Ocean on 26 December 2004.

USS *GREENVILLE*. This U.S. Navy submarine struck a Japanese fishing boat called the *Ehime Maru* off the coast of Oahu, Hawaii, on 9 February 2001. The collision was caused when the submarine let off its ballast from the main tank. The Japanese ship sank within minutes. Nine of the *Ehime Maru*'s crew died. The commander of the *Greenville* was not court-martialed but accepted full responsibility and retired after the incident. The U.S. government paid more than $25 million to the Japanese government and to the families of the victims.

– V –

VENEMAN, ANN MARGARET (1949–). A native of Modesto, California, Veneman holds an undergraduate degree from the University of California, Davis, a master's degree from the University of California, Berkeley, and a law degree from the University of California (Hastings College of Law). She began a public service career with the Bay Area Rapid Transit (BART) system in the San Francisco Bay area in the 1970s. She worked for the US Department of Agriculture in the 1980s, helping to negotiate elements of the General Agreement on Tariffs and Trade (GATT) and serving as deputy secretary before joining the California Department of Agriculture as secretary.

President **George W. Bush** appointed Veneman as secretary of agriculture in January 2001, and she served through his first term. In January 2005, she was appointed by **United Nations** Secretary General **Kofi Annan** to head the United Nations Children's Fund, which aids children and **women** with humanitarian aid and relief.

VENEZUELA. This coastal country in northern South America has a population of approximately 28 million and is rich in oil reserves. Venezuela is the fifth-largest petroleum exporting country in the world. As of 2008, Venezuela is the fourth-largest exporter of oil to the United States behind **Canada**, Saudi Arabia, and **Mexico**, respectively.

Tensions between the United States and Venezuela were palpable during the presidency of **George W. Bush**. Venezuela's charismatic socialist leader, **Hugo Chávez**, was an ardent critic of the Bush administration's **foreign policy**. He accused the Bush administration of "neocolonialism" and, in a dramatic speech in the **United Nations** (UN) in 2006, called Bush "el Diablo," or the devil. Working with other oil-producing nations, Chávez worked to ensure high oil prices beginning in 2002. His announcement that Venezuela would import arms from **Russia** in 2006, followed by joint military maneuvers with Russia off the coast of Venezuela in 2008, further strained bilateral relations.

VIEIRA DE MELLO, SÉRGIO (1948–2003). A Brazilian national, Vieira was a prominent career official with the **United Nations** (UN). He started his career in 1969, working for programs concerning refugees and the clearing of land mines in southeast Asia, and he was a special envoy to **Kosovo** in 1999. He was killed on 19 August 2003, in a bombing by **insurgents** at the Canal Hotel in **Baghdad**, **Iraq**. The bomb targeted the UN assistance mission to Iraq, which had been created just five days earlier. Twenty-one others were killed in the bombing. A second bombing in September 2003 forced the UN to close the mission. *See also* WAR IN IRAQ.

VIRGINIA TECH UNIVERSITY. Formally known as the Virginia Polytechnic Institute and State University, the campus is located in Blacksburg, Virginia. There are more than 1,300 faculty and 30,000 students. On 16 April 2007, Seung-Hui Cho, a Korean student attending the university, engaged in a bloody shooting rampage. Cho, who suffered from mental disorders, used firearms to kill 32 students and faculty in a two-hour-long massacre before taking his own life. The incident was the worst shooting at a postsecondary institution in US history.

VOLCKER, PAUL ADOLPH (1927–). A native of Cape May, New Jersey, he earned an undergraduate degree from Princeton (1949), a master's degree in economics from Harvard University (1951), and was a fellow at the London School of Economics. He worked as an economist for the **Federal Reserve** Board of New York in the 1950s and for the US Department of the Treasury in the 1960s. From 1969 to 1974, he served as undersecretary for the Treasury Department. He was president of the Federal Reserve Board of New York from 1974 to 1979. In 1979, President Jimmy Carter appointed him as chair of the Federal Reserve system. President **Ronald Reagan** reappointed him in 1983. He was succeeded by **Alan Greenspan** in 1987.

The **United Nations** (UN) appointed Volcker to head an investigation of alleged corruption surrounding the UN **Oil for Food Program** in **Iraq**. While his final report did not allege improper influence between the UN and the company for which Secretary General **Kofi Annan**'s son worked (Swiss-based Cotecna, Inc.), Volcker's report did call into question the UN secretary general's overall management.

Volcker supported the presidential candidacy of Democrat **Barack Obama** in 2008. Upon Obama's victory in November 2008, Volcker became one of Obama's key economic advisors, and chairs the president's Economic Recovery Advisory Board.

– W –

WALTER REED ARMY MEDICAL CENTER. Located in Bethesda, Maryland, the Walter Reed Army Medical Center is the US Army's premier medical facility. It provides medical care to active and retired military personnel. The facility was at the center of a scandal when the *Washington Post* newspaper ran a series of stories outlining alleged neglect and inadequate treatment of soldiers. Secretary of Defense **Robert Gates** took immediate action, and the commanding officer of the facility, Major General George Weightman, was subsequently fired in the wake of the revelations. The internal management of the care provided to soldiers was the subject of a congressional investigation, and President **George W. Bush** also appointed a Commission on Care for America's Returning Wounded Soldiers, headed by former secretary of health and human services Donna Shalala and former senator and Republican presidential nominee Robert (Bob) Dole to recommend reforms.

WALTERS, JOHN P. (1952–). A graduate of Michigan State University and the University of Toronto, Walters served as an assistant to the secretary of education under President **Ronald Reagan**. In the administration of **George H.W. Bush**, he served as chief of staff to William Bennett, the first "drug czar" or director of the **Office of National Drug Control Policy** (ONDCP). From 1996 to 2001, he was president of the Philanthropy Roundtable, an organization that promotes volunteerism and fund-raising. President **George W. Bush** tapped Walters to head the ONDCP in 2001, and he remained in that post throughout Bush's two terms. Walters's major efforts centered on drug prevention among youths, the eradication of coca fields in Colombia, and the interdiction of drugs from **Mexico**.

WAR IN IRAQ. The US-led invasion of **Iraq** commenced on 20 March 2003. A **Coalition of the Willing**—including Australia, Denmark, **Great Britain**, Spain, and **Poland**—supported the military invasion that toppled the regime of **Saddam Hussein**. On 1 May 2003, President **George W. Bush** announced the termination of major military operations. The occupation of Iraq continued, however, beyond the end of Bush's second term. A bilateral agreement between the United States and Iraq mandates the departure of US forces in 2011.

The roots of the invasion date to January 2002 when, in his State of the Union address, Bush contended that **Iran**, **Iraq**, and **North Korea** formed an **axis of evil** for these regimes' pursuit of **weapons of mass destruction** (WMDs). Bush asserted that Iraq had attempted to obtain uranium for its WMD program from **Niger**, a claim that was later refuted. Nonetheless, the speech marked an expansion of the **War on Terror** precipitated by the **11 September 2001 terrorist** attacks on New York City and the **Pentagon** in Washington, D.C. By September 2002, the Bush administration and Secretary of State **Colin Powell** began making a case to the **United Nations** (UN) that Iraqi dictator **Saddam Hussein**, who had expelled UN weapons inspectors, was not complying with the post-**Persian Gulf War** settlement of 1991 and had begun to stockpile chemical, biological, and other weapons. The UN adopted **United Nations Resolution 1441**, which mandated that Hussein comply with the agreement or face "serious consequences." UN chief weapons inspector **Hans Blix** and head of the **International Atomic Energy Agency** (IAEA) returned to Iraq in early 2003 but found no evidence of WMDs. Nonetheless, the US Congress authorized potential military action against Iraq in October 2002 by adopting the **Iraq War Resolution**.

Between October 2002 and March 2003, the Bush administration attempted to build a case that not only had Hussein stockpiled WMDs, but he had supported **terrorism** and **al-Qaeda**. The intelligence evidence was thin, as the British **Downing Street Memo**, leaked in 2005, revealed. In early 2003, the United States and other members of the UN Security Council—notably **Russia** and France—sparred over UN Resolution 1441 and the meaning of "serious consequences." French President **Jacques Chirac** ultimately threatened to veto any UN authorization of military action in March 2003.

Bush's decision to use unilateral force in Iraq and precipitate "regime change" solidified the so-called **Bush Doctrine**, a **neoconservative** approach to **foreign policy**. The United States would use force if international institutions or other countries declined to do so. Moreover, the United States would act preemptively when faced with an imminent threat to national security. **Preemptive warfare** conflicted with the policy of containment that had been used against the **Soviet Union** during the **Cold War**. A policy of containment had also been adopted against Iraq following the Persian Gulf War, as British and US forces imposed "no-fly" zones on Hussein's regime to guarantee he could not threaten neighbors in the Middle East.

The initial invasion—guided by overwhelming force, or **shock and awe**—devastated Iraq's army within six weeks, despite heavy fighting in areas like **Al-Anbar** Province. During the initial invasion, 139 US casualties occurred. Iraqi civilian and military casualties exceeded an estimated 16,000. However, 90 percent of all US and Iraqi casualties occurred after Bush declared an end to major military operations. Through December 2008, US deaths numbered 4,139 with more than 30,000 wounded. Iraqi civil deaths are estimated conservatively at more than 80,000.

The high toll on US forces and Iraqi civilians stemmed from a growing **insurgency** that began in 2004, and, according to some critics, a lack of **body armor** to protect troops. **Basra**, in the southern part of Iraq, and Najaf, in south-central Iraq, became hotbeds of insurgent activity. US forces battled **Muqtada al-Sadr**'s **Mahdi Army** in Najaf in 2004 until **Ayatollah Ali al-Sistani** successfully persuaded the Mahdi Army to turn in its arms. By 2007, the escalating violence from seemingly daily, random bombings and **improvised explosive devices** (IEDs) in **Baghdad, Mosul**, and in less populated parts of Iraq convinced Bush that a troop "surge" had become necessary. Some 20,000 additional US forces were sent to Iraq. Their success in quelling the violence was most notable in securing Baghdad and the so-called **Green Zone**, site of the new US Embassy and most international workers connected to the effort of rebuilding Iraq. In January 2008, Iraqi security forces battled with some success remnants of the Mahdi militia in Basra in a large-scale operation.

Critics contend that the War in Iraq was unnecessary and based on faulty intelligence or faulty interpretation of intelligence. Following the invasion, UN weapons inspector **David Kay** returned to Iraq and found no evidence of stockpiles of WMDs. Some critics charge that the invasion was a foregone conclusion in the minds of many of Bush's foreign policy advisors. Vice President **Richard B. (Dick) Cheney**, his chief of staff **I. Lewis (Scooter) Libby**, Secretary of Defense **Donald Rumsfeld**, Deputy Secretary of Defense **Paul Wolfowitz**, Deputy Secretary of State **Richard Armitage**, and Undersecretary of State and later UN Ambassador **John Bolton** were members of the **Project for the New American Century** (PNAC). Members of the PNAC think tank wrote a forceful letter to President William Clinton in 1998 urging military action to remove Saddam Hussein from power. Others, including former ambassador **Joseph Wilson**, disputed the administration's claims that Hussein had attempted to procure uranium from African countries. Finally, critics charged that no proven linkage existed between Hussein and the terrorist organization al-Qaeda. However, much of the post-invasion insurgency stemmed from an unpatrolled border with Iran over which many al-Qaeda operatives poured to oppose US forces.

One eventual political casualty of the War in Iraq was Secretary of Defense **Rumsfeld**. He was criticized by many, including Senator **John McCain**, for inadequate planning of the post-invasion phase of the military operations and for failing to send enough troops to secure peace. Rumsfeld resigned his post shortly after the **mid-term elections** of 2006. He was succeeded by **Robert Gates**. Another long-term political casualty was Bush's public approval. As the casualties mounted in Iraq, his job approval began to sink into the 40s beginning in 2005 and never recovered.

It was against the backdrop of increased violence by insurgents that a new Iraqi government set out to develop democratic institutions. Following the invasion, the United States set up the **Coalition Provisional Authority**, led first by **Jay Garner** and then his successor, **L. Paul Bremer**, to administer postwar Iraq. Power was transferred to the **Iraq Governing Council** in late 2003, a provisional government that included a new cadre of Iraqi leaders such as **Ahmed Chalabi**, **Jalal Talabani**, **Ibrahim al-Jaafari**, Ghazi Mashal Ajil al-Yawer, and **Iyad Allawi**. In 2005, Iraq held its first free elections and achieved some level of balance between **Sunni**, Shi'ite, and **Kurd**ish populations in a new parliamentary system headed by the government of **Nouri al-Maliki**. In January 2009, regional elections took place and were largely successful insofar as sustained violence was not a major factor. *See also* ARMED FORCES; BODY ARMOR; PREEMPTION.

WAR ON TERROR. The **11 September 2001 terrorist** attacks on New York and the **Pentagon** heralded the beginning of the War on Terror. The term connotes the general mobilization of governmental, diplomatic, and military resources in the administration of **George W. Bush** to prevent another major terrorist attack on US soil or on US interests overseas. Shortly after the 9/11 attacks, Congress passed the **Authorization for the Use of Military Force** (AUMF) legislation. The bill formed a key component of the so-called **Bush Doctrine** that the United States would take military action not only against terrorist organizations but also against those foreign governments that support them. Bush used the AUMF to lead an international force that invaded **Afghanistan** in October 2001 and toppled the **Taliban** regime, which had given **al-Qaeda** terrorists responsible for 9/11, including **Osama bin Laden** and **Abu Zubaydah**, safe haven to run terrorist training camps.

Bush broadened the War on Terror in his State of the Union address in January 2002, in which he called **Iraq**, **Iran**, and **North Korea** an **axis of evil** for these regimes pursuit of **weapons of mass destruction** (WMDs). Efforts at diplomatic sanctions against the three regimes were stepped up in the **United Nations** (UN). However, Iraqi dictator **Saddam Hussein**'s refusal to cooperate with UN weapons inspectors and comply with the post-**Persian Gulf War** settlement prompted Bush to contend, based on intelligence reports, that Hussein had stockpiled WMDs. Bush also asserted that Hussein had links with al-Qaeda, which were never proven.

The US-led invasion of Iraq confirmed two other facets of the Bush Doctrine that reflected a **neoconservative foreign policy**. The first was that the United States would act unilaterally against alleged state sponsors of terror if the UN and international institutions failed to do so. Bush was unable to procure a consensus on Iraq in the UN relative to **UN Resolution 1441**'s language that Hussein's failure to comply with weapons inspectors would lead to "serious consequences." French President **Jacques Chirac** opposed military intervention and threatened to veto any move by the United States for a military invasion. As a result, Bush eschewed the UN and assembled a **Coalition of the Willing** to invade Iraq.

The second additional element to the Bush Doctrine was the assertion that the United States had the right and responsibility to act preemptively to protect the national interest if an attack was deemed imminent. Despite questionable intelligence surrounding Hussein's WMD program, including the **Downing Street Memo**, Bush took military action, toppled Hussein's government, and imposed regime change in Iraq. This element of the Bush Doctrine conflicted with the doctrine of containment, which had been used against the **Soviet Union** during the **Cold War** and against Iraq following the Persian Gulf War to preclude Hussein from threatening his neighbors. Containment presumes military and diplomatic efforts to halt the expansion of rogue regimes. The **North Atlantic Treaty Organization** (NATO) was created as a buffer to halt potential military aggression by the Soviets into Western Europe. The "no-fly" zones imposed on Hussein's regime and enforced by **George H.W. Bush** and **William Clinton** are another example of a strategy of containment.

One central controversy surrounding the War on Terror included the detention of **enemy combatants** captured in Afghanistan and held at **Guantanamo Bay, Cuba**. Bush contended that detainees were illegal foreign enemy combatants who did not belong to a national army and were therefore not subject to the **Geneva Conventions**' protections as prisoners of war. Some detainees at Guantanamo, as well as others who were subject to **rendition** and interrogated by the **Central Intelligence Agency** (CIA) in so-called "black sites" outside the United States, contended they had been subjected to **torture**, including **waterboarding** or simulated drowning. Bush confirmed the use of "enhanced interrogation techniques" in 2006. Further, Bush planned to try the detainees before **military tribunals** and contended that the detainees had no recourse to civilian courts in the United States.

The Bush administration suffered a number of legal setbacks concerning detainees at Guantanamo. In *Rasul v. Bush* (2004), the **Supreme Court** ruled that detainees did have recourse to US civilian courts to challenge their detention. In *Hamdi v. Rumsfeld* (2004), the High Court confirmed that enemy combatants could be detained, but US citizens who were detained at Guantanamo had the right to **habeas corpus** (to have their case heard before a judge). In *Hamdan v. Rumsfeld* (2006), the Supreme Court struck down the military tribunals set up by the president, asserting that they violated the Uniform Code of Military Justice, as well as the Geneva Conventions. Congress subsequently passed the **Military Commissions Act** (2006) authorizing tribunals. In *Boumediene v. Bush* (2008), the Supreme Court struck down the Act, contending that the law violated rights to habeas corpus and reconfirming that detainees were subject to constitutional protections.

The "enhanced interrogation techniques" of the Bush administration, which detractors contended were tantamount to torture, prompted congressional action. In late 2005, Congress passed the **Detainee Treatment Act** sponsored by Arizona Senator and former Vietnam veteran prisoner of war **John McCain**. The act prohibited the inhumane treatment of prisoners and held that all interrogations were to be consistent with the US Army Field Manual. At the same time, the bill did not lend the right to habeas corpus to detainees. Bush challenged the law and argued that he would interpret its provisions vis-à-vis his constitutional authority as commander in chief to gather intelligence to thwart future terrorist attacks.

The War on Terror also had palpable implications for the civil liberties of US citizens. One controversy centered on **José Padilla**, a self-described sympathizer of al-Qaeda who planned a "dirty bomb" attack and was arrested by federal authorities in 2002. Padilla was held as a "material witness" and enemy combatant without charge. As such, he did not have recourse to the Sixth Amendment right to counsel or to habeas corpus. Critics charged that his indefinite detention was unconstitutional. Padilla was transferred to a military facility in South

Carolina, where he was held for five years. The matter was not put to rest until Padilla was ultimately charged on 11 counts, convicted in 2007, and sentenced to federal prison.

Other elements of the War on Terror domestically troubled civil libertarians. The **PATRIOT Act**, passed by Congress in October 2001, buttressed law enforcement agencies' ability to gather intelligence, detain immigrants indefinitely, and allow them to search electronic communications and financial records without a court order. Further, revelations by the *New York Times* in 2005 that the **National Security Agency** (NSA) had engaged in warrantless **wiretapping** of foreign nationals—including those in communication with US citizens—in violation of the **Foreign Intelligence Surveillance Act** (FISA) prompted one member of the FISA Court to resign in protest. Bush contended that the AUMF legislation authorized such actions. In 2007, Congress passed the **Protect America Act**, which clarified the process for complying with FISA requirements. *See also*; POWELL, COLIN; PROJECT FOR THE NEW AMERICAN CENTURY; RICE, CONDOLEEZZA.

WARSAW PACT. Signed on 14 May 1955, the Warsaw Pact was the military alliance of Eastern European countries under the aegis of Soviet domination during the **Cold War**. The Warsaw Pact was aimed at the Western alliance of the **North Atlantic Treaty Organization** (NATO) members. Members of the Warsaw Pact included **Bulgaria**, Czechoslovakia (now the independent nations of **Czech Republic** and **Slovakia**), East **Germany**, **Hungary**, **Poland**, and **Romania**. As with NATO signatories, the Warsaw Pact nations pledged to come to the aid of other member nations if attacked. The Warsaw Pact was formally dissolved on 1 July 1991, following the collapse of Communist regimes throughout Central and Eastern Europe, predating the eventual collapse of the **Soviet Union** in December 1991.

Many former Warsaw Pact nations have joined the **European Union** and NATO. **Russia** has opposed NATO membership, in particular, as a threat to its traditional sphere of influence. Russian President **Vladimir Putin** firmly opposed President **George W. Bush**'s plans to put an **anti-ballistic missile** system in Poland and the Czech Republic, and went so far as to suggest that European nations might be targeted by the Russian nuclear arsenal if the project went forward. *See also* GEORGIA; MEDVEDEV, DMITRI ANATOLYEVICH; STRATEGIC OFFENSIVE REDUCTION TREATY.

WASHINGTON MUTUAL. This lending institution, with assets of more than $300 billion, was one of the first major banks to fail in the wake of the **sub-prime mortgage crisis** that peaked in September 2008. Due to large-scale withdrawals from Washington Mutual, the Federal Deposit Insurance Corporation (FDIC) placed the bank in receivership and subsequently sold its assets to JP Morgan Chase. *See also* BERNANKE, BEN SHALOM; HOUSING AND ECONOMIC RECOVERY ACT (2008); PAULSON, HENRY MERRITT; TROUBLED ASSETS RELIEF PROGRAM (TARP).

WATERBOARDING. This controversial interrogation technique involves simulated drowning. Subjects are restrained and then water is poured over breathing passages to create the sensation of drowning. The technique is believed to date to the Spanish Inquisition.

Waterboarding by the **Central Intelligence Agency** (CIA) of suspected **terrorists** and **enemy combatants** captured following the **11 September 2001** attacks on New York and the Pentagon, the war in **Afghanistan**, and the **War in Iraq** made national and international headlines following a story in the publication *Newsweek* in 2004. The publication contended that the administration of **George W. Bush**, in an internal memo two years earlier, had sanctioned the practice. The memo implicated Attorney General **Alberto Gonzales** as well as Vice President **Richard B. (Dick) Cheney**'s counsel, **David Addington**, as having accepted waterboarding as a useful method of interrogation that was not tantamount to **torture** of prisoners. ABC News reported in 2005 that CIA agents confirmed this "enhanced interrogation method" was used against **al-Qaeda** operatives at secret prison sites or "black sites." Several terror suspects, including **Khalid Sheikh Mohammed** and **Abu Zubaydah**, were confirmed to have been subject to the practice.

International human rights organizations and many civil libertarians criticized the practice and called for its immediate halt. The major question was whether waterboarding violated the **Geneva Conventions** on **torture** of prisoners of war and the Eighth Amendment of the Constitution regarding "cruel and unusual punishment." In 2004, Arizona Senator **John McCain** and other legislators sponsored an amendment to a defense appropriations bill called the **Detainee Treatment Act** that prohibited inhumane treatment of prisoners and limited interrogation techniques to those outlined in the US Army Field Manual. In July 2007, President Bush signed an executive order banning torture. However, many human rights watch groups suggest that neither the Detainee Treatment Act nor the executive order specifically bans waterboarding. On 22 January 2009, by executive order, President **Barack Obama** outlawed the practice. *See also* GUANTANAMO BAY, CUBA; RENDITION.

WAZIRISTAN. This area of northwest **Pakistan** is controlled by tribal leaders and borders **Afghanistan**. The area became a point of controversy in the **War on Terror** as **Taliban** fighters fled to the region. Pakistani soldiers clashed with the Taliban fighters, and some were taken prisoner. When the Taliban stepped up cross-border attacks into Afghanistan, President **George W. Bush** ordered secret raids against the Taliban in Waziristan. Neither President **Pervez Musharraf** nor his successor, **Asif Ali Zadari**, would authorize the United States to hunt for **al-Qaeda** or Taliban operatives within Pakistan's borders. The policy put the United States at odds with Pakistani forces, who were ordered to fire back against US soldiers. The dispute over US operations in the region continued in late 2008 and early 2009, as US forces used automated drones to attack Taliban strongholds from the air. The raids caused a number of deaths, including civilians, sparking continued controversy.

WEAPONS OF MASS DESTRUCTION (WMDs). Weapons of mass destruction may include chemical, biological, and nuclear weapons that can cause catastrophic damage and significant loss of life or long-term injury. WMDs may also include so-called "dirty bombs," which mix conventional explosives with radiological material. The Bush administration remained highly concerned, following the **11 September 2001 terrorist** attacks on New York and the **Pentagon**, that terrorist organizations such as **al-Qaeda** were attempting to procure WMDs.

President **George W. Bush**, in his 2002 State of the Union address, considered three countries—**Iran**, **Iraq**, and **North Korea**—an **axis of evil** for these regimes' quest to develop or procure WMDs. The Bush administration's belief that Iraqi dictator **Saddam Hussein** had procured WMDs prompted a **preemptive** invasion of Iraq led by the United States in March 2003. The supposition that Hussein had stockpiled WMDs—based on faulty intelligence or faulty interpretation of that intelligence—was not vindicated following the invasion. *See also* BIOTERRORISM; GADHAFI, MU'AMMAR; LIBYA; WAR IN IRAQ.

WEST BANK. Bordered by the Dead Sea to the west and the country of Jordan to the east, the West Bank is otherwise bordered by **Israel**. Israel transferred political control of the West Bank and the **Gaza Strip** to the **Palestinian National Authority** in 1994 as part of the Oslo Accords. The West Bank and Gaza are not contiguous.

The West Bank fell under the de facto control of the radical Islamist party **Hamas** following the 2006 elections in the Palestinian Territories. The United States, **Canada**, and the **European Union** considered Hamas a **terrorist** organization and rescinded all international aid. A centerpiece of Hamas's ideology is the call for the destruction of the Israeli state.

In 2007, the president of the Palestinian Authority, **Mahmoud Abbas**—a member of the moderate **Fatah** party who was supported by President **George W. Bush**—declared a state of emergency and dismissed Hamas leader **Ismail Haniya**, who many Palestinians believed was the legitimate prime minister of the Palestinian Authority. Months of fighting in what amounted to a civil war between Hamas and Fatah militias eventually left Haniya in control of the Gaza Strip and Fatah in control of the West Bank. The split in control left a central component of President **George W. Bush**'s **foreign policy** goals in the Middle East, the **Road Map for Peace**, very much in question. *See also* FAYYAD, SALAM; OLMERT, EHUD; SHARON, ARIEL.

WHITMAN, CHRISTINE TODD (1946–). Born in New York City and raised in New Jersey, Whitman is a graduate of Wheaton College

(1968). She entered politics after graduation, working on Republican Nelson Rockefeller's presidential bid and later for the Nixon administration in the Office of Economic Opportunity, where she reported to **Donald Rumsfeld**. She later served in local government in New Jersey and was president of the New Jersey Board of Utilities from 1988 to 1990. Following a failed bid for a US Senate seat in 1990, in 1993 she successfully ran against incumbent Democratic New Jersey Governor Jim Florio and became the first female governor in the state's history. She was re-elected in 1997. Among her most central accomplishments were environmental policies that placed New Jersey in far greater compliance with federal standards on air and water pollution.

President **George W. Bush** appointed Whitman to head the **Environmental Protection Agency** (EPA) in 2001. She was caught up almost immediately in controversy surrounding an EPA rule promulgated by the outgoing administration of **William Clinton** restricting levels of arsenic in drinking water. Following the **11 September 2001 terrorist** attacks on New York and the **Pentagon**, Whitman publicly stated that the debris from the collapse of the **World Trade Center** did not pose immediate risks to residents or firefighters. She testified later about her comments before Congress, and was eventually exempted from a class-action lawsuit brought about by victims of the hazardous material from the collapse of the Twin Towers.

Whitman disagreed most vigorously with the Bush administration on clear air standards and resigned in June 2003. She was succeeded by **Michael Leavitt**. In 2005, she published a book entitled *It's My Party, Too: Taking Back the Republican Party. . . And Bringing the Country Together Again* in which she was critical of the Bush administration, its **neoconservative** philosophy, and its electoral strategy.

WILSON, JOSEPH CHARLES IV (1949–). A Connecticut native, Wilson earned a bachelor's degree from the University of California, Santa Barbara (1971). His career in the foreign service began in 1976. For the next two decades, he was stationed in Niger, Togo, South Africa, Baghdad, Iraq, and Congo, among other places. From 1985 to 1986, he worked as a congressional fellow in the offices of Democrats **Al Gore** and Tom Foley. Prior to the 1991 **Persian Gulf War**, Wilson made international headlines by defying Iraqi dictator **Saddam Hussein**, who pledged to execute anyone harboring "foreigners" in Iraq. In the administration of **William Clinton**, Wilson served as ambassador to Gabon and São Tomé and Príncipe (1992–1995). In 1997, President **William Clinton** appointed Wilson to head African Affairs for the **National Security Council** (NSC). He left public service in 1998 to start his own international capital company.

Wilson supported Al Gore for president in 2000 and **John Kerry** in 2004. In 2002, the **Central Intelligence Agency** (CIA) asked Wilson to conduct a fact-finding mission in Niger to determine whether the Iraqi regime of Saddam Hussein had attempted to procure "yellowcake" uranium toward the production of **weapons of mass destruction** (WMDs). Wilson found no evidence to support the claim. He later publicly took issue with President **George W. Bush**'s contention in his 2003 State of the Union address in which the president contended that Hussein *had* sought significant quantities of uranium from African countries.

Wilson was at the center of controversy when, on 14 July 2003, journalist **Robert Novak** revealed in his column that Wilson's wife, **Valerie Plame** Wilson, was a covert CIA agent. The "outing" of Valerie Plame was subject to a grand jury investigation, caused Plame to resign from the agency in 2005, and was the subject of a federal lawsuit that was later dismissed, and as of 2009, was under appeal. Joseph Wilson had become an active and vocal critic of the **War in Iraq** following the US-led invasion of that country in March 2003. He considered that President Bush, Vice President **Richard B. (Dick) Cheney**, **I. Lewis (Scooter) Libby**, **Karl Rove**, and **Richard Armitage**—the White House parties named in the lawsuit—had orchestrated his wife's outing as political retribution. In 2004, Wilson published *The Politics of Truth: Inside the Lies that Led to War and Betrayed My Wife's CIA Identity: A Diplomat's Memoir*, which traces his view of "Plamegate." Armitage was later revealed as the primary source for Novak's article.

WIRETAPPING. Surveillance of electronic and telephonic communications without a court order became a central controversy in the administration of **George W. Bush**. The National Security Agency (NSA) wiretapped conversations and electronic communications of foreign individuals, including those communications between US citizens and foreign nationals, as a means of gathering foreign intelligence in the **War on Terror** following the **11 September 2001 terrorist** attacks. The *New York Times* reported the story in 2005, alleging that the Bush administration had circumvented the statutory requirement that the president report such wiretaps for review by the **Foreign Intelligence Surveillance Act** (FISA) Court. One member of the court resigned in protest. Bush and Attorney General **Alberto Gonzales** contended that the **Authorization for the Use of Military Force** (AUMF), passed by Congress shortly after 9/11, authorized such wiretaps and superseded the need to comply with FISA requirements.

Civil libertarians were most concerned about warrantless wiretaps of US citizens and argued that Bush had violated not only the FISA Court regulations but essential constitutional protections to privacy. In 2007, Congress passed the **Protect America Act**, which authorized warrantless wiretaps, including domestic surveillance, as long as one individual involved in the communications is reasonably believed to be abroad and not in the United States. The FISA Amendments of 2008 extended the major provisions of the **Protect America Act** (2007).

WOLFOWITZ, PAUL DUNDES (1943–). A native of Brooklyn, New York, Wolfowitz graduated from Cornell University (1965) and earned a doctoral degree in political science from the University of Chicago (1972). In the 1970s, he worked for the Arms Control and Disarmament Agency and for the Defense Department. Under President **Ronald Reagan** Wolfowitz took a position as director of policy planning in the State Department and later became assistant secretary for East Asian and Pacific Affairs before he was appointed as ambassador to Indonesia in 1986. In the administration of **George H.W. Bush**, he served under Secretary of Defense **Richard B. (Dick) Cheney** as undersecretary for planning. From 1994 to 2001, he took an academic position at Johns Hopkins University in international relations. While at Johns Hopkins, Wolfowitz became part of the **Project for the New American Century** (PNAC), a grouping of **neoconservatives** who criticized the **foreign policy** of President **William Clinton** and called upon him to take action against Iraqi dictator **Saddam Hussein** in 1998.

In the administration of **George W. Bush**, Wolfowitz was appointed deputy secretary of defense in 2001 and served under **Donald Rumsfeld**. He was one of the administration's most vocal advocates for the **War in Iraq** and was part of a small group of administration officials who investigated alleged connections between Hussein and the **terrorist** organization **al-Qaeda** and Hussein's alleged possession of **weapons of mass destruction** (WMDs). He also articulated the administration's argument that Iraqi oil revenue would be sufficient to pay for the US-led invasion of **Iraq**.

In 2005, Bush appointed Wolfowitz to head the World Bank. His conservative stances on social policy proved controversial, as did his lack of experience in economic matters. Wolfowitz resigned from the World Bank in 2007 after revelations that he had arranged a promotion for his girlfriend. He joined the American Enterprise Institute, a conservative think tank, following his resignation.

WOMEN. The status of women in the United States was a central issue during the **George W. Bush** era. On the campaign trail in 2000, Bush's record as governor of Texas was criticized by many women's organizations, including the National Organization for Women (NOW) and pro-choice groups such as the National Abortion and Reproductive Rights Action League (NARAL Pro Choice America). As Texas governor, Bush was staunchly against **abortion** and signed a total of 13 antiabortion measures. He also supported a constitutional ban on abortions except in the case of rape, incest, or when the life of the mother was in danger, and favored a ban on third-trimester or so-called partial-birth abortions. As president, **William Clinton** had vetoed such a measure in 1995 and 1997. Critics also charged that as Texas governor, Bush had not done enough to ensure pay equity for women or health insurance for women and children.

The abortion debate figured prominently in Bush's two terms as president. In 2003, he signed the **Partial-Birth Abortion Ban Act**, the constitutionality of which was upheld in the Supreme Court decision *Gonzales v. Carhart* in 2007. In 2006, Bush cast his first veto on **stem-cell research**. The bill would have enabled researchers to use aborted fetuses produced from in vitro fertilization in their quest to find a cure for a host of diseases such as diabetes, Alzheimer's disease, and Parkinson's disease. Bush vetoed a similar bill for a second time in 2007.

While critics posited that Bush's policies retarded women's social advancement and right to choice, women nonetheless reached significant heights both substantively and symbolically during his two terms. First Lady **Laura Bush** played a prominent role in her husband's administration and was regarded as a role model of **compassionate conservatism** by many Americans. She was lauded for her public call to attention of the plight of Afghan women oppressed under the **Taliban** regime. Just several weeks after the US-led invasion of **Afghanistan**, Laura Bush became the first woman to give the president's weekly radio address and called the treatment of women under the Taliban "brutal." She was a steadfast supporter of breast cancer research and worked to cement international support for the Partnership for Breast Cancer Awareness and Research of the Americas. And she spent much of her time as first lady supporting women's health and **education** issues. According to the Gallup Poll, her popularity ranks among the highest for recent first ladies. The Bush's eldest daughter, **Barbara Pierce Bush**, played an active role in combating the spread of **acquired immune deficiency syndrome** (AIDS) in Africa and frequently accompanied her mother on diplomatic missions, including a visit to the Vatican to meet Pope **Benedict XVI** in 2006.

Women were also prominent in President George W. Bush's White House and Cabinet. **Condoleezza Rice** became the first female **national security advisor** and later the first secretary of state. Bush also appointed women as secretary of agriculture (**Ann Veneman**), secretary of education (**Margaret Spellings**), secretary of the interior (**Gale Norton**), secretary of labor (**Elaine Chao**), secretary of transportation (**Mary Peters**), and as White House press secretary (**Dana Perino**).

Finally, women also reached new heights elsewhere in the political system. **Hillary Clinton** was very narrowly defeated by **Barack Obama** in the 2008 Democratic presidential nomination contest. **Nancy Pelosi** became the first female speaker of the House of Representatives when Democrats captured Congress in the **mid-term elections** of 2006.

WORLD TRADE CENTER. Completed in 1971, this complex of seven buildings was notable for two 110-story towers (the Twin

Towers) that were a world-renown landmark in New York City. On 26 February 1993, Ramzi Yousef, a Kuwaiti national and self-described **terrorist**, drove a truck bomb to the World Trade Center in an effort to bring down one of the towers. The blast caused six deaths and some structural damage to the north tower, but did not destroy it.

On **11 September 2001**, nineteen **al-Qaeda** terrorists hijacked four aircraft from Boston, Newark, and Washington, D.C., en route to the West Coast. They crashed one fuel-laden Boeing 767 aircraft into each tower. Within several hours, the intense heat from the conflagration caused the towers to collapse. More than 2,700 workers from 80 countries died in the buildings, in the worst terrorist attack on US soil. Some in the buildings jumped out windows rather than succumb to flames and smoke. Ash and debris from the collapse of the towers spread throughout Manhattan.

President **George W. Bush** visited the site where the towers stood, dubbed "ground zero," as a massive cleanup effort got underway. Groundbreaking for a new set of towers, as well as a national memorial, at ground zero began in 2006. *See also* AFGHANISTAN; BIN LADEN, OSAMA; MOHAMMED, KHALID SHEIKH; OMAR, MULLAH MUHAMMED; PENTAGON; TALIBAN; UNITED FLIGHT 93; WAR ON TERROR.

WORLDCOM. The bankruptcy filing by this telecommunication provider in July 2002 was the largest in US history until **Lehman Brothers** filed for Chapter 11 bankruptcy protection in 2008. The company's cofounder, Bernard Ebbers, was convicted of fraud and conspiracy in an accounting scandal that resulted in $11 billion in losses to stockholders and implicated the accounting firm **Arthur Andersen**. *See also* ENRON.

WURZELBACHER, SAMUEL JOSEPH. Branded as "Joe the Plumber" by the news media, Wurzelbacher is the owner of a plumbing business in Ohio. In October 2008, during the presidential campaign, he drew nationwide attention for an exchange with Democratic presidential nominee **Barack Obama** in his Holland, Ohio, neighborhood. Wurzelbacher challenged Obama's tax plan, suggesting it would force his business to pay higher taxes and impede hiring. Obama responded that he did not wish to hamper the success of businesses, but that he wanted to "spread the wealth." The exchange sparked a firestorm of controversy, with some conservatives contending that Obama favored socialism. Wurzelbacher became a staple on the campaign trail with his support of Republican presidential nominee **John McCain**. He was rumored to have considered a run for an Ohio congressional seat in 2010. Following the election, he took a position as a reporter covering the conflict between **Israel** and **Hamas**, despite having no substantial journalism or foreign policy experience.

– Y –

YUGOSLAVIA. This country on the Balkan Peninsula was originally created in 1918, in the aftermath of World War I, out of the remnants of the Hapsburg Empire. Following World War II, Josef Broz Tito established an independent, nonaligned communist government, ruled from 1946 to 1980, and resisted domination by the **Soviet Union** during the **Cold War**. Tito's Socialist Federal Republic of Yugoslavia comprised the republics of Bosnia-Herzegovina, Croatia, Macedonia, Montenegro, Serbia, and Slovenia, in addition to the autonomous provinces of Kosovo and Vojvodina.

The collapse of the Socialist Federal Republic of Yugoslavia began in 1991. As individual republics clamored for greater autonomy, the country descended into civil war. Slovenia declared its independence in June 1991 and was briefly occupied by federal troops before a settlement was reached on its independent status. That same year ethnic Serbs (typically Eastern Orthodox Christians) opposed Croatians' (typically Roman Catholic) move for independence. By 1992, the two groups battled for territory in a full-scale civil war, placing Bosnia—with its large Muslim population—at the center of a bloody campaign rife with atrocities perpetrated largely by Serbs, including torture, murder, mass executions, and rape of Bosnian Muslims that was tantamount to genocide. Civilian casualties were particularly widespread in the cities of Sarajevo and Srbrenica.

The **United Nations** intervened to set up "protected areas" for "ethnic enclaves" in Bosnia as a means to halt the death toll. Members of the **North Atlantic Treaty Organization** (NATO), led by the United States and President **William Clinton**, engaged in selective air strikes against Bosnian Serbs to force a termination of hostilities in 1994. The United States brokered a settlement, dubbed the Dayton Agreement, in late 1994 that provided for an autonomous government for Serbs within Bosnia and ended much of the conflict between Serbs, Croats, and Bosnian Muslims. Serbia and Montenegro dissolved their union in 2003 (the Federal Republic of Yugoslavia), with both countries declaring independence. Croatia had declared its independence in 1991.

Ethnic strife between Serbs and ethnic Albanians, however, broke out by 1996. Serbian President **Slobodan Milošević**, supported by Macedonia (frequently referred to as the former Yugoslav Republic of Macedonia, which declared independence in 1991), imposed harsh political repression on ethnic Albanians in the region of **Kosovo** in an attempt to thwart calls for greater autonomy. Kosovar Albanians responded by forming an army of liberation that clashed with Serbian forces. In 1999, NATO forces intervened to halt the bloodshed and pushed Serbian forces out of Kosovo. The region was subsequently administered by UN peacekeeping forces, and a provisional transitional government was elected in 2001. In 2008, Kosovo formally declared its independence, which Serbia refused to recognize.

Allegations of genocide and violations of the **Geneva Conventions** by Serbians in the Bosnian conflict led the UN's **International Criminal Court** (ICC) to launch investigations and ad hoc tribunals for the perpetrators of war crimes. In 1993, the UN set up the International Criminal Tribunal for the former Yugoslavia. Serbian leader Slobodan Milošević was arrested and sent to the Tribunal in The Hague, Netherlands, in 2001, but died in 2006 before his trial terminated. **Radovan Karadžić**, who was president of the Federal Republic of Yugoslavia from 1992 to 1996, was arrested in 2008 and sent to The Hague for trial. As of 2009, he awaited trial. *See also* ARMED FORCES; VIERA DE MELLO, SÉRGIO.

– Z –

ZAPATERO, JOSÉ LUIS RODRÍGUEZ (1960–). Born in Valladolid, Spain, Zapatero led his Spanish socialist party to victory in 2004 and again in 2008 as was prime minister. He defeated the incumbent government of **José María Aznar** in 2004, running on a platform that included opposition to the **War in Iraq**. Much to the consternation of President **George W. Bush**, Zapatero removed all Spanish troops from **Iraq** within a month of taking office, further dividing **North Atlantic Treaty Organization** (NATO) countries on the war and the US-led invasion and occupation. *See also* MADRID (BOMBINGS).

ZARDARI, ASIF ALI (1955–). The widower of **Benazir Bhutto**, who was assassinated in December 2007, Zardari was elected president of **Pakistan** in 2008 following the forced exit of **Pervez Musharraf**, who faced imminent impeachment. Although an opponent of the **Taliban**, Zardari was critical of US incursions into and drone attacks on suspected **terrorist** bases in **Waziristan** from neighboring **Afghanistan**.

ZOELLICK, ROBERT BRUCE (1953–). Born in Naperville, Illinois, Zoellick is a graduate of Swarthmore College (1975) and earned a law degree and master's degree in public policy from Harvard (1981). After taking a clerkship at the US Court of Appeals in Washington, D.C., he served at the Department of the Treasury and in the Department of State under Presidents **Ronald Reagan** and **George H.W. Bush** from 1985 to 1992. From 1993 to 1997, he served as executive vice president of the **Federal National Mortgage Association** (Fannie Mae). In 1998, he was a signatory to the letter written to President **William Clinton** by the **neoconservative** think tank **Project for the New American Century** (PNAC) that proposed military action against **Iraq**'s dictator, **Saddam Hussein**.

During the 2000 presidential election, Zoellick served as a **foreign policy** advisor to **George W. Bush** and was also a key advisor during the 36-day **Florida recount**. In 2001, Bush named him as US Trade Representative, and he served in that position until 2005, at which time he moved to the Department of State as deputy secretary. In 2007, Bush appointed Zoellick to succeed **Paul Wolfowitz** at the World Bank.

ZUBAYDAH, ABU (1971–). A native of Saudi Arabia, Zubaydah became a member of the **terrorist** organization **al-Qaeda** in the 1990s. A close associate of **Osama bin Laden**, he ran a terrorist training camp in **Afghanistan** and is thought to have been involved in the planning of the **11 September 2001** attacks on New York and the **Pentagon**. He was captured in a joint operation between the **Central Intelligence Agency** (CIA) and Pakistani secret intelligence services in Faisalabad, **Pakistan**, in March 2002. President **George W. Bush** made public in 2006 that Zubaydah had been transferred to **Guantanamo Bay, Cuba**, and detained as an **enemy combatant**. Zubaydah claimed that he had been subjected to **torture** and the technique of **waterboarding**, or simulated drowning, as the CIA attempted to extract vital intelligence information from him regarding the 9/11 and other attacks. Bush justified the use of such "enhanced interrogation techniques," noting that they had compelled Zubaydah to convey information on the whereabouts of al-Qaeda operatives, including **Khalid Sheikh Mohammed**, who was captured in March 2003. *See also* DETAINEE TREATMENT ACT (2005).

President George W. Bush and
His Administration, 2001–2009

Presidential Election Results (2000)

	Popular Votes	Electoral Votes
George W. Bush	50,456,002	271
Albert Gore, Jr.	50,999,897	267

Presidential Election Results (2004)

	Popular Votes	Electoral Votes
George W. Bush	62,040,610	286
John Kerry	59,028,444	251

Vice President:
Richard B. Cheney (2001–2009)

Cabinet

Agriculture, Secretary of:
Ann M. Veneman (2001–2005)
Mike Johanns (2005–2007)
Ed Schafer (2008–2009)

Attorney General:
John Ashcroft (2001–2005)
Alberto Gonzales (2005–2007)
Michael B. Mukasey (2007–2009)

Commerce, Secretary of:
Don Evans (2001–2005)
Carlos M. Gutierrez (2005–2009)

Defense, Secretary of:
Donald H. Rumsfeld (2001–2006)
Robert M. Gates (2006–2009)

Education, Secretary of:
Rod Paige (2001–2005)
Margaret Spellings (2005–2009)

Energy, Secretary of:
Spencer Abraham (2001–2005)
Samuel W. Bodman (2005–2009)

Health and Human Services, Secretary of:
Tommy G. Thompson (2001–2005)
Michael O. Leavitt (2005–2009)

Homeland Security, Secretary of:
Tom Ridge (2003–2005)
Michael Chertoff (2005–2009)

Housing and Urban Development, Secretary of:
Melquiades Martinez (2001–2003)
Alphonso Jackson (2004–2008)
Steve Preston (2008–2009)

Interior, Secretary of the:
Gale Norton (2001–2006)
Dirk Kempthorne (2006–2009)

Labor, Secretary of:
Elaine Chao (2001–2009)

State, Secretary of:
Colin L. Powell (2001–2005)
Condoleezza Rice (2005–2009)

Transportation, Secretary of:
Norman Y. Mineta (2001–2006)
Mary E. Peters (2006–2009)

Treasury, Secretary of the:
Paul H. O'Neill (2001–2003)
John W. Snow (2003–2006)
Henry M. Paulson, Jr. (2006–2009)

Veterans' Affairs, Secretary of:
Anthony Principi (2001–2005)
R. James Nicholson (2005–2007)
James B. Peake (2007–2009)

Key White House Advisors and Staff

Chief of Staff:
Andrew Card (2001–2006)
Joshua Bolten (2006–2009)

Deputy Chief of Staff:
Joseph Hagin (2001–2008)
Karl Rove (2001–2007)

Office of Communications, Director:
Nicolle Devenish Wallace (2001–2006)
Kevin Sullivan (2006–2009)

Counsel:
Alberto Gonzales (2001–2005)
Harriet Miers (2005–2007)
Fred Fielding (2007–2009)

Press Secretary:
Ari Fleischer (2001–2003)
Scott McClellan (2003–2006)
Tony Snow (2006–2007)
Dana Perino (2007–2009)

Office of National Drug Control Policy, Director:
John Walters (2001–2009)

National Security Council (NSC), Assistant to the President for National Security Affairs:
Condoleezza Rice (2001–2005)
Stephen Hadley (2005–2009)

US Trade Representative:
Robert Zoellick (2001–2005)
Robert Portman (2005–2006)
Susan Schwab (2006–2009)

White House Office of Faith-Based and Community Initiatives
John DiLulio (2001)
Don Willett (2001–2002)
Jim Towey (2002–2006)
Jay Hein (2006–2009)

Appendix B

George W. Bush's
Success Rate in Congress

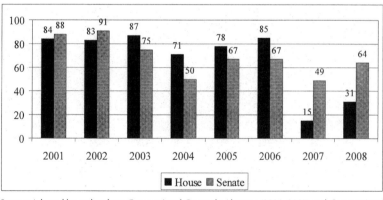

Source: Adapted by author from *Congressional Quarterly Almanac* (2001–2007) and *Congressional Quarterly Weekly Reports* (2008).

Appendix C

Vetoes of Public Bills Cast by President George W. Bush, 2001–2008

107th Congress (2001–2002)
None

108th Congress (2003–2004)
None

109th Congress (2005–2006)
H.R. 810. 19 July 2006. Embryonic stem-cell research.

110th Congress (2007–2008)

H.R.1591.	1 May 2007. Emergency supplemental appropriations.
S.5.	20 June 2007. Embryonic stem-cell research.
H.R.976.	3 October 2007. Children's Health Insurance Program/ Social Security.
* H.R.1495.	2 November 2007. Rivers and harbors.
H.R.3043.	13 November 2007. Labor, HHS, and Education appropriations.
H.R.3963.	12 December 2007. Children's Health Insurance Program/Social Security.
H.R.1585.	28 December 2007. Defense authorization for FY 2008.
H.R.2082.	8 March 2008. Intelligence appropriations.
* H.R.2419.	21 May 2008. Agricultural programs.
* H.R.6124.	18 June 2008. Agricultural programs.
* H.R.6331.	15 July 2008. Social Security/Medicare.

Note:

* Veto overridden, became public law.

Appendix D

President George W. Bush's
Public Approval (percent), 2001–2009

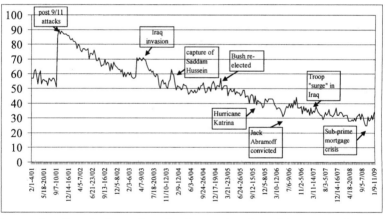

Source: Adapted by author from Gallup Poll and *USA Today* Gallup Poll, http://www.pollingreport .com/BushJob1.htm

Appendix E

George W. Bush's
Monthly Approval Data (percent), 2001–2009

2/1–4/01	57	12/6–9/01	86
2/9–11/01	57	12/14–16/01	86
2/19–21/01	62	1/7–9/02	84
3/5–7/01	63	1/11–14/02	83
3/9–11/01	58	1/25–27/02	84
3/26–28/01	53	2/4–6/02	82
4/6–8/01	59	2/8–10/02	82
4/20–22/01	62	3/1–3/02	81
5/7–9/01	53	3/4–7/02	77
5/10–14/01	56	3/8–9/02	80
5/18–20/01	56	3/22–24/02	79
6/8–10/01	55	4/5–7/02	76
6/11–17/01	55	4/8–11/02	75
6/28–7/1/01	52	4/22–24/02	77
7/10–11/01	57	4/29–5/1/02	77
7/19–22/01	56	5/6–9/02	76
8/3–5/01	55	5/20–22/02	76
8/10–12/01	57	5/28–29/02	77
8/16–19/01	57	6/3–6/02	70
8/24–26/01	55	6/7–8/02	74
9/7–10/01	51	6/17–19/02	74
9/14–15/01	86	6/21–23/02	73
9/21–22/01	90	6/28–30/02	76
10/5–6/01	87	7/9–11/02	73
10/11–14/01	89	7/22–24/02	69
10/19–21/01	88	7/26–28/02	69
11/2–4/01	87	7/29–31/02	71
11/8–11/01	87	8/5–8/02	68
11/26–27/01	87	8/19–21/02	65

9/2–4/02	66		6/9–10/03	62
9/5–8/02	66		6/12–15/03	63
9/13–16/02	70		6/27–29/03	61
9/20–22/02	66		7/7–9/03	62
9/23–26/02	68		7/18–20/03	59
10/3–6/02	67		7/25–27/03	58
10/14–17/02	62		8/4–6/03	60
10/21–22/02	67		8/25–26/03	59
10/31–11/3/02	63		9/8–10/03	52
11/8–10/02	68		9/19–21/03	50
11/11–14/02	66		10/6–8/03	55
11/22–24/02	65		10/10–12/03	56
12/5–8/02	64		10/24–26/03	53
12/9–10/02	63		11/3–5/03	54
12/16–17/02	63		11/10–12/03	51
12/19–22/02	61		11/14–16/03	50
1/3–5/03	63		12/5–7/03	55
1/10–12/03	58		12/11–14/03	56
1/13–16/03	61		12/15–16/03	63
1/20–22/03	58		1/2–5/04	60
1/23–25/03	60		1/9–11/04	59
1/31–2/2/03	61		1/12–15/04	53
2/3–6/03	59		1/29–2/1/04	49
2/7–9/03	61		2/6–8/04	52
2/17–19/03	58		2/9–12/04	51
2/24–26/03	57		2/16–17/04	51
3/3–5/03	57		3/5–7/04	49
3/14–15/03	58		3/8–11/04	50
3/22–23/03	71		3/26–28/04	53
3/24–25/03	69		4/5–8/04	52
3/29–30/03	71		4/16–18/04	52
4/5–6/03	70		5/2–4/04	49
4/7–9/03	69		5/7–9/04	46
4/14–16/03	71		5/21–23/04	47
4/22–23/03	70		6/3–6/04	49
5/5–7/03	69		6/21–23/04	48
5/19–21/03	66		7/8–11/04	47
5/30–6/1/03	64		7/19–21/04	49

7/30–31/04	47	7/7–10/05	49
7/30–8/1/04	48	7/22–24/05	49
8/9–11/04	51	7/25–28/05	44
8/23–25/04	49	8/5–7/05	45
9/3–5/04	52	8/8–11/05	45
9/13–15/04	52	8/22–25/05	40
9/24–26/04	54	8/28–30/05	45
10/1–3/04	50	9/8–11/05	46
10/9–10/04	47	9/12–15/05	45
10/11–14/04	48	9/16–18/05	40
10/14–16/04	51	9/26–28/05	45
10/22–24/04	51	10/13–16/05	39
10/29–31/04	48	10/21–23/05	42
11/7–10/04	53	10/24–26/05	41
11/19–21/04	55	10/28–30/05	41
12/5–8/04	53	11/7–10/05	40
12/17–19/04	49	11/11–13/05	37
1/3–5/05	52	11/17–20/05	38
1/7–9/05	52	12/5–8/05	43
1/14–16/05	51	12/9–11/05	42
2/4–6/05	57	12/16–18/05	41
2/7–10/05	49	12/19–22/05	43
2/21–24/05	51	1/6–8/06	43
2/25–27/05	52	1/9–12/06	43
3/7–10/05	52	1/20–22/06	43
3/18–20/05	52	2/6–9/06	42
3/21–23/05	45	2/9–12/06	39
4/1–2/05	48	2/28–3/1/06	38
4/4–7/05	50	3/10–12/06	36
4/18–21/05	48	3/13–16/06	37
4/29–5/1/05	48	4/7–9/06	37
5/2–5/05	50	4/10–13/06	36
5/20–22/05	46	4/28–30/06	34
5/23–26/05	48	5/5–7/06	31
6/6–8/05	47	5/8–11/06	33
6/16–19/05	47	6/1–4/06	36
6/24–26/05	45	6/9–11/06	38
6/29–30/05	46	6/23–25/06	37

7/6–9/06	40	11/2–4/07	31
7/21–23/06	37	11/11–14/07	32
7/28–30/06	40	11/30–12/2/07	34
8/7–10/06	37	12/6–9/07	37
8/18–20/06	42	12/14–16/07	32
9/7–10/06	39	1/4–6/08	32
9/15–17/06	44	1/10–13/08	34
10/6–8/06	37	1/30–2/2/08	34
10/9–12/06	37	2/8–10/08	33
10/20–22/06	37	2/11–14/08	31
11/2–5/06	38	2/21–24/08	32
11/9–12/06	33	3/6–9/08	32
12/8–10/06	38	3/14–16/08	32
12/11–14/06	35	4/6–9/08	28
1/5–7/07	37	4/18–20/08	28
1/12–14/07	34	5/1–3/08	28
1/15–18/07	36	5/8–11/08	29
2/1–4/07	32	5/30–6/1/08	28
2/9–11/07	37	6/9–12/08	30
3/2–4/07	33	6/15–19/08	28
3/11–14/07	35	7/10–13/08	31
3/23–25/07	34	7/25–27/08	32
4/2–5/07	38	8/7–10/08	33
4/13–15/07	36	8/21–23/08	29
5/4–6/07	34	9/5–7/08	33
5/10–13/07	33	9/8–11/08	31
6/1–3/07	32	9/26–27/08	27
6/11–14/07	32	10/3–5/08	25
7/6–8/07	29	10/10–12/08	25
7/12–15/07	31	10/23–26/08	31
8/3–5/07	34	11/7–9/08	28
8/13–16/07	32	11/13–16/08	29
9/7–8/07	33	12/4–7/08	32
9/14–16/07	36	12/12–14/08	29
10/4–7/07	32	1/9–11/09	34
10/12–14/07	32		

Source: Gallup Poll and *USA Today* Gallup Poll, http://www.pollingreport.com/BushJob1.htm

Appendix F

US Troops in Iraq, 2003–2008

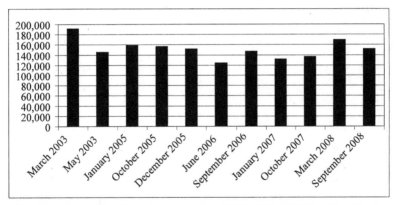

Adapted by author from http://www.foxnews.com/wires/2008Apr08/0,4670,USIraqTroopsTimeline, 00.html; http://www.usatoday.com/news/washington/2008–09–30–iraq-troops_N.htm?csp=34

Appendix G

US Military Wounded and Dead
in Iraq, March 2003–January 2009

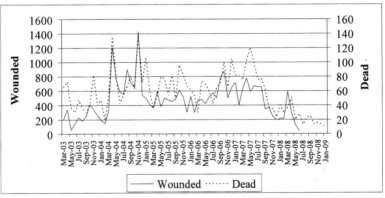

Adapted by author from http://www.globalsecurity.org/military/ops/iraq_casualties.htm

Appendix H
Estimated Civilian Deaths in Iraq, 2003–2008

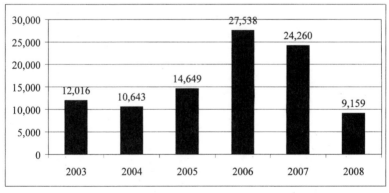

Adapted by author from http://www.iraqbodycount.org/database/

Appendix I

US and International Troops in Afghanistan, 2002–June 2008

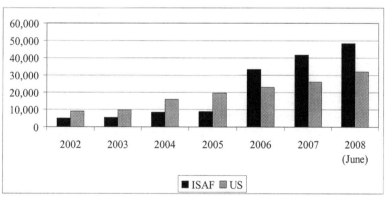

Adapted by author from http://www.afghanconflictmonitor.org/securityforces.html#docs4; http://www
.heritage.org/Research/NationalSecurity/troopMarch2005.xls; http://abcnews.go.com/Politics/wire
Story?id=3996596; http://www.usatoday.com/news/military/2008-04-10-afghanistan-troop-levels_
N.htm

Appendix J

Military Casualties in Afghanistan: US and Other International Security Assistance Force (ISAF) Countries

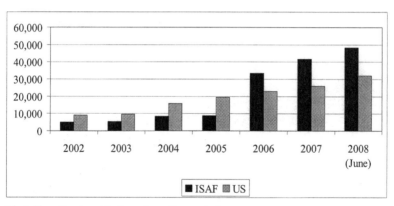

Adapted by author from http://www.icasualties.com/oef

Bibliography

CONTENTS

INTRODUCTION

The politics of the George W. Bush era generated a significant amount of scholarship during Bush's two terms. The books, peer-reviewed articles in social science and interdisciplinary journals, and memoirs presented below are arranged by theme. All were published between 1999 and early 2009. The focus of the bibliography is on scholarly research in political science and public administration.

As such, the works cited represent contemporary perspectives on the Bush era from the time shortly before he took office in January 2001 until his departure from the Oval Office in January 2009. Researchers are thus advised to consider the following bibliography within this boundary of time, and as a starting point for bibliographical material—not as a comprehensive guide to analyses of the Bush era.

As of early Spring 2009, new scholarship on Bush's presidency is produced monthly in book form and in peer-reviewed journals. This trend will continue for years to come. The political science journals *Presidential Studies Quarterly*, *Congress and the Presidency*, and *White House Studies* have been and will continue to be critical venues for the publication of research on Bush's terms in office. Other journals to consider include *American Journal of Political Science*, *American Political Science Review*, *American Politics Research*, *International Affairs*, *International Studies Quarterly*, *Journal of Politics*, *Perspectives on Politics*, *Political Research Quarterly*, *Political Science Quarterly*, *Politics & Policy*, *Public Administration Review*, and *Public Opinion Quarterly*. With the passage of time historians will also produce invaluable research, already in progress, that places the Bush era within the larger sweep of history. Journals to consider in this respect include *American Historical Review*, *History*, *Journal of American History*, and *Past and Present*, to name a few.

Many notable works in political science offer vital lenses through which to assess the presidency of George W. Bush as we await future scholarship. These titles are not included in the bibliography below, but serve as an excellent reference point to place Bush's presidency in the constitutional order over time. Richard Neustadt's *Presidential Power and the Modern Presidents* (New York: Free Press, 1991) remains a classic, prescriptive work even if it does not analyze the Bush presidency specifically. Stephen Skowronek's *The Politics Presidents Make: Leadership from John Adams to George Bush* (Cambridge, Mass.: Harvard University Press, 1993) emphasizes "regime cycles" and seeks to reconcile studies of the modern presidency following Franklin Roosevelt with earlier presidents. Where George W. Bush fits in this framework of "political time" remains very much an open question to be explored.

Other general works use the presidency of George W. Bush as a "case study" or otherwise integrate his administration in the study of presidential politics generally. Such works include Michael Genovese (ed.), *The Presidency and the Political System* (Washington, D.C.: Congressional Quarterly, 2005); Joseph Pika and John Maltese, *The Politics of the Presidency* (Washington, D.C.: Congressional Quarterly, 2009); George C. Edwards and Philip John Davies, *New Challenges for the American Presidency* (New York: Longman, 2003); George C. Edwards, *The Strategic President: Persuasion and Opportunity in Presidential Leadership* (Princeton, N.J.: Princeton University Press, 2009); and Shirley Anne Warshaw, *The Co-Presidency of Bush and Cheney* (Stanford, Calif.: Stanford University Press, 2009).

Bush's relations with the media have already been examined in some detail by scholars. The articles cited below give particular emphasis to the White House communications structure and efforts to manage the president's image. For a more general treatment of presidential press relations and public outreach, readers are advised to consult Samuel Kernell, *Going Public: New Strategies of Presidential Leadership* (Washington, D.C.: Congressional Quarterly 2006), which contains some data for Bush's first term regarding press conferences, public activities, and the like. Further, George C. Edwards' *On Deaf Ears: The Limits of the Bully Pulpit* (New Haven, Conn.: Yale University Press, 2003) includes some early data on

Bush's public activities but most importantly accentuates presidents' general frustration in attempting to move public opinion through the use of the bully pulpit.

Bush's use of executive power, in the domestic as well as the foreign policy realm—has received ample attention in the scholarly literature. Many works emphasize Bush's unilateral actions, from executive orders to "signing statements" issued by the president to challenge congressional legislation. Others accentuate the secrecy of the Bush White House and challenge the notion of "unitary executive theory." James P. Pfiffner's work entitled *Power Play: The Bush Presidency and the Constitution* (Washington, D.C.: Brookings Institution Press, 2008) is an excellent starting point to assess Bush's use of executive power from a constitutional perspective. More generally, scholars have begun to examine the unilateral powers of the presidency in greater depth, and Bush's actions should be juxtaposed with prior works that cover a significant swath of history. Kenneth R. Mayer's *With a Stroke of a Pen: Executive Orders and Presidential Power* (Princeton, N.J.: Princeton University Press, 2001), Philip J. Cooper's *By Order of the President: The Use and Abuse of Executive Direct Action* (Lawrence, Kan.: University Press of Kansas, 2002), and William G. Howell's *Power without Persuasion: The Politics of Direct Presidential Action* (Princeton, N.J.: Princeton University Press, 2003) provide a substantial basis from which to theorize about Bush's use of executive orders and independent actions. Further, Mark J. Rozell's oeuvre *Executive Privilege: Presidential Power, Secrecy, and Accountability* (Lawrence, Kan.: University Press of Kansas, 2002) provides a rich foundation to assess how Bush's use of executive privilege differs from or is similar to that of his predecessors.

Bush's relations with Congress must also be understood within the context of theories of the modern legislative presidency, using both quantitative and qualitative approaches. Bush's two terms ran the gamut of possible partisan configurations between the White House and Capitol Hill—from 2001 to 2002, party control was split between the Democrats in the Senate and the Republicans in the House; unified Republican control of Congress prevailed from 2003 to 2006; and divided government, with the Democrats in charge of Congress, returned from 2007 to 2008. The articles in the bibliography provide a well-rounded perspective, from "insider" perspectives on presidential confirmations to Bush's early legislative agenda and veto threat strategy. Readers are advised to consult other seminal works that place presidential–congressional relations into a more historical perspective. Jon R. Bond and Richard Fleisher's work *The President in the Legis-*

lative Arena (Chicago: University of Chicago Press, 1991), Paul C. Light's *The President's Agenda: Domestic Policy Choice from Kennedy to Clinton* (Baltimore: Johns Hopkins University Press, 1998), Andrew Rudalevige's *Managing the President's Program: Presidential Leadership and Legislative Policy Formulation* (Princeton, N.J.: Princeton University Press, 2002), and Richard S. Conley's *The Presidency, Congress, and Divided Government: A Postwar Assessment* (College Station, Tex.: Texas A&M University Press, 2002) all contribute vital theoretical approaches to presidential legislative leadership. On veto politics, readers are encouraged to consult Charles C. Cameron's *Veto Bargaining: Presidents and the Politics of Negative Power* (New York: Cambridge University Press, 2000).

A relatively rich literature exists at present on the staffing and structure of the Bush White House. Articles by John P. Burke, Martha Joynt Kumar, and Bradley Patterson focus on the presidential transition of 2000; these scholars have contributed significant works on presidential transitions in the past. Kumar's book *The White House World* is particularly notable for pragmatic accounts of presidential staffing. Howard Relyea's work on the establishment of the homeland security apparatus in the Executive Office of the President is an excellent starting point to understand the basis for the eventual Department of Homeland Security. Readers should also consult prior works on the administrative presidency, including Stephen Hess's updated volume *Organizing the Presidency* (Washington, D.C.: Brookings Institution, 2002) and John P. Burke's *The Institutional Presidency* (Baltimore: Johns Hopkins University Press, 2000) to place Bush's organization in comparative perspective.

The elections of 2000 and 2004 have already generated a plethora of scholarly literature, noted below. Larry Sabato's *Overtime!* (New York: Longman, 2002) offers an excellent starting point to review the 36-day battle for the 2000 election. Other volumes on the Florida Recount of 2000, such as Robert Zelnick's book *Winning Florida* (Stanford, Calif.: Hoover Institution Press, 2001) and Julian Pleasants's *Hanging Chads* (New York: Palgrave/Macmillan, 2004) provide superlative insight into the Bush team's management of the Florida fiasco. Notable judicial scholars, including Cass Sunstein and Bruce Ackerman, review in great detail the pivotal Supreme Court case of *Bush v. Gore* that halted the Florida recount. If the definitive volume on Bush's re-election has not yet been written, the articles cited in the bibliography below on the 2004 election emphasize not only the impact of the War on Terror and the War in Iraq on Bush's campaign but also potentially important changes in the landscape of campaign politics, including the impact of the Internet and Hispanic voters.

Foreign policy, the War on Terror, and the wars in Afghanistan and Iraq have already produced many scholarly manuscripts. The edited volume by Ivo H. Daalder and James M. Lindsay, *America Unbound: The Bush Revolution in Foreign Policy* (New York: Wiley, 2005), provides a detailed overview of the theories and strategies and informed Bush's foreign policy. Robert G. Kaufman's thoughtful work *In Defense of the Bush Doctrine* (Lexington, Ky.: University Press of Kentucky, 2007) challenges typical scholarly critiques of Bush's neoconservative stances. Journalist Bob Woodward's four volumes on the wars in Afghanistan and Iraq—*Bush at War*, *Plan of Attack*, *State of Denial*, and *The War Within*—purport to offer readers an in-depth perspective on Bush's role as commander in chief. Louis Fisher's contributions on the issue of military tribunals, both in book and article form, offer a scathing critique. Fisher's prior work—*Presidential War Power* (Lawrence, Kan.: University Press of Kansas, 2004) is a "must read" for those interested in understanding how George W. Bush's legacy fits within a much longer historical frame of reference.

Groundbreaking for the George W. Bush Presidential Center at Southern Methodist University in Dallas, Texas, is scheduled for 2010, with a completion date expected a few years thereafter. Records at the new library, which is administered by the National Archives and Records Administration, will become subject to public access and Freedom of Information Act requests on 20 January 2014. More information is available at www.georgewbushlibrary.gov. As primary documents become available to researchers in the coming years, the holdings of the Bush Library will produce significant "second-generation" scholarship among both historians and political scientists.

Researchers interested in Bush's governorship of Texas are advised to consider the holdings of the Texas State Archives at the University of Texas at Austin. Bush's papers—some 2,100 cubic feet of material—include correspondence, memoranda, legal records, legislative records, financial records, speeches, reports, meeting records, publications, printed material, lists, calendars and schedules, electronic records, audio and video tapes, and photographs for George W. Bush's tenure as governor of Texas from 17 January 1995 to 21 December 2000. The Texas State Archives website (http://www.lib.utexas.edu/taro/tslac/40078/tsl-40078.html) has extensive finding aids available electronically.

Internet sites also provide useful information on the Bush presidency. The White House Web Pages from Bush's two terms have been "archived" virtually at http://www.whitehouse.gov. Other helpful sites include:

American Presidency Project:
http://www.presidency.ucsb.edu/index.php

Executive Orders (National Archives and Records Administration):
http://www.archives.gov/federal-register/executive-orders/disposition
.html

Library of Congress, THOMAS (Legislation):
http://thomas.loc.gov/bss/110search.html

Miller Center Project on the American President, University of Virginia:
http://www.millercenter.virginia.edu/academic/americanpresident/

National Security Directives (Truman–George W. Bush, American Federation of Scientists):
http://www.fas.org/irp/offdocs/direct.htm

Office of Management and Budget Statements of Administrative Policy,
2001– :
http://www.whitehouse.gov/omb/legislative/sap/index.html

Polling Data, Real Clear Politics:
http://www.realclearpolitics.com/polls/

Presidential Pardons, University of Pittsburgh:
http://jurist.law.pitt.edu/pardons.htm

Presidential Speech Archive, Texas A&M University:
http://comm.tamu.edu/pres/speech.html

ADMINISTRATIVE PRESIDENCY

Albright, Robert R. "The U.S. Department of Transportation's Partnership Experience: Implications for the Future." *Journal of Labor Research* 25 (2004): 43–54.
Breul, Jonathan D., and John M. Kamensky. "Federal Government Reform: Lessons from Clinton's 'Reinventing Government' and Bush's 'Management Agenda' Initiatives." *Public Administration Review* 68 (2008): 1009–26.
Burke, John P. "The Bush Transition in Historical Context." *PS: Political Science & Politics* (2002): 23–26.

Copeland, Curtis W. "The Law: Executive Order 13422: An Expansion of Presidential Influence in the Rulemaking Process." *Presidential Studies Quarterly* 37 (2007): 531–44.

Eksterowicz, Anthony J., and Glenn P. Hastedt. "The George W. Bush Presidential Transition: The Disconnect Between Politics and Policy." *White House Studies* 5 (2005): 79–93.

Hurd, Richard W., and Sharon Pinnock. "Public Sector Unions: Will They Thrive or Struggle to Survive?" *Journal of Labor Research* 25 (2004): 211–21.

Johnson, Clay. "The 2000–01 Presidential Transition: Planning, Goals and Reality." *PS: Political Science & Politics* 35 (2002): 51–53.

Kumar, Martha Joynt. "Recruiting and Organizing the White House Staff." *PS: Political Science & Politics* 35 (2002): 35–40.

Kumar, Martha Joynt, and Terry Sullivan. *The White House World: Transitions, Organization, and Office Operations.* College Station: Texas A&M University Press, 2003.

Patterson, Bradley H. "The New Bush White House Staff: Choices Being Made." *White House Studies* 1 (2001): 225–37.

Pfiffner, James P. "The First MBA President: George W. Bush as Public Administrator." *Public Administration Review* 67 (2007): 6–20.

Relyea, Harold C. "The Law: Homeland Security: The Concept and the Presidential Coordination Office—First Assessment." *Presidential Studies Quarterly* 32 (2002): 397–411.

———. "Organizing for Homeland Security." *Presidential Studies Quarterly* 33 (2003): 602–24.

Tobias, Robert M. "The Future of Federal Government Labor Relations and the Mutual Interests of Congress, the Administration, and Unions." *Journal of Labor Research* 25 (2004): 19–41.

ADVISORY STRUCTURE

Burke, John P. "The Neutral/Honest Broker Role in Foreign-Policy Decision Making: A Reassessment." *Presidential Studies Quarterly* 35 (2005): 229–58.

———. "The Contemporary Presidency: Condoleezza Rice as NSC Advisor: A Case Study of the Honest Broker Role." *Presidential Studies Quarterly* 35 (2005): 554–75.

Dolan, Chris J., and David B. Cohen. "The War About the War: Iraq and the Politics of National Security Advising in the G.W. Bush Administration's First Term." *Politics & Policy* 34 (2006): 30–64.

Fisher, Louis. "Deciding on War Against Iraq: Institutional Failures." *Political Science Quarterly* 118 (2003): 389–410.

Haney, Patrick J. "Foreign-Policy Advising: Models and Mysteries from the Bush Administration." *Presidential Studies Quarterly* 35 (2005): 289–302.

Heilbrunn, Jacob. "Condoleezza Rice: George W.'s Realist." *World Policy Journal* 16 (1999/2000): 49–54.

Mann, James. *Rise of the Vulcans: The History of Bush's War Cabinet.* New York: Viking, 2004.

AFRICA

Adams, Melinda, and Jonathan Keller. "Rhetoric vs. Reality: U.S. Foreign Assistance to Africa under Bush 41 and Bush 43." *White House Studies* 8 (2008): 191–96.

Adebajo, Adekeye. "Africa, African Americans, and the Avuncular Sam." *Africa Today* 50 (2004): 92–110.

Heinze, Eric A. "The Rhetoric of Genocide in U.S. Foreign Policy: Rwanda and Darfur Compared." *Political Science Quarterly* 122 (2007): 359–83.

Keller, Jonathan, and Melinda Adams. "From Benign Neglect to Strategic Interest: The Role of Africa in the Foreign Polices of Bush 41 and 43." *White House Studies* 7 (2007): 35–85.

Owusu, Francis Y. "Post-9/11 U.S. Foreign Aid, the Millennium Challenge Account, and Africa: How Many Birds Can One Stone Kill?" *Africa Today* 54 (2007): 3–26.

Patterson, Amy S. *The Politics of AIDS in Africa.* Boulder, Colo.: Lynne Rienner Publishers, 2006.

ASIA

Beeson, Mark. *Bush and Asia: America's Evolving Relations with East Asia.* New York: Routledge, 2006.

Ollapally, Deepa. "America's War on Terrorism in Southern Asia: Political and Military Dilemmas." *White House Studies* 3 (2003): 445–58.

AUSTRALIA

Garran, Robert. *True Believer: John Howard, George Bush, and the American Alliance*. Crows Nest, New South Wales (Australia): Allen & Unwin, 2004.

AUTOBIOGRAPHY

Bush, George W. *A Charge to Keep*. New York: Morrow, 1999.

BUDGET AND ECONOMIC POLICY

Altman, Daniel. *Neoconomy: George Bush's Revolutionary Gamble with America's Future*. New York: Public Affairs, 2004.

Begala, Paul. *It's Still the Economy, Stupid: George W. Bush, the GOP's CEO*. New York: Simon & Schuster, 2002.

Béland, Daniel, and Alex Waddan. "Taking 'Big Government Conservatism' Seriously? The Bush Presidency Reconsidered." *Political Quarterly* 79 (2008): 109–18.

Dolan, Chris J. "In His Shadow: The Impact of the Reagan Economic Regime and Institutional Structure on the Bush Administration." *White House Studies* 7 (2007): 235–50.

Dull, Matthew. "Why PART? The Institutional Politics of Presidential Budget Reform." *Journal of Public Administration Research and Theory* 16 (2006): 187–215.

Galbraith, James K. *Unbearable Cost: Bush, Greenspan and the Economics of Empire*. New York: Palgrave McMillan, 2006.

Krugman, Paul. *Fuzzy Math: The Essential Guide to the Bush Tax Plan*. New York: Norton, 2001.

Patterson, Bradley H. "The White House Budget—What It Isn't, What It Is: And a Five-Year Comparison." *White House Studies* 5 (2005): 95–103.

Piven, Frances Fox. *The War at Home: The Domestic Costs of Bush's Militarism*. New York: Norton, 2004.

White, Joseph. "What Not to Ask of Budget Processes: Lessons from George W. Bush's Years." *Public Administration Review* 69 (2009): 224–32.

CABINET AND ADVISORS

Brown, Mary Beth. *Condi: The Life of a Steel Magnolia.* Nashville, Tenn.: Thomas Nelson, 2007.

Bumiller, Elisabeth. *Condoleezza Rice: An American Life: A Biography.* New York: Random House, 2007.

Cockburn, Andrew. *Rumsfeld: His Rise, Fall, and Catastrophic Legacy.* New York: Scribner, 2007.

DeYoung, Karen. *Soldier: The Life of Colin Powell.* New York: Knopf, 2006.

Dubose, Lou, Jan Reid, and Carl M. Cannon. *Boy Genius: Karl Rove, The Brains Behind the Remarkable Political Triumph of George W. Bush.* New York: Public Affairs, 2003.

Graham, Bradley. *By His Own Rules: The Story of Donald Rumsfeld.* New York: Public Affairs, 2009.

Hughes, Karen. *Ten Minutes from Normal.* New York: Viking, 2004.

Kessler, Glenn. *The Confidante: Condoleezza Rice and the Creation of the Bush Legacy.* New York: St. Martin's Press, 2007.

Lusane, Clarence. *Colin Powell and Condoleezza Rice: Foreign Policy, Race, and the New American Century.* Westport, Conn.: Praeger Publishers, 2006.

Minutaglio, Bill. *The President's Counselor: The Rise to Power of Alberto Gonzales.* New York: Rayo, 2006.

Suskind, Ron. *The Price of Loyalty: George W. Bush, the White House, and the Education of Paul O'Neill.* New York: Simon & Schuster, 2004.

CIVIL SERVICE REFORM

Breul, Jonathan D. "Three Bush Administration Management Reform Initiatives: The President's Management Agenda, Freedom to Manage Legislative Proposals, and the Program Assessment Rating Tool." *Public Administration Review* 67 (2007): 21–26.

Conley, Richard S. "Reform, Reorganization, and the Renaissance of the Managerial Presidency: The Impact of 9/11 on the Executive Establishment." *Politics & Policy* 34 (2006): 304–42.

Riccucci, Norma M., and Frank J. Thompson. "The New Public Management, Homeland Security, and the Politics of Civil Service Reform." *Public Administration Review* 68 (2008): 877–90.

COMPARATIVE PERSPECTIVES

Auer, Matthew R. "Presidential Environmental Appointees in Comparative Perspective." *Public Administration Review* 68 (2008): 68–80.

Brands, H. W. "FDR and GWB: Unlearned Lessons of a Wartime Presidency." *World Affairs* 170 (2008): 83–90.

Brzezinski, Zbigniew. *Second Chance: Three Presidents and the Crisis of American Superpower.* New York: Basic Books, 2008.

Davis, John. "The Evolution of American Grand Strategy and the War on Terrorism: Clinton and Bush Perspectives. *White House Studies* 3 (2003): 459–77.

Daynes, Byron W., and Glen Sussman. "Comparing the Environmental Policies of Presidents George H.W. Bush and George W. Bush." *White House Studies* 7 (2007): 163–79.

Farnsworth, Stephen J., and Robert S. Lichter. "Source Material: New Presidents and Network News: Covering the First Year in Office of Ronald Reagan, Bill Clinton, and George W. Bush." *Presidential Studies Quarterly* 34 (2004): 674–90.

Haley, P. Edward. *Strategies of Dominance.* Baltimore: Johns Hopkins University Press, 2006.

Judis, John B. *The Folly of Empire: What George W. Bush Could Learn from Theodore Roosevelt and Woodrow Wilson.* New York: Scribner, 2004.

Lansford, Tom. "Homeland Security from Clinton to Bush: An Assessment." *White House Studies* 3 (2003): 385–402.

Oliver, James K. "The Foreign Policy Architecture of the Clinton and Bush Administrations." *White House Studies* 4 (2004): 47–69.

———. "Pragmatic Fathers and Ideological Sons: Foreign Policy in the Administrations of George H.W. Bush and George W. Bush." *White House Studies* 7 (2007): 199–216.

Shannon, Vaughn P. "On the Same Page? Narrative Interactions and Middle East Policy in the Two Bush Presidencies." *White House Studies* 7 (2007): 267–88.

Strong, Robert A. "Deposing Dictators: The Bush Presidents, Saddam Hussein and Manuel Noriega." *White House Studies* 7 (2007): 217–33.

Wekkin, Gary D. "George H.W. Bush and George W. Bush: Puzzling Presidencies, or the Puzzle of the Presidency?" *White House Studies* 7 (2007): 113–24.

Yan, Yi Edward. "Two Tales of Engagement: A Comparison of China Policies Between the George H.W. Bush and George W. Bush Administrations." *White House Studies* 7 (2007): 251–66.

CONGRESSIONAL RELATIONS

Andres, Gary J. "Postcards from Sisyphus: What I Saw During the Confirmation Wars." *PS: Political Science & Politics* 35 (2002): 55–57.

———."The Contemporary Presidency: Parties, Process, and Presidential Power: Learning From Confirmation Politics in the U.S. Senate." *Presidential Studies Quarterly* 32 (2002): 147–56.

———. "The Contemporary Presidency: Polarization and White House/ Legislative Relations: Causes and Consequences of Elite-Level Conflict." *Presidential Studies Quarterly* 35 (2005): 761–70.

Collier, Ken. "Between the Bushes: The Evolution of Legislative Affairs." *White House Studies* 7 (2007): 181–94.

Conley, Richard S., and Richard M. Yon. "In the Shadow or the Sunshine of the Father? Veto Threats in the Administration of George W. Bush, 2001–2006." *White House Studies* 7 (2007): 125–39.

Crockett, David A. "The Contemporary President: Should the Senate Take a Floor Vote on a Presidential Judicial Nominee?" *Presidential Studies Quarterly* 37 (2007): 313–30.

Edwards, George C. "Strategic Choices and the Early Bush Legislative Agenda." *PS: Political Science & Politics* 35 (2002): 41–45.

Haider-Markel, Donald P., and Carol K. Carr. "The Political Fallout of Taking a Stand: The President, Congress, and the Schiavo Case." *Presidential Studies Quarterly* 37 (2007): 449–67.

Hartley, Roger E., and Lisa M. Holmes. "The Increasing Senate Scrutiny of Lower Federal Court Nominees." *Political Science Quarterly* 117 (2002): 259–78.

Lindsay, James M. "Deference and Defiance: The Shifting Rhythms of Executive-Legislative Relations in Foreign Policy." *Presidential Studies Quarterly* 33 (2003): 530–46.

Mackenzie, G. Calvin. "The Real Invisible Hand: Presidential Appointees in the Administration of George W. Bush." *PS: Political Science and Politics* 35 (2002): 27–30.

Mycoff, Jason D., and Joseph A. Pika. "President Bush and the 110th Congress: Prospects for Compromise or Conflict." *White House Studies* 7 (2007): 1–31.

Ornstein, Norman, and John Fortier. "Relations with Congress." *PS: Political Science & Politics* 35 (2002): 47–50.

Sollenberger, Mitchel A. "The Law: Must the Senate Take a Floor Vote on a Presidential Judicial Nominee?" *Presidential Studies Quarterly* 34 (2004): 420–36.

Sullivan, Terry. "Already Buried and Sinking Fast: Presidential Nominees and Inquiry." *PS: Political Science & Politics* 35 (2002): 31–33.

EDUCATION POLICY

McAndrews, Lawrence J. "Choosing 'Choice': George Bush and Federal Aid to Nonpublic Schools." *The Catholic Historical Review* 87 (2001): 453–69.

Miskel, Cecil, and Mengli Song. "Passing Reading First: Prominence and Processes in an Elite Policy Network." *Educational Evaluation and Policy Analysis* 26 (2004): 89–109.

ELECTION 2000

Anand, Sowmya, and Jon A. Krosnick. "The Impact of Attitudes toward Foreign Policy Goals on Public Preferences among Presidential Candidates: A Study of Issue Publics and the Attentive Public in the 2000 U.S. Presidential Election." *Presidential Studies Quarterly* 33 (2003): 31–71.

Bartels, Larry M., and John Zaller. "Presidential Vote Models: A Recount." *PS: Political Science & Politics* 34 (2001): 8–20.

Bishin, Benjamin G., et al. "Character Counts? Honesty and Fairness in Election 2000." *The Public Opinion Quarterly* 70 (2006): 235–48.

Brians, Craig Leonard, and Steven Greene. "Elections: Voter Support and Partisans' (Mis)Perceptions of Presidential Candidates' Abortion Views in 2000." *Presidential Studies Quarterly* 34 (2004): 412–19.

Grossback, Lawrence, and Allan Hammock. "Overcoming One-Party Dominance: How Contextual Politics and West Virginia Helped Put George Bush in the White House." *Politics & Policy* 31 (2003): 406–31.

Hughes, Paul. "Do EPA Defendants Prefer Republicans? Evidence from the 2000 Election." *Economic Inquiry* 44 (2006): 579–85.

Hutchings, Vincent L., et al. "The Compassion Strategy: Race and the Gender Gap in Campaign 2000." *The Public Opinion Quarterly* 68 (2004): 512–41.

Imai, Kosuke, and Gary King. "Did Illegal Overseas Absentee Ballots Decide the 2000 U.S. Presidential Election?" *Perspectives on Politics* 2 (2004): 537–49.

Jacobson, Gary C. "The Bush Presidency and the American Electorate." *Presidential Studies Quarterly* 33 (2003): 701–29.

Magee, Christopher S. P. "Third-Party Candidates and the 2000 Presidential Election." *Social Science Quarterly* 84 (2003): 574–95.

Miller, Arthur H., and Thomas F. Klobucar. "The Role of Issues in the 2000 U.S. Presidential Election." *Presidential Studies Quarterly* 33 (2003): 101–24.

Mixon, J. Wilson, et al. "Are the Networks Biased? 'Calling' States in the 2000 Presidential Election." *Public Choice* 118 (2004): 53–59.

O'Connor, Brendan. "Back to the Future, Again: Reagan, Bush, and Nader." *Australian Journal of Politics & History* 47 (2001): 594–600.

Pomper, Gerald M. "The 2000 Presidential Election: Why Gore Lost." *Political Science Quarterly* 116 (2001): 210–23.

Sabato, Larry J. (ed.). *Overtime! The Election 2000 Thriller.* New York: Longman, 2002.

Smith, Troy E. "Federalism in the 2000 Presidential Election." *Publius* 31 (2001): 71–95.

Southwell, Priscilla L. "Nader Voters in the 2000 Presidential Election: What Would They Have Done Without Him?" *The Social Science Journal* 41 (2004): 423–31.

Valentino, Nicholas A., et al. "The Compassion Strategy: Race and the Gender Gap in Campaign 2000." *Public Opinion Quarterly* 68 (2004): 512–41.

Waldman, Paul, and Kathleen Hall Jamieson. "Rhetorical Convergence and Issue Knowledge in the 2000 Presidential Election." *Presidential Studies Quarterly* 33 (2003): 145–63.

Wand, Jonathan N., et al. "The Butterfly Did It: The Aberrant Vote for Buchanan in Palm Beach County, Florida." *American Political Science Review* 95 (2001): 793–810.

Wattenberg, Martin P. "Elections: Tax Cut Versus Lockbox: Did the Voters Grasp the Tradeoff in 2000?" *Presidential Studies Quarterly* 34 (2004): 838–48.

ELECTION 2004

Abramowitz, Alan I., and Walter J. Stone. "The Bush Effect: Polarization, Turnout, and Activism in the 2004 Presidential Election." *Presidential Studies Quarterly* 36 (2006): 141–54.

Abramson, Paul R., et al. "The 2004 Presidential Election: The Emergence of a Permanent Majority?" *Political Science Quarterly* 120 (2005): 33–57.

Bichard, Shannon L. "Building Blogs: A Multi-Dimensional Analysis of the Distribution of Frames on the 2004 Presidential Candidate Web Sites." *Journalism and Mass Communication Quarterly* 83 (2006): 329–45.

Campbell, James E. "Why Bush Won the Presidential Election of 2004: Incumbency, Ideology, Terrorism, and Turnout." *Political Science Quarterly* 120 (2005): 219–41.

Cohen, Florette, et al. "American Roulette: The Effect of Reminders of Death on Support for George W. Bush in the 2004 Presidential Election." *Analyses of Social Issues and Public Policy* 5 (2005): 177–87.

Drew, Dan, and David Weaver. "Voter Learning in the 2004 Presidential Election: Did the Media Matter?" *Journalism and Mass Communication Quarterly* 83 (2006): 25–42.

Hodgson, Godfrey. "'Great Vote, Grisly Result': Europe's Reaction to the Reelection of George Bush." *World Policy Journal* 21 (4) (Winter 2004/2005): 13–18.

Jacobson, Gary C. "Polarized Politics and the 2004 Congressional and Presidential Elections." *Political Science Quarterly* 120 (2005): 199–218.

Keeter, Scott. "The Impact of Cell Phone Noncoverage Bias on Polling in the 2004 Presidential Election." *The Public Opinion Quarterly* 70 (2006): 88–98.

Kenski, Kate, and Kathleen Hall Jamieson. "Issue Knowledge and Perceptions of Agreement in the 2004 Presidential General Election." *Presidential Studies Quarterly* 36 (2006): 243–59.

Kenski, Kate, and Russell Tisinger. "Hispanic Voters in the 2000 and 2004 Presidential General Elections." *Presidential Studies Quarterly* 36 (2006): 189–202.

Klinkner, Philip A. "Mr. Bush's War: Foreign Policy in the 2004 Election." *Presidential Studies Quarterly* 36 (2006): 281–96.

Langer, Gary, and Jon Cohen. "Voters and Values in the 2004 Election." *The Public Opinion Quarterly* 69 (2005): 744–59.

McAllister, Ian. "A War Too Far? Bush, Iraq, and the 2004 U.S. Presidential Election." *Presidential Studies Quarterly* 36 (2006): 260–80.

Panagopoulos, Costas, and Daniel Bergan. "Contributions and Contributors in the 2004 Presidential Election Cycle." *Presidential Studies Quarterly* 36 (2006): 155–71.

Wattenberg, Martin P. "Elections: Turnout in the 2004 Presidential Election." *Presidential Studies Quarterly* 35 (2005): 138–46.

———. "Elections: Reliability Trumps Competence: Personal Attributes in the 2004 Presidential Election." *Presidential Studies Quarterly* 36 (2006): 705–13.

EXECUTIVE POWER, THE WAR POWER, AND CONSTITUTIONAL ISSUES

Aberbach, Joel D., et al. "The Contemporary Presidency: Who Wants Presidential Supremacy? Findings from the Institutions of American Democracy Project." *Presidential Studies Quarterly* 37 (2007): 515–30.

Adler, David Gray. "The Law: George Bush as Commander in Chief: Toward the Nether World of Constitutionalism." *Presidential Studies Quarterly* 36 (2006): 525–40.

Byrd, Robert C. *Losing America: Confronting a Reckless and Arrogant Presidency.* New York: W.W. Norton, 2004.

Cooper, Philip J. "George W. Bush, Edgar Allan Poe, and the Use and Abuse of Presidential Signing Statements." *Presidential Studies Quarterly* 35 (2005): 515–32.

Cornelius, Erika N., and Ryan C. Hendrickson. "George W. Bush, Haiti and Presidential War Powers." *White House Studies* 8 (2008): 57–69.

Dean, John W. *Worse than Watergate: The Secret Presidency of George W. Bush.* New York: Little, Brown, 2004.

Fein, Bruce. "Presidential Authority to Gather Foreign Intelligence." *Presidential Studies Quarterly* 37 (2007): 23–36.

Kassop, Nancy. "The War Power and Its Limits." *Presidential Studies Quarterly* 33 (2003): 509–29.

Kelley, Christopher S. "The Law: Contextualizing the Signing Statement." *Presidential Studies Quarterly* 37 (2007): 737–48.

Montgomery, Bruce P. "Source Material: Nixon's Ghost Haunts the Presidential Records Act: The Reagan and George W. Bush Administrations." *Presidential Studies Quarterly* 32 (2002): 789–809.

———. *The Bush-Cheney Administration's Assault on Open Government.* Westport, Conn.: Praeger, 2008.

Owens, John E. "Presidential Power and Congressional Acquiescence in the 'War' on Terrorism: A New Constitutional Equilibrium?" *Politics & Policy* 34 (2006): 258–303.

Paust, Jordan J. *Beyond the Law: The Bush Administration's Unlawful Responses in the 'War' on Terror.* New York: Cambridge University Press, 2007.

Perret, Geoffrey. *Commander in Chief: How Truman, Johnson, and Bush Turned a Presidential Power into a Threat to America's Future.* New York: Farrar, Straus & Giroux, 2007.

Pfiffner, James P. "The Contemporary Presidency: Constraining Executive Power: George W. Bush and the Constitution." *Presidential Studies Quarterly* 38 (2008): 123–43.

———. *Power Play: The Bush Presidency and the Constitution.* Washington, D.C.: Brookings Institution Press, 2008.

———. "Presidential Signing Statements and Their Implications for Public Administration." *Public Administration Review* 69 (2009): 249–55.

Saldin, Robert P. "Executive Power and the Constitution in Times of Crisis." *White House Studies* 4 (2004): 489–504.

Savage, Charlie. *Takeover: The Return of the Imperial Presidency and the Subversion of American Democracy.* New York: Little, Brown, 2007.

Tiefer, Charles. *Veering Right: How the Bush Administration Subverts the Law for Conservative Causes.* Berkeley, Calif.: University of California Press, 2004.

Weaver, William G., and Robert M. Pallitto. "The Law: 'Extraordinary Rendition' and Presidential Fiat." *Presidential Studies Quarterly* 36 (2006): 102–16.

EXECUTIVE PRIVILEGE

Harriger, Katy J. "Executive Power and Prosecution: Lessons from the Libby Trial and the U.S. Attorney Firings." *Presidential Studies Quarterly* 38 (2008): 491–505.

Rozell, Mark J., and Mitchel A. Sollenberger. "Executive Privilege and the U.S. Attorneys Firings." *Presidential Studies Quarterly* 38 (2008): 315–28.

Tiefer, Charles. "The Law: President Bush's First Executive Privilege Claim: The FBI/Boston Investigation." *Presidential Studies Quarterly* 33 (2003): 201–10.

FLORIDA RECOUNT AND *BUSH V. GORE*

Ackerman, Bruce. *Bush v. Gore: The Question of Legitimacy*. New Haven, Conn.: Yale University Press, 2002.

Banks, Christopher P., David B. Cohen, and John C. Green. *The Final Arbiter: The Consequences of Bush v. Gore for Law and Politics*. Albany: State University of New York Press, 2005.

Dershowitz, Alan M. *Supreme Injustice: How the High Court Hijacked Election 2000*. New York: Oxford University Press, 2001.

Dionne, E. J., and William Kristol. *Bush v. Gore: The Court Cases and the Commentary*. Washington, D.C.: Brookings Institution Press, 2001.

Dover, E. D. *The Disputed Presidential Election of 2000: A History and Reference Guide*. Westport, Conn.: Greenwood Press, 2003.

Dworkin, Ronald. *A Badly Flawed Election: Debating Bush v. Gore, the Supreme Court, and American Democracy*. New York: Norton, 2002.

Gillman, Howard. *The Votes that Counted: How the Court Decided the 2000 Presidential Election*. Chicago: University of Chicago Press, 2001.

Greene, Abner. *Understanding the 2000 Election: A Guide to the Legal Battles that Decided the Presidency*. New York: New York University Press, 2001.

Pleasants, Julian M. *Hanging Chads: The Inside Story of the 2000 Presidential Recount in Florida*. New York: Palgrave Macmillan, 2004.

Posner, Richard A. *Breaking the Deadlock: The 2000 Election, the Constitution, and the Courts*. Princeton, N.J.: Princeton University Press, 2001.

Rountree, Clarke. *Judging the Supreme Court: Constructions of Motives in Bush v. Gore*. East Lansing, Mich.: Michigan State University Press, 2007.

Sunstein, Cass R., and Richard A. Epstein (eds.). *The Vote: Bush, Gore, and the Supreme Court*. Chicago: University of Chicago Press, 2001.

Toobin, Jeffrey. *Too Close to Call: The Thirty-Six-Day Battle to Decide the 2000 Election*. New York: Random House, 2001.

Von Drehle, Dave. *Deadlock: The Inside Story of America's Closest Election.* New York: Public Affairs, 2001.

Whitman, Mark. *Florida 2000: A Sourcebook on the Contested Presidential Election.* Boulder, Colo.: Lynne Rienner, 2003.

Zelden, Charles L. *Bush v. Gore: Exposing the Hidden Crisis in American Democracy.* Lawrence, Kan.: University Press of Kansas, 2008.

Zelnick, Robert. *Winning Florida: How the Bush Team Fought the Battle.* Stanford, Calif.: Hoover Institution Press, 2001.

FOREIGN POLICY

Daalder, Ivo H., and James M. Lindsay (eds.). *America Unbound: The Bush Revolution in Foreign Policy.* New York: Wiley, 2005.

Dietrich, John W. *The George W. Bush Foreign Policy Reader: Presidential Speeches and Commentary.* Armonk, N.Y.: M.E. Sharpe, 2005.

Gaddis, John Lewis. "A Grand Strategy of Transformation." *Foreign Policy* 133 (2002): 50–57.

Gitlin, Todd. "The Politics of National Security: An Unabashed Liberal View." *World Policy Journal* 24 (2007): 45–53.

Groves, Sharon. "Sex Workers, USAID, and Brazilian Resistance." *Feminist Studies* 31 (2005): 445–47.

Haley, P. Edward. *Strategies of Dominance: The Misdirection of U.S. Foreign Policy.* Baltimore: Johns Hopkins University Press, 2006.

Hendrickson, David C. "Preserving the Imbalance of Power." *Ethics & International Affairs* 17 (2003): 157–62.

Jackson, Robert J., and Philip Towle. *Temptations of Power: The United States in Global Politics after 9/11.* New York: Palgrave Macmillan, 2006.

Jervis, Robert. "The Compulsive Empire." *Foreign Policy* 137 (2003): 82–87.

———. *American Foreign Policy in a New Era.* New York: Routledge, 2005.

Judis, John B. "Imperial Amnesia." *Foreign Policy* 143 (2004): 50–59.

Kane, John. "American Values or Human Rights? U.S. Foreign Policy and the Fractured Myth of Virtuous Power." *Presidential Studies Quarterly* 33 (2003): 772–800.

Kazin, M. "What Lies Beneath: Bush and the Liberal Idealists." *World Affairs* 170 (2008): 81–90.

Leffler, Melvyn P. "Bush's Foreign Policy." *Foreign Policy* 144 (2004): 22–28.

Leffler, Melvyn P., and Jeffrey W. Legro. *To Lead the World: American Strategy after the Bush Doctrine.* New York: Oxford University Press, 2008.

McCartney, Paul T. "American Nationalism and U.S. Foreign Policy from September 11 to the Iraq War." *Political Science Quarterly* 119 (2004): 399–423.

Moens, Alexander. *The Foreign Policy of George W. Bush: Values, Strategy and Loyalty.* Burlington, Vt.: Ashgate, 2004.

Mowthorpe, Matthew. "The United States Post Cold War Military Space Policy." *The Journal of Social, Political and Economic Studies* 28 (2003): 3–29.

Owens, John, and John Dumbrell (eds.). *America's 'War' on Terrorism and New Directions in US Government and National Security Policy.* Lanham, Md.: Lexington Books, 2008.

Schlesinger, Stephen. "Bush's Stealth United Nations Policy." *World Policy Journal* 25 (2008): 1–9.

Schwenninger, Sherle R. "Revamping American Grand Strategy." *World Policy Journal* 20 (2003): 25–44.

Seigfried, Charlene Haddock. "The Dangers of Unilateralism." *NWSA Journal* 18 (2006): 20–32.

Shapiro, Ian. *Containment.* Princeton, N.J.: Princeton University Press, 2007.

Soederberg, Susanne. "American Empire and 'Excluded States': The Millennium Challenge Account and the Shift to Pre-Emptive Development." *Third World Quarterly* 25 (2004): 279–302.

Walker, Martin. "Bush v. Annan: Taming the United Nations." *World Policy Journal* 22 (2005): 9–18.

GREAT BRITAIN

Dumbrell, John. "Working with Allies: The United States, the United Kingdom, and the War on Terror." *Politics & Policy* 34 (2006): 452–72.

Marsden, Lee. "Promoting Democracy in Northern Ireland: George Bush and the Peace Process." *The Political Quarterly* 77 (2006): 61–70.

Parmar, Inderjeet. "'I'm Proud of the British Empire': Why Tony Blair Backs George W. Bush." *The Political Quarterly* 76 (2005): 218–31.

HURRICANE KATRINA

Derthick, Martha. "Where Federalism Didn't Fail." *Public Administration Review* 67 (2007): 36–47.

Dyson, Michael Eric. *Come Hell or High Water: Hurricane Katrina and the Color of Disaster.* New York: Basic Civitas, 2006.

King, C. Richard. "George Bush May Not Like Black People, but No One Gives a Damn about Indigenous Peoples: Visibility and Indianness after the Hurricanes." *American Indian Culture and Research Journal* 32 (2008): 35–42.

Tynes, Brendesha, et al. "'Bush Doesn't Care About Black People': Race, Class, and Attributions of Responsibility in the Aftermath of Hurricane Katrina." *The Black Scholar* 36 (2006): 32–42.

ISRAELI–PALESTINIAN CONFLICT

Christison, Kathleen. "'All Those Old Issues': George W. Bush and the Palestinian-Israeli Conflict." *Journal of Palestine Studies* 33 (2004): 36–50.

Matthews, Mark. *Lost Years: Bush, Sharon, and Failure in the Middle East.* New York: Nation Books, 2007.

"The Road Map." *Journal of Palestine Studies* 32 (2003): 83–99.

Stewart, Dona J. "The Greater Middle East and Reform in the Bush Administration's Ideological Imagination." *The Geographical Review* 95 (2005): 400–24.

LATIN AMERICA

Feinberg, Richard E. "Regionalism and Domestic Politics: U.S.–Latin American Trade Policy in the Bush Era." *Latin American Politics and Society* 44 (2002): 127–51.

Golinger, Eva. *Bush versus Chávez: Washington's War on Venezuela.* New York: Monthly Review Press, 2008.

Leogrande, William M. "From the Red Menace to Radical Populism: U.S. Insecurity in Latin America." *World Policy Journal* 22 (2005/2006): 25–35.

LEADERSHIP AND GENERAL PERSPECTIVES

Blumenthal, Sidney. *How Bush Rules: Chronicles of a Radical Regime.* Princeton, N.J.: Princeton University Press, 2006.

Campbell, Colin, and Bert A. Rockman (eds.). *The George W. Bush Presidency: Appraisals and Prospects.* Washington, D.C.: Congressional Quarterly Press, 2004.

Campbell, Colin, et al. (eds.). *The George W. Bush Legacy.* Washington, D.C.: Congressional Quarterly Press, 2007.

Cannon, Lou, and Carl Cannon. *Reagan's Disciple: George W. Bush's Troubled Quest for a Presidential Legacy.* New York: Public Affairs, 2008.

Draper, Robert. *Dead Certain: The Presidency of George W. Bush.* New York: Free Press, 2007.

Edwards, George C. *Governing by Campaigning: The Politics of the Bush Presidency.* New York: Longman, 2007.

Edwards, George C., and Desmond S. King (eds.). *The Polarized Presidency of George W. Bush.* New York: Oxford University Press, 2007.

Fortier, John C., and Norman J. Ornstein (eds.). *Second-Term Blues: How George W. Bush Has Governed.* Washington, D.C.: American Enterprise Institute/ Brookings Institution Press, 2007.

Frum, David. *The Right Man: The Surprise Presidency of George W. Bush.* New York: Random House, 2003.

Gore, Al. *The Assault on Reason.* New York: Penguin Press, 2007.

Greenstein, Fred I. "George W. Bush and the Ghosts of Presidents Past." *PS: Political Science and Politics* 34 (2001): 77–80.

——. "The Contemporary Presidency: The Changing Leadership of George W. Bush: A Pre- and Post-9/11 Comparison." *Presidential Studies Quarterly* 32 (2002): 387–96.

——. "The Strong Leadership of George W. Bush." *International Journal of Applied Psychoanalytic Studies* 5 (2008): 171–90.

Gregg, Gary L., and Mark J. Rozell (eds.). *Considering the Bush Presidency.* New York: Oxford University Press, 2004.

Hoopes, James. *Hail to the CEO: The Failure of George W. Bush and the Cult of Moral Leadership.* Westport, Conn.: Praeger, 2008.

Kessler, Ronald. *A Matter of Character: Inside the White House of George W. Bush.* New York: Sentinel, 2004.

Kettl, Donald F. *Team Bush: Leadership Lessons from the Bush White House.* New York: McGraw-Hill, 2003.

Lansford, Tom, and Robert P. Watson (eds.). *George W. Bush: A Political and Ethical Assessment at Mid-Term.* Albany, N.Y.: SUNY Press, 2004.

Lind, Michael. *Made in Texas: George W. Bush and the Southern Takeover of American Politics.* New York: Basic Books, 2003.

Phillips, Kevin. *American Dynasty: Aristocracy, Fortune, and the Politics of Deceit in the House of Bush.* New York: Viking, 2004.

Renshon, Stanley A. *In His Father's Shadow: The Transformations of George W. Bush.* New York: Palgrave Macmillan, 2004.

———. "George W. Bush's Cowboy Politics: An Inquiry." *Political Psychology* 26 (2005): 585–614.

Rich, Frank. *The Greatest Story Ever Sold: The Decline and Fall of Truth from 9/11 to Katrina.* New York: Penguin Press, 2006.

Roper, Jon. The Contemporary Presidency: George W. Bush and the Myth of Heroic Presidential Leadership." *Presidential Studies Quarterly* 34 (2004): 132–42.

Schier, Steven E. *High Risk and Big Ambition: The Presidency of George W. Bush.* Pittsburgh: University of Pittsburgh Press, 2004.

Singer, Peter. *The President of Good & Evil: The Ethics of George W. Bush.* New York: Dutton, 2004.

Tenpas, Kathryn Dunn, and Stephen Hess. "The Contemporary Presidency: The Bush White House: First Appraisals." *Presidential Studies Quarterly* 32 (2002): 577–85.

Thompson, Carolyn B., and James W. Ware. *The Leadership Genius of George W. Bush: 10 Commonsense Lessons from the Commander in Chief.* New York: Wiley, 2003.

MEDIA RELATIONS

Boehlert, Eric. *Lapdogs: How the Press Rolled Over for Bush.* New York: Free Press, 2006.

Coleman, Renita, and Stephen Banning. "Network TV News' Affective Framing of the Presidential Candidates: Evidence for a Second-Level Agenda-Setting Effect through Visual Framing." *Journalism and Mass Communication Quarterly* 83 (2006): 313–28.

Eshbaugh-Soha, Matthew, and Jeffrey S. Peake. "The Contemporary Presidency: 'Going Local' to Reform Social Security." *Presidential Studies Quarterly* 36 (2006): 689–704.

———. "The Presidency and Local Media: Local Newspaper Coverage of President George W. Bush." *Presidential Studies Quarterly* 38 (2008): 609–30.

Kull, Steven, et al. "Misperceptions, the Media, and the Iraq War." *Political Science Quarterly* 118 (2003/2004): 569–98.

Kumar, Martha Joynt. "The Contemporary Presidency: Communications Operations in the White House of President George W. Bush: Making News on His Terms." *Presidential Studies Quarterly* 33 (2003): 366–93.

Malphurs, Ryan. "The Media's Frontier Construction of President George W. Bush." *The Journal of American Culture* 31 (2008): 185–201.

Mapes, Mary. *Truth and Duty: The Press, the President, and the Privilege of Power*. New York: St. Martin's Press, 2005.

Mayer, Jeremy D. "The Contemporary Presidency: The Presidency and Image Management: Discipline in Pursuit of Illusion." *Presidential Studies Quarterly* 34 (2004): 620–31.

Mueller, James E. *Towel Snapping the Press: Bush's Journey from Locker-Room Antics to Message Control*. Lanham, Md.: Rowman & Littlefield, 2006.

Sigelman, Lee, and Cynthia Whissell. "Projecting Presidential Personas on the Radio: An Addendum on the Bushes." *Presidential Studies Quarterly* 32 (2002): 572–76.

MIDDLE EAST

Cordesman, Anthony H. "Saudi Arabia: Friend or Foe in the War on Terror?" *Middle East Policy* 13 (2006): 28–41.

Greenwood, Scott. "Jordan, The Al-Aqsa Intifada and America's 'War on Terror.'" *Middle East Policy* 10 (2003): 90–111.

Unger, Craig. *House of Bush, House of Saud: The Secret Relationship Between the World's Two Most Powerful Dynasties*. New York: Scribner, 2004.

MID-TERM ELECTIONS OF 2002 AND 2006

Cohen, Jeffrey E. "The Polls: Presidential Referendum Effects in the 2006 Midterm Elections." *Presidential Studies Quarterly* 37 (2007): 545–57.

Jacobson, Gary C. "Referendum: The 2006 Midterm Congressional Elections." *Political Science Quarterly* 122 (2007): 1–24.

———. *A Divider, Not a Uniter: George W. Bush and the American People: The 2006 Election and Beyond.* New York: Pearson Longman, 2008.

Mondak, Jeffrey J., and Dona-Gene Mitchell (eds.). *Fault Lines: Why the Republicans Lost Congress.* New York: Routledge, 2009.

Sabato, Larry (ed.). *The Sixth Year Itch: The Rise and Fall of the George W. Bush Presidency.* New York: Pearson Longman, 2008.

MILITARY TRIBUNALS AND ENEMY COMBATANTS

Belknap, Michal R. "Alarm Bells from the Past: The Troubling History of American Military Commissions." *Journal of Supreme Court History* 28 (2003): 300–22.

Bellamy, Alex J. "No Pain, No Gain? Torture and Ethics in the War on Terror." *International Affairs* 82 (2006): 121–48.

Dorf, Michael C. "The Detention and Trial of Enemy Combatants: A Drama in Three Branches." *Political Science Quarterly* 122 (2007): 47–58.

Elsea, Jennifer K. "Presidential Authority to Detain 'Enemy Combatants.'" *Presidential Studies Quarterly* 33 (2003): 568–601.

———. *Military Tribunals And Presidential Power: American Revolution To The War On Terrorism.* Lawrence, Kan.: University Press of Kansas, 2005.

Fisher, Louis. "Military Tribunals: A Sorry History." *Presidential Studies Quarterly* 33 (2003): 484–508.

Massimino, Elisa. "Leading by Example? U.S. Interrogation of Prisoners in the War on Terror." *Criminal Justice Ethics* 23 (2004): 74–76.

MISSILE DEFENSE

Adler, David Gray. "The Law: Termination of the ABM Treaty and the Political Question Doctrine: Judicial Succor for Presidential Power." *Presidential Studies Quarterly* 34 (2004): 156–66.

Mowthorpe, Matthew. "President G.W. Bush and Missile Defense in the Aftermath of 9/11." *The Journal of Social, Political and Economic Studies* 29 (2004): 327–37.

NATURAL RESOURCES

Davis, Charles. "Preemptive Federalism or Regulatory Dismantlement? The Bush Administration's Implementation of the Federal Coal Mining Reclamation Program." *Politics & Policy* 36 (2008): 400–18.

Vaughn, Jacqueline, and Hanna Cortner. "Using Parallel Strategies to Promote Change: Forest Policymaking under George W. Bush." *The Review of Policy Research* 21 (2004): 767–82.

NEOCONSERVATISM

Bartlett, Bruce R. *Impostor: How George W. Bush Bankrupted America and Betrayed the Reagan Legacy.* New York: Doubleday, 2006.

Benn, David Wedgwood. "Neo-Conservatives and Their American Critics." *International Affairs* 80 (2004): 963–69.

Buchanan, Patrick J. *Where the Right Went Wrong: How Neoconservatives Subverted the Reagan Revolution and Hijacked the Bush Presidency.* New York: Thomas Dunne Books, 2004.

Fukuyama, Francis. *America at the Crossroads: Democracy, Power, and the Neoconservative Legacy.* New Haven, Conn.: Yale University Press, 2007.

Halper, Stephen, and Jonathan Clarke. *America Alone: The Neo-Conservatives and the Global Order.* New York: Cambridge University Press, 2005.

Nuruzzaman, Mohammed. "Beyond the Realist Theories: 'Neo-Conservative Realism' and the American Invasion of Iraq." *International Studies Perspectives* 7 (2006): 239–53.

Peleg, Ilan. *The Legacy of George W. Bush's Foreign Policy: Moving beyond Neoconservatism.* Boulder, Colo.: Westview Press, 2009.

NORTH KOREA

Choi, Jinwood. "The Second Term Bush Administration and the North Korean Nuclear Crisis." *Pacific Focus* 20 (2005): 257–83.

Hwang, Jihwan. "Realism and U.S. Foreign Policy toward North Korea: The Clinton and Bush Administrations in Comparative Perspective." *World Affairs* 167 (2004): 15–29.

Kang, C. S. Eliot. "U.S.-Korean Relations Post September 11." *Pacific Focus* 17 (2002): 35–60.

Kim, Ilsu. "A Comparative Analysis of President Clinton and Bush's Handling of the North Korean Nuclear Weapons Program: Power and Strategy." *Pacific Focus* 19 (2004): 69–106.

Martin, Curtis H. "G.W. Bush and North Korea: A Levels of Analysis View." *Pacific Focus* 22 (2007): 111–36.

PUBLIC OPINION

Brewer, Paul R., et al. "International Trust and Public Opinion about World Affairs." *American Journal of Political Science* 48 (2004): 93–109.

Crowson, H. Michael, et al. "The Role of Authoritarianism, Perceived Threat, and Need for Closure or Structure in Predicting Post-9/11 Attitudes and Beliefs." *The Journal of Social Psychology* 146 (2006): 733–50.

Frantzich, Stephen E. "September 11th and the Bush Presidency: Rally-Round-the-Rubble." (Scholarship). *White House Studies* 4 (2004): 217–30.

Gaines, Brian J. "Where's the Rally? Approval and Trust of the President, Cabinet, Congress, and Government Since September 11." *PS: Political Science & Politics* 35 (2002): 530–6.

Hardy, Bruce W., and Kathleen Hall Jamieson. "Can a Poll Affect Perception of Candidate Traits?" *The Public Opinion Quarterly* 69 (2005): 725–43.

Hetherington, Marc J., and Michael Nelson. "Anatomy of a Rally Effect: George W. Bush and the War on Terrorism." *PS: Political Science and Politics* 36 (2003): 37–42.

Jacobson, Gary C. "The Polls: Polarized Opinion in the States: Partisan Differences in Approval Ratings of Governors, Senators, and George W. Bush." *Presidential Studies Quarterly* 36 (2006): 732–57.

Panagopoulos, Costas. "The Polls: Cabinet Member and Presidential Approval." *Presidential Studies Quarterly* 37 (2007): 153–62.

Schubert, James N., et al. "A Defining Presidential Moment: 9/11 and the Rally Effect." *Political Psychology* 23 (2002): 559–83.

Wolf, Michael R. "Polls, Elite Opinion, and the President: How Information and Issue Saliency Affect Approval." *Presidential Studies Quarterly* 36 (2006): 584–605.

RELIGION AND FAITH

Berggren, D. Jason, and Nicol C. Rae. "Jimmy Carter and George W. Bush: Faith, Foreign Policy, and an Evangelical Presidential Style." *Presidential Studies Quarterly* 36 (2006): 606–32.

Black, Amy E., Douglas L. Koopman, and David K. Ryden. *Of Little Faith: The Politics of George W. Bush's Faith-Based Initiatives*. Washington, D.C.: Georgetown University Press, 2004.

Coe, Kevin, and David Domke. "Petitioners or Prophets? Presidential Discourse, God, and the Ascendancy of Religious Conservatives." *Journal of Communication* 56 (2006): 309–30.

Demerath, N. J. III. "Dear President Bush: Assessing Religion and Politics during Your Administration for 'Posteriority.'" *Sociology of Religion* 68 (2007): 5–25.

Jelen, Ted G. "Catholic Priests and the Political Order: The Political Behavior of Catholic Pastors." *Journal for the Scientific Study of Religion* 42 (2003): 591–604.

Kaplan, Esther. *With God on Their Side: How Christian Fundamentalists Trampled Science, Policy, and Democracy in George W. Bush's White House*. New York: Norton, 2004.

Kengor, Paul. *God and George W. Bush: A Spiritual Life*. New York: ReganBooks, 2004.

Linker, Damon. *The Theocons: Secular America under Siege*. New York: Doubleday, 2006.

Mansfield, Stephen. *The Faith of George W. Bush*. Lake Mary, Fla.: Charisma House, 2004.

Philips, Kevin P. *American Theocracy: The Peril and Politics of Radical Religion, Oil, and Borrowed Money in the 21st Century*. New York: Viking, 2006.

Rozell, Mark J., and Gleaves Whitney. *Religion and the Bush Presidency*. Bastingstoke, England: Palgrave Macmillan, 2007.

RHETORICAL PRESIDENCY

Bhatia, Aditi. "Religious Metaphor in the Discourse of Illusion: George W. Bush and Osama bin Laden." *World Englishes* 26 (2007): 507–24.

Cook, Corey. "The Contemporary Presidency: The Permanence of the 'Permanent Campaign': George W. Bush's Public Presidency." *Presidential Studies Quarterly* 32 (2002): 753–64.

Hall, Wynton C. "'Reflections of Yesterday': George H. W. Bush's Instrumental Use of Public Opinion Research in Presidential Discourse." *Presidential Studies Quarterly* 32 (2002): 531–58.

Harnett, Stephen John, et al. "'A Discovered Dissembler Can Achieve Nothing Great'; Or, Four Theses on the Death of Presidential Rhetoric in an Age of Empire." *Presidential Studies Quarterly* 37 (2007): 599–621.

Hart, Roderick P., and Jay P. Childers. "Verbal Certainty in American Politics: An Overview and Extension." *Presidential Studies Quarterly* 34 (2004): 516–35.

Hasian, Marouf Jr. "Dangerous Supplements, Inventive Dissent, and Military Critiques of the Bush Administration's Unitary Executive Theories." *Presidential Studies Quarterly* 37 (2007): 693–716.

Ivie, Robert L., and Oscar Giner. "Hunting the Devil: Democracy's Rhetorical Impulse to War." *Presidential Studies Quarterly* 37 (2007): 580–98.

Kellner, Douglas. "Bushspeak and the Politics of Lying: Presidential Rhetoric in the 'War on Terror.'" *Presidential Studies Quarterly* 37 (2007): 622–45.

Lyons, Paul. "George W. Bush's City on a Hill." *The Journal of The Historical Society* 6 (2006): 119–31.

Maggio, J. "The Presidential Rhetoric of Terror: The (Re)Creation of Reality Immediately after 9/11." *Politics & Policy* 35 (2007): 810–35.

Sigelman, Lee, and Cynthia Whissell. "Projecting Presidential Personas on the Radio: An Addendum on the Bushes." *Presidential Studies Quarterly* 32 (2002): 572–76.

Stuckey, Mary E., and Joshua R. Ritter. "George Bush, Human Rights, and American Democracy." *Presidential Studies Quarterly* 37 (2007): 646–66.

Taylor, Bryan C. "'The Means to Match Their Hatred': Nuclear Weapons, Rhetorical Democracy, and Presidential Discourse." *Presidential Studies Quarterly* 37 (2007): 667–92.

Vaughn, Justin S., and Jose D. Villalobos. "Conceptualizing and Measuring White House Staff Influence on Presidential Rhetoric." *Presidential Studies Quarterly* 36 (2006): 681–88.

Weisberg, Jacob. *George W. Bushisms: The Slate Book of the Accidental Wit and Wisdom of Our Forty-Third President.* New York: Fireside, 2001.

—— (ed.). *Still More George W. Bushisms: Neither in French, nor in English, nor in Mexican.* New York: Simon & Schuster, 2003.

Zarefsky, David. "Presidential Rhetoric and the Power of Definition." *Presidential Studies Quarterly* 34 (2004): 607–19.

SOCIAL POLICY

Aberbach, Joel D. "The Political Significance of the George W. Bush Administration." *Social Policy & Administration* 39 (2005): 130–49.

Ashbee, Edward. *The Bush Administration, Sex and the Moral Agenda.* Manchester, England: Manchester University Press, 2007.

Béland, Daniel, and Alex Waddan. "Conservative Ideas and Social Policy in the United States." *Social Policy & Administration* 41 (2007): 768–86.

Buchanan, Robert J., and William Hatcher. "Compassionate Conservatism: Federal Funding for the Ryan White CARE Act During the Bush Administration." *American Journal of Public Health* 97 (2007): 2013–16.

Claude, Judy. "Bush's Social Security Plan: Gambling Away the Nest-Egg." *The Black Scholar* 35 (2005): 21–25.

Dierenfield, Bruce J. *The Battle Over School Prayer.* Lawrence, Kan.: University Press of Kansas, 2007.

Gillman, Sander L. "What Is the Color of the Gonorrhea Ribbon? Stigma, Sexual Diseases, and Popular Culture in George Bush's World." *Cultural Politics* 3 (2007): 175–202.

Patel, Kant, and Mark Rushefsky. "President Bush and Stem Cell Policy: The Politics of Policy Making." *White House Studies* 5 (2005): 37–50.

Weiner, Terry. "Touching the Third Rail: Explaining the Failure of Bush's Social Security Initiative." *Politics & Policy* 35 (2007): 872–97.

TEXAS GOVERNORSHIP AND EARLY CAREER

Abraham, Rick. *The Dirty Truth: George W. Bush's Oil and Chemical Dependency: How He Sold Out Texans and the Environment to Big Business Polluters.* Houston, Tex.: Mainstream Publishers, 2000.

Girdner, Eddie J. "Texas as a Third World State: Governor George W. Bush and the Environment." *Scandinavian Journal of Development Alternatives and Area Studies* 19 (2000): 57–74.

Ivins, Molly, and Lou Dubose. *Shrub: The Short but Happy Political Life of George W. Bush.* New York: Random House, 2000.

Minutaglio, Bill. *First Son: George W. Bush and the Bush Family Dynasty.* New York: Times Books, 1999.

WAR IN IRAQ

Buckley, Kevin. "'The Graham Greene Argument': A Vietnam Parallel that Escaped George W. Bush." *World Policy Journal* 24 (2007): 89–98.

Gewen, Barry. "Why Are We in Iraq? A Realpolitik Perspective." *World Policy Journal* 24 (2007): 8–22.

Hersh, Seymour M. *Chain of Command: The Road from 9/11 to Abu Ghraib.* New York: HarperCollins, 2004.

Hess, Gary R. "Presidents and the Congressional War Resolutions of 1991 and 2002." *Political Science Quarterly* 121 (2006): 93–118.

Isikoff, Michael, and David Corn. *Hubris: The Inside Story of Spin, Scandal, and the Selling of the Iraq War.* New York: Crown Publishers, 2006.

Miller, T. Christian. *Blood Money: Wasted Billions, Lost Lives, and Corporate Greed in Iraq.* Boston: Little, Brown, 2006.

Pfiffner, James P. "Did President Bush Mislead the Country in His Arguments for War with Iraq?" *Presidential Studies Quarterly* 34 (2004): 25–46.

Puar, Jasbir K. "Abu Ghraib: Arguing against Exceptionalism." *Feminist Studies* 30 (2004): 522–34.

Ricks, Thomas W. *Fiasco.* New York: Penguin Press, 2006.

Ritchie, Nick, and Paul Rogers. *The Political Road to War with Iraq: Bush, 9/11 and the Drive to Overthrow Saddam.* New York: Routledge, 2007.

Russell, Richard L. "CIA's Strategic Intelligence in Iraq." *Political Science Quarterly* 117 (2002): 191–207.

Sheehan, Cindy. *Not One More Mother's Child.* Kihei, Hawaii: Koa Books, 2005.

Vanzo, John P. "A Geopolitical Analysis of a Partitioned Iraq." *World Affairs* 169 (2007): 155–60.

Woodward, Bob. *Plan of Attack.* New York: Simon & Schuster, 2004.

——. *State of Denial.* New York: Simon & Schuster, 2006.

——. *The War Within: A Secret White House History, 2006–2008.* New York: Simon & Schuster, 2008.

WAR ON TERROR

Ayub, Fatima, and Sari Kouvo. "Righting the Course? Humanitarian Intervention, the War on Terror and the Future of Afghanistan." *International Affairs* 84: (2008): 641–57.

Barak, Aharon. "Human Rights in Times of Terror—A Judicial Point of View." *Legal Studies* 28 (2008): 493–505.

Barber, Benjamin R. *Fear's Empire: War, Terrorism, and Democracy.* New York: W.W. Norton, 2004.

Beard, Jack M. "The Presidency and Building a Coalition to Wage a War on al Qaeda and the Taliban Regime." *White House Studies* 4 (2004): 159–77.

Byman, Daniel. "Do Counterproliferation and Counterterrorism Go Together?" *Political Science Quarterly* 122 (2007): 25–46.

Byman, Daniel, et al. "Iraq, Afghanistan and the War on 'Terror.'" *Middle East Policy* 12 (2005): 1–24.

Colucci, Lamont. *Crusading Realism: The Bush Doctrine and American Core Values after 9/11.* Lanham, Md.: University Press of America, 2008.

Conley, Richard S. (ed.). *Transforming the American Polity: The Presidency of George W. Bush and the War on Terrorism.* Englewood Cliffs, N.J.: Prentice Hall, 2005.

Cooper, Belinda. "Torture: Now Congress Is Accountable." *World Policy Journal* 23 (2006/2007): 64–69.

Crawford, Neta C. "Just War Theory and the U.S. Counterterror War." *Perspectives on Politics* 1 (2003): 5–25.

Crotty, William. "Presidential Policymaking in Crisis Situations: 9/11 and Its Aftermath." *Policy Studies Journal* 31 (2003): 451–64.

Davis, Darren W., and Brian D. Silver. "Civil Liberties vs. Security: Public Opinion in the Context of the Terrorist Attacks on America." *American Journal of Political Science* 48 (2004): 28–46.

De Castro, Renato Cruz. "U.S. War on Terror in East Asia: The Perils of Preemptive Defense in Waging a War of the Third Kind." *Asian Affairs* 31 (2005): 212–31.

Huddy, Leonie, et al. "Threat, Anxiety, and Support of Antiterrorism Policies Threat, Anxiety, and Support of Antiterrorism Policies." *American Journal of Political Science* 49 (2005): 593–608.

Isaac, Jeffrey C. "Social Science and Liberal Values in a Time of War." *Perspectives on Politics* 2 (2004): 475–83.

Jervis, Robert. "Understanding the Bush Doctrine." *Political Science Quarterly* 118 (2003): 365–88.

———. "Why the Bush Doctrine Cannot Be Sustained." *Political Science Quarterly* 120 (2005): 351–77.

Kaufman, Robert G. *In Defense of the Bush Doctrine.* Lexington, Ky.: University Press of Kentucky, 2007.

Kellner, Douglas. *From 9/11 to Terror War: The Dangers of the Bush Legacy.* Lanham, Md.: Rowman & Littlefield, 2003.

McCormick, James M. "The War on Terror and Contemporary U.S.–European Relations." *Politics & Policy* 34 (2006): 426–50.

Meyer, Karl E. "America Unlimited: The Radical Sources of the Bush Doctrine." *World Policy Journal* 21 (2004): 1–13.

Putzel, James. "Cracks in the US Empire: Unilateralism, The War on Terror and the Developing World." *Journal of International Development* 18 (2006): 69–85.

Renshon, Stanley A., and Peter Suedfeld. *Understanding the Bush Doctrine: Psychology and Strategy in an Age of Terrorism.* New York: Routledge, 2007.

Risen, James. *State of War: The Secret History of the CIA and the Bush Administration.* New York: Free Press, 2006.

Woodward, Bob. *Bush at War.* New York: Simon & Schuster, 2002.

Wrage, Stephen D. "Civil-Military Relations and the War on Terror." *White House Studies* 4 (2004): 197–215.

WOMEN'S ISSUES

Ferguson, Michaele L., and Lori Jo Marso. *W Stands for Women: How the George W. Bush Presidency Shaped a New Politics of Gender.* Durham, N.C.: Duke University Press, 2007.

Finlay, Barbara. *George W. Bush and the War on Women: Turning Back the Clock on Women's Progress.* New York: Palgrave Macmillan, 2006.

About the Author

Richard S. Conley was born in 1967 in southern California. He attended the University of California, Irvine, from 1985 to 1989, and majored in political science. He earned a master's degree from McGill University in Montréal, Québec, Canada, in 1993, and completed his doctorate in political science at the University of Maryland in 1998. His dissertation, which focused on presidential–congressional relations in the post-World War II era during periods of divided government, won the Department of Government and Politics' Dillon Award.

Dr. Conley took up an appointment as an assistant professor in political science at the University of Florida in 1998. He subsequently earned tenure and was promoted to associate professor in 2004. Dr. Conley routinely teaches courses in American politics, and is a specialist on the US presidency and executive–legislative relations. He also has an interest in comparative politics and teaches courses on Canadian, French, and Irish politics. He has led numerous study-abroad programs in France and Ireland.

Dr. Conley is author of *The Presidency, Congress, and Divided Government: A Post-War Assessment* (2002); *Historical Dictionary of the Reagan–Bush Era* (2007); and editor of *Reassessing the Reagan Presidency* (2003) and *Transforming the American Polity: The Presidency of George W. Bush and the War on Terrorism* (2005). His scholarly articles on American and comparative politics have appeared in *American Politics Research*, *Comparative Political Studies*, *Congress and the Presidency*, *Political Research Quarterly*, *Political Science Quarterly*, *Politics & Policy*, *Presidential Studies Quarterly*, and *White House Studies*. He has also authored more than a dozen book chapters on presidential politics. He is currently working on several archival projects concerning presidential–congressional relations in the Truman and Eisenhower presidencies, as well as a book on Republican presidents and conservatism in the postwar period.